Serial Crime

Serial Crime

Theoretical and Practical Issues in Behavioral Profiling

Second Edition

Wayne Petherick, PhD, editor

Contributors

Wayne Petherick, PhD
Claire Ferguson, MCrim
Terry Goldsworthy, PhD
Brent Turvey, MS (Forensic Science)
Barry Woodhouse, MPsych (Forensic)
Ross Brogan, MA (Fire Investigation)
Gareth Norris, PhD
Daniel B. Kennedy, PhD
Robert Homant, PhD
Michael McGrath, MD
David Field, LLB
Andrew Lowe, BS (Criminology)
Elizabeth Fry, MCrim

ELSEVIER

AMSTERDAM • BOSTON • HEIDELBERG • LONDON
NEW YORK • OXFORD • PARIS • SAN DIEGO
SAN FRANCISCO • SINGAPORE • SYDNEY • TOKYO
Academic Press is an imprint of Elsevier

Elsevier Academic Press
30 Corporate Drive, Suite 400, Burlington, MA 01803, USA
525 B Street, Suite 1900, San Diego, California 92101-4495, USA
84 Theobald's Road, London WC1X 8RR, UK

This book is printed on acid-free paper. ∞

Library of Congress Cataloging-in-Publication Data
Serial crime : theoretical and practical issues in behavioral profiling/Wayne Petherick ... [et al.].
–2nd ed.
       p. cm.
    Includes bibliographical references and index.
    ISBN 978-0-12-374998-7 (hard cover : alk. paper) 1. Criminal behavior, Prediction of.
2. Criminal investigation–Psychological aspects. 3. Recidivism. 4. Serial murder investigation.
5. Stalking. 6. Serial rape investigation. 7. Arson investigation. I. Petherick Wayne.
    HV6080. S47 2009
    364.3–dc22

                                                                                2009010549

British Library Cataloguing in Publication Data
A catalogue record for this book is available from the British Library.

ISBN 13: 978-0-12-374998-7

For all information on all Elsevier Academic Press publications
visit our Web site at www.elsevierdirect.com

Printed in the United States of America

09 10 9 8 7 6 5 4 3 2 1

Contents

Foreword to the Second Edition

It was with delight that I accepted Wayne Petherick's offer to write the foreword to the second edition of *Serial Crime: Theoretical and Practical Issues in Behavioral Profiling*. Having known Wayne for at least 8 years, I have seen firsthand his energy, intellect, and passion devoted to trying to educate others regarding criminal profiling.

As a forensic psychiatrist, I had harbored an interest in the art of criminal profiling, especially aware that a psychiatrist had done some profiling in relation to the New York City Mad Bomber and the Boston Strangler cases in the 1950s and 1960s. I had never delved much further, other than enjoying Hannibal Lector in *The Silence of the Lambs*. Approximately 12 years ago, I began my education in criminal profiling, as did many, by reading some of the career memoir paperbacks by ex-FBI profilers. After reading several, I began to notice that different people took credit for solving the same crimes, but more important, the criminal profiles offered appeared generally vague, unhelpful, and essentially investigatively useless. It dawned on me that despite claims of accuracy, the profiles did not have anything to do with the apprehension of the "Unsub." I obtained a copy of the original FBI study purportedly intended to validate the organized/disorganized dichotomy used by the FBI profilers. After reviewing this, I had no doubt that profiling as practiced by the FBI simply had no supportable basis. The more I learned about profiling, the less I was impressed, especially as taught and practiced by the FBI.

Another front was so-called geographic profiling, derived from crime pattern studies that had nothing to do with sexual and/or serial homicides. I sent off for the PhD thesis of Kim Rossmo, the most visible proponent of geographic profiling. His PhD thesis was very critical of the FBI method of profiling, but this criticism disappeared when he published his textbook on the subject. In his thesis, Rossmo pointed out why the studies he was basing his theories on had limited applicability to what he was doing, and then he used them anyway. As a final flaw, he used the cases he had employed to develop his theories to then prove them, which is scholarly circular reasoning, at best. Again, I was disappointed.

Across the ocean (from me), research was apace in Liverpool, with paper after paper appearing regarding criminal profiling. A new field called Investigative Psychology (IP), spearheaded by David Canter, had arisen. Looking into it, I believed I had come across something that was neither investigation nor psychology, yet the papers and books continue to flow. It seemed to be a "scientification" of criminal profiling, substituting statistical analysis of crime scenes and behaviors, as potentially useless as the organized/disorganized FBI model IP derides.

What could possibly be left?

As luck would have it, I fell in with a group of individuals, of whom Wayne Petherick is one, sharing similar concerns about the state of criminal profiling. We have come to believe that the profiling method offering the most promise is Behavioral Evidence Analysis as described by Brent Turvey. This paradigm offers less in the quantity of opinions generated in a case, but the product is more reliable and has greater investigative relevance.

There are too few helpful texts available regarding criminal profiling, and it is here that this book shines. Packed into 14 chapters is an education into the theoretical and investigative issues in criminal profiling that one can actually use. Although the level of authorship is quite scholarly, the material remains accessible to all levels of readership.

This second edition retains the original 11 chapters with significant updating of the theory and case studies used to highlight concepts. In addition, there are 3 completely new chapters that alone justify a new edition of this text. In "Behavioral Consistency, the Homology Assumption, and the Problems of induction," Petherick and Ferguson delve even further into the difficulties of relying on inductive techniques, essentially warning us away from them, and with good reason. "Investigative Relevance," by Ferguson, presents the findings of her study analyzing the investigative relevance of the various profiling paradigms. In "Metacognition in Criminal Profiling," Woodhouse and Petherick cut to the chase, identifying a major problem with criminal profiling—ignorant and inept practitioners who are unaware of their deficits. This chapter alone is worth the price of admission.

I cannot stress enough the relevance of this text to those interested in moving criminal profiling from a poorly understood and practiced art toward a more meaningful field slowly approaching the boundaries of a science. Wayne Petherick has made a masterful step in the right direction with the first edition of this work and a significant leap forward with this second edition. I feel proud to count him as a colleague and a friend.

Friday, July 25, 2008
Michael McGrath, MD
Webster, New York

Preface

Intellectual Honesty, Research, and Practice
Wayne Petherick

Three years have passed since the publication of the first edition of this text. This has been a time of learning, growth, and reflection. It has been a time to think critically about where we have come from and about where we are going. It has been, to be fair, a curious and winding path. At moments the path was bright and well lit, and at others the path was dark and frankly overgrown.

There have been significant developments and even scientific advances in profiling methodology and related literature, such as the publication of the third edition of Turvey's *Criminal Profiling: An Introduction to Behavioral Evidence Analysis*. Principles, practices, and terminology were refined, evidence-based methods of case examination were given greater structure and focus, and the contributions of cognitive psychology were embraced. Further still was the publication of *Forensic Victimology*, a collaborative effort by Turvey, myself, and other case-working professionals, which redefined victim study as a means of addressing investigative and forensic issues such as suspect development, modus operandi analysis, and case linkage. Both works have advanced the cause of investigating and examining serial crime for the better—emphasizing critical thinking and the scientific method.

Other publications in recent years were less helpful. Bad habits have developed or been revealed in the research community among many criminologists. Specifically, many publications have been selective in attention to the broad spectrum of published research—focusing on only certain authors or data that support their positions; they have also been narrow in their areas of study—replicating the same kinds of research over and over again while failing to learn what they have learned; and not least important, they are often found lacking in a basic understanding of science and the scientific method. Even worse, they have failed to see that their own research invalidates their approach—even though they continue unabated as though nothing were wrong.

This trend can be seen in many journal articles and book publications. Contrary data are studied thinly or ignored entirely; incomplete case information and data are presented to shore up weak theories that have become deeply held beliefs; and pedantic statistical analysis, rather than data interpretation and testing through falsification, is confused for science. The result has been students that are less informed, researchers who are not learning from their research, and a community that suffers from the intellectual dishonesty and scientific illiteracy of those whom it trusts to advance and educate it. The end result of this can only be a lack of faith among the consumers of profiling because the soil in the field fails to foster growth.

We need to do better, and so we have in this second edition of *Serial Crime*. Although this edition cannot remedy or solve the problems created by a flood of bad research that has and continues to drown students and practitioners in this field, it does promote a more rational and logical approach to criminal profiling and the examination of serial crime. It is also critical in its presentation because it needs to be. For too long, dated and even disproved theories and methods have predominated when they should have been discarded. Too many assumptions have been published as fact, and too many theories have been published as conclusions. This edition, in its critical orientation, will help students navigate the rising waters and provide them with tools that allow for discrimination between that which is useful and scientific and that which is not.

It is time to move beyond the intellectually dishonest research that seeks to overwhelm us. It is time for researchers to pause and reflect on their findings and what they mean. It is time for a more holistic and scientific approach to the study and investigation of crime. As researchers, let's seek falsification and not verification as the scientific method demands. As profilers, let's become the objective foil of the police rather than its lackey; let's do the job of narrowing suspect pools rather than pointing at individuals; let's accept our limitations and discriminate between fact and beliefs, between theories and proofs. And at all times let us practice in an intellectually honest manner, both knowing our limits and presenting them rather than pretending they do not exist. Only in this way can this field advance and present as the valid tool in reality it claims to be in theory.

With this in mind, *Serial Crime*, second edition, has the following structure and rationale.

Norris opens with a discussion on the history of criminal profiling in Chapter 1. This begins with the early work of anthropologists such as Lombroso through to the first contemporary example of criminal profiling by police surgeons on Jack the Ripper in Whitechapel, London. Following the works of Langer and Brussels, the early work of the FBI is examined, leading into discussions on the latest profiling methods of Canter and Turvey. This chapter terminates with a snapshot of the current position and likely future directions.

In Chapter 2, Petherick presents those concepts in logic and reasoning that are important to the profiling process. This includes an extensive coverage of induction and deduction as theoretical constructs, and it also shows how they operate in practice through both hypothetical and real cases.

Behavioral consistency and the homology assumption are examined by Petherick and Ferguson in the first new chapter of the second edition. As the basis for all inductive methods, behavioral consistency and the homology assumption are examined, as well as the assumptions they bring to the table of behavioral analysis.

Petherick then presents the different profiling methods with reference to the style of logic or reasoning they employ. Chapter 4 begins by defining criminal profiling and who can consider themselves a profiler before discussing the major paradigms involved. This includes the FBI's Criminal Investigative Analysis, the Diagnostic Evaluations of individual psychologists and psychiatrists, the Investigative Psychology of David Canter, and Turvey's Behavioral Evidence Analysis.

Following this, Petherick provides a discussion of accuracy and utility. Although profiling has been the focus of much research and debate, there is still some debate as to the best way to gauge the success of a profile. Should we claim success when an offender is simply caught, or should we wait and only claim success when an offender's characteristics can be matched unequivocally to those offered in the profile? These and a number of other questions are addressed in Chapter 5, "The Fallacy of Accuracy in Criminal Profiling." This critical overview examines the host of studies that have been done and suggests that the current yardsticks employed in determining a profile's utility are flawed, further suggesting a more suitable approach to not only determining success but also best practice when profilers become involved in an investigation.

In one of the first comprehensive analyses of investigative relevance (IR), Ferguson examines the degree to which a sample of profiles contain characteristics that may actually be used to advance the investigative endeavor. Beyond just looking at IR as a concept, Ferguson presents the results of a study of published criminal profiles and suggests ways in which profilers could advance the relevance of their investigative advice, thus making it more useful to the consumer.

In Chapter 7, Woodhouse and Petherick present the concept of metacognition in criminal profiling as well as the results of Woodhouse's study. This study examined the differences in knowledge between novice and expert groups on the perceived utility of two different criminal profiles. In short, experts were better equipped to differentiate between a "good" and a "bad" profile because they are able to recognize both competence and incompetence when they see it.

As our awareness and receptiveness to profiling increases, it stands to reason that it may become a form of expert evidence adopted by the courts to assist the judiciary in complex matters involving the interpretation of behavior and behavioral evidence. This has already occurred in a number of Western jurisdictions, and Chapter 8 examines the rules relating to expert testimony, how profiling may meet the threshold of expert testimony, and a selection of cases in which profiling evidence has been given.

Chapter 9, "Where to from Here?" considers not only the current state of affairs in profiling but also its future. Professionalization, the application of rigorous scientific processes, research, ethics, accountability, and education are all considered herein, and some future direction in each area is proposed.

In Chapter 10, Turvey and McGrath discuss the greatest recent exposure of criminal profiling in the media involving the Washington Snipers. What makes this case all the more interesting is that this happened in real time in countries throughout the world. Here, the authors explore the role and responsibilities of profilers in this case, the public's reaction to them, and the aftermath of their commentaries. Readers will find it to be one of the most insightful pieces on this aspect of profiling.

Chapter 11 focuses on serial stalking and discusses the behaviors constituting the offense of stalking, its incidence and prevalence, and what features of a crime make it a serial offense. This chapter also briefly examines the application of profiling to the crime of stalking and closes with two case studies of serial stalkers—those stalkers who pursue more than one victim. Both cases involve a large number of victims over an extended period of time, and the cases highlight several aspects of serial stalkers' behavior, including types of pursuit, victim selection, perceptions of their offending, and remorse.

Following this, Terry Goldsworthy, a seasoned investigator of the Queensland Police Service, examines rape, with a specific discussion of the serial variant of this interpersonal crime. Included are demographics and dynamics of the offense, followed by a suggested investigative model arising out of research conducted for his Master of Criminology award.

The penultimate chapter by Dan Kennedy and Robert Homant details the variety of factors involved in serial murder from its definition and classification to a comprehensive case study encompassing those facets covered throughout their chapter.

Last but by no means least, Ross Brogan, an arson investigator of considerable talent in both the theoretical and practical aspects of serial arson, discusses the issue of serial arson. This chapter focuses on arson as a behavior and is interspersed with a number of important case studies showing a variety of different types of serial arsonists.

As with the first edition, it has been a pleasure to work with this collection of authors. To work with them has been an experience of magnitude, to know they are in the field has been reassuring, and to think of the field without them is more than a little disheartening. The knowledge they possess in their respective areas is both considerable and impressive, and their continued dedication to evidence-based approaches will only serve to ensure that the field has a future. Collectively, these authors are a formidable intellectual group. Students of this text will therefore be well served in their approach, professionalism, and dedication, and subsequently well prepared to enter and further advance the field.

Acknowledgments

Any project like this ostensibly involves dozens (if not hundreds) of people at all levels. There are your family who work toward putting you where you are. There are your friends who push you along the way with encouragement and joy. Then there are your colleagues with whom you interact; they provide support, teaching, guidance, and give much needed advice along the path to keep you invigorated and on task. Then there are the students who use the work, who learn from what you have to offer, and who are inspired to discuss, absorb, and, it is hoped, advance what you give them. Then, of course, are the publishers for whom the work is compiled. They provide much needed structural guidance and the oft reminder of deadlines and necessary tasks to bring the work to fruition.

None are more important than others, and each will contribute their own little piece to the work, from encouragement to energy, to drive and passion. Each could be considered a contributor in their own way. I would love to name them all, but to do so would result, inevitably, in a volume of its own merit. The following is a short list and by no means exhaustive.

Brent Turvey has always been available for consultation and guidance, and I cannot name a personal or professional association that has borne more fruit, provided more strength and guidance, and encouraged me to be better. Brent's company has been invaluable in times of dark and light, and I am only the better for it. To many other members of the Academy of Behavioral Profiling, colleagues and friends all, I say thanks for your involvement in the community, for your encouragement to strive for excellence, and for the direction you have provided in terms of support and achievement in the professional community. This list includes in no small way Mike McGrath, Jerry Chisum, Ron Miller, Angela Torres, Dan Kennedy, John Baeza, and the multitude of other professionals and students who give of their time to participate in the evidence-based profiling community. They have shown that, no matter the adversity, it is possible to excel and advance, to pursue, and to shine. All this and more is available to anyone who should stand before their peers and not simply accept the minimum as the standard where you do what you are asked, but bow before the evidence and all that it can, and cannot, tell you.

But the list could go on, and on, and on.

It would be remiss of me not to give specific mention to the outstanding staff at Academic Press. I have been involved with them for many years now, and I am always encouraged by their enthusiasm and assistance. I thank the past staff, Kelly Weaver and Jen Soucy, and the new, Liz Brown, Acquisitions Editor, and Renske van Dijk, Development Editor, for their tolerance and encouragement. A good and worthwhile project is one thing, but a project without a home is like a ship without a port.

To forget the future would be as catastrophic as dismissing the past. In this vein, there are the students. Of particular mention here are Claire Ferguson and Amber McKinley-George, doctoral students who serve as constant and daily reminders of why we do what we do. Their courage and passion has been as much an inspiration as anything else. I was once told that today's student is tomorrow's colleague, and these two have frequently proven this as much, if not more, than any others. With them and others lie the future of this field, and I feel confident that we can only get better over time because they won't allow anything less.

There are undoubtedly more, but these provide the bones on which the flesh grows. Without them, there would be little incentive or growth. Without their input, the field would undoubtedly stay where it is and where it has been for long enough to be of concern.

This should serve as no small reminder that, as our time is short, we should do our best to pursue, advance, and excel. Most of all, we should think, and think constantly, about what we are doing, why, and where we are trying to go. Only then will we be able to identify the problems we have had, the problems we currently endure, and the problems we may face in the future.

Wayne Petherick

About the Authors

Wayne Petherick, PhD

Wayne is Associate Professor of Criminology at Bond University on the Gold Coast, Queensland, Australia. Wayne is a member of the board of the Academy of Behavioral Profiling and assistant journal editor for the *Journal of Behavioral Profiling*. He teaches in the areas of criminal profiling, behavioral evidence analysis, criminal motivations, case studies in forensic science, and crime and deviance. Wayne has consulted on many cases for state law enforcement and the private sector on stalking, sexual assault, and homicide. He has lectured at the Australian Federal Police Academy in Canberra and to state law enforcement groups in Australia and the United States. Wayne can be contacted at wpetheri@staff.bond.edu.au or wpetheri@me.com.

Claire Ferguson, MCrim

Claire holds a Bachelor of Arts degree (Honours) in Psychology from the University of Western Ontario in Canada and a Masters of Criminology from Bond University in Australia. She is currently a doctoral candidate in the Criminology Department at Bond University, where she is studying staged crime scenes. Claire worked for St. Leonard's Society in 2006, writing a narrative to be used for training purposes for homicide cases. In 2007, she undertook an internship with Queensland Fire and Rescue in the Fire Investigation Unit and recently completed a crime scene analysis internship with Forensic Solutions in 2008. Claire works at Bond University as an Adjunct Teaching Fellow in the Criminology Department. Claire can be contacted at clfergus@staff.bond.edu.au.

Terry Goldsworthy, PhD

Terry has completed a Bachelor of Commerce, Bachelor of Laws, Advanced Diploma of Investigative Practice, and a Diploma of Policing. As a result of his law studies, Terry was admitted to the bar in the Queensland and Federal Courts as a barrister in 1999. Terry then completed a Master of Criminology at Bond University. He later undertook his PhD focusing on the concept of evil and its relevance from a criminological and sociological viewpoint. In particular, Terry examined the link between evil and armed conflicts using the Waffen-SS as a case study. Terry is currently a Detective Senior Sergeant with more than 24 years policing experience in the Queensland Police Service. He served in general duties, the watch house, and the traffic branch before moving to the Criminal Investigation Branch in 1994. He is currently stationed at the Gold Coast Criminal Investigation Branch. Terry has recently published his first book titled *Valhalla's Warriors*, which examines the genocidal actions of the SS in Russia during World War II. He has also contributed a chapter to the tertiary textbook, *Serial Crime*, published by Academic Press. He has also had a number of articles published in the *Australian Police Journal* and the *Journal of Behavioral Profiling*.

Brent Turvey, MS (Forensic Science)

Brent holds a Bachelor of Science in History, a Bachelor of Science in Psychology, and a Master of Science in Forensic Science. He is author of *Criminal Profiling: An Introduction to Behavioral Evidence Analysis*, first, second, and third editions (1999, 2002, and 2008). He is coauthor of the *Rape Investigation Handbook* (2004), *Crime Reconstruction* (2006), and *Forensic Victimology* (2008). He is currently a full partner, forensic scientist, criminal profiler, and instructor with Forensic Solutions, LLC, and Adjunct Professor in Criminology at Oklahoma City University. He has consulted with many agencies, attorneys, and police departments in the United States and throughout the world on a wide range of rape and homicide cases as a forensic scientist and criminal profiler. He has also been court qualified as an expert in the areas of criminal profiling, forensic science, victimology, and crime reconstruction. He can be contacted at bturvey@forensic-science.com.

Barry Woodhouse, MPsych (Forensic)

Barry holds a Postgraduate Diploma in Psychology and recently graduated with the degree Master of Forensic (Psychology) at Bond University on the Gold Coast, Australia. Barry has experience working with offenders in a variety of contexts, and his areas of interest include working with victims and perpetrators of sexual abuse, drug and alcohol rehabilitation, posttraumatic stress disorder, and other areas of forensic psychology. He is currently working for the Sentencing Advisory Committee in Victoria, Australia.

Ross Brogan, MA (Fire Investigation)

Ross joined the New South Wales (NSW) Fire Brigades, in Australia, in 1970 and worked as a firefighter and officer throughout NSW during that period. Ross was awarded the Australian Fire Service Medal in 2005 for his contribution to fire investigation with the NSW Fire Brigades. He retired in December 2007 after serving the community of NSW for more than 37 years. In June 1987, he successfully completed the Arson Awareness section of NSW Police Detective training course; in August he was appointed to NSW Fire Brigades Fire Investigation Unit as an investigator, a position he held until 2003. In January 1999, Ross was awarded a Graduate Certificate in Fire Investigation; in 2004, he graduated with a Graduate Diploma of Fire Investigation; and in 2008, he graduated with a Master of Arts (Fire Investigation). Since March 2003, Ross has co-presented a 6-day practical fire investigation course for Charles Sturt University to students from the police, the fire service, private investigators, insurance investigators, and forensic science students. Ross continues to teach for Charles Sturt University. Ross is currently a member of the International Association of Arson Investigators, NSW, Victoria, and Queensland chapters; a USA International member; and a member of the Australian & New Zealand Forensic Science Society. He has been qualified by voir dire in both the criminal and the civil jurisdiction of the Supreme Court in NSW to give opinion evidence as an expert witness in fire matters. In all, Ross has attended and given evidence in excess of 100 matters throughout Australia.

Gareth Norris, PhD

Gareth is a lecturer in criminology at Aberystwyth University, Wales, UK. He was previously a lecturer in forensic psychology at Liverpool Hope University, UK, and a teaching fellow at Bond University, Australia, where he completed his doctoral thesis examining authoritarianism. Gareth has worked with a variety of criminal justice agencies, including the Metropolitan Police Service and HM Prison Service. He is a graduate of the MSc Investigative Psychology program at the University of Liverpool, and he has an interest in the use of psychology in investigations and the legal process.

Daniel B. Kennedy, PhD

Daniel is a forensic criminologist specializing in security and police issues. Before joining the sociology and criminal justice faculty at the University of Detroit Mercy in 1976, he was employed as an urban renewal worker, probation officer, and police academy director. Daniel has served as an expert witness throughout the United States, Canada, Mexico, and the Caribbean. He is board certified in security management and has published widely in various issues of *Security Journal, Journal of Security Administration, Journal of Criminal Justice, Crime and Delinquency, Criminal Justice and Behavior, Justice Quarterly, Professional Psychology, Victimology,* and *Security Management.*

Robert Homant, PhD

Robert has a PhD in Clinical Psychology. After 4 years as a staff psychologist at Michigan State Prison where he was director of the Sex Offender Program, he moved to Wisconsin State Prison as Chief Psychologist. He is currently full professor and chair of the Department of Sociology and Criminal Justice at the University of Detroit Mercy, where he teaches courses in deviant behavior, psychology and law, and corrections. His research interests include workplace violence and suicide by cop, and he has written a number of articles on criminal profiling and factors affecting criminally deviant behavior.

Michael McGrath, MD

Michael McGrath is a Board Certified Forensic Psychiatrist, licensed in the State of New York. He is a Clinical Associate Professor in the Department of Psychiatry, University of Rochester School of Medicine and Dentistry, Rochester, NY, and Medical Director & Chair, Department of Behavioral Health, Unity Health System, Rochester, NY.

Dr. McGrath divides his time among administrative, clinical, research and teaching activities. His areas of expertise include forensic psychiatry and criminal profiling. He has lectured on three continents and is a founding member of the Academy of Behavioral Profiling. He can be contacted at: mmcgrath @profiling.org.

David Field, LLB

David Field is an Associate Professor of Law at Bond University in Gold Coast, Australia. Former Solicitor for Prosecutions for Queensland, stipendiary magistrate for Glasgow, also former prosecutor and defense trial attorney in both Scotland and Australia (Qld and NSW). Author of *Evidence Law in Queensland,* as well as numerous textbook chapters relating to law end evidence.

Kind to children, considerate towards animals, and environmentally friendly. Available for funerals and bah mitzvas. Happily married, although my wife may not be.

Andrew Lowe, BS (Criminology)

Andrew is a police officer with the Queensland Police Service. He holds a Bachelor of Social Science (Criminology) qualification, and has published in the area of stalking. His interests include stalking, criminal profiling and forensic science. Andrew is currently and investigator working in child protection.

Elizabeth Fry, MCrim

Elizabeth completed a Joint Honors degree in Criminology and Sociology including a thesis on Education in a Young Offender Institute in the United Kingdom. She has also completed a Master of Criminology which included a thesis on Consistencies in Crime Scene Characteristics and Offender Behavior in Intimate Partner Homicide in Queensland, Australia. Elizabeth's current interests include criminal profiling, forensic criminology and juvenile homicide and she is actively continuing research into these areas.

CHAPTER 1

Criminal Profiling: A Continuing History

Gareth Norris

KEY TERMS

Cesare Lombroso: An early anthropometrician who attempted to infer criminality from bodily features.

Thomas Bond: A police surgeon who provided an ad hoc profile of Jack the Ripper, a serial murderer from Whitechapel, in the late 1800s.

Walter Langer: A psychiatrist who was asked by the Office of Strategic Services to provide a profile of Adolf Hitler, including his future actions.

James Brussel: A New York-based psychiatrist who provided the profile of the Mad Bomber of New York, George Metesky, in the 1950s.

Howard Teten and Pat Mullany: FBI agents who started profiling in the FBI in the 1970s.

David Canter: A British psychologist who provided the profile of the Railway Rapist, John Duffy, for Scotland Yard and later developed investigative psychology.

Kim Rossmo: Developed Criminal Geographic Targeting and is an advocate for geographic profiling.

Brent Turvey: A forensic scientist from the United States who developed the deductive profiling method called behavioral evidence analysis.

CONTENTS

1

INTRODUCTION

To the viewer of Hollywood thrillers or television crime dramas, the idea that an offender type can be identified through his or her behaviors at the crime scene—very often with little or no accompanying forensic evidence—understandably captivates one's attention. A certain air of mystique often surrounds the "profiler" in these instances, who is usually portrayed as a humble yet troubled individual in possession of an innate ability to decipher behavioral cues that ultimately leads to the capture of the suspect. Numerous accounts of the accurate representation of profiling and its depiction in mainstream media precede this writing (Alison & Canter, 1999; Petherick, 2003); however, the technique we now refer to as profiling has a relatively short but fascinating history, drawing on a range of diverse disciplines throughout its inception and evolution. Some of the first attempts at profiling could feasibly be attributed to early anthropologists, such as *Cesare Lombroso* and his attempts to link physical attributes to criminal activity (Turvey, 2008; Woodworth & Porter, 1999). Others even associate the basic principles to fictional characters such as Sir Arthur Conan Doyle's *Sherlock Holmes* (Egger, 1999). Although these may fit into many of the definitions of what profiling aims to be, they are often too simplistic in their portrayal, and a wide range of scholarly and professional debate has developed to encompass this absorbing and important field of criminal investigation.

Criminal profiling has been referred to by many other titles, such as psychological profiling, offender analysis, behavioral profiling, or offender profiling, and these terms are often used interchangeably. Likewise there exist numerous definitions of what actually constitutes a profile and what its overriding aims are deemed to be. One of the most cited is from Geberth (1996, p. 492), who defines it as "an educated attempt to provide investigative agencies with specific information as to the type of individual who would have committed a certain crime." Although others offer variations to this, the general aim of a profile is to provide the police with a composite "sketch" of the likely offender. This usually includes common demographic variables, such as age, ethnicity, and marital status, and the more specific considerations of past criminal history, possible motivation, and likely area of residence (Ault & Reese, 1980). The level of detail, and indeed the overall style of a profile, will depend not just on the actual technique being utilized but also very much on the individual who is creating it. With a range of often conflicting schools of thought providing the theoretical paradigm on which profiling is based, there are often contradictory accounts of the various elements, from evidence examination to the nature of investigative advice. Depending on who is consulted to provide such a profile could therefore have a profound influence on the investigation of a crime—should it rely on the profile for guidance.

EARLY BEGINNINGS

One of the earliest examples of profiling comes from the infamous case of Jack the Ripper, who terrorized the streets of Whitechapel, London in the late 1800s. Police pathologist Dr. *Thomas Bond* was to infer that the offender may have been suffering from a condition known as *satyriasis*—excessive and uncontrollable sexual desire in males (Rumbelow, 1988, p. 140). Contrary to popular belief, Bond also cast doubt on previous speculation that the offender was a surgeon or butcher due to the deft use of his weapon of choice (or, in his opinion, the lack thereof). Whereas some had speculated over the proficiency of dismemberment, the physical evidence suggested to Bond that the offender did not have particularly specialized anatomical knowledge. Unfortunately, and in a similar vein to many modern attempts at profiling, the offender in this case has never been identified, and people still speculate as to the likely perpetrator to this day. A similar case involving early manifestations of profiling—the Dusseldorf Vampire, Peter Kurten—also included a number of psychological considerations by pathologist Dr. Karl Berg in 1929. In this case, Berg believed the offender to be a narcissistic psychopath due to the degrading treatment of his victims (Berg, 1945). Both of these examples demonstrate how the two pathologists speculated as to the *type* of individual who was likely to have committed these crimes. Somewhat unintentionally, the opinion served to indicate who the authorities should be looking for, even though these affirmations may have been uninformed.

Although medical doctors made what we identify as the first criminal profiles,[1] as a branch of medicine, *psychiatrists* have also engaged in various forms of assessment. Whereas pathologists and other medical specialists are occasionally involved in criminal investigations, psychiatrists are more often involved in forensic settings, such as in the assessment of mental illness and fitness to plead/stand trial. Similarly, military psychiatrists/psychologists are more often employed in the assessment of personnel, although one other aspect of their work may involve the creation of propaganda materials, such as creating information for leaflet drops behind enemy lines. Judging the opinions of those involved in a conflict has often been used to guide strategy, and there are numerous accounts of German psychologists who were involved (involuntary or otherwise) in the Nazi war effort (Billig, 1978).

In 1943, a psychiatrist named *Walter Langer*[2] was asked to provide a psychological profile by the Office of Strategic Services.[3] With psychodynamic theory being at the

---

[1]Interestingly, Arthur Conan Doyle's fictional detective Sherlock Holmes was based on one of Doyle's instructors, a doctor, at the Edinburgh Royal Infirmary.

[2]The actual document was authored with the collaboration of Henry Murray, Ernst Kris, and Bertram Lawin.

[3]The Office of Strategic Services was a part of the U.S. Army in charge of gathering intelligence during the war effort. It disbanded in 1945, and many of its functions were taken over by the Central Intelligence Agency.

forefront of behavioral analysis at the time, the resulting assessment indicated the individual to be a *neurotic psychopath* and in dire need of expressing his manliness to his mother. He predicted that at the ultimate climax to conflict, the individual would most likely commit suicide. The focus of this profile was Adolf Hitler, and although a thorough comparative clinical examination could not be performed, Langer was at the very least correct about Hitler committing suicide, who did so in his Berlin bunker 2 years later. Interestingly, commentators place much emphasis on the suicidal realization of Hitler when, in fact, the prediction was the most probable in a list of eight such scenarios:

1. *Hitler may die of natural causes*—deemed to be a remote possibility because he was in good health aside from a stomach ailment, probably linked to a psychosomatic disturbance.
2. *Hitler might seek refuge in a neutral country*—unlikely because it would cast doubt on his myth of immortality by fleeing at the critical moment.
3. *Hitler might be killed in battle*—a possibility because he may desire to expose himself as a fearless leader and may have the adverse effect of binding the German people to his legend.
4. *Hitler might be assassinated*—another plausible outcome, which he himself had speculated over.
5. *Hitler may go insane*—he was believed to exhibit many characteristics of a borderline schizophrenic, and if faced with defeat, it was likely his psychological structure would collapse.
6. *German military might revolt and seize him*—an unlikely event due to the unique position he enjoyed in the eyes of the German people, but he may be confined in secret should he become unstable.
7. *Hitler may fall into our hands*—the most unlikely eventuality because this would be the scenario he personally would do his utmost to avoid.
8. *Hitler might commit suicide*—the most conceivable conclusion due to his inordinate fear of death, which he had already envisaged, stating "Yes, in the hour of supreme peril I must sacrifice myself for the people."

What is important to understand at this period in time is that although clinical assessment was becoming an important and emerging field, seldom was any evaluation conducted with the person not *in situ*. What Langer was attempting to provide was a psychological picture of someone whom he had not physically examined and also to provide some indication of his likely future actions. Indeed, Langer was to comment that such as study "was a far cry from the first-hand data with which a psycho-analyst usually works" (Langer, 1972, p. 26). Langer's eventual profile was exhaustive and included a number of sections on how the German people viewed Hitler, the way in which his associates regarded him, and the way Hitler believed himself to be. The overall aim was to both tentatively guide future dealings with him and, specifically, to aid in the propaganda effort against him.

Although Langer documents each circumstance and its likelihood of occurrence, a more detailed review of the text indicates the tenuous nature of the profile in general. There is some level of psychiatric assessment—for example, that he could be a borderline schizophrenic or a hysteric—but significant interpretation on his actual behavior relies on Hitler's own assertions, gleaned primarily from his writings and speeches. Nevertheless, Langer's work was to lead the way for others to analyze "unknown" individuals based on the observation of their behavior. Similar evaluations of major political leaders have also been constructed, including Freud's seldom cited psychological profile of former U.S. president, Thomas Woodrow Wilson (Freud & Bullitt, 1966).

JAMES BRUSSEL AND FORENSIC PSYCHIATRY

Following the work of Langer, the New York-based psychiatrist *James Brussel* was to provide a profile of the Mad Bomber, who had been terrorizing the city for a number of years (Brussel, 1968). The apprehension of George Metesky in 1956, being almost the mirror image of Brussel's prediction, right down to the legendary double-breasted suit Brussel predicted he would be wearing,[4] was to guide profiling into a new era. Whereas Langer had information on his subject and was aware of him as a person in the physical sense, Brussel had been able to provide his assessment on the basis of other information and with no prior knowledge of the actual offender. From his examination of the crime scene actions and other materials (e.g., the letters sent to the police), Brussel suggested that the offender was suffering from paranoia and most probably held a grudge against the Edison electrical company (the company was defamed in numerous letters discovered at the bomb sites and also the target of the first bomb). In particular, the letters written by Metesky to the police contained numerous phrases that were uncommon among the colloquial language of resident Americans and led to the (correct) assumption that the bomber was therefore more likely an overseas immigrant. Geographically, Brussel also examined the locations where the letters were posted and determined that he was most likely to commute to Manhattan by train and therefore could quite probably live somewhere in Connecticut. According to Brussel, when apprehended and taken in for questioning, Metesky appeared almost relieved that his vendetta could now come to an end (Brussel, 1968). Confined to a secure facility, Brussel would sporadically come into contact with Metesky, who he described as a gentleman and model patient.

---

[4]Contrary to popular belief, Metesky was apprehended at his home and answered the door to the police wearing his pajamas. He requested he be allowed to change, and he emerged wearing a buttoned double-breasted suit.

Criminal profiling was now becoming largely the property of a number of leading psychiatrists, who through relative genius, educated guesswork, or just plain luck were assisting the police in some high-profile cases. This method of profiling has since been termed *diagnostic evaluation* (Wilson, Lincoln, & Kocsis, 1997) and is essentially the psychologist's or psychiatrist's evaluation of the offender based on, for example, developmental and/or clinical issues (Badcock, 1997). Developmental (the personal needs and life experiences) and clinical (patterns of offending associated with mental illness) analyses are the cornerstone of forensic practitioners, enabling their expertise and training to be utilized in identifying possible aspects of the offender's psyche. Aside from theorizing over these developmental, clinical, and other related issues, forensic consultants have also attempted to marry theories of personality with those of the likely individual involved in a crime (Boon, 1997; Copson, Badcock, Boon, & Britton, 1997). Personality theories provide a framework for assessing what are commonly regarded as relatively consistent patterns of behavior present in an individual that cause him or her to behave in certain ways in certain situations. Therefore, theoretically at least, their application to criminal profiling would seem pertinent.

The forensic practitioner's main strengths perhaps lie in providing insight into the more bizarre cases. Indeed, some believe profiling should only be undertaken when there are signs of psychopathology (Pinizzotto, 1984) or else support the work of nonforensic profilers by providing them with insights into personality and abnormal psychology (McGrath, 2000). Liebert (1985, p. 294) is critical and suggests that "if investigative personnel believe that a serial murderer is basically a bad person who behaves offensively because he has chosen a particularly nefarious habit, the psychiatrist can be of little assistance." The general consensus appears to be that although most crimes can be profiled, it is the more atypical and disturbing ones that hold a place for the opinion of the forensic clinician. Their understanding of psychopathology gleaned from clinical assessment of their patients, coupled with their extensive training in abnormal psychology, is unparalleled in assessing the behavior of such criminals. Although other methods may have a more practical application within the investigative process, the consultation with forensic psychologists and psychiatrists still has a valuable role.

THE FEDERAL BUREAU OF INVESTIGATION AND CRIME SCENE ANALYSIS

When in 1964 Albert DeSalvo was apprehended and charged with being the "Green Man" rapist, it was largely Brussel's profile that provided the police with the confidence to also charge him with being the Boston Strangler, following his confession to his psychiatrist, so similar was he to the profile (Brussel, 1968).[5] Additional cases such as the Son of Sam[6] also indicated that profiling had a lasting utility in the investigation of many serious criminal episodes. Brussel was involved in the advent of what is regarded by many as the first serious attempt to standardize and validate the profiling process and provide some theoretical and empirical base for its predictions. Collaboration between Brussel and two members of the newly emerging Federal Bureau of Investigation (FBI) Academy, Special Agents *Howard Teten* and *Pat Mullany*, led the organization to create a systematized basis for the understanding of criminal behavior in the early 1970s (Turvey, 2008). Teten and Mullany established the Behavioral Science Unit (BSU)—immortalized in the movie *The Silence of the Lambs*—at Quantico, Virginia. The unit still exists as the National Center for the Analysis of Violent Crime.

Although it would still be some years before the term *profiling* would be officially accepted into wider discourse, Teten and Mullany essentially instructed new recruits at the academy about profiling, under the banners of *applied criminology* and *abnormal psychology*. Although these two individuals were the forefathers of this program, credit for the program usually falls to a number of other members of the unit. The initial results of the first main study on profiling, with the aid of a grant from the National Institute of Justice, were published in May 1985 (Ressler & Burgess, 1985). The original document is a relatively technical script, complete with pages devoted to statistical analysis; however, included within is a separate section titled *Crime Scene and Profile Characteristics of Organized and Disorganized Murderers*. The edited report was later published as the text, *Sexual Homicide: Patterns and Motives* (Ressler, Burgess, & Douglas, 1988). Primarily, it is the significance of the organized/disorganized dichotomy that is of particular importance in understanding the history of this branch of profiling.

Now termed *Criminal Investigative Analysis*, the technique has transformed from humble beginnings as an exploratory study of incarcerated offenders to using this information as a base for inferring characteristics of past offenders. In 1979, the BSU began the Criminal Personality Research Project, which was a precursor to the Institute of Justice-funded project (Ressler et al., 1988, p. 104). Eventual data collection took 4 years (1979–1983) and involved, by its eventual completion, 36 individuals, including a number of professional staff from the Boston City Hospital (Ressler & Burgess, 1985). Interviews were conducted

---

[5]DeSalvo was never actually tried with the Boston murders, following his violent death at the hands of another inmate while on remand. Some controversy still surrounds whether he was actually the culprit.

[6]Profiled by Dr. Murray Miron (from Geberth, 1996).

with 36 incarcerated sexual killers[7] and revealed a number of generalizable patterns of behavior. These were subsequently separated by what was perceived at the time to be a function of the level of organization that had been extended to the commission of the crime by the offender. The approach resulted in a checklist of behaviors, each categorized as being associated with an organized or a disorganized offender. These crime scene behaviors were then mapped onto the list of characteristics of that particular style of offender. It is documented that as early as 1978, BSU agents were profiling not only murders but also rape, arson, extortion, and a range of other violent and nonviolent offenses (Ressler et al., 1988, p. 104). Although in 1978 the actual organized/disorganized system had not been formally confirmed, its practical application had already been firmly established.

Their work also spawned many interesting concepts, including the *Crime Classification Manual* (CCM) (Ressler, Douglas, Burgess, & Burgess, 1992). Another FBI agent, Roy Hazelwood, later developed a categorization system for rapists whereby he classified them as being either selfish or unselfish according to their level of interaction with the victim (Hazelwood, 1987). Within this classification, Hazelwood further categorized them into a number of more detailed typologies[8] that were believed to reveal significant clues as to the type of offender concerned. The CCM set about providing detailed characteristics of offenders who committed various subtypes of behaviors (e.g., anger excitation) within the more general crime type (e.g., rape). Whereas the original study had focused on sexual murderers, there was now an attempt to give a more comprehensive understanding to many other types of criminal behavior. This has been likened by some to what the *Diagnostic and Statistical Manual* did for the assessment and treatment of clinical patients in psychology and psychiatry (McGrath, 2000). The CCM aimed to allow investigators to look up the behaviors of a particular crime and then map these onto the type of offender they were looking for. The FBI's study was one of the most innovative and pioneering approaches to the study of crime at the time, and credit should be awarded to the collaborators on the project. Agents from the FBI have consulted on major crimes throughout the world, and many past agents have attained almost celebrity status in the field of crime analysis, producing many semi-autobiographical accounts of their cases. In addition to these memoirs, they are often available for comment on many high-profile incidents for which their expert opinion is still widely sought.

---

[7]Although legend has it that 36 of the United States' most prolific serial murderers were examined, there were in fact only 36 multiple killers, and not all the sample agreed to be interviewed; instead, their data were gleaned from official documents.

[8]Labeled as power reassurance, power assertive, anger retaliatory, and anger excitation (developed from Groth, 1979).

DAVID CANTER AND INVESTIGATIVE PSYCHOLOGY

In November 1985, Professor *David Canter* from the University of Surrey, England, was contacted by two senior detectives from New Scotland Yard to discuss the viability of adopting the new method of criminal detection being developed by the FBI in the United Kingdom.[9] According to Canter (1994), these meetings were fairly casual from their outset until concern rose over a spate of violent rapes and murders in Greater London. The media had coined the name "Railway Rapist" to describe John Duffy, who was later apprehended with the assistance of the profile created by Canter. In particular, the locations of Duffy's offenses, being near railway lines and stations, enabled a reasonably accurate prediction of his home location by Canter. Other features of the profile—that Duffy would be in a troubled marriage, would be interested in martial arts, and would collect pornography—proved similarly accurate. While on trial for an assault on his wife, the police brought a previous victim to the court in an attempt to identify Duffy. Realizing the victim may have recognized him, Duffy's behavior escalated and he began to murder his future victims to hinder subsequent identifications. It was at this point, armed with forensic evidence and the information from Canter's profile, that Duffy was arrested. This early success led to further explorations into this emerging field, which was to be named *Investigative Psychology* (IP) and taught as a postgraduate course at the University of Surrey.[10]

The profile that Canter constructed of Duffy was, by his own admission, a very rudimentary document; as an environmental psychologist, Canter was at this time not fully acquainted with the workings of the criminal mind (Canter, 1994). Despite obvious apprehension, Canter, with the aid of two seconded police officers, began a systematic review of past cases in order to analyze them and provide a logical pattern. Although taken for granted in the age of the Internet, Canter used computer technology available at the time to search for patterns in the offender's behavior, revealing a subset of practically identical patterns. One important feature to emerge was that it appeared the individual in question was learning from his mistakes as the crime series progressed. The most striking aspect, however, was that although descriptions of offenders usually include height and hair color and are notoriously inaccurate (as in this case), a composite sketch of the *type* of person who was committing these rapes and

---

[9]The FBI had prior to this been consulted by the Metropolitan Police on a number of rapes in the Surrey district of Guildford.

[10]The Master's of Science in Investigative Psychology program ran from 1992 to 1994 at the University of Surrey before moving to its current base at the University of Liverpool.

murders was beginning to emerge. The main tenet of Canter's theory was that offenders do not live and operate in a vacuum but, rather, their criminal behavior mirrors their noncriminal behavior. This led to what Canter referred to as a "criminal shadow." Canter's theory of criminal narratives, as explained by his five factor model of interpersonal coherence, time and place, criminal career, forensic awareness, and criminal characteristics, has a strong psychological basis and is regarded as being a relatively robust and viable way of classifying offenders (West, 2000). As the more academic of the three disciplines discussed so far, IP has a continually evolving theory base, and research continues on its applicability and utility in investigations.

KIM ROSSMO AND GEOGRAPHICAL PROFILING

Although Canter's explorations into spatial behavior form a major part of the overall profiling process within the five factor model of offending behavior he proposed (Canter, 1994), others have further developed an almost separate branch of the profiling tradition. In particular, *Kim Rossmo* advocates his technique of *geographical profiling* as a distinct subdiscipline of profiling (Rossmo, 2000). The use of crime mapping in the more general sense has become a prominent tool in the police arsenal. Emanating from environmental criminology, and with particular reference to the work of Brantingham and Brantingham (1982), the majority of spatial theories share the same theoretical underpinning, namely that the farther an offender is away from his or her home location, the less likely he or she is to offend. This is commonly referred to as *distance decay* and relies on the assumption that not only do criminals prefer to operate in areas that they are familiar with but also these areas where they offend share distinct overlap with the places they attend as noncriminals. Rossmo's Criminal Geographic Targeting computer simulation uses an algorithm based on the Brantinghams' notion of distance decay and buffer zones. Indeed, comparative analysis of a number of such systems revealed a surprising similarity in their levels of accuracy (Levine, 1999). Geographic profiling has developed out of a distinct psychological theory base, and it is incorrectly considered by some to be the most "scientific" of the methodologies in that it relies on a number of mainstream psychological and behavioral principles, such as routine activity theory (Rossmo, 2000).

Prior to these computer simulations, Kind (1987) reported his retrospective prediction of the home location of the Yorkshire Ripper, Peter Sutcliffe. Navigational techniques, particularly the notion of a center of gravity, enabled Kind to accurately calculate Sutcliffe's home location. The accuracy of geographical profiling, however, is in some instances less impressive. For this reason, it is seldom used in isolation, instead frequently forming a subsection of an overall profile. Cases such as the "Beltway Sniper" in Washington, DC (see Chapter 10) are useful illustrations of the limitations of this particular method; in many instances, the crime is so unusual that nobody could realistically predict the spatial behavior of the offender(s) (Canter, 2003). Rossmo and Canter have been at the forefront of geographical profiling research, and their consultation with law enforcement agencies has helped to bring this technique into the public eye. Other applications of geographical profiling are regularly used by crime analysts and others interested in geographical crime trends (Ainsworth, 2001). Although it is unlikely that such a profile would be sufficient to apprehend a suspect in its own right, some continue to argue that it is a particularly useful way of prioritizing suspects through geographic location rather than through more subjective personal characteristics.

BRENT TURVEY AND BEHAVIORAL EVIDENCE ANALYSIS

Concerned that these relatively reductionist methods of analyzing criminal behavior were largely based on biographical narratives of a small number of incarcerated offenders, forensic scientist *Brent Turvey* created another addition to the profiling portfolio. In the mid-1990s, following an interview of convicted murderer Jerome Brudos, Turvey rejected these statistical evaluations on the basis that the accounts on which they were largely based could not be accurately relied on (Turvey, 2008). Reviewing the interview material from Brudos, Turvey discovered some major discrepancies in comparison with the police case files. This led him to the conclusion that it was inappropriate to accept the premises on which the profiles were usually based because the data analyzed were equivocal at best and, more often than not, factually incorrect. The method that arose from these concerns was termed *Behavioral Evidence Analysis* (BEA). It is distanced somewhat from the other methods in that it is viewed as deductive rather than inductive, the distinction being the specificity of the former and the generalizability of the latter (and the subsequent "certainty" with which the premises of any prediction can be made). Whereas diagnostic evaluations, CSI, and IP aim to provide guidance and focus to police investigations, BEA purports to be more of a holistic philosophy of criminal investigation (Turvey, 2008).

Regardless of its philosophy or content, BEA embraces a comprehensive and methodological approach to profiling, alongside the forensic science backdrop on which it is based. Particular emphasis is placed on such facets of the criminal event as victimology and motivation, which run parallel to such features of the BEA profile as wound pattern analysis and crime scene reconstruction. The cornerstone of this approach is not only the desire to give the police some guidance in their investigation or to narrow suspect pools but also to provide a comprehensive reconstruction of each criminal event. In contrast, CSA or IP, for example, provides a more general picture of the likely offender based on the analysis of past cases and assumes to a large degree that the police and forensic experts have made available all the information relating to the investigation. Although this reconstruction process should not be overlooked, BEA is still a relatively new concept; however, a third edition of the *Criminal Profiling* text and other publications continue to add to its theoretical foundation (Chisum & Turvey, 2007; Turvey, 2008). Courses in BEA are also taught to students and professionals in a range of jurisdictions, including the United States, China, Singapore, and Australia.

CONCLUSION

For an historical review to be of any practical utility, the conclusion to it must provide a snapshot of not only the current position but also likely future directions. The four main methodologies documented currently operate in relative isolation from each other; indeed, much acrimony exists between the many proponents from each camp as to who has constructed the most valid and reliable technique. As has been illustrated, each theory has developed in part by drawing upon each other in at least one respect, if only to capitalize on the inherent weaknesses present in each. The early explorations into the criminal mind by forensic practitioners such as Brussel paved the way for the agents from the FBI to develop these principles into a more structured and systematized approach to classifying criminals and identifying their likely attributes. The work of David Canter has further refined these early explorations into a rigorous and comprehensive methodology that has been applied to many different crime types and situations. Canter has been a strong proponent of the importance of time and space, and these ideas resonate in the work on geographical profiling by Kim Rossmo. Although the work of Brent Turvey somewhat distances itself from these methods, it was born of the concern that the generalizations on which they are based may be the result of inaccurate data, and it provides a healthy warning on the nature of being too complacent in the profiling process.

The term profiling has been extended into other areas of the legal system, has become increasingly linked with the notions of "jury" and "racial" profiling, and is now almost synonymous with terrorism. The methodologies involved can also take on the form of data-driven, statistical generalizations or the hunches of the individuals believing themselves to be gifted in such perceptions (Wrightsman, Greene, Nietzel, & Fortune, 2002). For the profiling of suspects in criminal cases, attempts to evaluate such approaches for their validity or accuracy have been largely inconclusive (Copson, 1995). One reason for this has been a general reluctance by most practitioners to reveal their methods, let alone their results. Comparisons between the different methods in experimental situations have been rare, if not nonexistent, but evaluations between trained profilers, detectives, psychologists, and other groups have met with unconvincing results (Kocsis, Irwin, Hayes, & Nunn, 2000; Pinizzotto & Finkel, 1990). Some high-profile cases have highlighted other issues with profiling that have cast their own limitations on such practices. In particular, ethical and legal concerns have been prominent in shaping the direction of professional profiling practice. As noted by Alison, McLean, and Almond (2007), there has been a general reluctance by either the British Psychological Society or the American Psychological Association to devote attention to profiling as a specific subdiscipline of forensic psychology, with the exception of the usual cursory note regarding members engaging in activities outside of their training or expertise. However, in the United States, the FBI has its own training program, and in the United Kingdom the National Centre for Policing Excellence holds lists of accredited profilers. Other organizations, such as the Academy of Behavioral Profiling, also seek to add some level of professionalism and accountability to the work of its members.

Perhaps, as has been demonstrated in The Netherlands, a more integrated approach could provide more utility. The Dutch police have set up the Offender Profiling Unit within their National Criminal Intelligence Division of the National Police Agency. Although parallels can be drawn between it and the FBI style of profiling, it adopts a far more multidisciplinary approach to the investigation of crime (Ainsworth, 2001; Jackson, van den Eshof, & de Kleuver, 1997). Forensic professionals, rather than being consulted by the investigating officers, are instead involved in the investigation from the outset. Again, rather than profiling being a panacea for apprehending an offender, profilers and psychologists work throughout the entire investigative process, offering guidance and assistance, up to and including the eventual interrogation and prosecution. Other developments, such as the emphasis on profiling as a decision support tool and its role in critical incident management, serve to integrate profiling into existing investigative frameworks rather than maintain it as a stand-alone endeavor (Alison, 2005). Profiling methodologies and techniques are now quite commonly being applied to high-volume crime, such as burglary (Bennell & Jones, 2005). Establishing closer and rewarding collaboration between the police and social scientists also breaks down many of the barriers that exist between each group. Where traditionally the police have been relatively closed to the idea of the need for outside help, similarly many social scientists and profilers have been seen to display an air of arrogance with their offers of assistance. Dispelling these prejudices and myths can only provide a more fruitful and lasting contribution to the field in the long term.

Questions

1. One of the earliest examples of criminal profiling was:
   a. Peter Kurten (The Dusseldorf Vampire)
   b. Jack the Ripper
   c. Adolf Hitler
   d. Woodrow Wilson
   e. None of the above
2. The criminal profiling program in the FBI was primarily started by:
   a. John Douglas and Robert Ressler
   b. Robert Ressler and Roy Hazelwood
   c. Howard Teten and Pat Mullany
   d. Jack Kirsch and Brent Turvey
   e. Maurice Godwin and David Canter
3. The terms offender profiling, behavioral profiling, offender analysis, and psychological profiling have all been used interchangeably over time. *True or false?*
4. The Washington sniper case is a useful illustration of the utility of geographic profiling. *True or false?*
5. Provide a brief overview of each of the major profiling paradigms presented in this chapter.

REFERENCES

Ainsworth, P. B. (2001). Offender Profiling and Crime Analysis. Cullompton, UK: Willan.

Alison, L. (2005). From trait-based profiling to psychological contributions to apprehension models. In L. Alison (Ed.), The Forensic Psychologist's Casebook: Psychological Profiling and Criminal Investigation (pp. 3–23). Cullompton, UK: Willan.

Alison, L., & Canter, D. (1999). Profiling in policy and practice. In D. Canter & L. Alison (Eds.), Profiling in Policy and Practice (pp. 3–22). Aldershot, UK: Dartmouth.

Alison, L., McLean, C., & Almond, L. (2007). Profiling suspects. In T. Newburn, T. Williamson, & A. Wright (Eds.), Handbook of Criminal Investigation. Cullompton, UK: Willan.

Ault, R., & Reese, J. (1980). A psychological assessment of crime profiling. FBI Law Enforcement Bulletin, 49.

Badcock, R. (1997). Developmental and clinical issues in relation to offending in the individual. In J. L. Jackson & D. A. Bekerian (Eds.), Offender Profiling: Theory, Research and Practice (pp. 9–42). Chichester, UK: Wiley.

Bennell, C., & Jones, N. J. (2005). Between a rock and a hard place: A method for linking serial burglaries by modus operandi. Journal of Investigative Psychology and Offender Profiling, 2, 23–41.

Berg, K. (1945). The Sadist: An Account of the Crimes of a Serial Killer. London: Heineman.

Billig, M. (1978). Fascists: A Social Psychological View of the National Front. London: Academic Press.

Boon, J. C. W. (1997). The contribution of personality theories to psychological profiling. In J. L. Jackson & D. A. Bekerian (Eds.), Offender Profiling: Theory, Research and Practice (pp. 43–60). Chichester, UK: Wiley.

Brantingham, P. L., & Brantingham, P. J. (1982). Mobility, notoriety and crime: A study of crime patterns in urban nodal points. Journal of Environmental Systems, 11, 89–99.

Brussel, J. (1968). Casebook of a Crime Psychiatrist. New York: Bernard Geis.

Canter, D. (1994). Criminal Shadows. London: HarperCollins.

Canter, D. (2003). Mapping Murder: The Secrets of Geographical Profiling. London: Virgin Books.

Chisum, W. J., & Turvey, B. E. (2007). Crime Reconstruction. London: Academic Press.

Copson, G. (1995). Coals to Newcastle? Part 1: A Study of Offender Profiling (Police Research Group Special Interest Series No. 7). London: Home Office.

Copson, G., Badcock, R., Boon, J., & Britton, P. (1997). Articulating a systematic approach to clinical crime profiling. Criminal Behaviour & Mental Health, 7, 13–17.

Egger, S. A. (1999). Psychological profiling: Past, present and future. Journal of Contemporary Criminal Justice, 15(3), 242–261.

Freud, S., & Bullit, W. C. (1966). Thomas Woodrow Wilson: A Psychological Profile Study. Boston: Houghton.

Geberth, V. J. (1996). Practical Homicide Investigation (3rd ed.). New York: CRC Press.

Groth, A. N. (1979). Men Who Rape: The Psychology of the Offender. New York: Plenum.

Hazelwood, R. R. (1987). Analyzing the rape and profiling the offender. In R. R. Hazelwood & A. W. Burgess (Eds.), Practical Aspects of Rape Investigation: A Multidisciplinary Approach. New York: Elsevier.

Jackson, J. L., van den Eshof, P., & de Kleuver, E. E. (1997). A research approach to offender profiling. In J. L. Jackson & D. A. Bekerian (Eds.), Offender Profiling: Theory, Research and Practice (pp. 107–132). Chichester, UK: Wiley.

Kind, S. (1987). Navigational ideas and the Yorkshire Ripper investigation. Journal of Navigation, 40, 385–393.

Kocsis, R. N., Irwin, H. J., Hayes, A. F., & Nunn, R. (2000). Expertise in psychological profiling: A comparative assessment. Journal of Interpersonal Violence, 15(3), 311–331.

Langer, W. (1972). The Mind of Adolf Hitler. New York: Basic Books.

Levine, N. (1999). Crimestat: A Spatial Statistics Program for the Analysis of Crime Incident Locations. Washington, DC: National Institute of Justice.

Liebert, J. (1985). Contributions of psychiatric consultation in the investigation of serial murder. International Journal of Offender Therapy and Comparative Criminology, 29(3), 187–199.

McGrath, M. G. (2000). Criminal profiling: Is there a role for the forensic psychiatrist? Journal of the American Academy of Psychiatry and Law, 28(3), 315–324.

Petherick, W. (2003). Criminal profiling: What's in a name? Comparing applied profiling methodologies. Journal of Law and Social Challenges, 5(1), 173–188.

Pinizzotto, A. J. (1984). Forensic psychology: Criminal personality profiling. Journal of Police Science and Administration, 12(1), 32–39.

Pinizzotto, A. J., & Finkel, N. J. (1990). Criminal personality profiling: An outcome and process study. Law and Human Behavior, 14, 215–233.

Ressler, R. K., & Burgess, A. W. (1985). Sexual Homicide Crime Scenes and Patterns of Criminal Behavior [Final Report]. Boston: National Institute of Justice.

Ressler, R. K., Burgess, A. W., & Douglas, J. E. (1988). Sexual Homicide: Patterns and Motives. New York: Lexington Books.

Ressler, R. K., Douglas, J. E., Burgess, A. W., & Burgess, A. G. (1992). The Crime Classification Manual. New York: Simon & Schuster.

Rossmo, K. (2000). Geographic Profiling. Boca Raton, FL: CRC Press.

Rumbelow, D. (1988). The Complete Jack the Ripper. London: Penguin Books.

Turvey, B. (2008). Criminal Profiling: An Introduction to Behavioral Evidence Analysis (3rd ed.). Burlington, MA: Academic Press.

West, A. (2000). Clinical assessment of homicide offenders: The significance of crime scene in offence and offender analysis. Homicide Studies, 4(3), 219–233.

Wilson, P., Lincoln, R., & Kocsis, R. (1997). Validity, utility and ethics of profiling for serial violent and sexual offenders. Psychiatry, Psychology and Law, 4, 1–12.

Woodworth, M., & Porter, S. (1999). Historical foundations and current applications of criminal profiling in violent crime investigations. Expert Evidence, 7, 214–264.

Wrightsman, L. S., Greene, E., Nietzel, M. T., & Fortune, W. H. (2002). Psychology and the Legal System (5th ed.). Belmont, CA: Wadsworth.

CHAPTER 2

Induction and Deduction in Criminal Profiling

Wayne Petherick

KEY TERMS

Logic: The science of valid thought and the process of argumentation.

Non sequitur: An argument in which the conclusion does not follow logically from the premise(s).

Premise: The evidence, information, or reasons that support the main claim of an argument.

Induction: Where the conclusion is made likely by the supporting evidence or premises.

Deduction: Where the conclusion is made certain by the supporting evidence or premises.

CONTENTS

INTRODUCTION

Literature on criminal profiling has reached a considerable volume, including not only a quantity of true crime works but also numerous scholarly texts and articles. The casual reader will be familiar with some aspects of profiling, with the more discerning reader being familiar with the steps involved in the profiling process (Holmes & Holmes, 2002; Ressler, Burgess, & Douglas, 1988; Turvey, 2008), the so-called "inputs" and "outputs" of a criminal profile (Davis, 1999; Egger, 1999; Geberth, 1996; Ressler & Burgess, 1985; Ressler et al., 1988), and the personality and grandiosity of profilers (see a variety of memoirs, such as Canter, 1994; Douglas & Olshaker, 1996, 1997, 1998; and Ressler & Shachtman, 1992).

However, beyond a few works (Petherick, 2006; Turvey, 2008) there has been less written in any valid way about the logical processes employed by the profiler when drawing conclusions about the offender.[1] This chapter provides an in-depth examination of the two main approaches used by profilers to arrive at their conclusions: *induction* and *deduction*. First, a general commentary on the logic of criminal profiling is provided, followed by a detailed discussion of induction and deduction, illustrating the fundamental differences between the two forms of reasoning. Finally, a hypothetical case scenario highlights the procedural aspects of how hypotheses are generated and a deductive conclusion is drawn.

LOGIC AND CRIMINAL PROFILING

This section begins by providing an introduction to logic and continues with the application of logic in criminal profiling. This is based on Petherick (2007, 2008) and Petherick and Turvey (2008a). As an introduction to logic only, the reader is encouraged to seek out Petherick and Turvey (2008a) for a more detailed treatment of the subject.

Logic may be defined as the process of argumentation or as a "unified discipline which investigates the structure and validity of ordered knowledge" (Farber, 1942, p. 41). Bhattacharyya (1958) suggests that logic is the science of valid thought, and Stock (2004) claims that logic is both science and art. More than simply providing a theoretical foundation on which to structure arguments, the basic principles and precepts of logic allow for a more thorough and rigorous testing of any argument put forth in a profile. In short, we can establish the veracity of a conclusion by juxtaposing the theory of logic onto that conclusion to determine whether it comports to good reasoning.

As a good starting point, McInerney (2004) provides three basic principles of logic that all profilers should avail themselves of. In this author's experience of peer review and examination of written profiles, many errors of logic fall into at least one of the following categories:

> *The principle of identity*: A thing is what it is. Existing reality is not a homogeneous mass, but it is composed of a variety of individuals. In profiling, this argument may be best used to argue for the independence of thought in regard to profiling particular crimes. That is, each case should be treated as an individual rather than a simple extension of other similar crimes. In other words, each crime represents its own universe of evidence, behavior, and victim–offender interactions.

---

[1]There has actually been quite a lot written on logic in profiling, but much of it relies on subjective or personal accounts with little recourse to foundational theoretical works on the subject. This results in a skewed, often biased, and largely invalid account of logic and reasoning.

The principle of the excluded middle: Between being and nonbeing, there is no middle state. Perhaps the best way to view this in the context of profiling is "either a crime (or an action/behavior) has occurred, or it hasn't." The key to establishing the validity of this *premise* is in carrying out a detailed and complete reconstruction to establish exactly what has occurred and what has not. Only through a proper forensic evaluation can the true nature and quality of the thing being examined be gauged.

The principle of sufficient reason: There is sufficient reason for everything. This may also be called the principle of causality. This principle states that everything in the known universe has an explanation for its existence. Implied here is that nothing is self-explanatory or the cause of itself, and perhaps most important, that all instances of a known thing must have an explanation that is realistic within accepted bodies of knowledge. Farber (1942) suggests that knowledge in its primary sense means true knowledge, in that it conforms to established facts of reality. In short, any argument put forth must not be sensational or rely on phenomenological explanations for cause or existence.

It would not be an understatement to claim that there is confusion surrounding logic within profiling. This goes way beyond a lack of theoretical understanding and extends into a total lack of regard for the practical implications of sound logic and reasoning. Before further considering the differences between the two main types of logic and reasoning, it is necessary to first understand the confusion and its subsequent impact.[2]

This confusion is not peculiar to initiates in the profiling community but is also prevalent among practicing profilers. Deduction, a specific type of reasoning, has taken on a casual meaning, with the majority treating it as synonymous with a conclusion, thereby believing that any conclusion is a deduction. For example, the following extract provides a "profile" and a brief commentary boldly claiming the conclusion is deductive, when in fact it is not (Klump, 1997, p. 123):

"You didn't have a burglary," I told the caller. "It was an employee, a man who has worked for you about 4 months. He's an assistant manager or a shift leader, probably between the age of 25 and 30, a loner and a quiet person. He's usually broke, but does not borrow money from other employees. He probably drives an older car that doesn't run very well; he may have trouble getting to work on time because of it. He's probably married and has young children. Do you have anyone like that?"

---

[2]This section is adapted from Petherick (2007, 2008).

"Yes we do," the owner answered, "The assistant manager. He closed on Friday night. How do you know all this?"

"Well, actually, you told me."

Deduction is a mental art investigators should cultivate. When they are evaluating a business crime, deducing the meaning of seemingly insignificant verbal or physical clues can trigger a chain of insights that lead directly to the perpetrator.

Even Brussel, the famous psychiatrist who profiled the Mad Bomber, adopts a rather casual usage (Brussel, 1968, p. 44):

Next I risked a deduction about the Bomber's age. I said, "He's middle aged."

The plainclothes detectives looked dubious again. Inspector Finney asked, "How do you figure that?"

"Well," I said, "Paranoia develops slowly. It doesn't usually erupt in its full force before the person is 35. This man has been making and planting his devices for 16 years."

If this were a valid deduction, the development of paranoia would have to follow such a predictable course that the age of onset occurred so often, and had been studied so extensively, that it had become law or principle (the age of onset may differ depending on the severity of the condition, whether medication is involved, and the biochemistry of the individual). Furthermore, it must have been established that the offender produced no bombs prior to those showing up in New York (so that the spree could not predate the 16-year mark). Even then, the nature of the deduction would be dubious (it would actually be a non-demonstrative inference or *false deduction* because many of the premises could not be reliably established). Therefore, the argument is *non sequitur*, meaning the conclusion does not necessarily follow logically from the premise.

In *Hunting Serial Predators*, Godwin (1999, p. iii) provides his view on induction and deduction:

Profiles constructed by the FBI profilers, clinical psychologists, criminologists, and the police routinely draw inferences about, for example, serial murderers and their behaviors based solely on work experience, gut feelings, and the motivation of the offender. This form of deductive profiling is where the profiler assumes one or more facts as self-evident about a crime or offender and then, following work experience and hunches, arrives at other facts commonly called conclusions. Hence, the FBI profiles are deductive rather than inductive. However, some argue that the FBI profiling method is inductive.

> Broadly, the argument put forward for the FBI method being inductive
> is since the FBI relies on data collected from interviews with serial
> murderers, as a foundation for developing their profiles, then their
> reasoning must be inductive. The basis for this argument is flawed,
> because the data collected by the FBI has never been empirically
> analyzed, nor has it been properly organized in a systematic manner so
> that profilers could refer to it in the future.

Godwin suggests that the Federal Bureau of Investigation's (FBI) method is deductive, and the basis for this seems to be because the FBI relies on experience and "gut feelings." He also notes profilers using deduction make assumptions about facts as being self-evident, even though such assumptions are contradictory to both theoretical and applied logic. Godwin, like Canter (1995), goes on to explain how others consider the FBI to be deductive because it relies on data collected from interviews with offenders. He notes that this is incorrect because the data has never been empirically analyzed or organized in such a way that it could be referred to in the future. This is also incorrect. First, the data was statistically analyzed and presented by Burgess and Ressler (1985), and second, inductive analyses need not be subjected to any high-level statistical procedures. A conclusion is inductive, at the most basic level, because it is probabilistic and uncertain, representing only one possibility of many. However, at the most basic level, a deduction is not a matter of statistical probability but, rather, a certain conclusion based on the established validity of the premises.

In 2002, Godwin published "Reliability, Validity, and Utility of Criminal Profiling Typologies." This article seeks to address the problems with a number of profiling methods, including those prescribed by the FBI (2002), Holmes and Holmes (2002), and Hickey (2002). Therein, he provides a number of critiques of what is referred to erroneously as "deduction." For example (Godwin, 2002, p. 13),

> As previously discussed, the reliability, validity, and utility of deductive
> profiles generally offered to police investigations are weak and have
> met with continual criticisms. For example, Godwin (1978) argues that
> profilers are playing blind man's bluff, groping in all directions in the
> hope of touching a sleeve. Levin and Fox (1985) point out that offender
> profiling as we know it today is vague and general and basically
> useless in identifying a killer.

As discussed in Chapter 3, there are very few criticisms of deductive (rational/concrete/case-oriented) profiling methods in the literature. Godwin, in fact, appears to be referring to profiling methods, such as those taught by the FBI, which are not actually deductive. This is a case of mistaken identity on Godwin's part because FBI methods are inductive (statistical/abstract/group-oriented). Subsequently, his claims of their weakness and other criticisms are misdirected.

It is also useful to note that Godwin's critique of profiles, which references material that dates back to 1978, predates the development of literature and theoretical foundation for the current application of deductive logic to profiling (Petherick & Turvey, 2008b). As such, his use of Godwin (1978) is entirely misplaced and all but moot. Levin and Fox's (1985) claim is similarly dated in light of modern developments. It would seem that these researchers would do well to invest in updated reference material in that regard.

However, all of these critiques could be legitimately levied at inductive profiling approaches, even those in use today. To do this, however, authors would need to correctly identify the differences, advantages, and disadvantages of each. This has yet to occur in the literature.

Interestingly, Godwin (2002) goes on to cite a number of other problems, including bias, selective thinking, and a particular logical fallacy—post hoc ergo propter hoc (it is actually cited as post hoc ergo proper hoc, which is incorrect). Of bias and selective thinking, Godwin is actually referring to adductive reasoning. This is a well-known concept in the science of logic, wherein a conclusion is developed without a full appreciation of the facts, and the reasoner then seeks out only confirmatory evidence. An example is the case in which a female homicide victim is found and the police believe it is a domestic homicide. The husband cannot provide an alibi, which it is believed "proves" their theory. This despite the fact that the victim was in a relationship with another male and has been receiving threatening and abusive e-mails and telephone calls and has been the subject of physical stalking. This information is ignored because it does not conform to the prevailing theory. Such reasoning, again, is emblematic of inductive profiling methods.

Of additional concern in this article is Godwin's constant reference to psychics and visions. In the discussion on the post hoc fallacy, Godwin (2002, p. 14) suggests that

> this form of reasoning in profiling is the basis for many erroneous conclusions. For example, you have a "vision" that a body is going to be found in the water near a tree and later a body is found in the water near a tree.

I do not disagree at all with the first assertion, that the post hoc fallacy is a problem in the profiling community, but to suggest that deductive reasoning is in any way associated with psychics or visions is an error of considerable note.

The safeguard against all of this is thorough application of the scientific method. It is the cornerstone of deductive profiling and by nature devoid of weak or biased inductive profiling conclusions. However, the problem does not end there, and things definitely do not get any better.

Godwin is not alone in claiming that deduction revolves around experience, and Canter (2000, p. 24) also uses this as the basis to determine whether something is inductive or deductive. For example, "deduction is a form of implicit reasoning in which whatever experience or logic the reasoner can draw upon will be used to derive inferences about the culprit from aspects of the crime." This will be faulty in part because of the failure to subject theories to falsification, a core component of any deductive argument.[2] As a form of personally experienced average such conclusions are actually inductive, with experience failing to meet the threshold of a deductive conclusion. Canter (2000, p. 24) also supplies the following:

> An example that illustrates this well is a case in which the victim of an unidentified assailant noticed that the offender had short fingernails on his right hand and long fingernails on his left hand. Somebody with specialist knowledge suggested that this was a characteristic of people who are serious guitar players. It was therefore a reasonable deduction that the assailant was somebody who played the guitar.

As with Godwin's argument about reasoning, Canter is simply providing one explanation out of any possible number of offender characteristics. This example is actually using Holmesian logic to draw conclusions about what is inductive and deductive, and this is perhaps not the best position from which to argue the point. Despite the prima facie validity of some of Holmes' arguments, many of his assertions were inductive hypotheses awaiting testing and are not deductions in their own right (the style of logic employed by Sherlock Holmes is referred to as hypothetico-deduction). Another discussion given on this case shows a further lack of understanding regarding proper logic (p. 24):

> This example shows the fundamental weaknesses of the deductive approach. Without clear empirical evidence about the prevalence of this particular pattern of nail length it is difficult to know whether the claim that it is unique to guitar players is valid. It may not be true of many guitar players and it may be a pattern that exists in many other individuals. In fact, in the case in question, the offender who was eventually identified had no contact with guitars and had this peculiar pattern of nail length because of his job in repairing old tires.

By Canter's own admission, there are other possibilities, one of which was discovered after the apprehension of the offender. For this to be a proper deduction, there would have to be a universal law or principle governing the situation in which someone's fingernails were shorter on one hand than on the other,

---

[2]There is nothing inherently wrong with using experience to inform opinions because it is intuition and experience that may tell a detective what question to ask or where to look for evidence. However, when conclusions are based only on experience, the process, regardless of good intent, will likely be flawed.

as well as the subsequent reason for this. Furthermore, it would have to be established that this is true in every single case. Even carrying out research on this particular constellation of nail length, as suggested, would not make the conclusion deductive because other possibilities may explain the difference.

In an earlier piece, Canter (1995, p. 343) likens deduction to commonsense reasoning as if the employment of common sense is a sufficient condition to meet the strict requirements of putting forward a deductive argument:

> Although the inference processes on which the FBI agents drew were illuminated by interviews they themselves had conducted with a few dozen convicted offenders, and by their own experiences of investigating many crimes, their processes of inference derivation were broadly *deductive*, being based upon common sense as might be the basis of judicial decisions. In the tradition of the detective novel, and other less fictional accounts of the solving of crimes, the processes that the FBI agents used focused on the clues derived directly from the crime scene. They drew upon general principles, drawn from everyday experience, to deduce the implications that the internal logic of a crime might have.

It seems that a good deal of the confusion comes from the definitions of induction and deduction used (if any), or indeed, whether one simply makes up their own as is often the case. It is worth noting that very few authors operationalize their terminology, with most relying on an idiosyncratic interpretation of what induction and deduction mean. This need to operationalize definitions is more than a simple academic exercise. It avoids ambiguity, communicates meaning, and enables the end user to understand exactly how the conclusion arose from the available evidence. As stated by McInerney (2004, p. 37),

> The most effective way to avoid vagueness or ambiguity in logical discourse is to define one's terms. We speak of defining terms, but actually what we are defining is the objects to which terms (words) refer. The process of definition, the mechanics of it, is the way we relate a particular object (the object to be defined) to other objects and thereby give it a precise "location." In defining a term or word, we relate it as rigorously as possible to the object to which it refers. There are two immediate practical benefits of carefully defining terms. Our own ideas are clarified, and, as a result, we can more effectively communicate them to others.

Strano (2004) shows similar confusion in his understanding of induction and deduction. Although accurately identifying that the criminal profile should be deduced from a forensic examination and behavioral reconstruction of the criminal event, Strano falls back into statements of probability where it is suggested that "from the combination of these data, a profiler attempts to deduce the characteristics of an offender who most *likely* [italics added] has committed a specific crime, with a specific victim, and under the distinctive conditions that characterize a particular crime scene" (p. 497).

Perhaps Strano's misunderstanding comes from the fact that he cites Godwin (1999), who is himself unaware of the finer points of logic:

> The criticisms of the deductive profiling model underline the fact that a deductive profiler's inferences about crime scene behavior may produce conclusions without any scientific basis. Occasionally, a profiler's deductive opinions about what may have happened at a crime scene are theoretically or empirically driven by research activity and hypothesis testing, but in many cases, they are based on personal experiences, a small number of cases (often closed, confidential information), and personal hunches.

It is true that a deductive process employs rigorous theory building and testing, and deductive conclusions are usually premised on inductively derived knowledge. However, the position that a deduction is based on personal experience belies a greater misunderstanding. Strano (2004) accurately suggests that the strength of the deductive method lies in the fact that if the premises are true, then the conclusions will also be true. However, he goes on to suggest that this is not always the case, which means the conclusion would not actually be deductive. This becomes a fault in understanding and application, not method.

In perhaps the most confusing discussion in the literature to date, Kocsis and Palermo (2007) discuss the different schools of thought in profiling without any detailed discussion of Behavioral Evidence Analysis, but of most concern is their take on deduction. They state the following (pp. 336–337):

> One recent development has been the suggestion that two distinct forms of profiling exist. The premise for this distinction is based on differing reasoning processes (i.e., inductive or deductive) that are argued to be in use by an individual when composing a profile. Inductive criminal profiling uses inductive reasoning, which in this context is defined as "reasoning involving broad generalizations or statistical reasoning, where it is possible for the premises to be true while the subsequent conclusion is false" (89, p. 686). Deductive criminal profiling, on the contrary, involves deductive reasoning, which is defined as "an argument where, if the premises are true, then the conclusions must also be true. In a deductive argument, the conclusions flow directly from the premises given" (89, p. 682). These distinctions form the basis of a method of profiling, referred to as behavior evidence analysis (BEA), which exclusively favors the use of deductive reasoning in combination with an understanding of the forensic sciences for the composition of a competent profile (90).

The problem with such distinctions is that it transposes philosophical paradigms onto the functional processes of the mind. Although the distinction between inductive or deductive reasoning is a well-established concept in the literature pertaining to critical thinking (91), there is debate in the cognitive psychology/psychiatry literature as to whether the mind functions in such a categorical fashion—that is, whether cognitive functions akin to inductive or deductive reasoning can be undertaken to the exclusion of one another (92,93). Unlike the autonomic functions of a computer, it is unlikely that the human mind is truly capable of engaging in such a discrete process of reasoning. Indeed, the brain itself, as a complex and highly active neuronal synaptic system, may subconsciously process diverse and/or intrusive thoughts that may increase the difficulty of full engagement in one or the other method. If the cognitive processes of the mind are incapable of engaging in this fashion, the suggestion of a method of profiling premised on the issue of one form of reasoning to the exclusion of the other is rendered highly problematic.

This provides yet another example of how these concepts get more than a little lost, with the most confusing assertion being that the human mind is not capable of thinking in such a discrete way. Readers should by now be more than familiar with, and critical of, the problem of taking such a position on the issue of induction and deduction.

Regardless of what profiling method is used, all approaches use logic to reach conclusions, with the logical structure of profiles being based on two components: premises and conclusions. The premises are the reasons that support the main claim of an argument (Alexandra, Matthews, & Miller, 2002), whereas the conclusions are what is inferred from them. For example, if a profiler argued that an offender was a male, there should be some support for that claim. This support may rely on physical evidence—semen found inside a sexual assault victim is a premise that supports such a conclusion—or the victim or a passerby may have identified the offender as a male. It is mainly in the strength of the link between premises (reasons) and conclusions (claims) that profiling methods significantly differ.

The reasons offered in support of the argument must directly contribute to strengthening the conclusion, and those reasons must be true. That is, the argument must link logically, and the arguments made must be true of the world (the *principle of sufficient reason*). For example, if the examination of a sexual assault victim did not yield any pubic hair, it is not logical to immediately argue that the offender did not have any pubic hair because other considerations and possible links should be explored. Also, if there is semen inside the vaginal vault, it is not sound reasoning to argue that women have semen, so it must have been a woman (because this would be unsupported by what is known to be true). What needs to be established is that the argument is valid (linkage) and sound (true of this world). Establishing the veracity of each component ensures that one's judgment has logical foundation.

As noted previously, an argument can be either inductive or deductive. Inductive arguments are *likely*, whereas sound deductive arguments are *certain*. These forms of reasoning are best thought of as representing different points of certainty along the same continuum. Although distinguishable along a continuum, both generally have, in their own right, an equally important function contingent on context.[3] Induction has a place in logical argumentation, but its place within the process of deriving profile characteristics is questionable beyond a certain point. In other words, a statistical probability is not a conclusion and should never be offered up as one.

INDUCTIVE CRIMINAL PROFILING

An *inductive argument* is one in which the conclusion is made likely by the supporting reasons or premises. A good inductive argument provides strong support for the conclusion, although the argument is not infallible. For example, U.S. crime statistics indicate that 90% of people who committed murder in 2002 were male (FBI, 2002). This does not guarantee the conclusion that an unknown offender for any given murder case will be a male; therefore, inductive premises provide varying degrees of certainty. In an inductive profile, the characteristics put forth in the profile are projective or predict some future event; they state what the offender will be like when he or she is found. As such, profile characteristics are a determination of offender traits evidenced at the crime scene and assumed to be relatively stable over time. For example, an offender who displays anger at the crime scene may be assumed to be a generally angry person in everyday life. An offender who treats his or her victims with care and attention may also be thought to exhibit these characteristics as part of his or her personality.

Inductive profiles rely on statistical and/or correlational reasoning (Petherick & Turvey, 2008c); thus, the information rendered in an inductive profile is based on probabilities. Induction is "a type of inference that proceeds from a set of specific observations to a generalization, called a premise, and this premise is a working assumption" (Thornton, 1997, p. 13).[4] Specific observations in a case are compared to the differences or similarities in past cases of the same or similar

---

[3]Induction is used to structure arguments typically concerning future events.

[4]Induction is not always identifiable, however, by whether the argument moves from the specific to the general.

nature, and these past cases serve as a generalization of typical offender characteristics. In terms of application, induction is also the simplest method to use.

It is the simplicity of this method that makes it more widely used in the profiling community because a vast amount of knowledge is not required in any one area. Instead, requisite skills include the ability to analyze statistics and prior crimes information as well as knowledge of where to find research when required. These two components are often an attribute of any profiling approach in which induction features prominently, as discussed by Kocsis (2001, p. 32):

> To use this model to produce a psychological profile, behaviors from any of the [behavior] patterns are compared and matched with those of the unsolved case. Once a behavior pattern has been matched with the unsolved case it can be cross-referenced with offender characteristics.

As illustrated by the sample size in the original FBI study of 36 offenders (Burgess & Ressler, 1985) and Hickey's (2002) study of serial murderers (62 women and 337 men over a period of 195 years), access to a large number of offenders or cases may not be possible, depending on the type of crime. Thus, the sample size of these studies is generally small, limiting studies to exploration, not explanation. Other authors are also concerned about the issue of sample size. For example, Canter et al. (2004) notes that the FBI agents who conducted the study did not use a random or even a large sample of offenders. One can never be certain, therefore, that the studies used as a point of reference are indeed reflective of the circumstances of a given case. Other factors may further hamper the application of generalizations, and Turvey (2008) identifies five scenarios in which averaged offender characteristics may not apply. The following are relevant to all inductive efforts:

- Anger retaliatory offenders who do not suffer from any kind of mental illness
- Domestic violence-related offenses
- Staged offenses
- Interrupted offenses
- Offenses involving controlled substances

Thus, although inductive generalizations may be true in some (even many) cases, there is no guarantee that they will apply in the current case, and before the offender is caught there is no real way to determine if they do apply.

APPLIED INDUCTIVE PROFILING

The following inductive profile was presented to a Coroner's Court in Australia in 2003. The testimony was offered by a state police profiler trained under the International Criminal Investigative Analysis Fellowship. When questioned on the racial extraction of the offender, the profiler reasoned as follows (p. 37):

> The likely characteristics of the person responsible are that he would be a male and [he] would be of white European racial extraction. That is based on the victim being white European and generally these crimes are committed intraracially and also you have the demographics of the area which was also predominately white European.

The logic of this style of profiling can be broken down as follows:

> Premise 1: The victim was a white European.
> Premise 2: Generally these crimes are committed intraracially.
> Premise 3: The demographics of the area are predominately white European.
> Conclusion: The likely person responsible is of white European racial extraction.

The conclusion is only probable because the profiler's primary source of guidance when determining the offender's racial or ethnic identity is Premise 2. This profiler has examined the case, referred to the research, and subsequently found that there is a general pattern of intraracial comparability, giving an opinion based on that comparability. Premise 3 is a supportive inference because presumably the demographics of a given geographical location are also indicative of offender racial extraction. Overall, the strength of the conclusion is contingent on the term *generally* in Premise 2. Thus, it should be clear how inductive reasoning guides the formulation of a profile.

Furthermore, if inductive arguments are linked together to support a conclusion, then one must be sure of the reliability of each premise. This is because a faulty chain of reasoning can lead from case observations to offender characteristics in a less than reliable manner. The following example illustrates how delicate final conclusions can be when contingent on a chain of *probable* reasoning. This example shows how age was reasoned in the same case (to reproduce the passage in its entirety would be awkward; see Coroner's Court [2003] for full details):

> Premise 1: During the course of the abduction, the victim was able to scream out twice, the second time longer and louder.
> Premise 2: The victim's property was left behind at the scene.
> Premise 3: There was a tearing of the shopping bag.
> *these indicate*
> Premise 4: The victim was able to struggle and resist up to a point.
> *also*

Premise 5: There were two male offenders.[5]
this suggests
Premise 6: Their execution plan was somewhat sloppy.
in turn
Premise 7: This reflects some inexperience in this area.
because
Premise 8: If the offenders had more experience in their backgrounds, one
    would not expect to see the victim scream and resist in this way.
therefore
Premise 9: It appears that they were inexperienced, probably immature.
Premise 10: These things contribute to the youthful age.
Conclusion: The (dominant) offender is most likely in his early twenties.

At first glance, the premises may appear to logically support the opinion. Yet, each step in the chain of reasoning weakens the strength of the overall conclusion because not every argument is deductive in its own right. Premises 1, 2, and 3 work to support Premise 4, and there are no obvious problems with the initial premises (unless the claims are rejected outright). However, Premises 4 and 5 argue that because the victim was able to struggle and resist against the offender(s), this supports Premise 6—that the offense plan was sloppy. This is questionable logic because the claim that the offenders insufficiently planned an abduction is reasoned on the basis of how the victim reacted at the time of the offense. This argues that such an interaction is indeed predictable. In turn, the assumption of predictability supports Premise 7 that the offenders were inexperienced, and Premise 8 states that experienced offenders do not allow Premise 4 to happen. Because the offenders are deemed to be inexperienced, they are *probably* immature. Premise 9 argues that experiential immaturity equals a youthful age, as stated in Premise 10. From this chain of causal reasoning, the conclusion is reached that the dominant offender is *most likely* in his early twenties. If any premise within the argument is found to be incorrect at any point (e.g., Premise 6), then the characteristic becomes questionable. This is because the conclusion is reliant on the entire chain of reasoning.

Any lack of certainty should be reflected in the end product by the language used to portray any thoughts the profiler has about the likely offender. Such statements as "the offender usually," "it would be typical to find," and "it is my belief that" must accompany inductive profiles in order to articulate the lack of certainty the profiler has about the conclusions. For example, if one were to assert that most murderers are male and, therefore, an unknown murderer

---

[5]Incidentally, the number of offenders in this case was not fully established, so this remains an assumption and any subsequent conclusions drawn are questionable.

is male, this is presenting an inductive argument as certain—the offender *is*—rather than a statement of probability—the offender *is likely to be*. It should be clear then that the principal purpose of inductive reasoning is the development of hypotheses and not conclusions.

DEDUCTIVE CRIMINAL PROFILING

Deductive profiling involves a more scientific approach and is a rational or logical process in which offender characteristics are a direct extension of the physical evidence (Petherick & Turvey, 2008b). Thus, if the premises are true, then the conclusions must also be true (Bevel & Gardiner, 1997). Neblett (1985, p. 114) goes further, stating that "if the conclusion is false, then at least one of the premises must be false." For this reason, it is incumbent on the profiler to establish the validity of each and every premise before drawing conclusions.

Because deductive arguments are structured so that the conclusion is implicitly contained within the premises, unless the reasoning is invalid, the conclusion follows as a matter of course. For example, if police enter a domestic dispute and find the husband in the process of stabbing his wife and she later dies from the severity of these stab wounds, it is valid to deductively reason that the husband killed his wife. One may argue that in fact the wife died as a result of blood loss or through the hemorrhaging of a vital organ and, therefore, not as a result of the husband's actions per se. However, as long as it can be proven that the husband's actions directly contributed to the death of his wife, one is entitled to deduce from the premises that the husband killed his wife.

Deductive arguments are designed to take us from truth to truth. That is, an argument is valid if (Alexandra et al., 2002, p. 65)

- It is not logically possible for its conclusion to be false if its premises are true
- Its conclusion must be true, if its premises are true
- It would be contradictory to assert its premises yet deny its conclusion

Applying this rationale to the prior example, it is not logically possible for the conclusion (that the husband killed his wife) to be false if the premises (the police caught the husband in the act and she died from the severity of the stab wounds) are true. Second, that the husband is responsible for the act of killing his wife must be true if one accepts the premises (that the police walked in on the husband stabbing his wife and she died as a result of these injuries). Third, it would be contradictory to assert that the police caught the husband in the process of stabbing his wife and she later died from the stab wounds, and then deny that the husband is the person who killed his wife. Thus, the argument is deductive.

Deductive profiling draws on the scientific method, which involves the testing of hypotheses through observation and experimentation. When a hypothesis has consistently withstood falsification, it can be presented using the appropriate deductive structure. In exactly the same manner, deductive profiling develops particular hypotheses about a case and then attempts to rule out competing hypotheses on the basis of the available physical evidence. However, simply submitting a hypothesis to falsification does not make it deductive. For this to happen, the certainty of the argument must be rationally unquestionable. This means that any subsequent falsification of the conclusion must not be undertaken with reference to the fantastical or phenomenological. In addition, the structure of the argument is critical and should conform to a specific standard. This can be found in any introductory text on logic and is also covered briefly next.

THE LOGIC OF DEDUCTIVE CRIMINAL PROFILING

A scientific profiling paradigm develops hypotheses about a case from which attempts are made to falsify competing hypotheses on the basis of the available physical evidence. The end result is a set of conclusions that is, on the basis of all available physical evidence, deductive. However, the resulting profile is by no means static, with new developments in logic challenging currently held hypotheses. A deductive profile will attempt to ascertain how this evidence fits the profile. That is, does this new knowledge change the current hypothesis? If so, the profile is updated to fit this new paradigm of understanding. If not, it is categorized as a weaker hypothesis but not discarded (an example of this process is provided at the end of this chapter).

An example of how a deductive profile is reasoned can be found in Turvey (2008, pp. 564–565). On the basis of the physical evidence, Turvey reasons from the hypothesis that "if an offender carefully disarticulates a victim, then, they have demonstrated some degree of medical knowledge" to the conclusion that "the crime evidences an offender with medical knowledge":

Premise 1: If an offender carefully disarticulates a victim, then, they have demonstrated some degree of medical knowledge.
Premise 2: The victim was not dismembered with commonly associated chopping instruments such as a hatchet, cleaver, or machete applied to areas of bone (such as a butcher might use).
Premise 3: There is no evidence that a sawing instrument such as a hacksaw, band saw, skill saw, or radial saw was used.
Premise 4: There is evidence that the offender(s) separated the victim's head, arms, legs, and feet at their respective joints with the utmost deliberation, precision, and care using a very sharp cutting instrument not unlike a scalpel.
Conclusion: The crime evidences an offender with medical knowledge.

The conclusion is a direct extension of the *available* physical evidence and does not make any conclusions outside the physical evidence, nor does it claim what level of medical knowledge the offender must have—only that the offender's behavior suggests that he or she has the requisite skill to perform the disarticulation. To reject the argument as deductive would require that the conclusion is not true due to rejection of the premises on which it is based. By extension, rejection of the premises would require rejection of the physical evidence. Because no interpretation has been placed on the evidence, this is not logical (the scalpel is an example of what tool may have been used to obtain that kind of precision). Second, one would have to argue that the conclusion could be false even on the acceptance of the premises. Because the argument leads directly from the physical evidence to the conclusion, any argument would have to suggest that the disarticulation of human joints with the utmost precision does not logically suggest (in any way) some degree of medical knowledge. Third, one would have to explain why it is not contradictory to assert the premises and subsequently deny the conclusion.

As a result, deductive profiling is typically less adventurous with its determinations, with Turvey (2008) citing four characteristics that can be deductively inferred[6]: knowledge of the scene, knowledge of the victim, knowledge of methods and materials, and criminal skill. Although it may appear at first to be a shortcoming, it must be remembered that a deductive profile works with physical evidence and will not venture into the unknown with supposition and assumption. To have 4 points about which one can be certain is better than having 40, the bases of which are questionable. It is also worth noting that the utility of a profile is largely a consequence of the surety of its conclusions. A profiler who is willing to venture into the unknown with his or her analysis runs the very real risk of leading investigations astray and wasting valuable time.

PRACTICAL APPLICATION OF DEDUCTIVE CRIMINAL PROFILING

The following is a scenario that illustrates how deductive profiling is applied. This example is not meant to be exhaustive, nor will it include every possibility from the evidence presented, but it is designed to be procedurally instructive. Note that more detail has been provided in this chapter regarding deduction because, comparatively speaking, deduction is far more complex than the application of statistical generalizations and therefore warrants greater explanation.

---

[6]It is possible to infer other offender characteristics deductively, such as the sex of the offender, if there is physical evidence, as will be shown. However, if physical evidence is present, one may not need a profile to state it.

Consider the following crime scene behavior:

> During an anal sexual assault, an offender approaches the victim from the front, allowing her to get a good look at him. He then wraps a belt around her neck, pulls down his pants before pulling her shirt up over her head, thereby revealing her breasts, which he manipulates. After completing the sodomy, the offender leaves the victim with her shirt in place, which covers her face.

Analyzing the case from a deductive perspective presents one with a number of hypotheses that can be measured against the evidence, including the following:

- The offender is a male.
- The belt was brought to the crime scene by the offender.
- The offender pulled the shirt up over the victim's head to help him believe the victim was somebody else.
- The offender pulled the shirt up over the victim's head to obscure identification.
- The offender pulled the shirt up to provide access to the victim's breasts.

These await testing against the available evidence and show the development of theories and, in the first instance, a deductive conclusion. Some of the hypotheses may or may not be borne out by further examination of the physical and behavioral evidence. These are considered in turn[7]:

1. The offender is a male: Following evidence at the crime scene and provided by the victim, it could be said that this hypothesis has been established. However, the ways in which this may be established through physical evidence include, for example, an examination that yields sperm in and around the victim's anus. This can be reasoned as follows:

   Premise 1: The victim was subjected to an anal sexual assault.
   Premise 2: The victim reports seeing the offender's penis.
   Premise 3: Semen was found around the victim's anus and vagina.
   Conclusion: The offender is a male.

2. The belt was brought to the crime scene by the offender. This can be reasoned as follows:

   Premise 1: The belt did not belong to the victim.
   Premise 2: The victim stated that the belt was not at the crime scene prior to the assault.

---

[7]Although this is how a deductive argument is structured in theory, it would not be usual to find the logic outlined in such a detailed way. To present each characteristic in this way may be cumbersome, and providing the argument is supported in a logical way, it may not be necessary to provide the full and complete logic for a given characteristic. However, there must be a minimum threshold providing support for the argument.

Premise 3: The victim reported seeing the offender remove the belt from around his waist.

Conclusion: The belt was brought to the crime scene by the offender.

3. The offender pulled the victim's shirt over her head to assist with the fantasy that the victim was someone else. This hypothesis can be reasoned as follows:

Premise 1: The offender did not call the victim by another name.

Premise 2: The offender did not engage in any other fantasy-related behavior.

Conclusion: At this point in time, there is no evidence to suggest that the offender pulled the victim's shirt over her head to assist with the fantasy that she was someone else.

4. The offender pulled the shirt up over the victim's head to obscure identification.[8] This hypothesis can be reasoned as follows:

Premise 1: The victim saw the offender on initial approach and a number of times before the shirt was pulled up.

Premise 2: The offender made no attempt to stop the victim from seeing him.

Premise 3: The offender did not engage in any other precautionary acts.

Premise 4: The offender left the victim alive and made no threats to her safety should she contact police.

Conclusion: The shirt was not pulled up over the victim's head to obscure identification.

5. The offender pulled the shirt up over the victim's head to provide access to the victim's breasts. This hypothesis can be reasoned as follows:

Premise 1: The offender did not pull the shirt up over the victim's head to assist with the fantasy that she was someone else.

Premise 2: The offender did not pull the shirt up over the victim's head to obscure his identification.

Premise 3: Once the shirt was raised over the victim's head, the offender immediately started fondling her breasts.

Conclusion: The offender pulled the shirt up to provide access to the victim's breasts.

Restated for absolute clarity, determining offense-related characteristics is about asking the right questions of offense-related behavior (Turvey, 2008). The first part of this process is defining the characteristic we are arguing, and the second

---

[8]As with everything in profiling, context is critical, and a determination of exactly when during the assault this was done would help discover the reason behind the action.

part involves determining which physical or behavioral evidence supports this. If the reconstruction of the offense includes those behaviors, then they can be argued. Considering and ruling out competing hypotheses is also important, as these examples and discussion have shown.

It should be apparent that this process is very systematic and thorough in developing knowledge about a particular case. Deduction utilizes a scientific approach for examining competing hypotheses and identifies certain arguments from the available physical evidence. In this way, not only can voids in knowledge be identified but also we can provide investigative strategies to overcome these voids. This leads to a more complete approach, leaving little to guesswork. Verifying the validity of the physical evidence also helps determine the veracity of the subsequent behavioral evidence and its interpretation, which is an extension of hypothesis generation.

CONCLUSION

This chapter has examined the logical structure of criminal profiling. Inductive profiling involves the application of statistical and probabilistic knowledge to a current case, and the source of this information is usually criminological studies, the profiler's own experience, intuition, bias, stereotypes, and generalizations. The strength of the conclusion reached through inductive profiling is contingent on the probability of the knowledge or research that has been utilized. Although useful in developing hypotheses, induction is not well suited to the final determination of offender characteristics. Conversely, deductive profiling involves the assessment of the physical material relating to the current case. Deductive profiling analyzes the evidence in the context of the case. Sound reasoning and critical thinking skills are applied to thus arrive at a logical conclusion.

Criminal profilers should not attempt to formulate a hypothesis about a case until they have examined all the physical evidence. Once the case has been thoroughly examined and hypotheses have been generated, then the profiler can attempt to provide a behavioral interpretation of the physical evidence. Apart from the practical implications, through an increased awareness of the logic and reasoning employed in the profiling process, we will also be better able to understand the individual methods and the utility they offer.

Questions

1. The two main types of logic used in criminal profiling are _____ and _____.
2. Explain the difference between inductive and deductive logic.
3. What are the five scenarios provided by Turvey that will effect the application of generalizations in a given case?

4. The argument that follows the format *If P then Q, P, therefore Q* is known as
_____.

5. In deductive logic, if the premises are true, then the conclusion will be true. *True or false?*

REFERENCES

Alexandra, A., Matthews, S., & Miller, M. (2002). Reasons, Values and Institutions. Melbourne: Tertiary Press.

Bevel, T., & Gardiner, R. (1997). Bloodstain Pattern Analysis: With an Introduction to Crime Scene Reconstruction. Boca Raton, FL: CRC Press.

Bhattacharyya, S. (1958). The concept of logic. Philosophy and Phenomenological Research, 18(3), 326–340.

Brussel, J. A. (1968). Casebook of a Crime Psychiatrist. New York: Dell Books.

Burgess, A. W., & Ressler, R. K. (1985). Sexual homicides crime scene and patterns of criminal behavior. National Institute of Justice Grant 82-IJ-CX-0065.

Canter, D. (1994). Criminal Shadows: Inside the Mind of the Serial Killer. London: HarperCollins.

Canter, D. (1995). Psychology of offender profiling. In R. Bull & D. Carson (Eds.), Handbook of Psychology in Legal Contexts. New York: Wiley.

Canter, D., Alison, L. J., Alison, E., & Wentink, N. (2000). Offender profiling and criminal differentiation. Legal and Criminological Psychology, 5, 23–46.

Canter, D. (2004). The organized/disorganized typology of serial murder. Psychology, Public Policy, and Law, 10, 293–320.

Coroner's Court. (2003). Transcript of Evidence: K. Illingsworth. N.S.W. Coroner's Court, 5th March.

Davis, J. (1999). Criminal personality profiling and crime scene assessment: A contemporary investigative tool to assist law enforcement public safety. Journal of Contemporary Criminal Justice, 15(3), 291–301.

Douglas, J. E., & Olshaker, M. (1996). Mindhunter: Inside the FBI Elite Serial Crime Unit. London: Mandarin Books.

Douglas, J. E., & Olshaker, M. (1997). Journey into Darkness: How the FBI's Premier Profiler Penetrates the Minds of the Most Terrifying Serial Criminals. London: Arrow Books.

Douglas, J. E., & Olshaker, M. (1998). Obsession: The FBI's Legendary Profiler Probes the Psyche of Killers, Rapists, and Stalkers and Their Victims and Tells How to Fight Back. New York: Pocket Books.

Egger, S. (1999). Psychological profiling: Past, present and future. Journal of Contemporary Criminal Justice, 15(3), 242–261.

Farber, M. (1942). Logical systems and the principles of logic. Philosophy of Science, 9(1), 40–54.

Federal Bureau of Investigation. (2002). Uniform Crime Report. Available at http://www.fbi.gov/ucr/cius_02/html/web/index.html. Accessed September 23, 2004.

Geberth, V. J. (1996). Practical Homicide Investigation: Tactics, Procedures and Forensic Techniques (3rd ed.). Boca Raton, FL: CRC Press.

Godwin, G. M. (1999). Hunting Serial Predators: A Multivariate Approach to Profiling Violent Behavior. Boca Raton, FL: CRC Press.

Godwin, G. M. (2002). Reliability, validity, and utility of criminal profiling typologies. Journal of Police and Criminal Psychology, 17, 1–18.

Hickey, E. (2002). Serial Murderers and Their Victims (3rd ed.). Belmont, CA: Wadsworth.

Holmes, R., & Holmes, S. (2002). Profiling Violent Crimes: An Investigative Tool (3rd ed.). Thousand Oaks, CA: Sage.

Klump, C. S. (1997). Taking your cue from the clues. Security Management, 41(9), 123–126.

Kocsis, R. N. (2001). Serial arsonist crime profiling. Firenews, Winter.

Kocsis, R. N., & Palermo, G. B. (2007). Contemporary problems in criminal profiling. In R. N. Kocsis (Ed.), Criminal Profiling: International Theory, Research, and Practice. New York: Humana.

McInerney, D. Q. (2004). Being Logical: A Guide to Good Thinking. Westminster, UK: Random House.

Neblett, W. (1985). Sherlock's Logic: Learn to Reason Like a Master Detective. New York: Barnes & Noble Books.

Petherick, W. A. (2006). Serial Crime: Theoretical and Practical Issues in Behavioral Profiling. Boston: Academic Press.

Petherick, W. A. (2007). Criminal profiling: A qualitative and quantitative analysis of methods and content. Unpublished doctoral dissertation, Bond University.

Petherick, W. A. (2008). Offender profiling in Australia. In K. Fritzon & P. Wilson (Eds.), Forensic Psychology and Criminology: An Australasian Perspective. North Ryde: McGraw Hill Australia.

Petherick, W. A., & Turvey, B. E. (2008a). Criminal profiling, the scientific method, and logic. In B. E. Turvey (Ed.), Criminal Profiling: An Introduction to Behavioral Evidence Analysis (3rd ed.). Boston: Academic Press.

Petherick, W. A., & Turvey, B. E. (2008). Behavioral Evidence Analysis: Ideo-deductive Method of Criminal Profiling. In B. E. Turvey (Ed.), Criminal Profiling: An Introduction to Behavioral Evidence Analysis (3rd ed.). Boston: Academic Press.

Petherick, W. A., & Turvey, B. E. (2008). Nomothetic Methods of Criminal Profiling. In B. E. Turvey (Ed.), Criminal Profiling: An Introduction to Behavioral Evidence Analysis (3rd ed.). Boston: Academic Press.

Ressler, R. K., & Burgess, A. W. (1985). Crime scene and profile characteristics of organized and disorganized murderers. FBI Law Enforcement Bulletin, 54(8), 18–25.

Ressler, R. K., Burgess, A. W., & Douglas, J. E. (1988). Sexual Homicides: Patterns and Motives. New York: Lexington Books.

Ressler, R. K., & Shachtman, T. (1992). Whoever Fights Monsters: The Brilliant FBI Detective Behind *The Silence of the Lambs*. New York: Simon & Schuster.

Stock, G. W. J. (2004). Deductive Logic. Oxford: Project Gutenberg Press.

Strano, M. (2004). A neural network applied to criminal psychological profiling: An Italian initiative. International Journal of Offender Therapy and Comparative Criminology, 48(4), 495–503.

Thornton, J. (1997). The general assumptions and rationale of forensic identification. In D. L. Faigman, D. H. Kaye, M. J. Saks, & J. Sanders (Eds.), Modern Scientific Evidence: The Law and Expert Testimony. St. Paul, MN: West.

Turvey, B. E. (2008). Criminal Profiling: An Introduction to Behavioral Evidence Analysis (3rd ed.). Burlington, MA: Academic Press.

CHAPTER 3

Behavioral Consistency, the Homology Assumption, and the Problems of Induction

Wayne Petherick and Claire Ferguson

KEY TERMS

Behavioral consistency: The theory that offenders will behave consistently between the offenses they commit.

Interpersonal coherence: A type of behavioral consistency, where offenders are theorized to behave consistently between their criminal and noncriminal behavior.

Homology assumption: A theory stating there is concordance between the behavior of two offenders and their subsequent demographic characteristics.

The problem of reliability: A problem of induction where the profiler will not know whether he or she is dealing with a statistical average or a statistical anomaly.

The problem of relevance: A problem of induction where the relevance of the literature used to provide an average for reference is not known.

The problem of trait reliance: A problem of induction where simplified trait descriptions are offered to describe how the offender will behave when found, based on the offender's crime scene behavior some time in the past.

The problem of case linkage: A problem of induction where case linkage is premised on the theory of behavioral consistency.

CONTENTS

INTRODUCTION

The ultimate goal of profiling is to identify the major behavioral and personality characteristics to narrow the suspect pool. Inferences about offender characteristics can be accomplished deductively, based on the analysis of discrete offender behaviors established within a particular case. They can also be accomplished inductively, involving prediction based on abstract offender averages from group data (these methods were detailed extensively in Chapter 2; see also Petherick & Turvey, 2008a). As discussed, these two approaches are by no means equal.

The reliability and validity of inductive profiling rest almost exclusively on two essentially weak theories: *behavioral consistency* and the *homology assumption*. Behavioral consistency posits that the same offender will do the same thing across the span of time during different offenses. The homology assumption suggests that, generally, there will be a similarity between different offenders who commit similar crimes. Without the ability to utilize either of these theories, comparing the current offender(s) to past offenders is essentially futile.

Although some in the profiling community understand the importance of these theories to actual casework, many do not. Either way, most are unaware of their limitations. This has serious implications for the legitimate role of inductive profiling when providing investigative or forensic inferences regarding behavioral evidence.

This chapter provides an in-depth discussion of both behavioral consistency and the homology assumption, outlining some of the research that has been done in the area. The purpose is to educate students and professionals regarding what these concepts are, why they are important, and the consequences to casework in light of their limitations. It builds on the discussion of inductive methods presented in Chapter 2.

BEHAVIORAL CONSISTENCY

There are essentially two types of consistency that are important to the application of profiling knowledge. The first is that an offender will show consistency between his or her noncriminal and criminal actions. This has been referred to as *interpersonal coherence* (Canter, 1994) and while discussed further, is not the type of consistency that is the focus of this chapter. The second type of consistency, and the subject of considerably more study in criminal profiling, is that a criminal will behave consistently across the offenses he or she commits.

The importance of consistency is related by Canter (1995, p. 347), who notes that

> one hypothesis central to profiling is that the way an offender carries out a crime on one occasion will have some characteristic similarities to the way he or she carries out crimes on other occasions. If the inherent

variations between contexts, for any aspect of human behavior, are greater than the variations between people then it is unlikely that clear differences between individuals will be found for those behaviors. This hypothesis is applicable to the situation in which a person has committed only one crime. Even in that case a "profile" has to be based upon the assumption that the criminal is exhibiting characteristics that are typical of that person, not of the situation in which the crime was committed.

Canter (2004, p. 4) also provides the following commentary:

> One aspect of these salient features that also needs to be determined as part of scientific development is that they are consistent enough from one context, or crime, to another to form the basis for considering those crimes and comparing them with other offenses. This issue of consistency turns out to be a complex one. Part of this complexity comes from weaknesses in the sources of data.
>
> A more conceptual challenge to determining consistency, as in all human activity, is that some variation and change is a natural aspect of human processes. There therefore will be criminals who are consistently variable or whose behavioral trajectories demonstrate some form of career development, as well as those whose criminal behavior will remain relatively stable over time. These questions are very similar indeed to those discussed in the more general personality literature about what is constant about people and what is variable, as Youngs (2004) explores. Research around all these possibilities of consistency is therefore central to any development of a scientific basis for offender profiling.[1]

Woodhams and Toye (2007, p. 3) provide the following discussion with regard to determining whether different crimes have been committed by the same individual. This process is known as *case linkage*:

> A second hypothesis of offender profiling is the offender (behavioral) consistency hypothesis (Canter, 1995). This hypothesis predicts that an offender will show consistency (or similarity) in their criminal behavior across their series of crimes. As explained by Mokros and Alison (2002), this hypothesis is necessary for offender profiling to work because "one person has to remain rather consistent in his or her actions if the correspondence of similarity associations holds between a person's characteristics and behavior" (p. 26).

---

[1] Canter is intimating that the "science" of profiling will come from the numbers. As with all endeavors, the science is in the interpretation, not the statistics.

The offender behavioral consistency hypothesis also underlies the practice of case linkage. If offenders were not consistent in their criminal behavior, it would be impossible to assign crimes to a common offender on the basis of their behavioral similarity.

Holmes and Holmes (2002) make this same assumption in *Profiling Violent Crimes*. Here, they suggest that not only does the crime scene reflect the personality (interpersonal coherence) but also the personality will stay the same (behavioral consistency), and the manifestation of the behavior at the crime (in both *modus operandi* and *signature*) will stay the same. It is necessary to provide their discussion in near fullness (Holmes & Holmes, 2002, pp. 41–44):

> Several assumptions can be made regarding psychological profiling. These assumptions are important to consider because they deal directly with the reasons why profiles are important and the manner in which certain information can be obtained and used to formulate a credible criminal investigative assessment. These assumptions are detailed next.
>
> **The Crime Scene Reflects the Personality**[2]
>
> The basic assumption of psychological profiling is that the crime scene reflects the personality of the offender. After all, how effective would profiling be if the crime itself was not indicative of the pathology assessment?[3] The assessment will aid in the direction and scope of the investigation of the crime.
>
> Not only is the manner in which the victim was fatally dispatched important, but the physical and nonphysical evidence will also lend, to some degree, an assessment of the type of personality involved in a particular murder. The amount of chaos, for example, might indicate that a disorganized personality was involved in this crime. If this is true, then we can make certain assumptions about particular social core variables of the unknown perpetrator. On the other hand, if the crime scene is "neat and clean" or thoroughly chaotic, then

---

[2]Although this is generally referred to as interpersonal coherence, the reader will recall that it is a form of behavioral consistency that occurs between the noncriminal and criminal behavior of the offender.

[3]It should be restated for clarification that this is the central question of this chapter. However, Holmes and Holmes' (2002) position appears to be at odds with our own. They suggest, with little qualification or clarification, that these theoretical assumptions be accepted uncritically. There is no discussion of how emotion, drugs, alcohol, staging, interruption, or anything else affect either behavior or personality in a given crime. It would seem that these things would need to be considered before any discussion of the temporal stability of personality could be embarked upon.

other assumptions might lead us to an offender who possesses a different set of social core variables.

The focus of the attack may also indicate certain information that aids in the apprehension of the unknown offender. For example, in a midwestern state, an elderly woman was killed in her own home. She was stabbed repeatedly and suffered multiple deep wounds to the upper legs and genital area. For reasons that we will further detail in a later chapter, the profile offered an assessment of the crime itself that, in part, resulted in the arrest of a man who was considered a suspect at the beginning stages of the law enforcement investigation.

. . .

The Method of Operation Remains Similar

The behavior of the perpetrator, as evidenced in the crime scene and not the offense per se, determines the degree of suitability of the case for profiling (Geberth, 1983, p. 401). The crime scene contains clues that experienced profilers determine to be signatures of the criminals. Because no two offenders are exactly alike, it is equally true that no two crime scenes are exactly alike.[4] As certain as a psychometric test reflects psychopathology, the crime scene reflects a person with a pathology.[5]

Many serial offenders themselves are very aware of the nonphysical evidence that is present at a crime scene. One murderer remarked,

> First of all, any investigative onlooker to my crime scene would have immediately deduced that the offender was extremely sadistic in nature. The visible markers of bondage, nature of the victims' wounds and evidence of unhurried, systematic abuse should have indicated that these sadistic acts were not new to me. And that I had committed such brutal crimes in the past and would likely do so again (Author's files).

. . .

---

[4]This alone questions the application of arbitrary generalizations when the crime itself has not come to be understood as its own universe. Furthermore, it appears that the authors of the text are getting confused about the concepts they are arguing: This section is about modus operandi (MO), yet they are arguing that an experienced profiler will be able to determine the signature. Nor will the MO always remain the same, which also seems to be a point of confusion.

[5]It is also prudent to discuss the issue of pathology. This word is derived from the Greek word *pathos*, meaning illness or sickness. However, it is more likely that in a crime involving true pathology, aspects of the offender's personality are likely to be obscured. This issue has not been significantly discussed in the literature.

The remarks from this killer show the one dimension of personality—the conscious dimension—that profiling often neglects. This murderer and rapist illustrates by his remarks the elements within his crime scenes that truly reflect his personality. The method of operation, the M.O., was repeated many times in the course of his rapes and murders.[6]

Addressing the stability of an individual's behavior across situations, Shoda, Mischel, and Wright (1994) delved into the behavior of schoolchildren in a summer camp setting. Although not examining criminal behavior, the opening paragraphs of their article are relevant to the current discussion. Not only do they suggest that idiographic analysis is of utmost importance in understanding a single case but also they highlight the importance of considering person–situation interactions (p. 674):

> Allport (1937) introduced the concept of idiographic analyses half a century ago, urging personologists to understand each individual deeply in terms of how that person functions, instead of just studying "operations of a hypothetical 'average' mind" (p. 61). Nonetheless, the idiographic focus has been bypassed by mainstream personality psychology. Probably this neglect reflects not a lack of interest but an absence of appropriate methods and theory for studying individual functioning in ways that are objective and scientific rather than intuitive and clinical. In our view, understanding individual functioning requires identifying first the psychological situations that engage a particular person's characteristic personality processes and the distinctive cognitions and affects that are experienced in them. Then, an individual's functioning should become visible in the distinctive or unique ways the person's behavior changes across situations, not just in its overall level or mean frequency. For example, a person may often behave in a warm and empathic way with her colleagues at work but almost always in a very critical manner with her family. Another person may show the opposite pattern so that he is warm and empathic with his family but critical with his professional colleagues. If two people are similar in their behaviors averaged across situations, but differ in the situations in which they display those behaviors, are these differences merely a reflection of momentary situational influences? Or do such differences reflect differences in enduring and meaningful aspects of their personality?

---

[6]The reader should refer to footnote 4. The case study as presented discusses the sadistic aspect of the offender's crimes, which is in turn more aligned to notions of signature. Why this is used as an example here is confusing and misleading.

To reiterate and expand on some of the issues this passage raises as relevant to profiling, consider the following:

1. Idiographic analysis provides a more thorough description and explanation of an individual situation compared to that afforded through hypothetical averages.
2. When considering the actions of one individual, situational variables play a pivotal role.
3. In profiling, the person–situation interactions must be accounted for in a detailed reconstruction of the criminal event. Without this, situational variables may not, or will not, be accounted for, rendering any conclusions about the offender potentially incorrect.
4. We cannot rely on the notion of behavioral consistency, given the differences between the public and private face of individuals over time. That is, what we see of a person in one environment will differ greatly from what we see of that person in another, and the behavior of an individual in one crime may differ greatly from that in another crime.

The main problem with consistency is that without performing a complete crime reconstruction, one cannot assume that there has been any level of consistency in the offender's behavior, either in single instances or across multiple offenses. Furthermore, we cannot assume that even though there may be consistency between two different crimes committed by the same offender, this will always be true. Consistency is a nice theory, but in practice, it will not be suitably or reliably predictive.

To round out this discussion, the variety of influences on consistency must be noted. For this purpose, we turn to Turvey's (2008a) commentary on the problems with the organized/disorganized dichotomy, which is perhaps the best known profiling approach relying on consistency. Turvey presents five events, although there are undoubtedly more, for which situational variables will greatly influence the offender's behavior, making it different from previous criminal or noncriminal behaviors. The assumption of behavioral consistency will therefore not be met. These events/offenders are as follows:

- Anger retaliatory offenders who do not suffer from any kind of mental illness
- Domestic violence-related offenses
- Staged offenses
- Interrupted offenses
- Offenses involving controlled substances

A relevant case example showing the fallibility of consistency is that of Louis Peoples. This was outlined by Petherick (2005, pp. 92–95) and was chronicled in the first instance with permission:

On the 16th of September, 1997, an unknown offender went onto the grounds of California Spray Dry Company, vandalizing vehicles parked in the employee lot and shooting at employees. Thomas Harrison, shot in the stomach and thigh, described the offender as a white adult male, 5 feet 9 inches tall, about 160 pounds in weight. He was wearing a dark baseball cap and dark clothes.

Approximately 5 weeks later, at 4:12 pm, the Stockton Branch of the Bank of the West was held up at gunpoint. A white male entered the bank wearing a black hat, black jacket, and dark glasses, approaching the teller at position 1, who was handed a note which read "give me all of your 100s, 50s, 20s, 10s and nobody will get shot." He took a small handgun from his jacket while the teller got the notes before fleeing the bank.

Five days later, a telephone call was made to Charter Way Tow of Stockton, California. Tow driver James Loper attended the scene. No reports of trouble were mentioned during the 3:30 am radio call to the dispatcher. Loper was later found by sheriff's deputies at 3:48 am. He had been shot 10 times.

The body of Stephen Chacko was found on the 4th of November 1997 in front of Mayfair Discount Liquors and Tobacco. Mr. Chacko was employed as the cashier at Mayfair, and was taken to St. Joseph's Medical Center where he was pronounced dead 20 minutes later from five gunshot wounds. It was found that during the robbery the offender fired at the cash register in a attempt to open it, but these attempts failed.

About a week later, Besun Yu and Jun Gao were shot and killed during a robbery at the Village Oaks Market, again in Stockton. Both victims were working in front of the store at the time of the robbery. The offender came in through the front door, shot Besun Yu at the cash register, and then shot Jun Gao in the aisle. The offender took the cash register out of the checkout stand and left the store.

The collection of facts in this case suggested to Turvey that the offender was becoming more desperate in their attempts. He had tried to open a cash register unsuccessfully by shooting at it, had stolen another cash register which he also couldn't open, and had shot staff at the places he had taken them from (when the simplest thing would be to get them to open the cash registers).

The offender took precautions in all of the above cases, such as wearing hats, sunglasses, and a jacket. In some cases he had a healthy knowledge of the layout of the premises and in some cases prepared an escape plan (such as cutting through chain link fences).

Oddly enough, despite the preparation evident in many of the cases, the offender did a number of things that seemed a contradiction to those precautionary acts intended to help him get away with his offenses. In the first case at Cal-Spray, he spent considerable time at the scene, thereby increasing his chances of apprehension. Also, the repeated use of a firearm, and a big one at that (.40 caliber), further increased his chances of getting caught owing to the noise it would generate. During the bank robbery, he waited in line to be seen by a teller, also increasing the risk of apprehension. If not for the severe nature of his act and the fact that someone died at his hand, his actions in relation to James Loper would have been comical: Shortly after shooting Mr. Loper, the offender rang Charter Way Towing looking for work claiming he had heard they were "short a man."

The cases were linked through the use of ballistics but the bank and Cal-Spray were not linked to the crime series until other ballistics tests tied them in just prior to Turvey's involvement. Looking back at the series of crimes, Turvey believed that the offender's actions at Cal-Spray provided the greatest insight into the crimes. Turvey suggested to investigators that the amount of time spent at Cal-Spray, the damage to cars, familiarity of the location, and ingress and egress routes all meant they should look for a former employee. When approached with this information, managers of the company informed police that they should seek out a former employee: Louis Peoples.

Peoples was a methamphetamine addict (which affected his behavior during the offense) and when arrested, he led police to the .40 caliber handgun used in the crimes which he had buried. He had also kept a diary of the media coverage of his crimes in the form of a scrapbook titled "Biography of a Crime Spree."

As can be noted from this example, it is both dangerous and inaccurate to assume behavioral consistency between a person's criminal behavior in one instance and their static personality and behavioral characteristics. There are too many factors that may be acting on the offender at the time of the crime which are unknown to the investigator that will influence the behavior of that offender. If these are not recognized and accommodated for, the inductive profiler will likely render an inaccurate assessment. That is, the behavior of an individual in one state cannot and should not be used to determine or predict trait characteristics.

THE HOMOLOGY ASSUMPTION

The homology assumption, put simply, refers to whether there is a concordance between the behavior of two offenders and their subsequent background characteristics. It could be argued that this is also a form of consistency—that is, consistency between the behaviors and backgrounds of different criminals. As stated by Mokros and Alison (2002, pp. 25–26),

> Offender profiling involves the process of predicting the characteristics of an offender based on information available at the crime scene. Decisions about the likely sociodemographic characteristics of that person are made on the basis of behavior. If it is possible to infer something about the person from what happened at the crime scene then any two persons who commit a particular type of crime in roughly the same way should be rather similar to each other.

> As a consequence, offender profiling in its conventional form is a nonconditional, linear process. If conditional "if ... then" rules were included to accommodate for individual peculiarities, situational influences or nondeterministic relations, the resulting profiles would contain "either ... or" predictions. To give an example: *If* excessive violence in cases of sexual assault could be associated with antisocial personality disorder or intoxication of the offender, the profile for a given case where increased levels of violence are present could predict *either* an antisocial perpetrator *or* a person with proneness to substance abuse *or* a combination of those two.

The homology assumption, as it stands, is not unique to the profiling approach known as investigative psychology. All inductive (trait) methods of profiling rely on there being concordance between the current offender and the characteristics of past offenders. Mokros and Alison (2002, p. 26) suggest that it is a "condition for the process of offender profiling to be feasible." In addition (p. 26),

> With respect to the assumptions that underlie offender profiling, this means that the degree of similarity in the offense behavior of any two perpetrators from a given category of crime will match the degree of similarity in their characteristics. In other words, there is an assumed sameness in the similarity relations between the domains of crime scene actions and demographic features. The more similar two offenders are, the higher the resemblance in their crimes will be.

This proposition extends beyond the degree of similarity between behaviorally similar offenders: The assumption holds not only that two offenders who are behaviorally similar will be demographically similar but also that offenders who behave similarly will be demographically similar to future offenders who exhibit this same behavior. Otherwise, the homology assumption would only be true of one group at one time, making the theory redundant. The authors suggest that (p. 26)

> the assumption of behavioral consistency does not subsume the second assumption (i.e., that of a correspondence in similarity of offense behavior and characteristics between offenders). If, however, the homology assumption is found to be valid, the assumption of behavioral consistency must be valid as well. The reason for this is the self-similarity of individuals. One person has to remain rather consistent in his or her actions if the correspondence of similarity relations holds between a person's characteristics and behavior.

To state the previous proposition another way, it could be argued that if the homology assumption does not hold, behavioral consistency will not either. As discussed later, research has largely failed to find support for the homology assumption.

This is not the last of the problems with the homology assumption, however. It also presupposes to a degree that the behavior of one offender that is similar to that of another will have a similar origin. That is, the cognition or motivation for the behavior is assumed to be similar given that the behavior is similar. This assumption is flawed because different offenders will do similar things for different reasons (Petherick & Turvey, 2008b). Furthermore, this assumption, and those made by Holmes and Holmes (2002) discussed previously, violates a principle of behavioral evidence—that modus operandi behavior is not static (Petherick & Turvey, 2008b).

Mokros and Alison (2002) tested the homology assumption with a sample of 100 male stranger rapes. The results were presented across three domains: age, sociodemographic features, and criminal history. The results show the following (pp. 37–39):

> **Test of the homology assumption with respect to age**
>
> If the homology assumption is correct, two offenders with close centroids will be within a similar age range. To test whether there is a positive correlation between centroid distance and age difference, two matrices were calculated. One contained the Euclidean distances between the centroids for each offender; the other comprised the age differences of all offenders.
>
> …
>
> The comparison of the two matrices yielded a Spearman's rho rank-ordered correlation of $r_s = -.01$ ($p < .001$). Hence, there is no linear

relationship between age and offense behavior: In the sample, offenders with smaller age differences did not have closer centroids. With respect to age, the null hypothesis must be retained.

Test of the homology assumption for sociodemographic features

Concerning sociodemographic features, the list of variables is limited to the following: non-European ethnic background, unemployment, unskilled labor, living circumstances (scored if the offender lived alone), and previous imprisonment/detention. This yields 48 offenders for whom information on all five variables was available.

. . .

Analogously, the same 48 offenders were compared with respect to their crime scene actions. . . . [This means that] there is no positive linear relationship between the five sociodemographic features analyzed and offense behavior. In the sample, offenders who are more similar with respect to sociodemographic features do not display any significant similarity in their style of offending. With respect to sociodemographic features, the null hypothesis must be retained.

Test of the homology assumption for previous convictions

The previous convictions were examined in 12 categories: theft, burglary (both dwelling and/or nondwelling), violence minor, violence major, criminal damage, damage endanger life, public order/drunkenness, motor vehicle crime, drugs (both possession and/or supply), indecent exposure, indecent assault, and rape of a female. They were coded as present if an offender had at least one conviction in a given category, either as a juvenile and/or as an adult.

. . .

In the sample, there is no positive linear relationship between the 12 previous conviction variables and the offender's crime scene actions. Offenders who display some resemblance in their criminal histories do not commit their rape offenses in similar ways. As is the case for the sociodemographic variables, the small correlation observed in the sample is in the direction opposite to the one predicted by the hypothesis. For previous convictions the null hypothesis cannot be refuted (i.e., there is no positive linear relationship with the domain of offense behavior).

Retaining the null hypothesis means that rapists who display a similar style of offending are not similar with respect to their background characteristics. In other words, there is no support for the homology assumption.

Woodhams and Toye (2007) also considered the homology assumption as part of their study on serial commercial robberies. As did Mokros and Alison (2002), Woodhams and Toye failed to find support for the homology assumption on the offender characteristics of age, ethnicity, employment status, criminal history, and distance traveled from home to the offense location. Woodhams and Toye suggest that it is possible that this relates to the three different robbery styles that share some offense characteristics, a result of the offense characteristics included, and the selection of just one offender from a team to represent the offense. Despite noting these possible reasons for the lack of support, it is also possible that there is another reason: The homology assumption is nothing more than a nice theory.

This all reduces to the following: Inductive methods rely almost exclusively on the comparison of a crime to other similar crimes. This must occur both within the offender's crimes (consistency) and between this offender's crimes and those of like offenders (homology). Without either two conditions, inductive profiling simply cannot be upheld. This chapter demonstrates the following in this regard: (1) Consistency simply cannot be assumed, especially in the absence of a thorough crime reconstruction, and (2) homology cannot ever be assumed, especially in light of the findings of Mokros and Alison (2002), Woodhams and Toye (2007), and an array of other research.

THE PROBLEMS OF INDUCTION

Inductive profiling as a means of forming theories is both necessary and useful, but using it as the sole basis for developing conclusions is improper. This section deals with the problems of induction as they relate specifically to consistency and homology.

The Problem of Reliability

The general "problem of induction," as Karl Popper (2003) put it, is that one can never know if one is dealing with a statistical average or a statistical anomaly (*reliability*). In reality, any inductive inference is an untested theory based on what has happened in the past; it may or may not have been studied or recalled properly, and it may or may not happen again. Hoping does not make it so.

Unfortunately, inductive profiling is easier and less time-consuming than its deductive counterpart. This makes it a more attractive prospect for anyone who prefers to expend little effort. Little to no examination of the physical evidence in a case need be conducted and subsequently less analyst training is required. In practice, the specific behavioral evidence in a particular case is often assumed by inductive analysts based on their research or experience rather than established by any scientific examination of case facts.

The inductive profiler also relies heavily, and even blindly, on the interpretations of others, which is a practice historically fraught with peril. The following provides one such case.

The USS Iowa

In 1989, an explosion aboard the USS *Iowa* prompted the Naval Investigative Service (NIS; now NCIS) to call for assistance from the Federal Bureau of Investigation (FBI). Roy Hazelwood and Richard Ault of the Behavioral Analysis Unit were sent to conduct an Equivocal Death Analysis of Clayton Hartwig who, it was assumed, caused the blast as a result of a rebuffed homosexual advance.

In this case, the Investigative Subcommittee and Defense Policy Panel of the Committee on Armed Services House of Representatives (1990, p. 39) found that the base investigation conducted by the Naval Investigative Service was lacking:

> The criminal investigation conducted by the NIS agents was a key part of the Navy's overall investigation of the USS *Iowa* explosion. The subcommittee staff investigation and our three days of hearings raised a number of important concerns relating to the conduct of the NIS investigation.

> The subcommittee believes the scope of the NIS investigation was too quickly narrowed to focus on Clayton Hartwig. This might have caused the NIS to miss evidence that would have implicated other individuals as suspects. Every one of the 1,000 crewmen had access to the turret and could have planted an explosion there. In addition, NIS agents seemed to focus almost exclusively on Hartwig's explosives knowledge and suicidal tendencies.

> This narrow focus became crucial to making the Navy's case that Hartwig committed suicide and murder.

Given that this criticism brings the known facts of the case into question, it would seem problematic to proceed with a profile on the basis of it. However, this is exactly what was done, and not surprisingly it brought scorn from the Committee (1990, p. 42):

> Because the FBI's psychological profile was key to making the Navy's case, the subcommittee examined the process used by the FBI to reach its conclusion. The two chief areas of concern were the quality of the material upon which the analysis was based and the degree of certainty of the opinion.

> To begin with, the profile was prepared by two FBI Special Agents assigned to the FBI National Center for the Analysis of Violent Crime.

An equivocal death is a death whose manner (i.e., homicide, suicide, or accident) has not been resolved through normal investigative activities. While these two Special Agents have experience working with such profiles, having compiled some 30 analyses in the last several years, neither of them are licensed psychologists with experience dealing with the multitude of behavior that may be manifest in an individual's personality. Both Special Agents have advanced degrees in counseling.

This lack of licensing is especially crucial when the material that they analyze becomes suspect. In this case the preponderance of the material came from interviews conducted and provided to the FBI by the NIS. As the subcommittee found earlier, serious questions were raised about the leading nature or bias introduced in the interviews by the NIS interviewing agents. Some witnesses denied making statements to NIS that are significant to the profile, chiefly that concerning Hartwig's alleged teenage suicide gesture. We know that, in at least one instance, the witness recanted several portions of his testimony, but was still considered as a reliable witness. The NIS inquiry was a criminal inquiry focused on some very specific aspects of Hartwig's and Kendall Truitt's personalities.[7] These interviews in no way serve as a collection of clinical information on which a reliable analysis may be based.

This leads to the second concern of the subcommittee—the degree of certainty of the opinion. Given the questionable nature of material upon which the analysis was based—and that FBI personnel in cases like these do not conduct an active investigation of themselves—it seems to the subcommittee that some caveats on the FBI's conclusion should have been made clear to the Navy, even if only that certain significant information, such as prior counseling and school records, interviews with teachers, parents and friends, was not available to the FBI for review.

In his excellent review of the case, Thompson (1999) provides a similarly scathing account of the inductive equivocal death analysis in this case and the lack of effort made to substantiate or corroborate witness statements and evidence (p. 356):

On December 21, the third and final day of the hearings held in the Rayburn House Office Building, FBI psychological profiler Richard

---

[7]Hartwig was the sailor accused of causing the explosion, whereas it was Truitt's alleged rebuff that led Hartwig to cause the explosion.

Ault was asked by Representative Mavroules if he had discussed the case with Dr. Froede. Ault said he had not. Had he even examined the autopsy reports? He hadn't done that, either. Mavroules told Ault that the medical examiner had ruled that all 47 deaths were accidental. "That is his opinion, and we have our opinion," Ault said, somewhat churlishly. Mavroules asked Hazelwood if he were sure that the material NIS had provided him was factual. "No, sir," Hazelwood replied, adding that it wasn't his job to corroborate information.

In fact, Hazelwood's specific justification for not questioning the evidence he and Ault were given was that when getting involved in an investigation with an outside agency, FBI profilers assume that they are working with professionals who have done their job. Therefore, no evaluation of the information coming from another agency is made.

The danger of relying blindly on information created by others should be perfectly clear. In fact, it violates the very standards of practice set out for those engaging in deductive profiling. As explained in Petherick & Turvey (2008b, pp. 146–147),

Criminal Profilers Are Responsible for Determining Whether the Evidence They Are Examining Is of Sufficient Quality to Provide the Basis for an Adequate Victimology, Crime Scene Analysis, or Criminal Profile.

The harsh reality is that crime scene processing and documentation efforts in the United States are often abysmal, if not completely absent, and in need of major reform (see DeForest, 2005). Crime scenes throughout the United States are commonly processed by police-employed technicians or sworn personnel with little or no formal education, to say nothing of training in the forensic sciences and crime scene processing techniques. The in-service forensic training available to law enforcement typically exists in the form of half-day seminars or short courses taught by nonscientists who, on their own, in no way impart the discipline and expertise necessary to process crime scenes adequately for the purposes of victimology, crime scene analysis, or criminal profiling.

...

If crime scene documentation and processing efforts are not sufficient to the task of allowing for the criminal profiler to establish the previously mentioned considerations, then those efforts were at best inadequate. Profilers must make note of such deficiencies in their analysis and factor them into their opinions and conclusions. They may even need to explain that certain conclusions are precluded because of them.

It is important to note that the profiler cannot know absolutely everything about any item of evidence. Nobody can. The challenge is to consider all that is known when performing an examination and be prepared to incorporate new information as it may come to light. This means appreciating that new information about any item of evidence, or its history, may affect any conclusions about what it means.

Without a competent investigation and forensic analysis to establish the facts of a case, and an evaluation of the quality of any evidence provided, it is not possible for the profiler to accurately infer related behavioral evidence. Conclusions about the meaning of behaviors in this context will be irrelevant when it cannot be reasonably established that they actually occurred. Such a context also makes comparisons between cases irrelevant because the analyst cannot be certain whether the behavior he or she is comparing from one case to another did in fact occur. In short, profilers have a duty to evaluate the quality of what they are given so any conclusions that follow will be based on accurate information and, therefore, relevant. They are admonished not to assume reliability, facts, or behaviors for the purposes of their analysis—an all too common practice.

If a profiler is unable to assess the quality of the evidence he or she has been given, then this identifies an important training need. The profiler should remove himself or herself as inexpert from any case when confronted with evidence that he or she is unfamiliar with or cannot evaluate with respect to quality, or the profiler may seek the advice of colleagues who are able to make such a determination.

The Problem of Relevance

A second major problem with inductive methods, and one that is directly aligned to notions of consistency and homology, is the *relevance* of the literature providing the average for reference. For a better understanding, consider the following example from Alison, Goodwill, and Alison (2005, p. 257):

- Offender's age

  - The offender is likely to be within an **age range of 28 to 35 (CATCHEM)**. However, age has proven an extremely difficult variable to "profile." **No suspect should be eliminated solely on the basis that he does not fall within the profiled age range.**

  - Although the average age of child sexual murderers in Boudreaux, Lord, and Dutra's (1999) study was 27 years old with the great majority under 30, the CATCHEM data indicates that when the victim's body is transported from the scene of the murder the offender's likely age group is around **30 to 35 years old**. Offenders who do not transport their victims tend to be younger, around age 18 to 25 years old.

Here, the CATCHEM database is used as the standard from which offender comparisons are drawn. These comparisons provide the basis for the offender characteristics given in the profile, which is simply a reiteration of past research findings. As seen, there is little reference to the evidence or victim in the case at hand, with much of the report being no more than a general summary of research conducted on similar crimes or crime in general. This is clearly problematic in that it presents this offender not as an individual but as an assembly of averages. This is especially apparent when it is noted that for each crime of a similar type, the profile offered using this method would be (and often is) virtually identical, regardless of case specifics. Perhaps most troubling is the authors' own admission that the research is drawn from jurisdictions different than that in which the crime being profiled was committed. This raises the question of cross-cultural validity and reliability.

The Problem of Trait Reliance

Another major problem with induction related to consistency and homology is the *reliance* on trait descriptions of the offender. What this means is that the behaviors of the offender at the time of the crime are believed to represent the offender's general personality, both at the time of the crime and in the future (Petherick, 2008; see Chapter 2). In other words, an offender who displays anger at the crime scene is believed to be generally angry in his or her daily life, as suggested by the theory of interpersonal coherence. The link between personality and profiling is made clear in Kocsis (2006, p. xii):

> Today, with the luxury of hindsight, the development of profiling can be seen as akin to the field of personality theory. Within the disciplines of psychology and psychiatry, there exists an accepted consensus in the existence of a conceptual construct known as the mind. Although there is agreement in the concept of the mind, there are numerous rival approaches or theories that attempt to explain the nature and operation of the mind. A few examples of these differing approaches or "personality theories" include the psychoanalytic, behaviorist, and biological theories. The work and research into profiling can be viewed in an analogous fashion. There appears to be a general consensus that profiling is a concept whereby crime behaviors can be interpreted for the purpose of making predictions concerning the probable offender's characteristics. Akin to the varying personality theories, differing approaches have evolved over time that propose how crime behaviors are interpreted or profiled.

The association between studies of criminal groups and the inference of the characteristics of one offender can be seen in Canter (1995, p. 344), where it is stated that "by considering empirical results from the study of actions of a large number of criminals it has been possible to propose both theories and methodologies that elaborate the relationship between an offender's actions and his or her characteristics." The problem inherent in this assumption is best stated by Theodore Reik in *The Unknown Murderer* (1945, p. 42): "It is still not sufficiently realized that the criminal at the moment of the act is a different man from what he is after it—so much so that one would sometimes think them two different beings."

The Relevance of Risk Assessment Research

The problem of relying too heavily on statistical averages is not peculiar to profiling, and one of the most damning indictments on using a statistical average comes from risk assessment. A prediction of whether someone poses a risk of violence in the future is not a far cry from the predictive analysis made by inductive profilers, who argue for the traits a person will exhibit at some point in the future. Risk assessment tools have come and gone, and like many areas of social science inquiry, this field has seen revision, evolution, and revolutions in the practices that are endorsed and applied.

Three generations of risk assessment practices have been identified (Ogloff & Davis, 2005), which have presumably come about because of changes in the way the risk assessment process is perceived and practiced. The first of these involved relatively unstructured assessments of an individual made by the clinician. These clinical assessments of risk have great similarity to diagnostic evaluations in criminal profiling, a method in which clinicians bring their experience with personality and psychopathology to bear in determining the profile of the current offender (Petherick & Turvey, 2008a; Wilson, Lincoln, & Kocsis, 1997). The second generation of risk assessment, brought about largely by dissatisfaction with previous idiosyncratic appraisals, utilized statistical models for risk assessment, which also considered situational factors in the determination of risk. The third generation saw a more critical application of risk assessment appraisals, moving beyond dichotomous classifications of "dangerous" or "not dangerous" to include risk factors for violence, harm, and risk level (Ogloff & Davis, 2005). Similar to the previous generation, predictive statistical models are employed to maintain an objective assessment of risk; however, these are balanced with the clinical judgment of the analyst. Thus, statistical assessments and clinical judgment work in concert to give an overall determination of a person's risk, providing a balance between clinical and statistical models.

This historical examination of risk assessment provides us with an enlightening view on modern practice and serves as more than a lesson in the determination of risk. This illustrates that over time, an opinion developed entirely through the experiences of an individual (the knowledge of one) was deemed to be inaccurate, and so debate turned to the suitability of research (the knowledge of many) for answers. However, years of practice also found that the knowledge of many was largely unsuited to predicting individual behaviors, and so the field turned to a combination of knowledge between one and many, weighing actuarial predictors against individual experiences. From this example, it can be suggested that idiosyncratic models provide for more bias and therefore more error. However, of greatest importance here is the recognition also of the dangers of actuarial judgment on its own, despite the fact that introducing this method was likely based on the goal of increased objectivity into the process as a whole. Most notably, the problem with actuarial methods lies in acknowledging the degree to which group studies can be used to predict the behavior of individuals.

This problem is best articulated by Arthur Conan Doyle through his fictional character Sherlock Holmes in *The Sign of Four* (Doyle, 2002, p. 60): "You can, for example, never foretell what any one man will do, but you can say with precision what an average number will be up to."

The relevance of group predictions to individual cases was put to the test by Hart, Michie, and Cooke (2007), who assessed two widely used and accepted actuarial instruments for the assessment of risk: the Violence Risk Appraisal Guide and the Static-99. Hart et al. provided in their literature review a summary of the risks posed by generalizing from the population to the individual (p. 61):

> Suppose a public opinion survey of 500 eligible voters found that 54% expressed their intent to cast ballots for candidate Smith in an upcoming election. This information allows one to forecast with reasonable confidence that candidate Smith will be elected by another group—namely, the general electorate. However, this same information does not allow one to predict the behavior of a randomly selected voter with great confidence. Even though, in the absence of other relevant information, the most rational prediction is that every single voter will cast a ballot for candidate Smith, these individual predictions frequently will be wrong. So, to return to the ARAI example above, we need to know the margin of error for predictions made using Test X that a given person, such as Jones, will commit violence.

It was these margins of error that Hart and colleagues examined. Without delving into the specific statistical results of the study, the confidence intervals of both instruments were examined. The results of the study and the suitability of group estimates to individual cases are best summarized in their discussion (p. 63):

> Our analyses indicated that two popular ARAIs used in risk assessment have poor precision. The margins of error for risk estimates made using the tests were substantial, even at the group level. At the individual level, the margins of error were so high as to render the test results virtually meaningless. Our findings are consistent with Bohr's conclusion that predicting the future is very difficult.

Our findings likely come as no surprise to many people. The difficulties of predicting the outcomes for groups versus individuals—whether in the context of games of chance or of violence risk assessments—are intuitively obvious.

In line with the findings of Hart et al. (2007), Meloy (1998, p. 8) provides a similar warning with regard to stalking:

Nomothetic (group) studies on threats and their relationship to behavior are not necessarily helpful in ideographic (single case) research on risk management, beyond the making of risk probability statements if the stalker fits closely into the reference group. Such studies may overshadow the commonsense premise that threats have one of three relationships to subsequent violence in single stalking cases: They exhibit violence, they disinhibit violence, or they have no relationship to the individual's violence. Careful scrutiny of the subject's threat/violence history should be the investigative focus when this relationship is analyzed in an individual stalking case; and the importance, or weight, of threats in a risk management situation should be determined by searching for the presence of other factors that may aggravate or mitigate violence (Monahan & Steadman, 1994).

The relevance of this passage to the current discussion on profiling is evident. However, to avoid any confusion, the following conclusions are restated:

1. Nomothetic knowledge is not necessarily helpful in understanding individual cases.
2. Probability statements can really only be made if the subject falls within the reference group; however, one can never know the degree to which the subject fits within the reference group in profiling until *after* the offender is caught.
3. A careful scrutiny of the individual case should be the investigative focus.

The Problem of Case Linkage

The previously discussed problems apply equally to the question of *case linkage* as to any other aspect of profiling endeavors, therefore it is necessary to further canvass this as a specific issue.

With inductive methods, case linkage rests almost entirely on the assumption of behavioral consistency—that is, offenders who commit two or more crimes will behave similarly, or consistently, between their various offenses. In fact, this is absolutely necessary in the statistical assessment of crimes to determine whether the same offender or group of offenders is responsible. However, the practice is also fraught with peril on a number of fronts.

The following discussion is by no means exhaustive, but it rounds out the discussion of consistency and homology. A number of factors need to be considered. First, although research has shown some evidence for consistency (see Woodhams and Toye (2007), Salfati and Bateman (2005), Santilla, Fritzon, and Tamelander (2005), among others), there are a number of methodological and practical problems that may render the research invalid. These include the type of crime involved, the target (property or personal), the inaccurate recording of information in police offense databases (e.g., the recording of preliminary, unverified data instead of established case facts), the use of controlled substances by offenders making their behavior more random, or the staging of crime scenes to mislead or hamper investigative efforts.

Perhaps most notable among the problems with extant research is the domains on which consistency has been found. To date, consistent offender behaviors are assessed or found on the basis of congruence in their modus operandi. These behaviors include anything that is done for the successful completion of the crime, such as disguising one's appearance or voice, cleaning up the crime scene and/or removing evidence, and planning. It is not a long bow to draw that the behavior of serial offenders will be more similar across offenses in those elements that allow them to successfully complete their crimes.

However, the cautious profiler will know that this cannot be assumed but must be investigated and established until all probabilities are exhausted. In other words, behaviors that help the offender evade capture are more likely to be repeated, whereas those that increase the offender's exposure to harm will be less likely to recur. Thus, using these behaviors as the basis for whether a series of crimes are linked borders on circular reasoning: Serial offenders are more likely to learn and adopt behaviors that are successful, behaviors that are successful are most predictive of case linkage, the crimes of serial offenders can be predictive of a given offender if measured on behaviors that are successful.

Grubin, Kelly, and Brundson (2001, p. 39) provide the following less than encouraging commentary on the issue of consistency and case linkage:

> While the preceding chapters have demonstrated that behavioral consistency can be described across serial sexual attacks, it remains to be seen whether this can be translated into a methodology to identify linked offenses which can act as a screening procedure for offenses.

> The methodology developed is based on the fact that the frequency with which each of the 256 possible combinations of domain types occurs can be easily determined. This allows a probability for each combination to be calculated. If the number of cases in the database was sufficiently large, then this probability would approach the actual rate that occurs in rape generally. Unfortunately, although large, data sets of this type,

both in the UK and ViCLAS databases, are small in relative terms; many of the 256 possible combinations simply do not occur, while random fluctuations may mean that others are overrepresented.

The authors go on to note that to account for this, they employed a statistical technique to smooth out the data. Having to potentially manipulate the data is one thing, but the larger problem that potentially leads to this manipulation is another. As discussed in Turvey (2008b, p. 60) in relation to victim crime data,

> much of the victim and offender data that is cited in the literature comes from the FBI's Uniform Crime Reports (UCR), which is a compilation of data from reporting law enforcement agencies around the United States. Not every law enforcement agency compiles this information every year, and not every agency that compiles numbers submits them to the FBI—especially if their numbers are bad and they don't want them made public. So the total number of reporting law enforcement agencies varies from state to state, and from year to year.

However, this problem is not confined to the UCR—or any other single database for that matter. Woodhams and Toye (2007) also note a number of problems with extracting data from such databases. ViCLAS (Violent Crime Linkage Analysis System), an adaptation of the FBI's Violent Criminal Apprehension Program system, despite being widely adopted, has also been criticized (McKenna, 2005):

> A national system to catch serial killers, rapists, and extortionists by "profiling" and comparing crimes across states has been slammed as ineffective because police in all but two states refuse to share information.
>
> Senior Queensland police have complained that the Violent Crime Linkage Analysis System—set-up in 1997 after several high-profile serial killer cases—is not being supported by law enforcement across Australia.
>
> The system, modeled on a hugely successful FBI program in the US, is coordinated by the Australian Crime Commission and involves an automated database that finds patterns between violent crimes.
>
> It is the only behavioral analysis carried out on crimes in Australia and focuses on cases of rape, murder, attempted murders, extortions, and sexual offenses.
>
> Each state police service, as well as the Australian Federal Police, is supposed to file detailed information on violent crime, which is then analyzed for similarities to other cases around the country.
>
> But a federal parliamentary inquiry into the ACC has been told that the system is not working to its potential because of a lack of police cooperation.

Detective Superintendent Stephan William, head of the Intelligence Support Group of the Queensland Police Service, told a parliamentary hearing that the ACC needed to take charge and overhaul the system. "The database is not well supported uniformly across Australia," he said.

"I think it is fair to say that some jurisdictions make no contributions at all, and it will never reach its full potential while that occurs."

"We need to have that addressed at a national level one way or another so that we can decide how we are going to take it forward."

Senior police told *The Australian* yesterday that only Queensland and Western Australia were "taking the database seriously."

Under the system, an investigator fills out a 140-strong questionnaire, covering all details of the method of the crime and any detected links between the offender and victim.

The ACC and NSW and Victorian police were yet to respond to the claims last night.

But it is understood many jurisdictions are not cooperating because of a perception that the ACC is not properly analyzing the case information because of their focus on tackling organized crime.

Superintendent William indicated to the inquiry that some of the blame could be directed to the ACC. "It is a difficult problem for them (ACC) because it does not really fit within their charter, but they have inherited it," he said.

"But we, as a jurisdiction which has committed fairly heavily towards it, would like to see some sort of resolution on what is going to happen."

At the time of the system's implementation, senior police said the high-profile cases of serial backpacker killer Ivan Milat and Sydney "granny killer" Kevin Glover had highlighted that Australian law enforcement lacked a capability for behavior analysis.

In Queensland, the system was first used to track and convict "granny rapist" Gilbert Atwell.

Atwell was sentenced to life imprisonment in 2000 for attacks on 11 elderly Brisbane woman.

However, the problem starts long before the database is scoured for information or similarities. As with any research endeavor, the initial information must be collected and classified correctly (including being accurately recorded initially). Then the information must be passed along to be entered into the database, where it must be correctly entered by an analyst. That information must then be searched, usually through an assembly of algorithms or search strings, in a meaningful way. Once mined, the data may then be passed along to a researcher who may also have to impart some level of interpretation during the coding that provides the data for analysis. The whole process is ripe for human error.

As with so many areas of criminal profiling, these problems could be overcome by discarding statistical averages and generalizations and conducting thorough analyses of the current case through the employ of critical thinking, analytical logic, and the scientific method. Being able to reconstruct a crime and therefore to become intimate with its peculiarities will not only answer investigative and forensic questions but also prove to be a more valid basis on which to determine those crimes in a series that are the work of the same offender.

CONCLUSION

In light of the problems discussed in this chapter, there can be no question that continued reliance on consistency and homology, and by extension inductive profiling, is an error of considerable proportions. That such practices continue unabated is a testament to the low quality of training available to profilers, to the absence of behavioral scientists engaged in casework, to entrenched mindsets and affiliations, and to the failure of those in the community to understand what they have read.

For behavioral consistency and the homology assumption to be even useful theories, a number of things must occur. First, a full and thorough reconstruction of the evidence must be undertaken to ensure that the behaviors being examined for consistency are valid. Similarly, one cannot assume that others are trained professionals who have done their jobs professionally. This is too often not the case. One also cannot assume that available research is representative or reflective of a particular offender or offender populations. For example, would research on single homicides be a suitable standard from which to assess the behavior of a serial murderer? Would general research on homicide, including domestic homicides, be a suitable standard from which to assess the behavior in a stranger killing? This problem has been best stated by Turvey (2008c, p. 629), who notes that

> serial crime refers to any series of two or more related crimes (Petherick, 2005, pp. 143–149). Despite the limits set upon us by traditional nomothetic reasoning, this does not mean two or more related crimes of the same type (i.e., rape, homicide, burglary, stalking, etc.). Unfortunately, many investigators and researchers are stuck in a nomothetic mode—a function of how crime has

been studied (chunked into similar groups), as opposed to how criminals actually behave and how each crime must subsequently be investigated. From a practical standpoint, it is not the type of crime that defines the existence of series, but the inference that the same offender is committing them. Nomothetic research and study have worked very hard to blind us to the reality that many offenders are not just a rapist, not just a murderer, not just an arsonist, not just a stalker, not just a burglar, and not just a bank robber. In fact, many serial offenders (a.k.a. serialists) commit crimes of multiple types in the course of a criminal season or career. Thinking this way is one of the steps that can lead to their identification and apprehension. And the opposite is also true.

Another problem is the assumption that the way an offender behaves at a crime scene is reflective of his or her general personality traits. The presence of extreme emotions, alcohol, or drugs, among others, can obscure an offender's personality, either at the time of the crime or some time in the future. The severity of mental illness may wax and wane, individuals can vary their medication regime, or what led an offender to be angry at the crime may be temporary or fleeting.

It would seem that after reviewing the literature in the previous discussions, continued use of inductive methods may be a function of (1) the seemingly "scientific" status of inductive methods (Hicks & Sales, 2006) afforded by the use of numbers, in no small way a view continually peddled by those who employ them, and (2) the ease with which these methods can be taught and applied, noting that no real expertise in the behavioral or forensic sciences is necessary to use them. Neither argument on its own or combined provides a sufficient reason for their continued use.

It should be clear at this point that inductive methods are not only incorrect in their presentation of nomothetic research as relevant to individual cases but also misleading in that they present each individual offender as a hypothetical average offender from previous crimes, where these characteristics may have little to do with the crime at hand. Undoubtedly, profilers should all endeavor to be more selective in their approach to the way offender characteristics in criminal profiles are derived.

Despite these limitations, there continues to be a proliferation of methods relying on both consistency and homology in determining the characteristics of an unknown offender. Until this practice stops, profiling as a whole will continue to be viewed with skepticism and maintain its position as an underutilized investigative tool.

As for change, there is no time like the present.

Questions

1. The theory that the same offender will do the same thing across the span of time during different offenses is known as:

   a. Behavioral homology

   b. Behavioral consistency

   c. Homology assumption

   d. Interpersonal consistency

   e. None of the above

2. The study conducted by Mokros and Alison (2002) on 100 male stranger rapes found:

   a. Support for the homology assumption with respect to age

   b. Support for the homology assumption for sociodemographic features

   c. Support for the homology assumption for previous convictions

   d. Limited support for the homology assumption

   e. No support for the homology assumption

3. The problem of relevance relates to the relevance of the literature used in providing an average for reference. *True or false?*

4. The only profiling method that relies on the homology assumption is investigative psychology. *True or false?*

5. Discuss some general problems with crime data.

REFERENCES

Alison, L., Goodwill, A., & Alison, E. (2005). Guidelines for profilers. In Alison, L. (ed.). The Forensic Psychologist's Casebook: Psychological Profiling and Criminal Investigation. Devon: Willan.

Canter, D. (1994). Criminal shadows: Inside the mind of the serial killer. London: Harper Collins.

Canter, D. (1995). Psychology of offender profiling. In R. Bull & D. Carson (Eds.), Handbook of Psychology in Legal Contexts. London: Wiley.

Canter, D. (2004). Offender profiling and investigative psychology. Journal of Investigative Psychology and Offender Profiling, 1, 1–15.

Doyle, A. D. (2002). The Complete Sherlock Holmes. New Lanark, UK: Geddes & Grosset.

Grubin, D., Kelly, P., & Brundson, C. (2001). Linking Serious Sexual Assault through Behavior. London: Home Office, Research Development and Statistics Directorate.

Hart, S. D., Michie, C., & Cooke, D. J. (2007). Precision of actuarial risk assessment instruments: Evaluating the "margins of error" of group v. individual predictions of violence. British Journal of Psychiatry, 190(49), 60–65.

Hicks, S. J., & Sales, B. D. (2006). Criminal Profiling: Developing an Effective Science and Practice. Washington, DC: American Psychological Association.

Holmes, R. M., & Holmes, S. T. (2002). Profiling Violent Crimes: An Investigative Tool. Thousand Oaks, CA: Sage.

Investigations Subcommittee and Defence Policy Panel of the Committee on Armed Services (1990). USS Iowa tragedy: An investigative failure. Washington DC: US Government Printing Office.

Kocsis, R. N. (2006). Criminal Profiling: Principles and Practice. Totowa, NJ: Humana Press.

McKenna, M. (2005, November 8). States refusing to share crime data. The Australian.

Meloy, J. R. (1998). The Psychology of Stalking: Clinical and Forensic Perspectives. Boston: Academic Press.

Mokros, A., & Alison, L. J. (2002). Is offender profiling possible? Testing the predicted homology of crime scene actions and background characteristics in a sample of rapists. Legal and Criminological Psychology, 7, 25–43.

Ogloff, J. R. P., & Davis, M. R. (2005). Assessing risk for violence in the Australian context. In D. Chappell & P. Wilson (Eds.), Issues in Australian Crime and Criminal Justice. Sydney: Butterworths.

Petherick, W. A. (2005). Serial Crime: Theoretical and Behavioral Issues in Behavioral Profiling. Boston: Academic Press.

Petherick, W. A. (2008). Criminal profiling. In P. R. Wilson & K. Fritzon (Eds.), Forensic and Criminal Psychology: An Australian Perspective. Melbourne: McGraw-Hill.

Petherick, W. A., & Turvey, B. E. (2008a). Nomothetic methods of criminal profiling. In B. E. Turvey (ed.). Criminal Profiling: An Introduction to Behavioral Evidence Analysis. (3rd. ed.). Burlington, MA: Academic Press.

Petherick, W. A., & Turvey, B. E. (2008b). Behavioral evidence analysis: An ideo deductive method of criminal profiling. In B. E. Turvey (ed.). Criminal Profiling: An Introduction to Behavioral Evidence Analysis. (3rd. ed.). Burlington, MA: Academic Press.

Popper, K. (2003). The logic of scientific discovery. London: Routledge Classics.

Reik, T. (1945). The Unknown Murderer. New York: Prentice Hall.

Salfati, G., & Bateman, A. L. (2005). Serial homicide: An investigation of behavioral consistency. Journal of Offender Psychology and Offender Profiling, 2, 121–144.

Santilla, P., Fritzon, K., & Tamelander, A. L. (2005). Linking arson incidents on the basis of crime scene behavior. Journal of Police and Criminological Psychology, 19, 1–16.

Shoda, Y., Mischel, W., & Wright, J. C. (1994). Personality processes and individual differences. Journal of Personality and Social Psychology, 67(4), 674–687.

Turvey, B. E. (2008a). Criminal Profiling: An Introduction to Behavioral Evidence Analysis. (3rd ed.). Burlington, MA: Academic Press.

Turvey, B. E. (2008b). Serial crime. In B. E. Turvey (ed.). Criminal Profiling: An Introduction to Behavioral Evidence Analysis. (3rd. ed.). Burlington, MA: Academic Press.

Turvey, B. E. (2008c). Victimity: Entering the criminal justice system. In B. E. Turvey & W. A. Petherick (Eds.), Forensic Victimology: Examining Violent Crime Victims in Investigative and Legal Contexts. San Diego: Academic Press.

Wilson, P., Lincoln, R., & Kocsis, R.N. (1997). Validity, utility and ethics of profiling for serial violent and sexual offenders. Psychiatry, Psychology and Law, 4(1), 1–12.

Woodhams, J., & Toye, K. (2007). An empirical test of the assumptions of case linkage and offender profiling with serial commercial robberies. Psychology, Public Policy, and Law, 13(1), 59–85.

CHAPTER 4

Criminal Profiling Methods

Wayne Petherick

KEY TERMS

Criminal profile: An attempt to provide personality and behavioral clues of an offender based on the offender's behavior and the evidence he or she leaves behind.

Criminal investigative analysis: A blanket term used by the FBI and FBI-trained profilers that incorporates profiling, indirect personality assessment, equivocal death analysis, and trial strategy.

Organized offender: An offender who may be psychopathic and is literally organized in his or her offense behavior, cleaning up the crime scene, removing weapons and evidence, and attempting to hide the body, among others.

Disorganized offender: An offender who may be psychotic and makes no attempt to clean up the crime scene, remove evidence, or hide the body, among others.

Investigative psychology: An inductive profiling method developed by David Canter based on psychological principles and research into various offense types.

Geographic profiling: A profiling method that focuses on the probable spatial behavior of the offender as a function of the locations of various crime sites.

Least effort principle: Given two alternative courses of action, people will choose the one that requires the least effort.

Distance decay: The theory that crimes will decrease in frequency the further away an offender travels from his or her home base.

CONTENTS

67

Circle theory: The theory that an offender's home may be found within an area prescribed by the two outermost offenses in the series.

Diagnostic evaluation: A general term for the profiling work of psychologists and psychiatrists done on an ad hoc basis.

Behavioral evidence analysis: A deductive profiling method based on the collection and interpretation of physical evidence and the application of deductive logic.

INTRODUCTION

As an investigative aid, criminal profiling has received a great deal of attention from academic audiences and popular culture (Petherick, 2003), and significant advances have been made in both practical and theoretical terms. Even though our collective knowledge about this area has grown, there is still much about the process that remains a mystery. For example, there is little acknowledgment or understanding of the logic or reasoning employed within the profiling process (see Chapter 2), or that there are indeed different methods employed within the profiling community. Of more concern is the fact that many practitioners continue to confuse these issues even in the face of overwhelming contradictory evidence. Just as serious is when they practice one method but pass it off as another, or when they cannot distinguish between methods. This may not necessarily be a conscious act, but either way, it suggests a problem.

It is the aim of this chapter to provide a theoretical and practical overview of the main criminal profiling methods in use. This includes a detailed analysis of the Federal Bureau of Investigation's (FBI) *Criminal Investigative Analysis*, Canter's *Investigative Psychology*, Rossmo's *Geographic Profiling*, and Turvey's *Behavioral Evidence Analysis*.[1] In addition, the generic method employed by mental health professionals known as *diagnostic evaluations* is also addressed. Each section provides not only a comprehensive review of the theoretical and practical underpinnings of each approach but also a summary of critiques.

CRIMINAL PROFILING: WHAT IS IT?

In a broad sense, a *criminal profile* is an attempt to provide personality and behavioral clues about offenders based on their behavior and the evidence they leave

---

[1]Although the individual proponents would probably argue that the individual methods do not "belong" to them, those listed are considered the primary or leading practitioners of each method and are generally accredited with their development.

behind. "It is an inferential process that involves an analysis of ... their interactions with the victim and crime scene, their choice of weapon and their use of language among other things" (Petherick, 2003, p. 173).

According to Geberth (1996, p. 710), "a criminal personality profile is an educated attempt to provide investigative agencies with specific information as to the type of individual who would have committed a certain crime." Holmes and Holmes (2002) simply cite this definition from Geberth. In their textbook on criminal investigation, Bennett and Hess (2001) do not specifically define profiling; instead, they classify it according to its goal, which is identifying an individual's mental, emotional, and psychological characteristics.

The FBI and its associates no longer use the term *criminal profiling* to describe their method of offender behavior analysis. This term and others (e.g., psychological profiling and behavioral profiling) have been replaced by the blanket term *Criminal Investigative Analysis* (CIA), which covers not only profiling but also other services such as indirect personality assessment, equivocal death analysis, and trial strategy. Criminal profiling under this paradigm is aimed at "providing the client agency with the characteristics and traits of an unidentified offender that differentiate him from the general population. These characteristics are set forth in such a manner as to allow those who know and/ or associate with the offender to readily recognize him" (Hazelwood, Ressler, Depue, & Douglas, 1995, p. 116).

Thus, it should be apparent that despite the differences in approach or author, there is a degree of unanimity in the ways profiling is defined. Generally, any attempt to interpret an offender's actions to suggest features of his or her personality and behavior constitutes criminal profiling. There is less agreement, however, about who may be a criminal profiler.

One need not call oneself a criminal profiler to offer profile characteristics. In fact, a number of other professions have trodden into areas that have historically been the province of criminal profilers. Consider the following example from Thomas Noguchi, M.D., Chief Medical Examiner (reproduced exactly as per the original document):

Medicolegal Opinion

For the purpose of assisting the investigation of law enforcement agencies on the death of Janine Katherine Kirk, I submit the following opinions.

My opinions were based on injury pattern, the circumstances surrounding the death, information during the discovery and the recovery of the body at the scene. The following observations were made to predict certain characteristics of the assailant involved in the case. This type of work has been known in a field of forensic sciences as a profiling of the assailant.

PHYSICAL CHARACTERISTICS OF THE ASSAILANT

1. The person is a male, strong and much taller than that of the decedent. In order to deliver a concentrated blunt force to a small target area, above mentioned physical characteristics would be required.
2. The person would be right-handed, thus, he would be able to deliver blows to the left side of the victim. The blows were delivered from his right to left direction.
3. The person delivered his blows to the face of the victim as he was facing the decedent.
4. Severe blows to the back of the neck causing severe bruises to the skin and underlining muscles.

PSYCHOLOGICAL CHARACTERISTICS

1. The person would be acquainted with and known by a decedent, thus, the assailant was able to approach her without difficulty.
2. The person, had ability to plan in advance and execute his plan, including the disposition of the body.

Furthermore, one need not be a capable or competent profiler to use the label. As in many areas of endeavor, this has led to a distinct stratification of skills and abilities. Unfortunately, a substandard practitioner in this area has the very real capacity to ruin not only his or her own reputation but also that of other practitioners and the field in general. One bad experience may lead all profilers to be tarred with the same brush and probably contributes to a great deal of the skepticism voiced by a number of critics. For instance, Godwin (1985, p. 276), in one widely cited criticism believes that profilers "play a blind man's bluff, groping in all directions in the hope of grabbing a sleeve. Occasionally they do, but not firmly enough to seize it, for the behaviorists producing them must necessarily deal in generalities and types." Liebert (1985) is also critical, stating that superficial behavioral profiling that rigidly reduces serial murder to a few observable parameters has the potential to lead an investigation astray.

Perhaps the most poignant discussion on what makes someone a criminal profiler was stated by Turvey (personal communication, July 25, 2004), who provides the following, reproduced almost in its entirety:

> Criminal profiling is a general term that can refer to any process of inferring the traits of criminals. It is not bound by method or organization.

> The first criminal profilers that we have a solid record of in the Western world were criminal investigators in Europe in the late 1800s (re: Hans Gross' *Criminal Investigation*). They were linking cases by MO, looking

for the signatures of burglars, and working to establish motive and personality characteristics before anyone heard of Dr. James Brussel or the Mad Bomber of New York in the 1950s.

Police investigators and forensic personnel (the pathologist in Whitechapel, for example) were the first to enter the profiling arena in the 1800s.

Forensic psychiatrists first entered in the 1940s–1950s with the Mad Bomber case and the Boston Strangler.

FBI agents of various investigative and noninvestigative backgrounds entered in the 1970s–1980s with the work of Teten and Mullany.

Criminologists and others have followed since.

Each related discipline has staked a legitimate claim to the profiling community, and any attempt by any one group to define profiling as strictly their game is probably not a very good student of history, or doesn't understand or accept the history.

In any case, if you are qualified or working in any of these disciplines, I would argue, and it is currently the position of the Academy of Behavioral Profiling,[2] that criminal profiling may be a legitimate extension of your work.

Rather than defining a criminal profiler by some subjective standard, it is better to measure the standard of the community that one is rooted in and how well one is grounded there. Otherwise the compound multidisciplinary requirements would be ridiculously prohibitive.

For example, to be a good criminal profiler, it is necessary to have an understanding of the forensic autopsy process, what it involves, how it is performed, how to read and question results. It is not, however, necessary to be a forensic pathologist. The more medico-legal knowledge you have, the better you will be at your profiling work there is no doubt. But in the end you will need to rely upon a forensic pathologist's conclusions in rendering your profile unless you are a forensic pathologist. To do otherwise would be inappropriate.

Another example: To be a good criminal profiler, it is necessary to have an understanding of blood stain pattern analysis and know that such things

---

[2] The Academy of Behavioral Profiling is a professional organization that was conceived as a forum for the discussion of evidenced-based profiling. It holds annual meetings and is the first profiling "community" to promote a code of ethics. See http://www.profiling.org.

are important to establishing events and sequences and the like. But one need not be an expert in bloodstain pattern analysis to write a competent profile. The more knowledge in this area that you have the better, but unless you are a bloodstain pattern expert you should really rely on someone that is and not make your own interpretations of such evidence.

What makes someone a criminal profiler? The answer would have to be that a criminal profiler is someone who constructs criminal profiles. There are good profilers, there are bad profilers; there are educated profilers, and there are ignorant profilers. Some are ethical. Some are not. All are defined by the work they do. When a detective is inferring criminal traits from the evidence in their investigation, they are profiling. When a criminologist is studying a group of similar offenders to infer common characteristics, they are profiling.

The purpose of the ABP in this regard is to develop uniform practice standards by which the work product of evidence-based profilers can be evaluated, and subsequently competency, knowledge, skill, and ability can be assessed. Yes there are educational and experience baselines, but even a student can render a profile ... that is of good quality and helpful to an investigative or forensic effort, which is as it should be.

So if you're profiling, you are a profiler. Though you may or may not be a very good one depending on the quality of your education, training, and experience.

Only an evaluation of your work product can tell.

The previous chapter discussed how a profile can be inductive or deductive, and it should be noted that the style of reasoning employed in a process can be identified even before the individual methods discussed next are considered. A method is identified as inductive or deductive based on the primary style of logic or reasoning employed in developing offender characteristics, with most methods being inductive. The first four methods presented here employ inductive reasoning. The last, behavioral evidence analysis, employs deductive reasoning.

CRIMINAL INVESTIGATIVE ANALYSIS

Perhaps one of the best known methods is that devised by the FBI. The method chiefly arose out of one core study conducted between 1979 and 1983, for which federal agents interviewed offenders about their crimes. The goal was to determine whether there are any consistent features across offenses that may be helpful in classifying these offenders, with a number of publications arising directly from this study (Burgess, Hartman, Ressler, Douglas, & McCormack,

1986; Douglas, Ressler, Burgess, & Hartman, 1986; Ressler & Burgess, 1985; Ressler, Burgess, & Douglas, 1988; Ressler, Burgess, Douglas, Hartman, & D'Agostino, 1986; Ressler, Burgess, Hartman, Douglas, & McCormack, 1986).

The mainstay of the FBI approach is the organized/disorganized dichotomy, which distinguishes offenders by virtue of the sophistication of their offenses. Because this system was in use before the research was conducted, this is perhaps best thought of as a validation study with the terminology first appearing in *The Lust Murderer* in 1980 by Hazelwood and Douglas. The researchers state that one of the quantitative goals of the study was to "identify the differentiating characteristics used by the BSU [Behavioral Sciences Unit] agents to classify sexual murderers and determine whether or not these variables were valid statistically" (Burgess & Ressler, 1985, p. 4).

An *organized offender* is often said to be psychopathic and is literally organized in most facets of his or her life, cleaning up his or her crime scenes, removing weapons and evidence, and even attempting to hide the body. *Disorganized offenders* are often said to be psychotic and make no such attempt to clean up their crime scenes, remove evidence, or hide the body. Although the association has been discarded in most publications on the subject, some authors continue to associate organized crimes with psychopathic offenders and disorganized crimes with psychotic offenders (Geberth, 1996; Holmes & Holmes, 2002), although whether this holds true in practice in contended. Ressler and Shachtman (1992, pp. 113–114) note that the terminology had to be "dumbed down" for the police, who typically lacked training in psychology and psychiatry:

> To characterize the types of offenders for police and other law
> enforcement people, we needed to have terminology that was not
> based on psychiatric jargon. It wouldn't do much good to say to a police
> officer that he was looking for a psychotic personality if that police
> officer had no training in psychology…. Instead of saying that a crime
> scene showed evidence of a psychopathic personality, we began to
> tell the police officer that such a crime scene was "organized" and so
> was the likely offender, while another and its perpetrator might be
> "disorganized," when mental disorder was present.

At its simplest, the model works by associating factors from the crime scene (Table 4.1) with a criminal's personality (Table 4.2).

Thus, if the crime scene appeared planned and controlled with restraints used, where there were aggressive acts with the body prior to death, and the weapon or evidence was absent (ergo, an organized crime scene), it could be said that the offender would be above average intelligence, socially competent, with a controlled mood during the crime, and so forth (ergo, an organized offender).

Table 4.1 Crime Scene Characteristics of the Organized and Disorganized Offender

Psychopathic (Organized) Crime Scene Characteristics	Psychotic (Disorganized) Crime Scene Characteristics
Offense planned	Offense spontaneous
Victim is a targeted stranger	Victim or location known
Personalizes victim	Depersonalizes victim
Controlled conversation	Minimal conversation
Crime scene reflects overall control	Crime scene random and sloppy
Demands submissive victim	Sudden violence to victim
Restraints used	Minimal restraints used
Aggressive acts prior to death	Sexual acts after death
Body hidden	Body left in plain view
Weapon/evidence absent	Evidence/weapon often present
Transports victim	Body left at the death scene

From Ressler and Burgess (1985).

Table 4.2 Offender Characteristics of the Organized and Disorganized Offender

Psychopathic (Organized) Offender Characteristics	Psychotic (Disorganized) Offender Characteristics
Average to above average intelligence	Below average intelligence
Socially competent	Socially inadequate
Skilled work preferred	Unskilled work
Sexually competent	Sexually incompetent
High birth order	Low birth order
Father's work stable	Father's work unstable
Inconsistent childhood discipline	Harsh discipline as a child
Controlled mood during crime	Anxious mood during crime
Use of alcohol with crime	Minimal use of alcohol
Precipitating situational stress	Minimal situational stress
Living with partner	Living alone
Mobility with car in good condition	Lives/works near the crime scene
Follows crime in news media	Minimal interest in the news media
May change jobs or leave town	Significant behavior change

From Ressler and Burgess (1985).

Confusingly, although the original sample was composed of offenders in sexual homicides, the terminology of the original FBI study has been adopted in the classification of other crimes. Despite the limitations of the original study, organized and disorganized labels have also appeared in the area of stalking (Wright, Burgess, Laszlo, McCrary, & Douglas, 1996; implied in Geberth, 1996) and arson (Douglas, Burgess, Burgess, & Ressler, 1992; Kocsis, Irwin, & Hayes, 1998).

According to Ressler et al. (1988), the CIA process is composed of six steps (ultimately five, with the final [ideal] stage being the apprehension of the offender).

Stage 1, profile inputs, involves the collection and integration of all of the known material relating to the criminal offense, including but not limited to the physical evidence, police reports, and photographs/videos. In addition to autopsy photographs, aerial photographs and pictures of the crime scene are also needed, along with crime scene sketches with distances, directions, and scale (Douglas et al., 1986). Also during this stage, the victim is examined, including his or her "domestic setting, employment, reputation, habits, fears, physical condition, personality, criminal history, family relationships, hobbies, and social conduct" (p. 405).

Decision process models, the second stage, involves the integration of the various profiling inputs into patterns that may assist in determining the homicide type and style, intent, victim and offender risk, escalation, and time and location factors. Although not specifically discussed, it is likely that much of this information was drawn on for the Crime Classification Manual, a tool designed to "make explicit crime categories that have been utilized informally" (Douglas et al., 1992, p. 6). These include the following (Ressler et al., 1988, pp. 138–142):

Homicide Type and Style: A single homicide involves one victim and one homicidal event. A double homicide is two victims, with one event and one location, and a triple homicide is three victims in one location during one event. More than three victims is classified as a mass homicide.

Primary Intent of the Murderer: The killer's primary intent could be criminal enterprise, emotional, selfish, cause specific, or sexual. Murder may not be the primary intent of the offender but may be engaged in to meet one of the above goals.

Victim Risk: The victim risk is determined by looking at the victim's age, occupation, lifestyle, and the physical stature of the victim. Low-risk victims include those whose daily lives do not usually put them in harms way, whereas a high-risk victim is targeted by a murderer who knows where they can find victims. Information about the victim can provide insight into the type of offender sought.

Offender Risk: Like victim risk, the actions of the offender that may place them at risk are also of interest. The risks an offender places themselves at may indicate emotional maturity, personal stress, or confidence in the police.

Escalation: This refers to the propensity of an offender to increase the nature of their criminal behavior, say, from voyeurism to rape, as well as an assessment of the likelihood of the offense being or becoming serial in nature.

Time Factors: Several factors need to be considered here, and these include the time it took to kill the victim, to commit any additional acts with the body, and to dispose of the body. Additionally, the time of the day or night might also be important as it may provide information on the lifestyle or employment of the offender.

Location Factors: Information about where the victim was first approached, and the location of the death and dump sites is similarly important. This may provide insight into whether the offender used a vehicle for transport.

The third stage is crime assessment, where an attempt is made to reconstruct the sequence of events and victim and offender behaviors. Based on this information and that of the previous stages, decisions are made about the level of organization or disorganization of the offense, so it is primarily during this stage that the application of the typology comes into play. Other considerations include crime scene dynamics, motivation, and considerations of staging.

Stage 4 involves the actual criminal profile and provides insight into the offender's background, physical characteristics, habits, beliefs, values, and pre-offense and postoffense behavior (Ressler et al., 1988). Once the profile has been compiled, it can be delivered to the investigative team and integrated into the inquiry by generating suspects and evaluating those already under consideration for their "fit." In a perfect world, this would lead to the final stage, apprehension. If a suspect is apprehended, the authors note that an interview should be conducted to establish the validity of the overall process.

Douglas and Burgess (1986, p. 9) suggest the following seven-step process, which they claim is similar to that used by clinicians in making a diagnosis:

1. Evaluation of the criminal act
2. Comprehensive evaluation of the specifics of the crime scene(s)
3. Comprehensive analysis of the victim
4. Evaluation of the preliminary police reports
5. Evaluation of the medical examiner's autopsy protocol
6. Development of profile with critical offender characteristics
7. Investigative suggestions predicated on the construction of the profile

Adapting the FBI's methodology, the Dutch profiling unit has taken this method a step further attempting to address some of the concerns raised about the approach. While being staffed in part by profilers trained by the FBI, the unit adopts a more multidisciplinary approach because these profilers also work closely with investigators, psychologists, and legal professionals. Discussing the increasing role of crime analysts within Dutch police organizations, Jackson, van den Eshof, and de Kleuver (1997, p. 107) note the following:

> This interest led to several initiatives, one of which was the setting up of an offender profiling unit within the National Criminal Intelligence Division of the National Police Agency. The task of that unit was to respond to requests from regional police forces for help and advice with criminal investigations, particularly for those involving serious contact crimes.

> When the service finally went into operation in September 1991, the unit's guiding principles and work methods bore a strong resemblance to FBI methods. However, from the beginning of the enterprise it was also recognized that to be effective, the unit had not only to be accountable to those it served, namely the Dutch police, but should also be actively involved in the scientific forum. This meant that research, including evaluation studies, should be carried out and the findings made public to ensure critical debate and opportunities for development.

Thus, instead of just relying on subjective interpretation, intuition, and investigative experience, this unit tests its range of hypotheses about offenders and publishes the results, allowing for transparency in its operations. Ainsworth (2001) suggests this stands in stark contrast to the FBI, which was largely secretive about its work until agents such as John Douglas published their memoirs (Douglas & Olshaker, 1995). These individual biographical accounts may not be a good judge of their success, however (Ainsworth, 2001, p. 135):

> This openness comes in marked contrast to the FBI's work where, in most cases, public scrutiny only became possible when ex-profilers wrote and published their memoirs.... Even in such cases, the amount of detail which was provided hardly allowed for the scientific assessment of many of the claims. In addition, it seems likely that ex-profilers will speak at length about their successes but be noticeably more reticent about their failures.

According to Jackson et al. (1997, p. 108), there are two principles guiding the development of the unit, each having consequences for their operations:

1. Offender profiling is a combination of detective experience and behavioral scientific knowledge. Given this perspective, it is not surprising that close links were quickly established with the Behavioral Science Unit of the FBI (as it was then called) and still continue to

be maintained. A further consequence of this view is that the unit should be organized on multidisciplinary lines. The team comprises a police officer (trained at the FBI Academy at Quantico) working closely together with a forensic psychologist who is also a qualified lawyer (a further footnote in the chapter states that a second psychologist has joined the profiling unit).

2. An offender profile is not an end in itself, but it is purely an instrument for steering an investigation in a particular direction. Within Dutch police practice, offender profiling is not viewed as a product in itself, but simply as another management instrument to further the work of the detective team. This principle means that the profiler's description of a possible offender must always be coupled with practical advice and suggestions about how to proceed with the investigation at hand.

As noted, this method is the most prevalent today and the reasons for this are many and varied, including its ease of use, the legitimacy afforded the near mythical status of its developers,[3] and the range of literature available on it. Not all of this literature is flattering, and CIA has attracted considerable criticism.

Petherick and Turvey (2008a) note a number of general shortcomings with this method, specifically citing problems with its application. Most notably, it is Turvey's concern that classifying an offender based solely on the presentation of the crime scene may in some instances lead investigators astray. This is likely to occur when the offender or evidence dynamics change or obscure the physical evidence on which the assessment is made. Crimes involving the use of drugs, those during which the offender is interrupted, anger-motivated offenses, and staged offenses can all change the presentation of the crime scene on which determination of the offender's level of sophistication is made (i.e., whether the offender is organized or disorganized). This may lead the profiler to believe that authorities are dealing with a disorganized offender because of the presentation of the scene when they are actually confronted with the crime of an organized offender.

Furthermore, Petherick and Turvey (2008a) suggest that the method revolves around the simple reduction of human behavior to a few observable parameters that subsequently lead to characteristics of the unknown offender. It should also be noted that the individual characteristics of each offender type are not weighted in terms of their importance, and in applying the model it is left to individual

---

[3]Jenkins (1994, p. 70) notes that "this meant presenting the FBI's behavioral scientists (the 'mind hunters') as uniquely qualified to deal with the serial murder menace, and this interpretation became very influential. The mind hunter image of the BSU was initially presented in a series of high laudatory media accounts, which reinforced the prestige of the unit as the world's leading experts on serial violence."

profilers to determine which characteristics they deem important or applicable to a specific crime. This introduces a level of subjectivity into the process that may adversely affect the outcome and strain the method's validity.

On a methodological level, the sample size was small ($N = 36$), the sample was not random, and the interviews relied heavily on self-report. In a small number of cases, the agents conducting the interview could not decide which category the offender fit into, so they were told to force the offender into either the organized or disorganized group (Ressler & Burgess, 1985). Each agent was essentially left to decide which category the offender belonged to, and no inter-rater reliability was conducted to determine if the offender had been correctly classified. With regard to the reliability of the study, it has never been replicated on an international level and so its application outside of the United States may also be questionable (Petherick, 2003; Woodworth & Porter, 2001).

Lastly, it has been noted that few offenders will fit neatly into either the organized or the disorganized category, and that most will fall somewhere between these two extremes (Canter, Alison, Alison, & Wentink, 2004; Ressler & Shachtman, 1992; Petherick & Turvey, 2008a). In the words of Ressler and Shachtman (p. 180), "As with most distinctions, this one is too simple and too perfect a dichotomy to describe every single case. Some crime scenes, and some murderers, display organized as well as disorganized characteristics and we call those 'mixed.'"

Baker (2001) claims that the mixed category is less helpful to investigators. Moving to a continuum may decrease the method's strength in discriminating between types because an offender may change from organized to disorganized and vice versa throughout the course of his or her criminal career. This concern does not only apply to the application of the mixed category though, and this evolution (or deevolution) represents a general problem with the approach.

In examining the literature on the involvement of FBI profilers in individual cases, there are a substantial number of less than flattering reports. It is not the purpose of this chapter to discuss these in-depth, but the interested reader should consult Investigations Subcommittee and Defense Policy Panel of the Committee on Armed Services (1990); Darkes, Otto, Poythress, and Starr (1993); Kopel and Blackman (1997); Fox and Levin (1996); Thompson (1999); and Petherick and Turvey (2008a).

INVESTIGATIVE PSYCHOLOGY

As with CIA, investigative psychology (IP) identifies profiling as only one part of the overall process. The main advocate of this method is David Canter, a British psychologist who promotes a research approach to offender behavior. It is inductive and dependent on the quality and amount of data accumulated

(McGrath, 2000). Although many inductive methods suffer from the same problems, Canter employs larger sample sizes than the FBI, continually conducting research and using more rigorous methodologies to expand knowledge (Egger, 1998; Petherick, 2003). Therefore, the conclusions are still inductive, but they are based on more empirically robust evaluations. According to the program's web site, IP provides a

> scientific and systematic basis to previously subjective approaches to all aspects of the detection, investigation, and prosecution of crimes. This behavioral science contribution can be thought of as operating at different stages of any investigation, from that of the crime itself, through the gathering of information and on to the actions of police officers working to identify the criminal then on to the preparation of a case for court.

Canter has gone to great pains to differentiate IP from everyday profiling (Canter, 1998, p. 11):

> So should psychologists be kept out of the investigation of crimes? Clearly, as the director of an institute of investigative psychology I do think that psychologists have much to offer to criminal, and other, investigations. My central point is to make a distinction between "profiling" and investigative psychology.

Furthermore, to distinguish between IP and profiling approaches that are more idiosyncratic, Canter (1998, p. 11) notes the following:

> Investigative psychology is a much more prosaic activity. It consists of the painstaking examination of patterns of criminal behavior and the testing out of those patterns of trends that may be of value to police investigators.... Investigative psychologists also accept that there are areas of criminal behavior that may be fundamentally enigmatic.

This approach has five main components that provide a theoretical backdrop, commonly referred to as the five-factor model, as being reflective of an offender's past and present: interpersonal coherence, significance of time and place, criminal characteristics, criminal career, and forensic awareness.

Interpersonal coherence refers to the way people adopt a style of interaction when dealing with others (Canter, 1995). Canter believes that an offender will treat his victims in a similar way to that in which he treats other people in his daily activities—that is, there is some consistency in his relationships with others between offending and nonoffending behavior. A rapist who exhibits selfishness with friends, family, and colleagues will also exhibit selfishness with his victims. This belief is not unique to IP, and most profiling approaches rely on the notion of interpersonal coherence in developing offender characteristics (Petherick, 2003).

Because "interpersonal processes gain much of their psychological nuance from the time and place in which they occur" (Canter, 1989, p. 14), the *significance of time and place* also reflects some aspects of the offender's personality. That is, the time and place are often specifically chosen and thus provide further insight into an offender's actions in the form of mental maps. The suggestion here is that "an offender will feel more comfortable and in control in areas which he knows well" (Ainsworth, 2001, p. 199). Two considerations are important here—the specific location and the general spatial behavior, which is a function of specific crime sites (Canter, 1989). Canter (2003) has dedicated an entire work to these aspects, which are largely based on the theory of environmental criminology.

Criminal characteristics provide investigators with some idea about the type of crime they are dealing with. The idea is to determine "whether the nature of the crime and the way it is committed can lead to some classifications of what is characteristic…based upon interviews with criminals and empirical studies" (Canter, 1989, p. 14). This is an inductive component of the approach and, as it stands, is similar to attempts made by the FBI in applying the organized/disorganized typology.

Criminal career suggests that a criminal will behave in a similar way throughout a crime series, although it is acknowledged that there is some room for adaptation and change. This adaptation and change may be reflective of past experiences while offending. For example, a criminal may bind and gag a current victim based on the screams and resistance of a past victim (Canter, 1989). This aspect may reflect an evolution of modus operandi displayed by many offenders who learn through subsequent offenses and continue to refine their criminal behaviors. In addition, the nature and type of precautionary behaviors may provide some insight into the type of contact the offender has had with the criminal justice system.

Finally, *forensic awareness* may show an increase in learning based on past experience with the criminal justice system. A rapist may turn to using condoms in order to prevent the transfer of biological fluids and prevent subsequent DNA analysis. Perpetrators may well be sophisticated in that they will use techniques that hinder police investigations, such as the wearing of a mask or gloves, or attempt to destroy other evidence (Ainsworth, 2000).

Furthermore, there are five characteristics or clusters that are instructive to investigators. These are self-explanatory and include residential location, criminal biography, domestic/social characteristics, personal characteristics, and occupation/education history (Ainsworth, 2000). Although there is not necessarily any greater weighting placed on any of these profile features, Boon and Davies (1993) suggest that residential location and criminal history are most beneficial (again highlighting the emphasis that IP places on crime geography). Even a cursory examination of the literature arising from this paradigm shows a considerable focus on examinations of the offender's geographic behavior. In this way, the method shares many similarities with other approaches to geographic profiling detailed subsequently.

The criticisms of IP parallel those of other inductive approaches but include others that are more unique to the method. Considerable emphasis is placed on the use of statistical procedures in determining offender characteristics, with the most notable being multidimensional scaling or smallest space analysis (SSA). An SSA provides a graphical representation of the relationships between variables, with those that are closely correlated appearing closer together in the plot, and those not correlated being further apart. The specific clustering of variables may also indicate those groups of behaviors that are related, thereby suggesting themes in offending behavior, crime, or offender characteristics.

As with any statistical procedure, it is possible to err in the interpretation of the data. For example, the SSA provides a graphical representation of correlations of every variable to every other variable in a data set. Because different offenders will do similar things for different reasons (Petherick & Turvey, 2008b), it may be possible in a given data set to misinterpret or overstate the correlation between two variables. Worse, because the context of the behavior is not established or poorly understood, the subsequent interpretation of the data may be incorrect. Consider the following example: During the course of a sexual assault, a rapist bites the breast of a rape victim in an attempt at foreplay. In another unrelated sexual assault, the rapist bites the victim's nipple as a form of gratification or stimulation, and in yet a third case, the biting behavior is intended to gain victim compliance. The same behaviors are borne of different motivations, mean different things to the offenders, and are intended to serve different functions or fantasy behavior. Simply reducing the variable to "biting" tells us little, if anything.

McGrath (2000) is concerned that predictions about offender behaviors or characteristics may not be applicable to a certain case because of a low baseline of occurrence. As a result, generalizations may or may not apply to a particular case in guiding the conclusion rather than the conclusion being case specific.

For a more detailed overview of application, see Canter (2003); Canter, Coffey, Huntley, and Missen (2000); and Snook, Canter, and Bennell (2002). Whatever the criticisms, IP at least introduces a systematic and scientific study of criminal behavior.

GEOGRAPHIC PROFILING (GEOPROFILING)

Whereas criminal profiling attempts to define a number of characteristics of the offender from his or her actions at the crime (e.g., age, sex, race, and intelligence), geographic profiling focuses on just one aspect of the crime: the offender's likely location. According to Rossmo (1997, p. 161), geographic profiling focuses on the "probable spatial behavior of the offender within the context of the locations of, and the spatial relationships between, the various crime sites." As with criminal profiling, it is not intended to be an investigative panacea but, rather, a tool that assists police and prioritizes search areas (Laverty & MacLaren, 2002; Ratcliffe, 2004; Rossmo, 1997, 2003). Ideally, a geoprofile should follow from and augment a full criminal profile, once done (Rossmo, 1997).[4]

Protagonists identify geographic profiling as a decision support system used to make estimates of the likely geographic region of an offender's home location (Rossmo, 2000), although it may also identify where the offender works (Ratcliffe, 2004) or some other location with which the offender is familiar (referred to as *activity nodes*). Essentially, geographic profiling makes use of the nonrandom nature of criminal behavior, presupposing that most crimes have rhyme or reason to them (Wilson, 2003):

> Crimes are not just random—there's a pattern. It has been said criminals are not so different from shoppers or even from lions hunting prey. When an offender has committed a number of crimes, they leave behind a fingerprint of their mental map, and you can decode certain things from that. We put every crime location into a computer program and it produces a map showing the most probable areas the police should target.

The provision of geographic profiling software, profiling units, and specialist geoprofilers gives the distinct impression that the approach is scientific and robust, but in reality the theories on which the practice rests are dated and the application of geoprofiling to individual cases has met with serious debate and criticism. For example, the *least effort principle*, which is a core component of Rossmo's approach in the form of the "nearness principle," was first suggested by Zipf in approximately 1950. *Distance decay*, the notion that crimes decrease in frequency the farther away an offender travels from home, has also been around for several decades.

The next section considers some of the theoretical underpinnings of geographic profiling.

---

[4] In Rossmo (1997, p. 161), it is noted that "a psychological profile is not a necessary precursor for a geographic profile," but this position later changed.

The Least Effort Principle

The least effort principle at its most fundamental level suggests that given two alternatives to a course of action, people will choose the one that requires least effort. That is, people will adopt the easiest course of action.

According to Rossmo (2000, pp. 87–88),

> When multiple destinations of equal desirability are available, the least effort principle suggests the closest one will be chosen. The determination of "closest," however, can be a problematic assessment. Isotropic surfaces, spaces exhibiting equal physical properties in all directions, are rarely found within the human geographic experience.

As Rossmo suggests, the ability to impose arbitrary concepts of nearness onto crime is made difficult by the fact that our geographic environment is largely nonuniform. This means that not only does the layout of our environment impact on offending decisions but also our physical location in a three-dimensional space will come into play.[5] This may be particularly critical in areas such as New York and other major cities where high-density housing is the norm. In rural areas where travel routes are typically straighter and naturally larger, the application of the least effort principle may also be problematic. The caution is not necessarily against the application of these principles generally, rather, applying the same principles in open environments that one may apply in city spaces.

The least effort principle may not account for other offense contingencies either, such as the lack of victim availability in certain areas, interrupted offenses, or any other event outside of the offender's immediate control. In addition to these constraints, Rossmo (2000) also suggests that a criminal's financial resources are a consideration in his or her journey to crime.[6]

Distance Decay

Distance decay refers to the idea that crimes will decrease in frequency the farther away an offender travels from his or her home (Rengert, Piquero, & Jones, 1999; van Koppen & de Keijser, 1997). Distance decay is a geographical expression of the principle of least effort (Harries, 1999) and results when an offender shows a preference for closer crime sites.

---

[5]For example, certain types of offenders may not select high-rise buildings for a variety of reasons, and in terms of opportunity factors in crime commission, high-rise buildings may not present the same opportunities because they are not typically thoroughfares.

[6]I am reminded of the burglar who used public transport to get to and from his crime sites and, in an attempt to return to his home base, offered the bus driver a stolen DVD player because he had no cash with which to pay his ticket.

This does not mean that crime sites are closely clustered around the offender's home because this would constitute a threat to the offender's anonymity and liberty. Because of this, Rossmo (2000) posits the existence of a comfort or "buffer zone" directly around the offender's home. Within this area, targets are viewed as less desirable because of the perceived risk associated with offending too close to home (Rossmo, 2000). This is confirmed by van Koppen and de Keijser (1997, p. 1), who note that "offenders rarely commit offences on their own doorstep, presumably because the chances of recognition by people who know them are higher."

Distance decay is also affected by opportunity in the same way as the least effort principle. According to Rengert et al. (1999, pp. 428–429), regardless of the degree to which criminals would like to choose the locations of their offenses, they are unable to do so given the lack of opportunities and the random and unpredictable behavior of others, which will often foil even the best laid plans:

> This is not to deny the "individuality" of criminals; each of them does indeed make separate decisions. However, each decision is made within the framework of constraints. For many criminals, a major aspect of these constraints is represented by distance. In other words, no matter how much one may wish to emphasize "free will" of the individual, in practice, criminals are not free to commit crime anywhere they wish. Their ethnic character may make them stand out in a strange neighborhood, their economic status will determine their access to different modes of transportation, and their past experiences (e.g., school, armed services, and so on) determine the area they have knowledge of. Criminologists can begin to understand the working of these constraints by measuring the *distance decay* effect exhibited in criminal spatial interaction.

The Circle Hypothesis

Those involved in geographic profiling seem to be preoccupied with the way in which geometric shapes are suggestive of a criminal's journey to crime. For example, Canter and Larkin (1993) proposed the "circle hypothesis," which was later tested by Kocsis and Irwin (1997) on a sample of Australian rapes, arsons, and burglaries. Snook et al. (2002) tested the utility of the circle hypothesis by giving a circle heuristic to a group of human judges and comparing their results to an actuarial computer-based model, and a similar study was later conducted by Snook, Taylor, and Bennell (2004).

The danger of overlaying arbitrary geometric shapes should be quite obvious, but the appeal of juxtaposing a circle, a square, or a wedge onto a map for a novice might be too much to avoid. One such example can be drawn from the author's own experience, in which an experienced intelligence analyst, in considering an extensive temporal and geographic crime series, proudly pronounced something like "we found a pattern. If you plot out all of the offenses on a map, you can draw a circle around them!" When questioned at greater length about what this might mean or the implications that it may have for the investigation as a whole, the question was greeted with stunned silence. When asked again what implications this might have, it was pronounced again, though in a more subdued tone, that you could draw a circle around the offenses once they were plotted on a map. This was, apparently, the extent of the revelation about the spatial pattern of the offending. Taken out of context, misinterpreted, or applied inconsistently, the actual meaning of any pattern will be nil.

Canter and Larkin (1993) proposed two types of offending based on the degree to which the offender was proximally tied to his or her home. The marauder hypothesis describes an offender who strikes out from his home location and then returns, with the home being within a circle defined by the two outermost offense locations. On the other hand, a commuter, still operating out of a home base, leaves the general location of this home to offend in a different geographic region, later leaving this area and returning to the locale of his home base. The two models are presented in Figure 4.1.

In Canter and Larkin's (1993) study, there was no support for a commuter model in a sample of 45 sexual assaulters, but in 41 of the 45 cases, the offender's home was located within the circle. Because of this, they suggested there is "strong support for the general marauder hypothesis as being the most applicable to these sets of offenders" (p. 67).

Although the theory seems plausible and attractive, there are a number of issues with the model. First, although Canter and Larkin (1993) identified 87% of offenders as marauders, the decision regarding whether one is dealing with a

FIGURE 4.1
The Marauder and
Commuter Models.

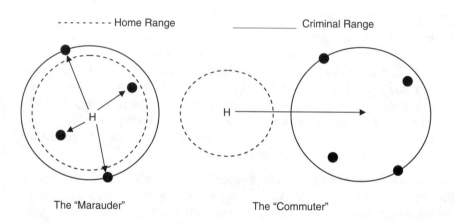

- - - - - - - - Home Range   _____ Criminal Range

The "Marauder"   The "Commuter"

marauder or a commuter when the offender's home base is not known may still be a matter of luck or educated guess. If the profiler relies on the statistical probability that the offender is a marauder, then the same general cautions apply as those for any inductive method, such as whether the case is statistically anomalous (in the Canter and Larkin study, this would mean that the offender was part of the 13%, or perhaps that the research did not apply in any meaningful way in this community or jurisdiction). In addition, the following points are raised, which may highlight limitations in this particular study (from the Discussion section):

- The base is not at the center of the circle of crimes (this will impact on search areas and population numbers in densely populated areas).
- The eccentricity of the model is important because it may reflect some developmental processes on the part of the offender whereby he or she sometimes travels further from home for offending than at other times.
- As a result, the differences between marauding and commuting could perhaps be explained by increasing criminal skill or confidence.
- The representation of ranges using circles is overly simplistic, and other research has suggested that in the United States, city expansion from downtown areas may be better indicated by elliptical or sectoral patterns.
- The number of offenses per offender in this sample was relatively small.
- It is possible that the information used in the modeling was not an accurate representation of all of the offenses committed by the offenders.

Geographic Profiling Computer Systems

In an effort to simplify the processes used in geographic profiling, geographic profilers have developed a variety of computer programs designed to assist in the process of calculating crime site information.

Dragnet, developed and offered by the University of Liverpool in the United Kingdom, is advertised as a "geographical prioritization package" that works by using the locations of a series of crimes and prioritizing areas around the offense locations containing the likely location of the offender's home.

Use of the program involves inputting data on the crime sites, which is ostensibly the first stage. This will produce little more than "dots on a plot" or a screen as shown in Figure 4.2 (unless otherwise stated, all of the following information is taken from http://www.i-psy.com/publications/publications_dragnet.php).

FIGURE 4.2

Crime Data Plot.

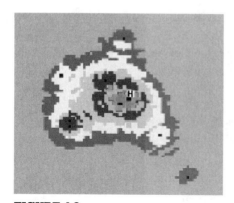

FIGURE 4.3
Prioritization Area.

Then the analyst produces a priority map as shown in Figure 4.3. The priorities are dictated by a legend, with the "hotter" colors suggesting high priority and "cooler" colors suggesting low priority. The map can indicate the presence of more than one focus for investigators, which may be suggestive of more than one offender (thus, in this capacity, it could be said that the system has case linkage ability). Figure 4.3 also shows the prioritization area with the offender's home marked "H." The produced search areas are usually overlaid with a standard street map.

As with many of its computerized counterparts, Dragnet can integrate information about the layout of certain areas, such as city blocks, incorporating a Manhattan metric designed to account for indirect distances encountered in the urban environment. Figure 4.4 shows the standard Euclidian distance, and Figure 4.5 shows a Manhattan metric accounting for streetscapes.

Based on his PhD research while at Simon Fraser University, Kim Rossmo developed Rigel Profiler, which is now sold through Environmental Criminology Research Incorporated (ECRI), a company set up to deliver the software. ECRI (2001) states that Rigel

- Is a system for geographic profiling designed to support serial crime investigations by prioritizing suspects and addresses and enabling investigators to focus their resources on specific locations.

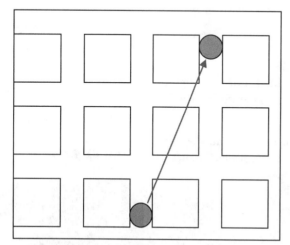

FIGURE 4.4
Euclidian Distances. These are usually point A to point B measurements, or "as the crow flies." This is problematic because it is not an accurate representation of how offenders travel or the layout of the spatial environment.

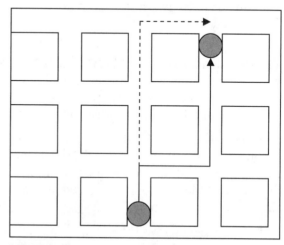

FIGURE 4.5
Manhattan Metrics. This is only a limited solution to the problems of a standard Euclidian distance because of the nonlinear and irregular layout of city spaces and the uncertainty of knowing which route the offender actually took.

- Uses ECRI's patented Criminal Geographic Targeting (CGT) algorithm and is Java based for platform independence.
- Supports a variety of GIS and text data sources and can be customized according to customer requirements. Rigel can effectively manage the integration of address and location information, as well as incorporate additional geographic layers (i.e., schools, shops, playgrounds, etc.) that are of interest.
- Is able to extract information from a case linkage system such as ViCLAS. Information can include crime locations, suspect information, case details, and investigator details.
- Presents the results in the form of two- or three-dimensional surface maps called "jeopardies" showing the most probable locations of an offender's residence. At the core of Rigel is the patented algorithm used to derive the output map from the set of input data.
- Enables law enforcement agencies to focus their search efforts on the most likely neighborhoods, thus making optimal use of their resources.
- Is used by leading police agencies and has been used in hundreds of cases throughout the world.

These are not the only programs available for use, although these would be the major systems in use or covered in the literature. The cost of some programs may make their use for either practical or research purposes prohibitive. Other commercial software, such as Microsoft Excel, can provide a similar level of analysis providing one knows how to input the algorithms and structure the output.

Santilla, Zappala, Laukkanen, and Picozzi (2003) conducted a study on the utility of geographic profiling in a series of three rapes in Italy. They found that although there was some limited support for certain distance decay functions, jurisdictions may be unique in travel patterns due to population size, road patterns, and physical geography. Because of this, they claim it is necessary to calibrate the parameters for individual jurisdictions before any attempt to isolate nodes is undertaken. They correctly claim that such calibration would make the "use of an empirical function resource demanding" (p. 51). This may be an insurmountable obstacle in jurisdictions with limited resources, such as funding or computer support, or where there is a lack of expertise. "Flying in" the technology or the expertise may be impossible or unrealistic in many such cases for many of the same reasons.

The practical shortcomings in individual cases have been discussed, but these are extended in a more general theoretical sense, as discussed by Rossmo (2000, pp. 208–209), to the reliability of geographic profiling. He notes that the following considerations may undermine suitability:

- Generally, there should be a minimum of five distinct locations, of the same type, available for analysis. It is usually assumed that the offender has not moved or been displaced during the time period of these crimes, but if this has occurred, then more locations are required. A geographic assessment may be appropriate in cases involving fewer locations.

- Only crime locations that are accurately known should be used. For example, encounter sites may be imprecise if they have to be inferred from last known victim sighting. In some investigations, the locations of certain sites may be completely unknown.

- Analysis of the crime site type with the most locations results in lower expected CGT hit score percentages. Multiple offenses in the same immediate area should not be double counted. The degree of spatial–temporal clustering must be assessed because crime sites too close in time and space are probably non-independent events.

- Combining different site types to increase the total number of locations available for analysis can be advantageous when the number of crimes is minimal. However, two potential problems exist with this approach. The first is that locations may be significantly correlated; this is particularly likely when the offender travels directly to the dump site from the encounter site. The second problem occurs when combined crime locations produce a hunting area larger than that found with a single site type, resulting in the possibility of a greater search area, even though the hit percentage is smaller. This problem is most likely to occur if the two crime site areas are incongruent.

- Preference should be given to the crime site type that affords the greatest degree of choice to the offender. Site types with constrained target backcloths[7] tell us little about the criminal. If victim specificity leads to spatial bias, then encounter locations may not be the best profiling option. Similarly, body dump sites in isolated areas may reveal only general detail about an urban killer.

The absence of any of the previous information would seriously impact on the ability of the profiler to accurately assess an offender's geographic behavior. Given the previous considerations, the following points should also be noted:

- The first of Rossmo's points assumes not only that the offender has not moved location but also that the crime series has been accurately linked to the one offender. In some cases, previously unlinked offenses may not be identified as the work of the same offender until some time after

---

[7]"Target or victim backcloth is important for an understanding of the geometric arrangement of crime sites; it is the equivalent of a spatial opportunity structure (Brantingham & Brantingham, 1993). It is configured by both geographic and temporal distributions of "suitable" (as seen from the offender's perspective) crime targets or victims across the physical landscape. The availability of particular targets may vary significantly according to neighborhood, area, or even city, and is influenced by time, day of week, and season; hence, the term structural backcloth is also used" (Rossmo, 2000, pp. 126–127).

the offender is caught. Behaviors indicative of escalation may also foil attempts here because the voyeurism and theft of personal belongings (e.g., underwear) by a serial rapist may go unreported or unnoticed. If the victim is killed, this information may never come to light, and so it is possible that the number of known offenses may not currently, if ever, reach a threshold where a geoprofile is possible. Also, given the previous considerations, it would seem that a profile of a serial criminal early in his or her criminal actions will be largely ineffective.

- In some serial murder cases, the only information police have to go on is the last seen locations. This, in theory at least, makes it difficult, if not impossible, to offer a geographic profile in such cases, unless the profiler chooses to advance without this information. Given Rossmo's warning, this would not be recommended.

- The degree of choice an offender has regarding a crime site may not be known at the time of the geoprofile, if ever; thus, although this would be important to know, it may be impossible to introduce into an analysis. For example, an offender plans to break into an apartment and rape the lone female occupant. Unbeknown to him, she has visitors and so his attempts are foiled. This crime site may provide the best insight into his behavior, but we would never know because the lack of an opportunity structure prohibited the crime from occurring. A similar lack of opportunity can be seen in the crimes of Berkowitz. On some nights, he would go looking for victims, but failure to find any would see him returning to previous crime sites where he masturbated. It may be that the crimes that would have occurred closest to his home were those that were foiled, and that those farthest away offered the best availability of victims and situations.

Turvey (1999, cited in Petherick & Turvey 2008a, pp. 99–100) expresses similar concerns about the utility and reliability of geographic profiling, including the following:

- This method breaks the same tenet of behavioral-evidence analysis as the others mentioned previously: It takes a single manifestation of offender behavior (offense location selection) and attempts to infer its meaning out of the overall behavioral and emotional context that it was produced in.

- This method is actually employed without the benefit of a psychological profile. Although Rossmo states that he requires a full psychological profile for a competent geographical analysis, he has been known to proceed without one or to construct his own.

- The result of ignoring overall behavioral evidence and case context and not utilizing full criminal profiles, geographic profiling cannot, and does not, distinguish between two or more offenders operating in the same area.

- This method assumes that all cases that are submitted have been positively linked by law enforcement. It does not check the veracity of this or any other information provided by law enforcement.

- This method assumes that offenders most often live near or within easy reach of their offense area.

- Rossmo's dissertation very competently outlines the weaknesses and the shortcomings of the published research on serial murder. Then, his dissertation goes on to base theories regarding geographic profiling, and the CGT software, on those admittedly flawed studies.

- The technology used in CGT is impressive but amounts to only so much scientification. Inferences regarding offender anchor points and spatial behavior must still be drawn by the analyst.

Despite an impressive array of costly computer solutions to the journey to crime problem, it is clear that, although a nice theory, the application of geographic profiling raises more questions than the theories on which it is based answer. As noted by Rengert et al. (1999), the decision where to offend is often outside of the offender's control and cannot, as some criminological theories would have us believe, be based strictly on free will. One of the factors in decisions to offend is the distance an offender will have to travel to commit his or her crimes.

It is also instructive to consider the viewpoints of others about specific geographic profiling units. Despite the positive press generated by a number of these, it is evident that not everyone associated with their use regard them so highly. For example, in *Rossmo v. Vancouver (City) Police Board* (2001, at ¶21 and ¶38, respectively), the following claims were made[8]:

- A cursory analysis seems to suggest that a choice to extend the contract would not be a good business decision. In short, there is little apparent evidence of enhanced policing outcomes. And establishing the extent and durability of prestige is problematic.[9]

- The question for the Vancouver Police Department and the Police Board is to what degree do we wish to continue what is essentially an international police program. There have been no definitive applications of geographic profiling in the [VPD] and the department is facing significant budget issues that require decisions on funding priorities.

---

[8]Rossmo was suing the Vancouver Police Department (VPD) for wrongful termination when his contract expired. He lost the suit and has since left the Geographic Profiling Unit.

[9]It was acknowledged that Rossmo's international celebrity was good for the VPD, but as this comment acknowledges, it is difficult to quantify celebrity and prestige and so actual return to the VPD was difficult to gauge.

Understandably, this case generated much media interest in what would, at least on the outside, appear to be the fall from grace of a very public internationally known figure. In "Profiling Section Wasn't Good Value," the Vancouver Sun (2001) reported the following:

> The contract of a detective–inspector in charge of the city police's geographic profiling section was terminated because the department felt it wasn't getting good value for its money, deputy chief Gary Greer testified Wednesday.
>
> The termination had nothing to do with jealousy or the existence of a so-called boy's club on the force, he said in B.C. Supreme Court.
>
> "It wasn't cost effective," he said.
>
> Kim Rossmo, a 22-year member of the force, is suing for wrongful dismissal after his 5-year contract wasn't renewed last Dec. 31.
>
> Greer was an inspector when he recommended that Rossmo's job be one of three positions the police department had to cut to meet budget requirements imposed on city hall.

DIAGNOSTIC EVALUATIONS

As discussed in Chapter 1, much of the earliest profiling work available for reference was by psychologists and psychiatrists. Indeed, many modern approaches to profiling are heavily grounded in psychological theory and practice. As a generic term for the "as needed" work by mental health practitioners, Wilson, Lincoln, and Kocsis (1997) identify diagnostic evaluations as a form of criminal profiling.

Although the approach and application of the various profiling paradigms are well enunciated, diagnostic evaluations are less defined, and there are no unified approaches under this "model." Instead, one's education, training, and experience dictate the approach one takes at a given point in time with a given case, with the profile being the result of the clinician's understanding of offenders, personality, and mental illness (Gudjonsson & Copson, 1997).

Representing the ruminations of psychologists and psychiatrists, Jackson and Bekerian (1997) dedicate sections of their work to developmental and clinical issues involved in profiling and also in the application of personality theories to psychological profiling. Boon (1997) explains how psychoanalytic/psychodynamic, learning, dispositional/trait, humanist/cognitive, and alternative/Eastern philosophies may assist in case disposition, and Woodworth and Porter (2001, p. 244) contend that "although the use of psychoanalytic concepts in profiling is rarely seen today, the Mad Bomber prediction remains an interesting highlight in the development of profiling."

Fritzon (2000) discusses a similar application of personality theories to the crime of arson. In examining arsonists, Fritzon suggests that it may be instructive to consider their motives within the framework of needs theories. Two of those considered are Maslow's hierarchy of needs and McClelland's learned needs. The application of Maslow's hierarchy is illustrated here (pp. 162–164):

> Maslow's theory explains human behavior in terms of a hierarchy of five general needs. The most basic of these are psychological needs, including food, water, oxygen, etc.... In some cases, serious fires can result from these individuals' efforts to stay warm when sheltered ... fires which are set for financial gain could also be said to be motivated by physiological need in that food and shelter are usually dependent on financial considerations.... The second level of the hierarchy of needs is safety and security needs. These include a desire for security, stability, and protection. In terms of arson, firesetting, which is motivated by crime concealment, fulfills the need for protection from the undesirable consequences of being caught and convicted of the primary crime. The next level of the hierarchy concerns social needs such as the need for love, affection, and a sense of belonging. Maslow states that individuals who are unable to satisfy this need will feel lonely, ostracized, and rejected.... Their behavior can be seen as resulting from frustration and dissatisfaction of these needs. It may be a way (albeit a dysfunctional one) of restoring the disequilibrium that such frustration causes.... The fourth level of Maslow's hierarch concerns ego and esteem needs, which can be focused either internally or externally.... This category of arson can be seen as an attempt to redress self-esteem by someone who feels they have been wronged.... The final stage of the need hierarchy is the need for self-actualization, which refers to the process of developing our true potential as individuals to the fullest extent.... Arson that is committed by political and extremist groups, such as the Animal Liberation Front, therefore, can be viewed as being motivated by the need for actualization of the particular goals and ideals propagated by that group.

McGrath (2002, p. 321) provides the following suggestions regarding the psychologist's or psychiatrist's role in profiling:

- Their background in the behavioral sciences and their training in psychopathology place them in an enviable position to deduce personality characteristics from crime scene information.
- The forensic psychiatrist is in a good position to infer the meaning behind signature behaviors.
- Given their training, education, and focus on critical and analytical thinking, forensic psychiatrists are in a good position to "channel their training into a new field."

Although these are obvious areas for forensic mental health specialists to apply their skills, McGrath also notes that any involvement in the profiling process should not be treatment oriented. It is critical that the psychiatrist or psychologist not fall prey to role confusion and descend into treatment advice when acting as a profiler.

Adding to the potential problems this may pose, those conducting diagnostic evaluations seldom have extensive experience in law enforcement or its related areas (Wilson et al., 1997). West (2000, p. 220) provides similar commentary:

> It has to be conceded that many clinicians, whatever their professional background, do not routinely review crime scene data or witness depositions.... Instead, the clinical approach ... tends to preclude consideration of more exact details of the offense. All too often it is easier to believe the offender than to read the witness depositions or observe the crime scene. It seems inevitable that such omissions might lead to serious errors in any assessment.

Because their involvement in profiling tends to be sporadic (Dietz, 1985), the mental health specialist may lose touch with the requirements of a police investigation and therefore offer vague and/or irrelevant suggestions. Ainsworth (2001) suggests that the profile produced by mental health workers may contain statements about the inner workings of the offender's mental processes that will not be directly observable, and that these explanations provided may not be as useful to investigators as those from other approaches. This is referred to as investigative relevance and is discussed elsewhere in this book. The problem may go further than the type of advice offered in diagnostic evaluation profiles and extend into difficulties of getting into police investigations. Canter (1989, p. 13) suggests the difficulty is that "police officers are unlikely to admit psychologists to their investigations unless some mutual trust and reciprocal benefit is expected" and that "it is difficult to make a contribution until some experience has been gained, yet difficult to gain experience until some contribution can be offered."

Despite West's (2000) concern that a profiler may come to believe the offender if given the opportunity to interface directly with the offender, Tamlyn (1999) claims that when the clinician is involved in the investigative phase of a profile, there is usually not an opportunity to directly assess or examine the subject of the analysis, perhaps more an artifact of profiling than diagnostic evaluations specifically. Gudjonsson and Copson (1997) agree, stating that criminal profilers have historically relied on indirect methods such as intuition, psychodynamic theories, behavioral analysis, and statistical reasoning.

With regard to their role, forensic clinicians in the United Kingdom often rely on the good will of their employer to allow them to undertake profiling duties at the potential expense of their employers (Tamlyn, 1999). This means that many will work in their own time and be largely unpaid. It is unlikely that this situation will differ from that of other countries where mental health experts act in the advisory capacity of profilers. In fact, many professionals will perform profiling as an adjunct to their usual duties rather than being employed in this capacity full-time. The reality is that there are very few full-time profilers in any agency throughout the world.

Although diagnostic evaluations are not a unified approach with a clear theoretical framework, Copson, Badcock, Boon, and Britton (1997, p. 16) outline the following principles of clinical profiling:

- Custom made: the advice should not rely on the recycling of some kind of generic violent antisocial criminal stereotype;
- Interactive: at a range of levels of sophistication, depending on the officers' understanding of the psychological concepts at issue; and
- Reflexive: the advice should be dynamic, insofar as every element has a knock-on effect on every other element, and evolving, in that new information must lead to reconsideration not only of the element(s) of advice affected but of the construct as a whole.

They also identify a number of dangers (p. 16):

- There is an imperative to please which must be recognized and overcome, otherwise objectivity will be undermined by tendencies to overinterpretation and unequivocality.
- Close interaction with the officers leaves the profiler open to allegations of improper collusion, such as tailoring a profile to fit a known suspect, or devising some interviewing strategy which is unethical or even unlawful.
- The mass of data which comes out of an interactive and reflexive process means that recording is an extremely difficult and time-consuming business, even to the extent that sometimes a written report never quite emerges.
- The reduction of a mass of data into a summary document—and more especially the failure to produce a summary document—leaves the profiler open to being misrepresented.

There are no specific critiques of diagnostic evaluations in the literature, but these may be easily extrapolated from the approach itself. For example, without a unified approach, the principles involved may not be clearly enunciated, and any attempt to study the efficacy of the approach may be hampered by the inability to reproduce the train of thought that led to particular conclusions. Ainsworth (2001) claims that the profile produced by mental health workers may contain statements about the workings of the offender's mental processes, and that the explanations they provide may not be as useful to investigators as those derived under other methods. Finally, certain aspects of psychological analysis may be difficult to integrate into a police investigation, bringing into question the utility of the profile and the profiler's involvement, such as Brussel's assertion that the "Mad Bomber" suffered from an Oedipal complex.[10]

BEHAVIORAL EVIDENCE ANALYSIS

In profiling terms, behavioral evidence analysis (BEA) is the most recent of the individual profiling methods. The method was developed by Turvey, and it is based on forensic science and the collection and interpretation of physical evidence and, by extension, what this means about an offender. BEA is primarily a deductive method and, as a result, will not make a conclusion about an offender unless specific physical evidence exists that suggests the characteristic. What this means is that instead of relying on averaged offender types, BEA profilers conduct a detailed examination of the scene and related behaviors and infer from this what offender characteristics are evidenced in the behavior and scene.

The strength of BEA lies in the fact that the profiler works only with what is known; nothing is assumed or surmised (Petherick, 2003), and a great deal of time is spent determining the veracity of the physical evidence and its relationship to the crime. In this way, evidence that is irrelevant or unrelated has little evidentiary value and is not given weight in the final analysis. This assists in maintaining objectivity and leads to a more accurate and useful end product.

Like its inductive counterparts, BEA involves a number of steps, with each building on previous stages to provide an overall picture. These can be represented graphically, as shown in Figure 4.6.

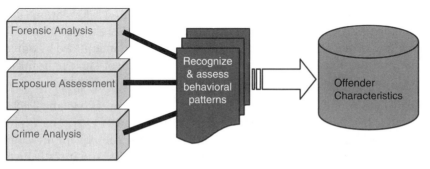

FIGURE 4.6
Stages of Behavioral Evidence Analysis.

---

[10]Although Freud is undoubtedly one of the fathers of modern psychology and his impact on psychology is considerable, many of his theories have been disputed or discredited because of their questionable basis.

The first stage of BEA is called the Forensic Analysis (EFA) and refers to the examination, testing, and interpretation of the physical evidence (Petherick & Turvey, 2008b). In this stage, all of the physical evidence surrounding a case is examined to assess its relevance and determine its overall nature and quality. This step also ensures the probative quality of the evidence should the case end up in court. Ultimately, the EFA informs the profiler what evidence he or she has to base a profile on, what evidence may be missing, what evidence may have been misinterpreted, and what value that evidence has in subsequent analyses. Thornton (2006, p. 37) contextualizes the importance of physical evidence:

> We are interested in physical evidence because it may tell a story. Physical evidence—properly collected, properly analyzed, and properly interpreted—may establish the factual circumstances at the time the crime occurred. In short, the crime may be reconstructed. Our principal interest is ultimately in the reconstruction, not the evidence per se.... Also, along with the ethos is an ethic—a moral obligation to maintain the integrity of the processes by means of which the reconstruction is accomplished. In short, the ethics of crime reconstruction represents an imperative to "get it right." "Getting it right" involves more than guessing correctly. It necessitates a systematic process. It involves the proper recognition of the evidence, the winnowing of the relevant wheat from the irrelevant chaff, and the precise application of logic, both inductive and deductive. The process is not trivial.

Because this stage relates to the examination of physical evidence, profilers who are not familiar with or qualified to interpret physical evidence should not undertake this task. Instead, they should work with trained professionals whom they trust to examine the evidence they are basing their conclusions on. The importance of establishing a set of given facts from information obtained during an investigation should be apparent, but this information is often assumed as correct without question. Two cases that exemplify the pitfalls of working with information that has been gathered and interpreted by others are the investigation of the explosion aboard the *USS Iowa* and the homicide of Joel Andrew Shanbrom, for which brief explanations are provided.

Early one morning in 1989, the number 2 turret on board the *USS Iowa* exploded, killing 47 of the ship's crew (Thompson, 1999). The explosion sent shockwaves throughout the U.S. Navy, with the subsequent investigation revealing dangerous practices, incompetence, cover-ups, and investigative failures, only some of which were related to the explosion and deaths. Given the magnitude of the disaster, the navy consulted agents from the FBI's Behavioral Analysis Unit to provide some insight into what it believed were the actions of a suicidal homosexual, Clayton Hartwig.

In an attempt to provide this insight, the FBI agents used a technique known as equivocal death analysis (EDA), essentially another name for a psychological autopsy (a profile of a deceased person). Although the EDA was not responsible for first bringing attention to Hartwig as the person responsible for the explosion, it was most certainly responsible for catalyzing this opinion in the minds of investigators and the naval executive. What followed was a series of events that perpetuated bad judgment and showed just how dangerous it can be to accept at face value information or evidence that one has not collected first-hand: Investigators from the Naval Investigative Service (NIS) started by assuming Hartwig's guilt and then provided this information to the FBI profilers, whose assessment fed this line of thinking back to the NIS and the Navy.

With regard to their analysis, a report of the Investigations Subcommittee of the Committee on Armed Services House of Representatives (1990) noted two important issues with the FBI's analysis (pp. 6–7):

- The procedures the FBI used in preparing the EDA were inadequate and unprofessional. As a matter of policy, the analysts do not state the speculative nature of their analyses. Moreover, the parameters that the FBI agents used, either provided to them or chosen by them, biased their results toward only one of three deleterious conclusions. Further biasing their conclusions, the agents relied on insufficient and sometimes suspect evidence. The FBI agents' EDA was invalidated by 10 of 14 professional psychologists and psychiatrists, heavily criticized even by those professionals who found the Hartwig possibility plausible.

- The FBI analysis gave the Navy false confidence in the validity of the FBI's work. If the Navy had relied solely on the work of the NIS's own staff psychologist—which emphasized that such psychological autopsies are by definition "speculative"—the Navy would likely not have found itself so committed to the Hartwig thesis.

Despite the questionable nature of the EDA process and its methodology, there were more fundamental concerns about the material on which the analysis was based. The following concerns were also raised by the Investigations Subcommittee about the process and results:

- Richard Ault admitted that the Navy had only provided him with fragments of the evidence assembled against Hartwig.
- Ault was asked who wrote the poem "Disposable Heroes," a key piece of information on which Hartwig's alleged homosexuality hinged, and he did not know.
- Asked whether the agents were aware that another gunner's mate told Admiral Milligan that another sailor had written the poem, Hazelwood stated that this was immaterial because Hartwig had the potential to see it.

- The agents were asked if they were aware that David Smith had recanted the testimony used in their EDA, and they claimed they were not sure what he had recanted.
- The agents had relied entirely on the information provided to them by the NIS and had not done any interviews themselves.

There were further concerns about the veracity of the information on which the profile was based (Investigations Subcommittee and Defense Policy Panel of the Committee on Armed Services, 1990, p. 42):

> The preponderance of material came from interviews conducted and provided to the FBI by the NIS. As the subcommittee found earlier, serious questions were raised about the leading nature or bias introduced in the interviews by the NIS interviewing agents. Some witnesses denied making statements to NIS that are significant to the profile.... In at least one instance, the witness recanted several portions of his testimony, but was still considered a valuable witness.

Another example stressing the importance of not only establishing a set of facts for oneself but also assessing evidence dynamics is the homicide of Joel Andrew Shanbrom, a school district police officer in California. Shanbrom's wife, Jennifer, claimed that she was upstairs bathing their son when she heard an altercation downstairs between her husband and some (black) men. A profile of the alleged offender was compiled by Mark Safarik of the FBI's Behavioral Analysis Unit.

Safarik's assessment gave considerable weight to the apparent ransacking of certain rooms in the house, including that of the son, Jacob:

> The dressers and night stands in the master bedroom, Gisondi's room, and Jacob's bedroom had been disturbed.... In Jacob's bedroom, a room clearly identified as a child's bedroom, the dresser drawers were pulled out to give the appearance they were searched. Such a room would not be expected to contain any valuables and this would have been passed over by offender(s) looking for valuables.

Although police had trouble with Jennifer Fletcher's story from the outset, particularly after discovering significant life insurance policies on her husband, the profile stuck steadfast to its assessment of ransacking. It was not until an expert profiler, in providing trial assistance to the defense, was able to establish through consideration of evidence dynamics that the scene had in fact been altered by a police officer in her search for clothing for Jacob Shanbrom, who was naked and cold from hiding in a bedroom closet with his mother since the alleged homicide. In a postscript to this case, Jennifer and Matthew Fletcher were both charged with the 1998 murder of Shanbrom after facing counts of murder, fraud, and conspiracy (Associated Press, 2002; Blankstein, 2002).

It is also necessary to establish the accuracy and quality of the information that serves as the basis of the profile because of the *evidence dynamics*. This refers to "any influence that changes, relocates, obscures, or obliterates physical evidence, regardless of intent" (Chisum & Turvey, 2008, p. 167). Thus, evidence dynamics may be the result of the offender moving from one room to another during an offense, a bleeding but not yet deceased victim crawling down a hallway, paramedics attending the scene of a violent crime, or firefighters attending a fire scene, among others. However, evidence dynamics is important in the case far beyond the extant circumstances of the crime scene, playing a role from the time the evidence is deposited until the final adjudication of the case (Chisum & Turvey, 2000). To provide some context to the way in which evidence dynamics may alter the physical presentation of crime scene actions, consider the following example from Chisum and Turvey (p. 9):

> A youth was stabbed several times by rival gang members. He ran for a home but collapsed in the walkway. A photo of the scene taken prior to the arrival of the EMT team shows a blood trail and that the victim was lying face down. Subsequent photos show the five EMT's working on the body on his back. He had been rolled over onto the blood pool. It became impossible for bloodstain patterns interpretation to be used to reconstruct the events leading to the death of the youth.

The importance of the EFA and establishing a set of facts for one's self should be clear. Although only two cases have been used as examples, there are a litany of others with a similar lack of critical appraisal of the presenting evidence (see also Superior Court of California, 1999).

The other aspect of the forensic analysis that is important and factors in evidence dynamics is crime reconstruction, which involves a determination of the actions surrounding the crime. Popular conceptions of crime reconstruction abound, with some believing the process involves the physical rebuilding of the crime scene in another location. Saferstein (2004) suggests that the reconstruction will support a sequence of events through the observation and evaluation of physical evidence, as well as any statements made by witnesses or those involved with the crime. Rynearson (2002) incorporates "commonsense reasoning" and its use with forensic science to interpret evidence as it resides at the crime scene. Cooley (1999, p. 1), in an excellent paper written while a graduate student at the University of New Haven, suggests that crime scene reconstruction is the foundation of the BEA method:

> Deductive reasoning, via crime scene reconstruction, can and will provide the profiler with the appropriate information allowing him or her to construct the most logical profile of an unknown offender. This will enable the profiler to supply the requesting agency with investigatively relevant information.

The second stage of the process, victimology, examines all aspects of the victim, including lifestyle, hobbies, habits, friends, enemies, and demographic features. The information derived through the victimology can help to determine the existence or extent of any relationship between the victim and the offender. Two other related components of the victimology are victim and offender exposure. Victim exposure refers to the possibility of suffering harm or loss by virtue of an individual's personal, professional, and social life (Petherick & Turvey, 2008c). This is further partitioned into lifestyle exposure and the exposure present at the moment of victimization, known as incident exposure. As a general rule, exposure can be low, medium, or high, indicating the level of risk a person is at by virtue of the person's personal, professional, and social life. In BEA, just as much time should be spent examining the victim's personality and behavioral characteristics as spent examining the offender.

In the third stage, crime analysis, the profiler determines factors such as the method of approach and attack, the method of control, location type, nature and sequence of any sexual acts, materials used, the type of verbal activity, and any precautionary acts the offender engaged in (Petherick & Turvey, 2008b). Precautionary acts may include wearing gloves or a balaclava, altering one's voice, or wearing a condom. This stage also sets out to determine what type of crime scenes are involved in a criminal event. These include the point of contact; primary, secondary, and tertiary scenes; and the dump or disposal site. For example, a victim with extensive wounds that would have produced a substantial amount of bleeding is found in an area devoid of bloodstains. This is suggestive of the victim being killed elsewhere (a primary crime scene) and then moved to the scene where the body was found (the dump or disposal site).

The final stage is the actual criminal profile, and is called offender characteristics. All of the information from the previous stages is integrated and assessed through the scientific method and deductive reasoning to determine what the physical evidence, victimology, and crime scene characteristics collectively argue about the offender. Turvey (2008) argues against offering the profile characteristics of age, sex, race, and intelligence because these are typically assessed inductively and not based on physical evidence.

Although BEA is a method that relies on deductive logic, it cannot be characterized as purely deductive. This is because the process of deduction relies in part on induction, which produces theories that may be tested against the evidence. This is confirmed by Stock (2004, p. 5), who writes, "In the natural order of treatment inductive logic precedes deductive, since it is induction which supplies us with the general truths, from which we reason down in our deductive inferences."

Because of the reliance on physical evidence and the reconstruction of the behavior involved in the criminal event, inductive reasoning will be employed.

Wound patterns and victimology are two such examples in which inductions may be used to form the basis of a later deduction. The type of knife used, its width, the length of the blade, and other characteristics of edged weapons have typically been determined through a study of known weapons and their features as well as their associated wound patterns. However, the application of this knowledge to the particular features of a set of wounds present on a victim's body involves the deductive application of this knowledge.

There are no direct criticisms of BEA in the literature, although there is some minor discussion of deductive approaches in general. Most seem to be quite confused by the application of the reasoning (see Chapter 2; Canter, 2004; Godwin, 1999), whereas others provide some cursory discussion of it but seem unsure of how the overall process operates. Holmes and Holmes (2002, p. 7) note that "much care is taken from the examination of forensic reports, victimology, and so forth and the report will take much longer to develop using only this approach." First, the authors seem largely unaware of the finer points of logic, such as induction being a component of and important to the overall process of deduction. The reader is also left with the distinct impression that the thoroughness of the approach (and the subsequent time involved) is pejorative. A final deductively rendered opinion will rely on inductively derived knowledge, although Holmes and Holmes tend to treat both processes as being dichotomous and largely exclusive. This suggests a fundamental lack of overall knowledge of the processes involved in reasoning.

Other assumptions made by Holmes and Holmes (2002) about this method suggest that the general understanding of the approach is wanting. For example, they note that "with the deductive approach ... one assumption is that any crime is accompanied by fantasy" (p. 7). A thorough examination of Turvey's *Criminal Profiling: An Introduction to Behavioral Evidence Analysis* (all three editions) failed to find any such claim. In addition, the value of the deductive method lies in the fact that such assumptions are not made, and they are guided by the case information rather than by preconceived theories about what might be the case.

However, McGrath (2000) has identified one critical observation of this method: If the initial premises on which conclusions are based are wrong, then the subsequent conclusions will also be wrong. Given that one of the primary purposes of the forensic analysis is to establish the veracity of the premises, this is not necessarily a problem as long as profilers are aware that it is incumbent on them to establish the basic information on which their decisions are based. If the basis of the premises cannot be established, then this may limit the amount of characteristics that can be offered (because deductive approaches will only derive conclusions on what has been unequivocally established). Beyond these observations, there has been little criticism of this approach.

CONCLUSION

Although there are commonalities among approaches, such as their goals, they are not as homogeneous as they may appear. Because there are significant shortcomings of some of the approaches detailed herein, anyone looking to invest time and resources in a profile should expend some effort on researching the differences and determining which approach might best serve their needs. Inductive methods, those relying on statistical reasoning or "averaged" offender types, appear to be the most problematic.

In contrast, deductive approaches provide the most potential for an accurate evaluation because of their reliance on examinations of physical evidence and its meaning and also because of the underlying power of deductive reasoning. Add to this the application of the scientific method and this may further strengthen the approach and its promise. Although deductive approaches are not without problems, their potential shortcomings are easily controlled. To be able to determine the approach that may provide the most help to police, more research must be conducted to ascertain not only the accuracy of profiling methods but also the operational utility each has to offer, and users are cautioned to educate themselves about the positive and negative aspects of each school of thought.

Questions

1. Regardless of individual method or author, the definition of criminal profiling is generally uniform. *True or false?*
2. The original study conducted by the FBI took place between _____ and _____.
3. BEA is currently the only profiling method that utilizes deductive logic. *True or false?*
4. Investigative psychology uses _____ _____ analysis in examining crime data.
5. What are the five factors in investigative psychology?
6. List and describe the stages of BEA.
7. List and briefly describe the criticisms of geographic profiling.

REFERENCES

Ainsworth, P. B. (2000). Psychology and Crime. Harlow, UK: Longman.

Ainsworth, P. B. (2001). Offender Profiling and Crime Analysis. Devon, UK: Willan.

Associated Press. (2002, March 2). Wife of slain man charged. Las Vegas Review-Journal. Available at http://www.reviewjournal.com. Accessed November 14, 2005.

Baker, T. E. (2001). Understanding and apprehending America's most dangerous criminals. Law and Order, 49(5), 43–48.

Bennett, W. W., & Hess, K. M. (2001). Criminal Investigation (6th ed.). Belmont, CA: Thompson Learning.

Blankstein, A. (2002). Couple charged in man's shooting: Jennifer and Matthew Fletcher are accused of murder in the 1998 death of her former husband, Joel Shanbrom. Available at http://articles.latimes.com/2002/mar/01/local/me-arrest1. Accessed November 15, 2005.

Boon, J., & Davies, G. (1993). Criminal profiling. Policing, 9(8), 1–13.

Boon, J. C. W. (1997). The contribution of personality theories to psychological profiling. In J. Jackson & D. Bekerian (Eds.), Offender Profiling: Theory, Research and Practice. Chichester, UK: Wiley.

Brantingham, P. L., & Brantingham, P. J. (1993). Environment, routine, and situation: Toward a pattern theory of crime. In R. V. Clarke & M. Felson (Eds.), Routine Activity and Rational Choice: Advances in Criminological Theory (Vol. 5, pp. 259–294). New Brunswick, NJ: Transaction Publishers.

Burgess, A. W., Hartman, C. R., Ressler, R. K., Douglas, J. E., & McCormack, A. (1986). Sexual homicide: A motivational model. Journal of Interpersonal Violence, 1(3), 251–272.

Burgess, A. W., & Ressler, R. K. (1985). Sexual homicides crime scenes and patterns of criminal behavior (Grant No. 82-IJ-CX-0065). Washington, DC: National Institute of Justice.

Canter, D. (1989). Offender profiles. The Psychologist, 2(1), 12–16.

Canter, D. (1995). Criminal Shadows: Inside the Mind of the Serial Killer. London: HarperCollins.

Canter, D. (1998). Profiling as poison. Inter Alia, 2(1), 10–11.

Canter, D. (2003). Mapping Murder. London: Virgin Books.

Canter, D. (2004). Offender profiling and investigative psychology. Journal of Investigative Psychology and Offender Profiling, 1, 1–15.

Canter, D., Alison, L. J., Alison, E., & Wentink, N. (2004). The organized/disorganized typology of serial murder: Myth or model? Psychology, Public Policy, and Law, 10, 293–320.

Canter, D., Coffey, T., Huntley, M., & Missen, C. (2000). Predicting serial killers' home base using a decision support system. Journal of Quantitative Criminology, 16(4), 457–478.

Canter, D., & Larkin, P. (1993). The environmental range of serial rapists. Journal of Environmental Psychology, 13, 93–99.

Chisum, W. J., & Turvey, B. E. (2000). Evidence dynamics: Locard's exchange principle and crime reconstruction. Journal of Behavioral Profiling, 1(1).

Chisum, W. J., & Turvey, B. E. (2002). Evidence dynamics. In B. E. Turvey (Ed.), Criminal Profiling: An Introduction to Behavioral Evidence Analysis (2nd ed.). London: Academic Press.

Chisum, W. J., & Turvey, B. E. (2008). An introduction to crime reconstruction. In Turvey, B. E. (ed.). Criminal Profiling: An Introduction to Behavioral Evidence Analysis. (3rd. ed.). Burlington, MA: Academic Press.

Cooley, C. (1999). Crime scene reconstruction: The foundation of behavioral evidence analysis. Paper presented at the University of New Haven. Unpublished.

Copson, G., Badcock, R., Boon, J., & Britton, P. (1997). Articulating a systematic approach to clinical crime profiling. Criminal Behaviour and Mental Health, 7, 13–17.

Darkes, J., Otto, R. K., Poythress, N., & Starr, L. (1993, January). APA's expert panel in the congressional review of the USS Iowa incident. American Psychologist, 8–15.

Dietz, P. E. (1985). Sex offender profiling by the FBI: Preliminary conceptual model. In M. H. Ben-Aron, S. J. Hucher, & C. D. Webster (Eds.), Clinical Criminology. Toronto: M & M Graphics.

Douglas, J. E., & Burgess, A. E. (1986). Criminal profiling: A viable investigative tool against violent crime. FBI Law Enforcement Bulletin, 55(12), 9–13.

Douglas, J. E., Burgess, A. W., Burgess, A. G., & Ressler, R. K. (1992). Crime Classification Manual: A Standard System for Investigating and Classifying Violent Crime. New York: Simon & Schuster.

Douglas, J. E., & Olshaker, M. (1995). Mindhunter: Inside the FBI Elite Serial Crime Unit. New York: Scribner.

Douglas, J. E., Ressler, R. K., Burgess, A. W., & Hartman, C. R. (1986). Criminal profiling from crime scene analysis. Behavioural Sciences and the Law, 4(4), 401–421.

Egger, S. A. (1998). The Killers among Us: An Examination of Serial Murder and Its Investigation. Upper Saddle River, NJ: Prentice Hall.

Environmental Criminology Research, Inc. (2001). What is Rigel? Available at http://www.geographicprofiling.com/rigel/index.html. Accessed April 10, 2009.

Fox, J. A., & Levin, J. (1996). Killer on Campus. New York: Avon Books.

Fritzon, K. (2000). The contribution of psychological research to arson investigation. In D. Canter & A. Alison (Eds.), Profiling Property Crimes. Aldershot, UK: Ashgate.

Geberth, V. J. (1996). Practical Homicide Investigation: Tactics, Procedures and Forensic Techniques (3rd ed.). Boca Raton, FL: CRC Press.

Godwin, G. M. (1999). Hunting Serial Predators: A Multivariate Classification Approach to Profiling Violent Behavior. Boca Raton, FL: CRC Press.

Godwin, J. (1985). Murder USA: The Ways We Kill Each Other. New York: Ballantine.

Gudjonsson, G., & Copson, G. (1997). The role of the expert in criminal investigation. In J. Jackson & D. Bekerian (Eds.), Offender Profiling: Theory, Research and Practice. Chichester, UK: Wiley.

Harries, K. (1999). Mapping Crime: Principles and Practice. Washington, DC: U.S. Department of Justice, Crime Mapping and Research Center.

Hazelwood, R. R., & Douglas, J. E. (1980). The lust murderer. FBI Law Enforcement Bulletin, 49(4), 1–5.

Hazelwood, R. R., Ressler, R. K., Depue, R. L., & Douglas, J. E. (1995). Criminal investigative analysis: An overview. In R. R. Hazelwood & A. W. Burgess (Eds.), Practical Aspects of Rape Investigation: A Multidisciplinary Approach (2nd ed.). Boca Raton, FL: CRC Press.

Holmes, R. M., & Holmes, S. T. (2002). Profiling Violent Crimes: An Investigative Tool. Thousand Oaks, CA: Sage.

Investigations Subcommittee and Defense Policy Panel of the Committee on Armed Services House of Representatives. (1990). USS Iowa Tragedy: An Investigative Failure. Washington, DC: U.S. Government Printing Office.

Jackson, J., & Bekerian, D. (Eds.). (1997). Offender Profiling: Theory, Research and Practice. Chichester, UK: Wiley.

Jackson, J. L., van den Eshof, P., & de Kleuver, E. E. (1997). A research approach to offender profiling. In J. L. Jackson & D. A. Bekerian (Eds.), Offender Profiling: Theory, Research and Practice. Chichester, UK: Wiley.

Jenkins, P. (1994). Using Murder: The Social Construction of Serial Homicide. New York: Aldine.

Kocsis, R. N., & Irwin, H. J. (1997). An analysis of spatial patterns in serial rape, arson, and burglary: The utility of the circle theory of environmental range for psychological profiling. Psychiatry, Psychology & Law, 4, 195–206.

Kocsis, R. N., Irwin, H. J., & Hayes, A. F. (1998). Organised and disorganised criminal behaviour syndromes in arsonists: A validation study of a psychological profiling concept. Psychology, Psychiatry and Law, 5(1), 117–131.

Kopel, D. B., & Blackman, P. H. (1997). No More Wacos: What's Wrong with Federal Law Enforcement and How to Fix It. New York: Prometheus.

Laverty, I., & MacLaren, P. (2002, Summer). Geographic profiling: A new tool for crime analysis. Crime Mapping News, 4, 5–8.

Liebert, J. A. (1985). Contributions of psychiatric consultations in the investigation of serial murder. International Journal of Offender Therapy and Comparative Criminology, 29, 187–199.

McGrath, M. G. (2000). Criminal profiling: Is there a role for the forensic psychiatrist? Journal of the American Academy of Psychiatry and Law, 28, 315–324.

Petherick, W. A. (2003, June). Criminal profiling: What's in a name? Comparing applied profiling methodologies. Journal of Law and Social Challenges, 173–188.

Petherick, W. A., & Turvey, B. E. (2008a). Nomothetic methods of criminal profiling. In Turvey, B. E. (ed.). Criminal Profiling: An Introduction to Behavioral Evidence Analysis. (3rd. ed.). Burlington, MA: Academic Press.

Petherick, W. A., & Turvey, B. E. (2008b). Behavioral evidence analysis: An ideo deductive method of criminal profiling. In Turvey, B. E. (ed.). Criminal Profiling: An Introduction to Behavioral Evidence Analysis. (3rd. ed.). Burlington, MA: Academic Press.

Petherick, W. A., & Turvey, B. E. (2008c). Victimology. In Turvey, B. E. (ed.). Criminal Profiling: An Introduction to Behavioral Evidence Analysis. (3rd. ed.). Burlington, MA: Academic Press.

Profiling section wasn't good value, Vancouver police deputy chief says. (2001, June 28). Vancouver Sun.

Ratcliffe, J. H. (2004). Crime mapping and the training needs of law enforcement. European Journal on Criminal Policy and Research, 10, 65–83.

Rengert, G. F., Piquero, A. R., & Jones, P. R. (1999). Distance decay reexamined. Criminology, 37(2), 427–445.

Ressler, R. K., & Burgess, A. W. (1985). Crime scene and profile characteristics of organized and disorganized serial murderers. FBI Law Enforcement Bulletin, 54(8), 18–25.

Ressler, R. K., Burgess, A. W., & Douglas, J. E. (1988). Sexual Homicides: Patterns and Motives. New York: Lexington Books.

Ressler, R. K., Burgess, A. W., Douglas, J. E., Hartman, C. R., & D'Agostino, R. B. (1986). Sexual killers and their victims: Identifying patterns through crime scene analysis. Journal of Interpersonal Violence, 1(3), 288–308.

Ressler, R. K., Burgess, A. W., Hartman, C. R., Douglas, J. E., & McCormack, A. (1986). Murderers who rape and mutilate. Journal of Interpersonal Violence, 1(3), 273–287.

Ressler, R. K., & Shachtman, T. (1992). Whoever Fights Monsters. New York: Pocket Books.

Rossmo, D. K. (1997). Geographic profiling. In J. Jackson & D. Bekerian (Eds.), Offender Profiling: Theory, Research and Practice. Chichester, UK: Wiley.

Rossmo, D. K. (2000). Geographic Profiling. Boca Raton, FL: CRC Press.

Rossmo v. Vancouver (City) Police Board. (2002). Available at http://www.hamilton-howell.ca/cases/rossmo.htm. Accessed June 16, 2005.

Rynearson, J. (2002). Evidence and Crime Scene Reconstruction: A Guide for Field Investigations (6th ed.). Redding, CA: National Crime Investigation and Training.

Saferstein, R. (2004). Criminalistics: An Introduction to Forensic Science (8th ed.). Upper Saddle River, NJ: Prentice Hall.

Santilla, P., Zappala, A., Laukannen, M., & Picozzi, M. (2003). Testing the utility of a geographical profiling approach in three rape series of a single offender: A case study. Forensic Science International, 131, 42–52.

Snook, B., Canter, D., & Bennell, C. (2002). Predicting the home location of serial offenders: A preliminary comparison of the accuracy of human judges with a geographic profiling system. Behavioural Sciences and the Law, 20, 109–118.

Snook, B., Taylor, P. J., & Bennell, C. (2004). Geographic profiling: The fast, frugal and accurate way. Applied Cognitive Psychology, 18, 105–121.

Stock, G. W. J. (2004). Deductive Logic. Oxford: Project Gutenberg Press.

Superior Court of California. (1999). The People of the State of California v. Douglas Scott Mouser. Available at http://www.corpus-delicti.com/mouser_101999_prodan_direct.html. Accessed November 11, 2005.

Tamlyn, D. (1999). Deductive profiling: A clinical perspective from the UK. In B. E. Turvey (Ed.), Criminal Profiling: An Introduction to Behavioral Evidence Analysis. London: Academic Press.

Thompson, C. C. (1999). A Glimpse of Hell: The Explosion on the USS Iowa and Its Cover-Up. New York: Norton.

Thornton, J. (2006). Crime reconstruction: Ethos and ethics. In J. Chisum & B. E. Turvey (Eds.), Crime Reconstruction. San Diego: Academic Press.

Turvey, B. E. (2008). Offender characteristics: Rendering the criminal profile. In Turvey, B. E. (ed.). Criminal Profiling: An Introduction to Behavioral Evidence Analysis (3rd ed.). Burlington, MA: Academic Press.

van Koppen, P. J., & de Keijser, J. (1997). Desisting distance decay: On the aggregation of individual crime trips. Criminology, 35, 505–515.

West, A. (2000). Clinical assessment of homicide offenders: The significance of crime scene in offense and offender analysis. Homicide Studies, 4(3), 219–233.

Wilson, C. (2003, April). Mapping the criminal mind. New Scientist, 178, 47.

Wilson, P., Lincoln, R., & Kocsis, R. (1997). Validity, utility and ethics of profiling for serial violent and sexual offenders. Psychology, Psychiatry and Law, 4(1), 1–12.

Woodworth, M., & Porter, S. (2001). Historical foundations and current applications of criminal profiling in violent crime investigations. Expert Evidence, 7, 241–264.

Wright, J. A., Burgess, A. G., Laszlo, A. T., McCrary, G. O., & Douglas, J. E. (1996). A typology of interpersonal stalking. Journal of Interpersonal Violence, 11(4), 487–503.

CHAPTER 5

The Fallacy of Accuracy in Criminal Profiling

Wayne Petherick

INTRODUCTION

The defining criterion by which the utility of a particular tool is often judged is its accuracy or sensitivity of detection. We place little faith in that which is inaccurate or in those things that do not detect what they are meant to detect. Things are no different in the profiling community, and the most common measure by which a profiler claims utility is how close his or her approximations are to an offender, if one is caught. As will be shown in this chapter, with the craft being the way it is, this is probably the worst possible way to declare one's success.

It has been noted in the preceding chapters that a criminal profile is an estimation (the differences in profiling methods aside) of an offender based on his or her behavior and interactions with a crime scene and a victim. Typically, the goal is to identify gross personality and behavioral characteristics that may set the criminal apart from other members of society.

109

The defining issue here is that any attempt to describe criminal profiling must include an understanding that it is an attempt to identify gross personality and behavioral types and states rather than pointing the finger at a specific individual. This differentiates the approach at a scientific level as class evidence, where one item can be placed in a class of similar items, rather than individuating evidence, which can differentiate between individuals, even of the same class (Inman & Rudin, 1997). Although profiling belongs to the former, practitioners often toe the line or attempt to leap majestically over it, and this clearly exceeds the limits of what can be legitimately achieved through the process (*New Jersey v. Fortin* [2000] is one such example, as is the profile prepared in *The Estate of Samuel H. Sheppard v. The State of Ohio* [Court TV Online, 1999], discussed subsequently). Signature evidence, a common form of profiling evidence, is often used in court to provide a basis for case linkage. If it can be shown by a profiler that the crimes of an accused are remarkably similar to other open cases, then these crimes may also be attributed to the same offender, or it may be possible to taint a jury by claiming that a current series of offenses is similar to those an accused has been previously charged with. This speaks to the ultimate issue, usurping the role of the jury and corrupting the flow of the criminal justice system.

The confusion regarding the ability of a profile to identify a specific person is evidenced in the criminal investigative analysis (CIA) submitted by Gregg McCrary in *The Estate of Samuel H. Sheppard v. The State of Ohio* (Court TV Online, 1999). Although a CIA is based on probabilities, the typical opening caveat in this report was conspicuously absent. Although it was noted throughout the report that "the more time an offender spends at a crime scene the higher the probability that the offender is comfortable and familiar with that scene" and "the totality of this evidence reveals that this crime was, in all probability, not a 'for-profit' or drug-related burglary, nor a sexually motivated crime," the report goes far beyond these statements of probability in closing, where it is noted that:

> the totality of the physical, forensic, and behavioral evidence allows for only one logical conclusion and that is that the homicide of Marilyn Reese Sheppard on July 4, 1954, was a staged domestic homicide committed by Dr. Samuel Sheppard. The known indicators for criminal staging as well as the known crime scene indicators consistent with a staged domestic homicide are abundantly present. This evidence not only supports no other logical conclusion but also significantly contradicts Dr. Samuel Sheppard's testimony and statements.

This is not only in opposition to assertions noted throughout the profile, which are correlations between this case and indicators provided in the *Crimes Classification Manual* (Douglas, Burgess, Burgess, & Ressler, 1992) but also far exceeds the certainty with which such a conclusion can be made. In this case, the profiler is attempting to individuate the offender from the evidence. Behavioral evidence simply cannot meet this threshold.

THE FALLACY OF ACCURACY

As criminal profiling methods and techniques permeate the academic and investigative communities, more is being learned about how offender characteristics are developed from the offender's crime scene and behavior. This may be attributed to the rise of a number of independent schools of thought in the criminal profiling community that are challenging long-held assumptions, including the criticisms levied against stagnating criminal profiling methods (Ainsworth, 2001; Petherick & Turvey, 2008).

Although there are many areas for improvement in this field, only one is the focus of this chapter—the *fallacy of accuracy*. This issue is not only important but also highly relevant to the current development of the field because it speaks directly to the utility of the end product—the final criminal profile.

The fallacy of accuracy encompasses two issues: actual accuracy and utility. First, we must address the issue of accuracy. When pressed on the witness stand, at professional meetings, or in interviews, some criminal profilers boldly claim 100% *accuracy rates*, that their methods and analysis are as good as fingerprints and DNA evidence (*New Jersey v. Fortin*, 2000), or that they "haven't been wrong yet" (McKnight, 2000). Other criminal profilers have suggested that accuracy equates to usefulness; if it was accurate, that means it must have been useful and vice versa. Still other criminal profilers argue that if criminal profiling was not accurate, they would not get so many requests for it. Would this same argument be accepted if put forth by a psychic? Clearly, none of this reasoning is valid. The only way to determine actual accuracy is to compare a criminal profile to an offender that has been unequivocally convicted of the crime that was profiled (and even under ideal conditions this may be a very subjective process). If this is not being done, then the full extent of a profiler's accuracy is unknown and any claims should be viewed with the appropriate skepticism.

What is often forgotten by zealous criminal profilers is that, as discussed in Hazelwood, Ressler, Depue, and Douglas (1995), a criminal profile, also referred to as a criminal investigative analysis (Cooper & King, 2001), is an investigative tool only that is designed to narrow and define suspect pools. As such, the following (or similar) disclaimer precedes each report prepared by members of the Federal Bureau of Investigation's (FBI) Investigative Support Unit (Hazelwood, 1995, pp. 176–177):

> It should be noted that the attached analysis is not a substitute for a thorough and well-planned investigation and should not be considered all inclusive. The information provided is based upon reviewing, analyzing, and researching criminal cases similar to the case submitted by the requesting agency. The final analysis is based

upon probabilities. Note, however, that no two criminal acts or criminal personalities are exactly alike and, therefore, the offender may not always fit the profile in every category.

The caution prescribed by the disclaimer is contextualized in Hazelwood et al. (1995, p. 125), in which it is stated that "CIA and profiling should be used to augment proven investigative techniques and must not be allowed to replace those methods; to do so would be counterproductive to the goal of identifying the unknown offender."

However, what is published in the literature and what is told to the court when expert qualification and testimony are on the line do not always add up.

According to a report filed in a U.S. criminal court, written by an expert criminal profiler called to review the work of the FBI in a serial murder case, the mandatory disclaimer previously discussed is not always present on work put before the court (Turvey, 2002, p. 7):

> This examiner has read this disclaimer on similar reports drawn up by FBI BSU [Behavioral Analysis Unit] personnel when reviewing their investigative reports. However, this examiner has made note that this disclaimer is absent from reports submitted by BSU personnel during a trial, when expert testimony may be needed. It could be argued that the inclusion of such a disclaimer at trial might tend to hamper admissibility because it addresses the issue of limited reliability. It seems significant, however, as the conclusions are based on the same methodology as reports prepared by the BSU during an investigation.

This kind of omission is fairly serious and speaks to the reluctance of those in the field to disclose or admit to the shortcomings of particular methods. In addition, the selectivity with which this caveat is used highlights a more insidious knowledge: that the product is flawed and airing this may prevent subsequent expert testimony. Good scientific practice[1] involves not only articulating conclusions based on evidence, arrived at from solid analytical reasoning, but also pointing out the limitations of any analysis conducted (see Inman and Rudin [2001] for a cogent discussion of this point). Profiling should be no different.

However, addressing the issue of accuracy is only half the battle. What help is an accurate profile that cannot be put to good use by anyone? Next, we must

---

[1]Now, it is acknowledged that profiling is not a science (Muller, 2000; Turvey, 2008), but this does not mean that we should not apply scientific principles to our analyses. The argument that profiling is not a science and therefore not bound by the same principles is vapid and used as an excuse for lackluster performance. It is argued that a stricter adherence to a scientific process will make the practice of profiling more accurate and better able to assist the police and courts in their determinations.

address the issue of utility. A criminal profile may be entirely accurate but so general in its characteristics that it is useless to those who need investigative guidance. This is a common complaint among end users of criminal profiles. For example, the leader of one major serial killer task force criticized the profile developed for the case as lacking utility. As reported in Ebnet (1998):

> Detectives also say their profile of the killer is of little help. The profile, which agents from FBI headquarters in Quantico, Va., crafted during a winter visit to Spokane, contains little detail. "The first thing (the agents) told us after they gave us the profile is not to use it," Silver said. "You hope it gives you direction. It just doesn't."

The purpose of a criminal profile is to reduce the suspect pool, not to be so inclusive that it applies to just about everyone. It should be of use to the investigation—something that investigators can put to work, advancing their inquiry. A criminal profile without utility can be a waste of valuable time and resources.

There is a general dearth of literature on this subject, and many individuals and agencies are reluctant to broadcast their accuracy figures. Inaccuracy may be perceived as ineffectiveness. If they are not seen as being effective by those who control funding, then budgets may be cut, positions eliminated, and roles diffused. For this reason, it is often prudent for these figures to be concealed, misplaced, misrepresented, or simply not gathered. As stated in Ainsworth (2001, 176), "There have been very few pieces of research which have looked at both the accuracy and usefulness of profiles used in 'live' criminal cases." This small handful of publications or studies examining the accuracy of criminal profiling includes most notably Darkes, Otto, Poythress, and Starr (1993); Homant and Kennedy (1998); Ingram (1998); and Turvey (2000, 2008).

THE MEASURE OF SUCCESS

Jackson, van den Eshof, and de Kleuver (1997) stated that the success of profiling can be defined as the number of hits scored by profiles. These authors later suggest that their definition is perhaps too restrictive, and that it should be extended to include the perceived value of advice in relation to investigative suggestions, crime assessment, and interview techniques. This is due to the fact that the work of their profiling unit "covers a wider scope of assistance than merely producing profiles" (p. 127). It is my opinion, however, that the former definition is not restrictive at all, that it is in fact far too general to be of much use in providing a measurable standard with which to gauge the accuracy of a profile. Rossmo (2000) suggests that for a profile to be useful, it must assist in the investigative decision-making process. He further notes that any suggestions that are vague, general, unworkable, or of low probability are not likely to produce helpful leads (Rossmo adopts a statistical approach in the profiling process and as such probabilities are all important). Rossmo's proposal that a profile must assist in the investigative decision-making process is fully supported herein.

Gudjonsson and Copson (1997, p. 73) have noted that "if success in profiling were synonymous with accurate prediction, then profilers could claim much success." Because this is simply not the case, there must be another yardstick with which to measure the assistance that a profile provides in an investigation. Unfortunately, some in the discipline may indeed measure their success in this way, which invariably leads to gratuitous self-promotion and an over-inflated sense of utility. Surely, Godwin's (1985) assertion in the early days of profiling that 9 out of 10 profiles were vapid and likened to a game of blind man's bluff still applies today. The analogy I have frequently used is that of the fisherman's net: If one uses a net that is big enough, and casts it over a wide area, surely one has an increased chance of catching fish. However, the size of the net or the width of the cast plays no part in the quality of the fish caught.

ACCURACY RATES

Alleged accuracy figures range from the sublime to the ridiculous. Although there are a variety of problems associated with determining statistical accuracy, it is clear that many estimates of accuracy are based solely on the "feel good" attractiveness of the profile and not necessarily on any actual benefit derived from its publication. That is, simply by virtue of having a profile done on a case, investigators may feel it has helped, regardless of whether it is even used during the investigation. This perception of assistance may be further heightened as a function of the complexity of the case or of a case that falls well outside of the experience of even the most sophisticated investigator. In addition, many investigators already employ a simplified form of profiling in their duties and may indeed arrive at many of the same conclusions. Although they may not know how they arrived at these conclusions, the involvement of a profiler might assist in articulating their thoughts. Having a third party reaffirm existing thoughts in this way can be quite reassuring.

In 1981, as part of regular management practices, the FBI conducted a cost–benefit study to determine the value of the service to consumers (Pinizzotto, 1984). In an effort to determine this, 192 end users (of 209 cases) were polled regarding the assistance provided by FBI-prepared profiles. The results suggested that only 46% of these crimes had been solved, which amounted to 88 investigations. Of these, it was further determined that they helped focus the investigation in 72% of the cases, helped locate a suspect in 20% of those cases, directly identified a suspect in 17% of cases, and assisted in the prosecution of suspects in 6% of cases. Interestingly, the profile was deemed to be of no assistance to the same degree that it helped directly identify a suspect (17%) (Rossmo, 2000).

Pinizzotto (1984) claims that, basing their decision on a combination of common sense, logic, intuition, and experience, the BSU has an accuracy rate in excess of 80%. Later, Pinizzotto teamed with Norman Finkel (Pinizzotto & Finkel, 1990) to assess the outcome and process differences in profiles among groups of profilers, detectives, psychologists, and students. This was assessed using the expert/novice approach (Pinizzotto & Finkel, 1990; Rossmo, 2000), in which the skills of qualified investigators are compared to those of neophytes. The results of the study suggest that of the four groups, profilers had the highest mean number of accurate predictions (29.1), with the detectives having the second highest (15.8), psychologists the third highest (10.8), and students the lowest number of mean accurate predictions (6.3). The finding that profilers are more accurate at profiling than other groups has also been reported elsewhere. It is hoped that this should come as no surprise.

In one study in the United Kingdom on the accuracy of profilers, the Coals to Newcastle project (Gudjonsson & Copson, 1997) found that the aggregate accuracy ratio among all groups studied was 2.2:1 (this means that for each 2.2 correct points, there was 1 incorrect point). Although individual accuracy rates were also calculated (e.g., between clinical and statistical profilers), the point is well illustrated by looking simply at these aggregate scores. Essentially, a 2.2:1 ratio suggests that only an approximate 66% accuracy rate can be established.

In cases in which criminal profiling has led to the apprehension of an offender, there is little explanation as to exactly how it was of help. For example, in the Coals to Newcastle project it was determined that in 5 out of the 184 cases the criminal profile led to the identification of the offender. Without knowing how such success was defined or established, the full utility of the criminal profile cannot be assessed, nor can successes be studied and replicated. Undoubtedly, the degree to which a profile helps "catch" an offender will also be dictated by the case at hand, with the evidence having a considerable impact. Also, if a prime suspect has already been identified or if there is supporting physical evidence, this may assist in case resolution despite the involvement of a profiler.

PROBLEMS

Perhaps the greatest obstacle to objectively examining this issue is the way in which criminal profiles are assessed for their accuracy. Should we simply compare the final profile to the offender once caught? Where do we then stand if the offender is not caught? As stated by Homant and Kennedy (1998, p. 324), "Even when the identity of the offender is unambiguously determined, there is still a large subjective element in deciding how well the person fits the profile." Also, providing a criminal profile may only confirm what investigators currently think. If the suspect is later arrested and charged, who then "gets the credit" for accuracy or utility (especially if the profile is merely tailored to fit a suspect rather than painstakingly compiled from a thorough analysis of the crime)—the investigating detective, the criminal profiler, or both?

One common method employed in determining the usefulness of profiling is studies of *consumer satisfaction*. Typically, this involves polling a select group of consumers of criminal profiling and asking questions related to their satisfaction with the results. This is inherently problematic for a number of reasons. First, virgin consumers may be so enamored with the information they receive that they inadvertently report their bedazzlement rather than their genuine satisfaction. This may be particularly the case where bizarre, novel, or unique information is provided, and this is similar to the concern voiced by Campbell (1976), who stated that police might be more seduced by the academic credentials of the profiler than by the profile itself. This belief has been affirmed by Kocsis and Hayes (2004), who found that a profiler's perceived accuracy is a function of the professional standing of its author (as a profiler or simply as some other person). Second, the studies may not consider longitudinal data, opting instead for a cross-sectional design. This would have the effect of providing information on satisfaction with limited cases, in a limited time frame, and possibly from limited sources, potentially biasing results due to restricted exposure to profiling. Last, a criminal profile in a particularly difficult case may provide the investigators with false hope, subsequently inflating their opinion of the profiling process.

One might argue that the best way to assess the utility of a criminal profile is to count the number of correct characteristics in the profile against the offender once apprehended. This may be illustrated as follows: One criminal profile may contain 10 characteristics and only be correct on 2 of them. However, 1 of these 2 accurate characteristics leads to the successful identification of the suspect pool, from which an offender is identified through other physical evidence. In another case, the same criminal profiler offers 10 characteristics and is correct on all of them, although the criminal profile has not assisted in developing or apprehending a suspect. In which case does the criminal profiler have the right to claim success and/or utility? Is it prudent for the profiler to claim an accurate profile in the second case as argument toward his or her overall success, or is it misleading? It should be clear that the process is not as simple as many would have us believe.

Controlled studies present problems of their own. For example, Kocsis, Irwin, Hayes, and Nunn (2001) attempted to qualitatively assess the differences between the abilities of students, detectives, psychologists, profilers, and psychics. Although the purpose of their study was not to determine the success of profiles per se, the nature of the study was to compare the abilities of these various groups and a measure of their abilities was indeed communicated in terms of their success. In this study, two measures of accuracy were used. First, total accuracy was measured and defined as "the total number of correct answers on four submeasures." The second measure used was Pinizzotto and Finkel accuracy, which was constructed using a set of questions similar to those used by Pinizzotto and Finkel (1990).

The study showed that the psychologists identified more of the physical behaviors and offense characteristics than did the police officers, and also that they identified more of the physical characteristics than did the psychics. None of the other characteristics were deemed to be statistically significant. Although the authors note that this casts serious doubt on the utility of profilers in investigations, it is equally likely that this was an artifact of the questionnaire used. For example, a closed-ended set of questions was asked rather than letting the participants define their own profile parameters. Under physical characteristics, study participants were asked the offender's age (bracketed to 1–12 years, 13–17 years, 18–25 years, and so forth) and the offender's build, height, hair color, eye color, and ethnic background. Under offense characteristics, study participants were asked questions regarding the distance the offender lived from the crime scene and method of approach, among others. The offender's history and habits were the last category of the questionnaire. Many of these characteristics were not directly inferable by offender behavior, and as a result, would have required a degree of guesswork, indicating that the accuracy assessed within this study was questionable.[2] For those characteristics for which only a limited number of options were present (e.g., sex), guesswork may have indeed played a major role, given that a smaller number of options increases one's chance of accuracy.

SUGGESTIONS

In search of success and celebrity, some criminal profilers may be too concerned with how accurate their profiles are (no matter how general, inclusive, and subjective) and broadcast this as evidence of their uncanny ability to identify an unknown offender through the offender's criminal behavior. A very relevant example is the activities of a cavalcade of so-called experts in the Washington Sniper case. Utility may take a back seat.

Based on the prior discussion, a number of suggestions can be proposed regarding the accuracy of a profile and, subsequent to this, the utility of a method in general and individual profiles in the specific. These are easy to consider and

---

[2]It is possible that some of the questions, such as those regarding hair and eye color, were intended more for the psychics, but asking the profilers to assess these still places their conclusions outside of the usual realms of profile characteristics.

implement when embarking on casework, and they should become the corner-stone of practice when engaging in operational profiling work. These can be summarized as follows:

1. Establish a clear set of guidelines for the development of the profile.
2. Consider how the profile may actually be used by the consumer.
3. It is perhaps easiest to keep your eye on the prize when it is known exactly what the prize is (i.e., without some clear direction or goal when preparing a profile, it is easy to fall into the trap of offering vague and irrelevant characteristics instead of relevant suggestions).
4. Be guided by ethical and practical considerations and constraints.
5. Have an enduring commitment to the assistance provided and be accountable for your conclusions.

The first point relates to some issues that were raised previously in this chapter. This includes discussing what evidence was and was not available, the ways in which this may affect subsequent conclusions, and being clear in outlining what information is required for the type of analysis to be performed. Also, the profiler should inform the end user of the reasoning process employed in developing the profile.

Consideration of how a profile might be used by the end consumer is paramount to utility. Without thinking about the variety of ways in which a profile may be acted upon, profilers may fall into the trap of providing ambiguous offender characteristics that may confuse rather than aid the investigation. To further highlight this point, consider an example from an oft-cited profiling text (Holmes & Holmes, 2002, p. 22):

> The killer is a seriously disturbed individual.... The manner in which he cuts the parts of the body shows determination and anger plus making the victim less than a human being: "Not only are you nothing, now you are little bits of nothing." What is especially interesting is that the person has kept, or at least it has not been found, the skin from the neck to the waist. This is the most important part for him. I can see him skinning this body part and wearing it at night around the house where he lives alone.

This profile comes across as intensely subjective and is full of supposition guided by what the author believes to have occurred. Indeed, if the skin mentioned had not been found, then the whole basis for the final opinion comes crashing down around its foundation. Last, how would detectives act on this information? Surely, if they found the skin in someone's possession this would leave little doubt they had their person, but how would they arrive at this point from the information provided? If an investigator cannot act on a characteristic, it is little more than clutter and should be left out.

This brings us to the third point. How, then, are we to determine what is clutter and what is useful? The answer is very simple and rests only on a determination of what investigators are seeking. Typically, they have some feature of the offense in mind that they are seeking assistance with, and it is this which should become the focus of the profile.[3] This may be a determination of precautionary acts, intent or premeditation, staging, or motive, to name but a few. This will ensure that both the profile and the investigation stay on track.

The well-known medical maxim "do no harm" may be appropriate for consideration. Not only must profilers consider the harmful effects that may come about from their involvement but also they must be constantly vigilant about the practical constraints of their craft, some of which have been discussed at length.

Because ethics is discussed elsewhere in this book, it will not be afforded a lengthy discussion here. Suffice it to say that although ethics is absent from many quarters in the profiling area, this does not absolve a profiler from behaving ethically. When life and/or liberty may hang on the words of any expert, that expert must do his or her utmost to behave properly, including behaving in a responsible and ethical manner. To do otherwise will only serve to bring the field (and the expert) into further disrepute.

Perhaps as a final consideration for developing valid profiles, it should be pointed out that the work of the profiler is not finished once the report has been drafted, or even submitted. First, the report should be subject to revision if and when new evidence comes to light. In this way, the profile becomes a dynamic document, not one that is outdated the moment evidence in a case changes. Also, and perhaps equally important, it should be incumbent on the profiler to take time with investigators to explain and detail his or her report and how best to implement its contents into their investigation. Furthermore, profilers should provide clear indications of how they arrived at their conclusions. There would be no greater shame than to have an investigator presented with a profile whose promise was high but was then not utilized as a result of confusion regarding its development or place within the investigative process.

CONCLUSION

If we are more concerned with the accuracy of a profile than we are with its investigative utility, we run the very real risk of failing to advance profiling beyond the personality and celebrity of those offering the service. Any criminal profiler who

---

[3]Some investigators may be seeking full profiles, but this should not be assumed.

undertakes casework without consideration of the usefulness of his or her end product is disregarding the very reason criminal profiles are constructed in the first place: to assist the investigative community in the identification of personality and behavioral characteristics that distinguish offenders from the general population. It is possible to advance the practice beyond its current state, although to do so practitioners must be cognizant of issues relating to utility and relevance. To ignore these is to remain ignorant of flaws in thinking and practice.

Questions

1. In the study conducted by Pinizzotto, what percentage of profiles were found to be of no assistance?
   a. 46%
   b. 72%
   c. 20%
   d. 6%
   e. 17%
2. The Coals to Newcastle project found that the aggregate accuracy ratio among all groups studied was:
   a. 2.2:1
   b. 1.7:1
   c. 2:1
   d. 4.3:1
   e. 1:1
3. If a criminal profile has 10 offender characteristics in it, and these characteristics prove to be accurate, it could be argued that the profile is useful. *True or false?*
4. Some criminal profilers suggest that accuracy equates to usefulness. *True or false?*
5. The fallacy of accuracy encompasses two issues. These are _____ and _____.

REFERENCES

Ainsworth, P. B. (2001). Offender Profiling and Crime Analysis. Devon, UK: Willan.

Campbell, C. (1976). Portraits of mass killers. Psychology Today, 9, 110–119.

Cooper, G., & King, M. (2001). Analyzing Criminal Behavior. Ogden, UT: IQ Design.

Court TV Online. (1999). State expert's new report implicating Sam Sheppard. Available at http://www.courttv.com/national/2000/0131/mccrary_ctv.html. Accessed June 28, 2002.

Darkes, J., Otto, R. K., Poythress, N., & Starr, L. (1993, January). APA's expert panel in the congressional review of the USS Iowa incident. American Psychologist, 8–15.

Douglas, J. E., Burgess, A. W., Burgess, A. G., & Ressler, R. K. (1992). Crime Classification Manual: A Standard System for Investigating and Classifying Violent Crime. New York: Lexington Books.

Ebnet, M. (1998, June 15). Spokane officials have few leads on serial killer. Seattle Times.

Godwin, J. (1985). Murder USA: The Ways We Kill Each Other. New York: Ballantine.

Gudjonsson, G. H., & Copson, G. (1997). The role of the expert in criminal investigation. In J. L. Jackson & D. A. Bekerian (Eds.), Offender Profiling: Theory, Research and Practice. Chichester, UK: Wiley.

Hazelwood, R. (1995) Analyzing the rape and profiling the offender. In A. Burgess & R. Hazelwood (Eds.), Practical Aspects of Rape Investigation (2nd ed.). Boca Raton, FL: CRC Press.

Hazelwood, R. R., Ressler, R. K., Depue, R. L., & Douglas, J. E. (1995). Criminal investigative analysis: An overview. In A. Burgess & R. Hazelwood (Eds.), Practical Aspects of Rape Investigation (2nd ed.). Boca Raton, FL: CRC Press.

Holmes, R. M., & Holmes, S. T. (2002). Profiling Violent Crimes: An Investigative Tool (3rd ed.). Thousand Oaks, CA: Sage.

Homant, R. J., & Kennedy, D. B. (1998). Psychological aspects of crime scene profiling: Validity research. Criminal Justice and Behavior, 25(3), 319–343.

Ingram, S. (1998). If the profile fits: Criminal psychological profiles into evidence in criminal trials. Journal of Urban and Contemporary Law, 54, 239–266.

Inman, K., & Rudin, N. (1997). An Introduction to Forensic DNA Analysis. New York: CRC Press.

Inman, K., & Rudin, N. (2001). Principles and Practice of Criminalistics: The Profession of Forensic Science. Boca Raton, FL: CRC Press.

Jackson, J. L., van den Eshof, P., & de Kleuver, E. E. (1997). A research approach to offender profiling. In J. L. Jackson & D. A. Bekerian (Eds.), Offender Profiling: Theory, Research and Practice. Chichester, UK: Wiley.

Kocsis, R. N., & Hayes, A. F. (2004). Believing is seeing? Investigating the perceived accuracy of psychological profiles. International Journal of Offender Therapy and Comparative Criminology, 48(2), 149–160.

Kocsis, R. N., Irwin, H. J., Hayes, A. F., & Nunn, R. (2001). Expertise in psychological profiling: A comparative assessment. Journal of Interpersonal Violence, 15(3), 311–331.

McKnight, K. (2000, April 1). Expert's opinion challenged. Ohio Beacon Journal.

Muller, D. (2000). Criminal profiling: Real science or just wishful thinking? Homicide Studies, 4(3), 234–264.

New Jersey v. Fortin, 745 A.2d 509, NJ (2000).

Petherick, W. A., & Turvey, B. E. (2008). Nomothetic methods of criminal profiling. In B. E. Turvey (ed.). Criminal Profiling: An Introduction to Behavioral Evidence Analysis. (3rd ed.). Burlington, MA: Academic Press.

Pinizzotto, A. J. (1984). Forensic psychology: Criminal personality profiling. Journal of Police Science and Administration, 12(1), 32–40.

Pinizzotto, A. J., & Finkel, N. J. (1990). Criminal personality profiling: An outcome and process study. Law and Human Behavior, 14, 215–233.

Rossmo, D. K. (2000). Geographical Profiling. Boca Raton, FL: CRC Press.

Turvey, B. (2000). Criminal profiling and the problem of forensic individuation. Journal of Behavioral Profiling, 1(2), 1–15.

Turvey, B. (2002, May 28). Memorandum Re: Washington v. Robert Yates.

Investigative Relevance

Claire Ferguson

KEY TERMS

Inputs of the profile: The information or evidence on which a profile is based.

Outputs of a profile: The conclusions given about offender characteristics based on the inputs.

Appeal to common practice: A logical fallacy stating that because most people engage in a particular practice, this provides evidence for the practice.

Investigative relevance: The degree to which a profile actually assists in the investigative decision-making process.

Criminal profiling is one tool available to investigative agencies that may assist in narrowing suspect pools, linking crimes, providing relevant leads and new investigative strategies, and keeping the overall investigation on track (Turvey, 2008). However, like a flashlight in a darkened room, profiling may not always provide valuable assistance if it shines in the wrong direction or fails to shine at all. In a perfect world, profiles are intended to provide investigators with a set of refined characteristics of the offender for a crime or a crime series that will assist their efforts. In contrast, it could be argued that profiles are not intended to provide information that may be irrelevant, unclear, confusing, or distracting to these efforts. Any information provided within the profile that does not assist in narrowing suspect pools or providing new avenues of inquiry is left open to misinterpretation and is therefore potentially damaging (Turvey, 2008). The degree to which information provided in a profile can actually be utilized by investigators to meet their goals is known as *investigative relevance*.

123

This chapter examines whether criminal profiles actually provide the assistance they are meant to provide—that is, whether they are investigatively relevant or whether they are distracting and of little value to investigators. This chapter discusses some of the critical issues in investigative relevance and presents the results of research conducted by the author. It is shown throughout that the various types of profiles differ greatly in how much they acknowledge, and strive toward, investigative relevance. Before examining the research on investigative relevance, the goals of profiling and the information used and subsequently provided are examined.

GOALS OF PROFILING AND INPUTS AND OUTPUTS

According to Homant and Kennedy (1998), criminal profiling was originally developed (1) to assist investigators in narrowing suspect pools to smaller, more workable numbers and (2) to provide new avenues of inquiry for investigators to follow. Despite the behavior of some practitioners to the contrary, it is important to note that profiling is not designed to implicate a certain individual as responsible for the crime, nor should it (Muller, 2000). Instead, profiling has more general goals.

Holmes and Holmes (2002) identify four main goals of criminal profiling, which are summarized as follows:

1. To provide investigating authorities with a social and psychological evaluation of the offender
2. To narrow the suspect pool
3. To provide a psychological assessment of items found in possession of the offender
4. To provide interviewing and interrogation strategies

Turvey (2008) similarly identifies a number of goals of profiling, during either the investigation or the trial that may follow. According to Turvey (p. 138), there are five main investigative goals for which identifying characteristics of the suspect pool is of primary importance:

1. To reduce the viable suspect pool in a criminal investigation and to help prioritize the investigation for those remaining suspects
2. To assist in the linkage of potentially related crimes by identifying crime scene indicators and behavior patterns (e.g., modus operandi and signature)
3. To assist in assessing the potential for escalation of nuisance criminal behavior to more serious or more violent crimes (e.g., harassment, stalking, and voyeurism)
4. To provide investigators with investigatively relevant leads and strategies
5. To help keep the overall investigation on track and undistracted

In the trial phase in which the offender is already known, the profile is used to assist in the preparation of interviews, hearings, and trials. For the trial stage, there are also five goals (Turvey, 2008, p. 138):

1. To assist in the process of evaluating the nature and value of forensic evidence in a particular case
2. To assist in the process of developing interview or interrogative strategy
3. To help develop insight into offender fantasy and motivations
4. To help develop insight into offender state of mind before, during, and after the commission of a crime (e.g., levels of planning, evidence of remorse, and precautionary acts)
5. To help elucidate crime scene linkage issues by examining modus operandi and signature behavior

Although helpful in many crimes, criminal profiling is not always suitable or necessary (Petherick, 2007). Simply requiring that suspect pools be narrowed or strategies be taken to interrogate an offender does not mean that criminal profiling is necessary in any one case. Also, although profiling may be beneficial to one type of case generally, not every case of this type will benefit from it (Petherick, 2007). Homicide is a prime example. Whereas a profile might provide some assistance in a stranger homicide, its use in a domestic homicide, where the link between the offender and victim is usually more clear, may be questionable. Whether or not a profile is called for depends on the goals of the investigating agency, the available evidence, case specifics, and whether a profiler is available. Unfortunately, profiling may also be used in error to "bootstrap" a case when the prosecution case is weak or lacking in physical evidence. In determining whether or not a profiler should be recruited, investigative agencies should first determine what information they can make available to the profiler and what advice they expect in return.

Inputs and Outputs

The quality of any profile is dictated by the information on which it is based; this information is known as the *inputs* of the profile. Profilers may request many different inputs or materials on which to base their conclusions, including autopsy reports, victim information, witness statements, crime scene photographs, and investigators' reports. Because the quality and quantity of the information available have a direct bearing on the profile, it is incumbent on profilers to ensure they get as much information as possible. In every case, the more available, the better.

Pinizzotto (1984, pp. 33–34) provides the following list of inputs as necessary to produce a complete profile. This list is fairly uniform across most sources (interestingly, Geberth [1996] provides a strikingly similar list of inputs, with almost identical wording. Neither author provides citation for the list, nor to an original source):

1. Photographs of the crime scene: This includes color photos of the victim, enlarged photos of the wounds on the victim's body, various angles and positions of the victim, and complete photos of the entire area of the crime.

2. Neighborhood and complex: This includes racial, ethnic, and social data.

3. Medical examiner's report: This includes photos depicting the full extent of damage to the body, toxicology reports, a report on the presence of any semen, and postmortem wounds.

4. Map of travel prior to death: This includes place employed, residence, and where last seen before the crime scene location.

5. Complete investigative report of the incident: This includes standard report of date, time, location, etc.; weapon if known; investigative officers' reconstruction of the sequence of events; and detailed interviews of witnesses.

6. Background of the victim: This includes age; sex; race; physical description including dress at the time of the incident; marital status/ adjustment; intelligence, scholastic achievement, and adjustment; lifestyle and recent changes in lifestyle, personality style, and characteristics; demeanor; residency, former and present, and its relation to the crime scene; sexual adjustment; occupation, former and present; reputation at home and at work; medical history, physical and mental; fears; personal habits, such as the use of alcohol or drugs; social habits; hobbies; friends and enemies; and recent court action.

In their discussion of criminal personality profiling, O'Hara and O'Hara (2003, p. 712) provide a much more vague list of factors to be considered when compiling a profile:

1. The activities of the criminal as evidenced by the arrangement and disposition of materials at the crime scene
2. The description of the criminal act by witnesses
3. The background and activities of the victim
4. Any other detail of the crime that could express the personality of the perpetrator, such as the type and condition of the getaway car

Once the information has been assessed and an analysis undertaken, the profiler can then move to interpretation and compilation of profile characteristics.

These offender characteristics are known as *outputs*. Despite the various approaches that use similar inputs in constructing a profile, the offender characteristics that make up the final product vary markedly between methods. For example, Turvey (2008) is very conservative in offering offender characteristics and believes that only four characteristics can be argued definitively from the evidence available: knowledge of the victim, knowledge of methods and materials, knowledge of the crime scene or location, and criminal skill.

Taking a far more liberal stance, Ault and Reese (1980) provide a detailed list of characteristics that may be offered that cover nearly every facet of the offender's past, present, and future behavior, such as sex, age, race, sexual maturity, and probable reaction to police interrogation. Several other authors also support the provision of a large number of potential characteristics of the offender, including Geberth (1996) and O'Toole (2004), who are seemingly of the opinion that the more one knows about the offender, the better. In fact, Geberth provides the following list of 22 factors that can be determined by a profile (pp. 780–781): age, sex, race, marital status, intelligence, scholastic achievement/adjustment, lifestyle, rearing environment, social adjustment, personality style/characteristics, demeanor, appearance and grooming, emotional adjustment, evidence of mental decompensation, pathological behavioral characteristics, employment/occupational history and adjustment, work habits, residence in relation to crime scene, socioeconomic status, sexual adjustment, type of sexual perversion or disturbance (if applicable), and motive. Although it may seem that more information about the offender is better, an excess of information that cannot be used by investigators has the potential to distract the inquiry and may therefore do more harm than good.

From an examination of profiling methods, it can be seen that inductive (nomothetic) methods (criminal investigative analysis [CIA] and investigative psychology [IP]) generally argue for a larger number of offender characteristics, whereas deductive (idiographic) methods that focus on individual cases (behavioral evidence analysis [BEA]) offer less. This is most likely because statistical methods compare characteristics of the current crime to a list of many *possible* characteristics present across a number of past cases, whereas BEA aims to examine the current crime to make conclusions about this offender, at this crime, with this victim, regardless of other similar crimes and criminals (Petherick, 2007).

The previous discussion leads to the question of accuracy, utility, and investigative relevance in criminal profiling. Are more characteristics in a profile more useful to investigators? Do characteristics presented in a profile that prove to be accurate necessarily indicate that a profile was helpful to the investigation? These issues are discussed in the following section.

ACCURACY, UTILITY, AND INVESTIGATIVE RELEVANCE

Accuracy and utility were detailed in Chapter 4, but a brief summary of each is provided for the sake of context.

According to Ainsworth (2001, p. 176), not enough research has been done comparing the accuracy and utility of criminal profiles. Despite little research in the area, the issue of accuracy must be discussed because it is generally these criteria that profiles have been measured against in the past (Petherick, 2007). Some profilers have claimed that the accuracy of their profiles is directly related to their usefulness, and that if profiles were inaccurate, then profilers would not be in such high demand (Petherick, 2007). This is a logical fallacy called an *appeal to common practice*, and it is not an acceptable argument to support the accuracy of criminal profiling. Actual accuracy can only be determined by comparing profile characteristics to offenders after they have been indisputably convicted of the crime that was profiled, and even this process may remain subjective because of the imprecise nature of many profile characteristics (e.g., intelligence). It should also be noted that in many cases in which a profile is written, the profile is used to determine who, specifically, committed the crime and to bootstrap the prosecution's case against the accused to secure a conviction. It is therefore not surprising, considering the profile was used to find the offender, that it is accurate. Any appeal to this argument for accuracy is therefore circular and redundant.

Rossmo (2000) proposes that for a profile to be useful to investigators, it must advance the decision-making process involved in the investigation. He suggests that offender characteristics presented in a profile need to be clear, be distinguishable from the general population, be probable, and be of use in order to assist investigators. This brings about the focus of this chapter—investigative relevance. If a profile is too vague or indiscriminate for an investigator to use, it is not investigatively relevant. In light of this, any attempt to gauge the advantages of criminal profiling should acknowledge that accuracy, utility, and investigative relevance are very clearly linked.

One of the few discussions on investigative relevance is provided by Turvey (2008), who maintains that it is the responsibility of the criminal profiler to demonstrate how the conclusions made in the profile are relevant to the current investigation. Petherick (2007; see also Chapter 4) suggests that investigative relevance is a two-part concept: (1) Profiles must include information that can be acted on by investigators, and (2) profiles must provide information that distinguishes the offender from the general population.

It should also be noted that the relevance of some offender characteristics may be case dependent. Baeza's (1999) discussion of investigative relevance suggests that different profile characteristics will be relevant for different cases, and that characteristics that are the product of guesswork or intuition will never be relevant. Because of this, he highlights the importance of assessing cases on an individual basis. Baeza also maintains that despite the perception that certain offender features are relevant, such as personality characteristics, marital status, education, intelligence, hobbies, personal interests, and transport, these features often do not provide the detail that would be necessary for investigators to act on. It is further noted that simply because an offender characteristic made a list of features that are generally included, this does not mean the characteristic should be included in every case, nor does it guarantee that the feature will be relevant to the current investigation.

In line with this discussion, the profile characteristics adopted in the research discussed next were deemed to be investigatively irrelevant based on any, or any combination, of the following:

1. The characteristic does not discriminate from the general public or offender population. For example, stating that an offender is married or involved in a serious and long-term relationship does not assist investigators in a case because many others in the suspect pool are also married or involved in serious relationships. This fact may be true of an offender, but identifying it does not assist the investigation and may instead distract investigators. These characteristics are therefore not relevant. Other such characteristics are socioeconomic status, whether the offender is employed, education level, whether the offender is a day or a night person, type of preferred dress, social skills, whether the offender has friends or is a loner, what social environments the offender prefers, whether the offender has an automobile and what condition it is in, and the condition of the offender's residence.

2. It is not clear how identifying the characteristic could be acted on by the investigating agency. For example, stating that an offender's mother was the dominant parent may be interesting, or ultimately correct; however, identifying such a characteristic does not allow investigators to further the decision-making process in an ongoing case. Other characteristics that were not included based on this were escalation of emotion; risk of future offenses; whether the offender has a history of sexual problems; whether the offender is known to carry/collect/display weapons and, if so, what type; any recent change in the offender's behavior; and personality type.

3. Stating any such characteristic is redundant. To lessen the chance of wasting crucial investigative time, characteristics should not be offered unless there is substantial and reliable evidence to indicate their presence. However, for certain characteristics, reliable and substantial evidence speaks for itself, and therefore it is not necessary for a profile

to restate that such a characteristic is present. For example, a profile will not assist investigators if it makes an educated guess or statistical inference regarding the race of the offender. In order for race to be inarguably inferred, physical evidence or eyewitness accounts must be present. However, if such evidence is present, it is not necessary for a profile to reiterate what investigators already know. Therefore, profiles should never contain information on such characteristics as the offender's name, age, race, sex, height, weight, whether the offender was under the influence of drugs or alcohol, or whether the offender has any physical abnormalities.

4. The characteristic does not describe the offender but describes his or her behavior during the crime or the crime itself. In order to be relevant, the profile should not only report the behaviors but also make a conclusion about the offender based on these behaviors and how they are reflected in the physical evidence at the scene. Although describing offender behaviors may be helpful in producing a profile, they are not considered offender characteristics. For example, describing the level of planning or control that was apparent in a crime may tell us about the offender and could be evidence of certain offender characteristics, but it is not a characteristic in and of itself. Describing such behaviors illustrates the offender's state at the time of the crime, but it does not go beyond this to make an inference about the offender's traits in general. This does not mean, however, that describing the behavior is unimportant, because this can provide crucial background information and context to the profile.

AN ANALYSIS OF INVESTIGATIVE RELEVANCE

As discussed previously, there have been many attempts to analyze and evaluate profiling methods and profiles in the past (Ainsworth, 2001; Petherick, 2007). These attempts, however, have generally focused on the accuracy of the profile based on a comparison with apprehended offenders (Pinizzotto & Finkel, 1990) or the perceived usefulness of the profile to the requesting agency (Copson, 1995). Only one study has focused on assessing whether offender characteristics given in profiles are relevant to ongoing investigations and what proportion of characteristics given can actually further the investigation. This study was undertaken as part of the author's master's thesis and is discussed in detail here.

For the purposes of the research, the definition of investigative relevance provided by Petherick (2007) as well as the discussion by Baeza (1999) was utilized. This definition maintains that investigatively relevant characteristics distinguish an offender from the general suspect pool or population and/or must provide enough detail to be acted on by law enforcement. Furthermore, characteristics that are the product of guesswork or intuition are never relevant. Identifying vague characteristics does not allow investigators to further the decision-making process in an ongoing case because, clearly, leaving the decision up to investigators to decide how ambiguous characteristics apply is fraught with problems.

To determine what characteristics fit this concept of investigative relevance, an exhaustive list of offender characteristics was compiled from a number of sources (Ault & Reese, 1980; Geberth, 1996; O'Toole, 2004; Turvey, 2002) as well as from the profiles. Each characteristic was then compared to the definition to determine whether it could be considered relevant. Any characteristic that was the product of guesswork or intuition, which could not be acted on by law enforcement, or could not distinguish from the general population was then eliminated from the list. Upon conducting this examination, two other factors were noted that affected the relevance of offender characteristics. Characteristics were further eliminated from the list if they simply restated what the physical evidence clearly showed without drawing any further conclusions from it, or if they described the offender's behavior during the crime without further interpretation. Stated simply, characteristics that provided information that was the product of guesswork, was not discriminating from the general public, which could not easily be acted on by investigators, or which simply restated the physical and behavioral evidence present at the crime scene were not viewed as relevant to an investigation and were therefore excluded from the list. After separating the irrelevant characteristics from the initial exhaustive list, five characteristics remained: Motive, Special Skills or Knowledge of Methods and Materials, Knowledge of or Relationship to the Victim, Knowledge of the Crime Scene or Location, and Criminal Skill/Forensic Awareness. A coding dictionary was prepared to define these five characteristics, which is summarized as follows:

Motive: This is defined as "the physical, psychological, or emotional needs that impel and drive behavior" (Turvey, 2008, p. 276). It may be a general or specific descriptor.

Special Skills or Knowledge of Methods and Materials: This is presented in the profile as being demonstrated in the criminal behavior by a very specific type of knowledge of some special skill, method, or material, such as flying an airplane, the ability to crack a safe, or hacking into a complex computer system.

Knowledge or Relationship to the Victim: Offender behaviors may indicate the offender(s) had knowledge of his or her victim, such as the victim's schedules, routes of travel, and other personal details. Evidence at the crime scene that may indicate that the victim was familiar with the offender includes a lack of forced entry, no signs of a struggle, or lack of defensive wounds.

Knowledge of Crime Scene or Location: This refers to specific knowledge an offender may display of the location where the crime took place. Examples include knowledge of the location of safes and valuables, cleaning products, knowledge of access to remote areas, as well as knowledge of security codes, or knowing the exact location in a multiroom dwelling of a specific victim.

Criminal Skill and Forensic Awareness: This is the degree of criminal knowledge an offender displays in committing the crime as well as knowledge of physical evidence and police or forensic procedures. This knowledge could be the result of time spent in prison or experience committing similar crimes. It may also reflect the general intelligence of the offender. Planning, precautionary acts, and deliberate acts to confuse and hamper investigations may reflect criminal skill and forensic awareness.

To assess the investigative relevance of criminal profiling, a number of profiles were collected. These consisted of written profiles from published works such as textbooks, web sites, biographies, and journal articles. Only cases in which the complete profile was given were included in the analysis because this provided not only a complete list of characteristics but also the greatest insight into the reasoning on which the characteristics were offered. This reasoning was necessary to examine because it allowed for a distinction to be made between those characteristics that were based on evidence and those that were the product of guesswork or intuition. Therefore, incomplete, summarized, or bullet-point profiles were excluded. A total of 59 profiles from four different profiling methods—diagnostic evaluations (DE), CIA, IP, and BEA—were analyzed for this study, drawn from various crime types and locations throughout Australia, Canada, the United Kingdom, and the United States.

Each profile was analyzed to determine the total number of offender characteristics present, how many of these characteristics were relevant as measured against the coding dictionary (i.e., to determine the number of relevant characteristics as a proportion of the total number of overall characteristics), as well as what type of evidence was used to support each characteristic. The types of justification used to code a characteristic were physical evidence, statistics or research, personal opinion or belief, or no justification. In short, each profile was first examined to determine how many characteristics were present. Each characteristic in the profile was then compared against the coding dictionary to determine if it fit the definition of any of the five relevant characteristics. If one of these definitions was met, the characteristic was further examined to determine what justification, if any, was used to support its presentation. This was done for all 59 of the profiles sampled in this study.

RESULTS

The results from the analysis are presented in two sections. The first section involves a qualitative assessment to describe general trends in the data. In the second section, the data are separated based on the methodology employed in the profile in order to perform a comparative analysis on the characteristics and justifications given by each profiling method.

Analysis of Overall Sample

The initial qualitative analysis provided a breakdown of the profiling methodology employed, as well as the mean number of characteristics given in the profiles of each type. A summary of the data is provided in Table 6.1.

CIA profiles comprised the largest proportion of the sample studied at 47%.[1] Profiles that did not fit into any known profiling methodology (referred to as *Other*) comprised the lowest proportion of the sample at 2%. Due to this, Other profiles were not analyzed further. The mean number of characteristics given in the whole sample was 25. The lowest number of characteristics given was from BEA profiles ($\bar{X} = 8$, $SD = 10$) and the highest from DE profiles ($n = 58$, $SD = 52$).

The initial analysis also involved assessing the frequencies of characteristics and justifications given in the profiles regardless of the profiling methodology used. A summary of these frequencies and their corresponding proportion of the total is provided in Table 6.2.

Table 6.1 Total Characteristics Given by Method

Method	Total No. of Profiles	% of Total	Mean No. of Characteristics Given	Standard Deviation
BEA	12	20	8	10
CIA	28	47	25	18
DE	10	17	58	52
IP	8	14	14	13
Other	1	2	6	0
Total	59	100	25	30

BEA, behavioral evidence analysis; CIA, criminal investigative analysis; DE, diagnostic evaluations; IP, investigative psychology.

[1]All figures were rounded up or down for ease of reporting; therefore, totals may not always equal 100.

Table 6.2 Frequency of Characteristics and Justification Used

	Motive		Methods/ Materials		Knowledge of Victim		Knowledge of Location		Criminal Skill	
	n	%	n	%	n	%	n	%	n	%
Not given	25	42	56	95	27	46	33	56	43	73
Given without justification	11	19	1	2	11	19	9	15	3	5
Given with physical evidence	17	29	2	3	9	15	10	17	10	17
Given with statistics or research	0	0	0	0	1	2	2	3	1	2
Given with personal opinion or belief	6	10	0	0	11	19	5	9	2	3
Total	59	100	59	100	59	100	59	100	59	100

As noted previously, many of the profiles examined (more than 40% for all characteristics) did not give the characteristics deemed investigatively relevant. The offender characteristics Motive and Knowledge of Victim were given in slightly more than half of the sample (58 and 54%, respectively). Knowledge of the Location was given less than half of the time (44%), whereas Criminal Skill was given in approximately one-fourth of the sample (27%). Offender Knowledge of Methods and Materials was rarely given (5%). When Motive was given in this sample, it was most likely to be justified with physical evidence (17 of 34 profiles) and was never justified with statistics or research. Offender Knowledge of Methods and Materials was given in very few profiles (only 3 of 59) and was most likely justified with physical evidence (2 of the 3) and never with statistics, research, personal belief, or opinion. The offender characteristic Knowledge of the Victim was given in 32 of 59 profiles. It was most likely to be unjustified, or justified with personal opinion or belief (11 profiles each), and was unlikely to be justified by statistics or research (1 profile). Finally, when Knowledge of Location and Criminal Skill were given as offender characteristics (in 26 and 16 profiles, respectively), they were most often justified with physical evidence (10 profiles each) and least often justified with research and statistics (2 and 1 profile, respectively).

Analysis of Sample by Method

After the preliminary analysis, the data was separated by method to compare the various profiling approaches. A cross-tabulation was conducted in which the data was analyzed separately to investigate which relevant offender characteristics were given and what type of justification was used to support each characteristic. The results for each profiling method are presented in turn.

Criminal Investigative Analysis

In this analysis, 28 CIA profiles were analyzed, which comprised nearly half of the total profiles (47%). As mentioned previously, of these 28 profiles, the average number of offender characteristics given was 25, with a minimum of 2 and a maximum of 69 characteristics offered. Table 6.3 presents the analysis of all CIA profiles to illustrate the frequency with which relevant characteristics were given and the justification used to support these characteristics.

Similar to the overall data in this study, CIA profiles did not offer the relevant offender characteristics in many cases. Motive was given in slightly more than half the profiles (16 of 28), was often unjustified (7 of 16), and was never justified with statistics or research. The offender characteristic Knowledge of Methods and Materials was not given in any of the CIA profiles. Knowledge of the Victim was the characteristic most likely to be present in the CIA profiles (19 of 28), and when it was given, it was often given without justification or with personal belief as justification (both 8 of 19). Knowledge of the Victim was never justified with research or statistics. Knowledge of the Location was given in 15 of 28 profiles and was likely to be unjustified (5 of 15) or justified with physical evidence (5 of 15). It was justified with statistics or research in only 1 case. Finally, Criminal Skill was given as an offender characteristic in approximately one-fifth of this sample (6 of 28 profiles). When given, it was likely to be unjustified, justified with physical evidence, or justified with personal opinion (2 profiles each), and it was never supported with research or statistics.

Behavioral Evidence Analysis

In this analysis, 12 BEA profiles were examined. These profiles comprised 20% of the total sample. As mentioned previously, the mean number of characteristics given in the BEA profiles studied was 8 ($SD = 10$), with a minimum of 3 and a maximum of 36 characteristics. Table 6.4 presents a summary of the analysis of the 12 BEA

Table 6.3 Frequency and Percentage of Characteristics and Justification Used in CIA Profiles

	Not Given		Given without Justification		Given with Physical Evidence		Given with Stats or Research		Given with Personal Belief or Opinion		
	n	%	*n*	%	*n*	%	*n*	%	*n*	%	Total
Motive	12	43	7	25	5	18	0	0	4	14	28
Methods/ Materials	28	100	0	0	0	0	0	0	0	0	28
Victim	9	32	8	29	3	11	0	0	8	29	28
Location	13	46	5	18	5	18	1	4	4	14	28
Skill	22	79	2	7	2	7	0	0	2	7	28

Table 6.4 Frequency and Percentage of Characteristics and Justification Used in BEA Profiles

	Not Given		Given without Justification		Given with Physical Evidence		Given with Stats or Research		Given with Personal Belief or Opinion		
	n	%	*n*	%	*n*	%	*n*	%	*n*	%	Total
Motive	1	8	0	0	11	92	0	0	0	0	12
Methods/ Materials	10	83	0	0	2	17	0	0	0	0	12
Victim	5	42	0	0	6	50	0	0	1	8	12
Location	5	42	2	17	5	42	0	0	0	0	12
Skill	5	42	0	0	7	58	0	0	0	0	12

profiles in this sample. This table presents the frequencies with which relevant characteristics were offered and the justification used to support these characteristics.

In the BEA profiles, all the relevant characteristics, with the exception of Knowledge of Methods and Materials, were given in more than half of the profiles (Motive = 92%, Knowledge of Victim = 68%, Knowledge of Location = 68%, Criminal Skill = 68%). Physical evidence was most likely used as justification for all relevant offender characteristics. In all 11 profiles in which Motive was given, it was justified using physical evidence. Similarly, physical evidence was used as justification in all 7 profiles that gave Criminal Skill as an offender characteristic, both profiles that gave offender Knowledge of Method and Materials, as well as 6 of 7 profiles that included Knowledge of the Victim. Knowledge of the Location was presented in 7 of the 12 profiles, and it was justified by physical evidence in 5 cases and unjustified in the other 2 cases.

Diagnostic Evaluations

For this study, 10 DE profiles were analyzed, comprising 17% of the total sample. As noted in the results section, the mean number of characteristics given in the DE profiles was 58 (*SD* = 52), with a large range (minimum, 6; maximum, 155). Table 6.5 provides a summary of the analysis of the DE profiles presenting the frequencies with which relevant characteristics were given and the justification offered in support.

In the 10 DE profiles, the frequency of presentation of the relevant characteristics was less than 40% for each. In fact, Criminal Skill was not present in any of the profiles. Similarly, for Knowledge of Methods and Materials and Knowledge of the Location, only 1 profile presented the characteristic, and it was not justified. Motive was given in only 4 profiles, and it was given with no justification in 2 of these 4, whereas physical evidence and personal belief were

Table 6.5 Frequency and Percentage of Characteristics Given and Justification Used in DE Profiles

	Not Given		Given without Justification		Given with Physical Evidence		Given with Stats or Research		Given with Personal Belief or Opinion		
	n	%	*n*	%	*n*	%	*n*	%	*n*	%	Total
Motive	6	60	2	20	1	10	0	0	1	10	10
Methods/ Materials	9	90	1	10	0	0	0	0	0	0	10
Victim	7	70	1	10	0	0	1	10	1	10	10
Location	9	90	1	10	0	0	0	0	0	0	10
Skill	10	100	0	0	0	0	0	0	0	0	10

given as justification in 1 case each. Knowledge of the Victim was given in 3 profiles, with justification being evenly split between no justification, research or statistics, and personal belief with 1 case each.

Investigative Psychology

This study analyzed eight IP profiles, which comprised 14% of the total sample. The mean number of characteristics given in these IP profiles was 14 ($SD = 14$), with a minimum of 2 and a maximum of 39 characteristics. Table 6.6 presents a summary of the analysis of the eight IP profiles, the frequencies with which relevant characteristics were given, and the justification used to support these characteristics.

Knowledge of Methods and Materials was not given in any of the eight IP profiles. Motive was presented in three of the eight profiles. Of these three,

Table 6.6 Frequency and Percentage of Characteristics Given and Justification Used in IP Profiles

	Not Given		Given without Justification		Given with Physical Evidence		Given with Stats or Research		Given with Personal Belief or Opinion		
	n	%	*n*	%	*n*	%	*n*	%	*n*	%	Total
Motive	5	63	2	25	0	0	0	0	1	13	8
Methods/ Materials	8	100	0	0	0	0	0	0	0	0	8
Victim	6	75	1	13	0	0	0	0	1	13	8
Location	5	63	1	13	0	0	1	13	1	13	8
Skill	5	63	1	13	1	13	1	13	0	0	8

Motive was unjustified in two cases, and it was justified by personal opinion in the remaining case. Knowledge of the Victim was present in two IP profiles, and it was unjustified in one case and justified with personal opinion in the other case. Knowledge of the Location and Criminal Skill were each present in three profiles. When Knowledge of the Location was given, it was unjustified in one case and justified by research or statistics and personal opinion in one case each. When Criminal Skill was given, it was unjustified in one case and justified by physical evidence and research or statistics in one case each.

DISCUSSION

To meet their goals, criminal profiles must offer offender characteristics that will assist the decision-making process in criminal investigations, thereby allowing the investigation to move forward. Profile characteristics that are confusing, unnecessary, distracting, or not detailed enough to be acted on will not allow the goals of profiling to be met and are therefore a waste of time and resources (Baeza, 1999). With that being the case, the current study examined whether the profile characteristics offered in profiles are, in fact, progressing the decision-making process in investigations.

In many practices, there is a major difference between theory and practice. This research also considered whether profiling is, in practice, based on the theories that underpin a particular method (i.e., does IP use research, and does BEA use evidence?). A validation study focusing strictly on investigative relevance has not been conducted on a criminal profiling sample in the past, and this research therefore fills an existing void. Although the background theory of many profiling methods may seem valid, it is crucial to examine whether these are being applied and, if so, to determine whether the approaches are actually helpful. This issue becomes more salient when issues of public safety and miscarriages of justice are factored in.

For the current study, 59 profiles were examined to determine how many offender characteristics were offered, what investigatively relevant characteristics were offered, and what justification was offered to support these characteristics. This information was then analyzed to determine what characteristics were generally offered in profiles as a whole and how the characteristics differed based on the varying methodologies employed by the profilers.

Interpretation of Results

In general, this research found that three of the four profiling methods provided more investigatively irrelevant characteristics than relevant ones, with

BEA being the exception. It has been shown in this research that for the most part, there are 5 characteristics that can be considered relevant to criminal investigations. However, the average number of characteristics given in the current sample was more than 25. Assuming that all 5 relevant characteristics were present (which was the case in very few profiles), there was still an average of 20 irrelevant characteristics given in these profiles that have the potential to confuse and distract investigators. However, as previously stated, different offender characteristics may be relevant depending on the case and the evidence provided in their support (Baeza, 1999). Therefore, in some of the sample the characteristics given above and beyond the relevant 5 may have been relevant to that case. However, this surely cannot be the case with all of the characteristics given. More important, this analysis showed that in many of the profiles, not only were there a large number of characteristics that were irrelevant but also the 5 deemed relevant were not provided. Certainly this presents a problem.

For the sample as a whole, more than 40% of the profiles did not offer at least one of the relevant characteristics. This percentage increased to almost 95% for the characteristic Knowledge of Methods and Materials. This illustrates a serious problem in the profiling community because it indicates that as many as 19 in 20 profiles may neglect to include at least one relevant offender characteristic that would assist the investigation. This may be a result of four factors. First, not enough evidence may be presented to the profiler, making it impossible for the profiler to give insight into certain behavior. Second, there is too much reliance on statistical comparison. If a comparison characteristic cannot be found in the chosen data set, that characteristic will not be offered by the statistical profiler. For instance, in the two research-based profiling methodologies (CIA and IP), Knowledge of Methods and Materials was not given in any of the profiles sampled. In the evidence-based BEA, it was offered in nearly 17% of profiles and was always justified with physical evidence. It may be that the research-based approaches' focus on previous cases leads profilers to fail to search for peculiar knowledge of methods and materials in each case. Third, not including one or more relevant characteristics may be due to the types of crimes and criminals that are being profiled. Perhaps the crimes profiled in this sample did not involve any behavior requiring specialized knowledge. Finally, the absence of these characteristics may be a reflection of the inherent lack of attention to detail, as well as the lack of specific knowledge that would be necessary for a profiler to recognize the offender characteristic. In statistical approaches, where the profiler often has little background in behavioral and forensic science, the profiler may be unqualified to conduct the requisite examination of the evidence and therefore unable to discern this characteristic when present. Any one of these four factors, or a combination of them, may explain the tendency to not recognize or include the characteristic. Identifying these elements highlights the need to not only understand the physical evidence and its meaning but also to work from a base of evidence and not just a degree of similarity.

Knowledge of Methods and Materials was not the only characteristic absent from much of the sample. Nearly three-fourths of the profiles did not provide an assessment of Criminal Skill, which may inform the profiler not only of past crimes committed but also of the offender's contact with the criminal justice system. This cannot be explained by an absence of criminal skill given the prevalence of past offending, especially in the case of serial offenders. In fact, any absence of criminal skill and the evidentiary basis for this should be clearly stated by the profiler and not just assumed or surmised. Twice as many BEA profiles offered Criminal Skill as did CIA profiles, and this was always justified by physical evidence when offered. CIA profiles offered this characteristic in only approximately 20% of profiles, and it was usually unjustified, justified with physical evidence, or justified with personal belief. IP offered Criminal Skill in 40% of the profiles, and when offered, it was unjustified, justified with physical evidence, and justified with research and statistics in one case each. This fact is notable because in theory, IP and CIA profiles are research based, and this characteristic is only justified by research in one case between the two methods.

The other relevant characteristics followed a similar pattern as the IP and CIA profiles. The fact that these offender characteristics are rarely justified by research means that it is impossible to trace a line of reasoning employed in producing the characteristics or to question the veracity of both the profile and the research on which they are meant to be based. Most often, all the characteristics in these profiles were unjustified or justified with personal belief (or physical evidence in a small number of cases). In fact, in none of these profiles was research and statistics the most likely justification for any characteristic. This is clearly not consistent with the research-based theories of CIA and IP. In both methods, the current case is compared with research on other similar cases to determine likely offender characteristics based on common characteristics of convicted offenders (Ainsworth, 2001; Ressler et al, 1988). The question that logically follows is that if IP and CIA profilers are not using research to justify these characteristics, what theories (if any) are being employed? Judging by the results, it appears that these methods are more likely to use personal belief as support for offender characteristics, when they employ any justification at all. This practice is not what each method promotes as its basis, also suggesting that these methods are much more idiosyncratic than these profilers claim. This mismatch between theory and practice clearly indicates a problem worthy of further investigation.

Conversely, the BEA method is in theory driven by evidence. The theoretical underpinnings of BEA were supported in this analysis because almost all of the relevant characteristics offered used physical evidence as justification for their inclusion. In fact, all but three characteristics in the BEA profiles used physical evidence as support. This match between theory and practice may suggest that BEA profiles are more likely to meet their intended goals.

By extension, BEA profiles were generally more likely to contain investigatively relevant characteristics. This can almost certainly be attributed to the fact that the characteristics deemed relevant in this analysis parallel those endorsed by BEA as being both necessary and inferable in a criminal profile (Turvey, 2008). As discussed, the list of characteristics deemed relevant in this study was produced after an independent and exhaustive process. A list of many offender characteristics given in criminal profiles was gathered, and each characteristic was then analyzed to determine relevance based on the definition proposed by Petherick (2007) and Baeza (1999). The similarities between the characteristics judged to be relevant and the BEA method is not surprising given that BEA is the only method that defines and strives for investigative relevance and decreasing investigative distractions.

CONCLUSION

Profiles are designed to assist investigators by narrowing suspect pools and providing new avenues of inquiry. Any information provided within the profile that does not assist in reaching these goals is left open to misinterpretation and is therefore potentially damaging to the investigative effort (Turvey, 2008).

Based on the findings of this study, it is clear that some profiling approaches maintain investigative relevance better than others. It has been illustrated herein that there is a major discrepancy between the theories and practice of research-based profiling methodologies. This issue needs to be addressed before the profiling community can move forward. It is imperative to the integrity of this community that those working within it adhere more strictly to the philosophies of examination they endorse. Simply relying on a statistical average may reduce the credibility of profiling, delay investigations, further endanger the public, and increase the possibility of a miscarriage of justice. Clearly, some individuals are aware of the issues of relevance, making concerted efforts to maintain relevance in every instance, whereas others are not so concerned with their blanket approach. The failure of many to recognize the importance of offering investigatively relevant investigative support is not only irresponsible but also may be unethical. This chapter has exposed such shortcomings, and in so doing it may lend a hand in bringing the importance of investigative relevance to the fore.

The study discussed here is the first of its kind, and it has opened the door for future research to further the criminal profiling process and therefore assist law enforcement in its investigations. It is hoped that in the future, investigative relevance will become the new measure on which profiling practices are gauged. This will further expose the shortcomings of some methods and perhaps bring about a resolution while acknowledging the usefulness of other methods and the assistance they may provide.

Questions

1. Which of the following is not an investigatively relevant characteristic according to Ferguson?
   a. Motive
   b. Knowledge of methods and materials
   c. Knowledge of the victim
   d. Intelligence
   e. Knowledge of the crime scene
2. Which of the following is not one of the goals of profiling according to Holmes and Holmes?
   a. To provide investigating authorities with a social and psychological evaluation of the offender
   b. To narrow the suspect pool
   c. To provide a psychological assessment of items found in possession of the offender
   d. To provide interviewing and interrogation strategies
   e. Identifying the suspect from a suspect pool
3. What does Rossmo argue of the decision-making process as far as profiling is concerned?
   a. That it must assist in the investigative decision-making process
   b. That it must help develop a suspect from the suspect pool
   c. That is must provide a probable list of characteristics
   d. That only criminal investigators should be trained as profilers
   e. None of the above
4. Criminal profiling is only of use in the investigative phase; beyond that, it has no use. *True or false?*
5. More information is not better in criminal profiling. *True or false?*
6. It is the responsibility of the criminal profiler to demonstrate how conclusions are relevant. *True or false?*
7. Inductive methods usually argue for a smaller number of offender characteristics. *True or false?*
8. With regard to investigative relevance, what is the difference between inductive and deductive methods in terms of the characteristics offered?
9. List and describe some of the inputs of criminal profiling.
10. List and describe the common outputs of criminal profiling.

REFERENCES

Ainsworth, P. (2001). Offender Profiling and Crime Analysis. Devon, UK: Willan.

Ault, R., & Reese, J. (1980). A psychological assessment of crime profiling. FBI Law Enforcement Bulletin, 49(3), 22–25.

Baeza, J. (1999). Investigative Relevance, Paper presented at the 1st Annual Academy of Behavioral Profiling Meeting, Monterey, CA.

Copson, G. (1995). Coals to Newcastle? Part 1: a study of offender profiling. Police Research Group Special Interest Series Paper 7. London: Home Office.

Geberth, V. (1996). Practical Homicide Investigation: Tactics, Procedures and Forensic Techniques (3rd ed.). Boca Raton, FL: CRC Press.

Holmes, R., & Holmes, S. (2002). Profiling Violent Crimes: An Investigative Tool (3rd ed.). Thousand Oaks, CA: Sage.

Homant, R., & Kennedy, D. (1998). Psychological aspects of crime scene profiling: Validity research. Criminal Justice and Behavior, 25(3), 319–343.

Muller, D. (2000). Criminal profiling: Real science or just wishful thinking? Homicide Studies, 4(3), 234–264.

O'Hara, C., & O'Hara, G. (2003). Fundamentals of Criminal Investigation (7th ed.). Springfield, IL: Thomas.

O'Toole, M. (2004). Criminal profiling: The FBI uses criminal investigative analysis to solve crimes. In J. Campbell & D. DeNevi (Eds.), Profilers: Leading Investigators Take You Inside the Criminal Mind. Amherst, MA: Prometheus.

Petherick, W. (2007). Critical profiling: A qualitative and quantitative analysis of methods and content. Unpublished doctoral dissertation. Bond University, Robina, Queensland, Australia.

Pinizzotto, A. (1984). Forensic psychology: Criminal personality profiling. Journal of Police Science and Administration, 12(1), 32–40.

Pinizzotto, A., & Finkel, N. (1990). Criminal personality profiling: An outcome and process study. Law and Human Behavior, 14(3), 215–233.

Ressler, R. K., Burgees, A. W., & Douglas, J. E. (1988). Sexual homicides: Patterns and motives.New York: Lexington Books.

Rossmo, D. (2000). Geographic Profiling. Boca Raton, FL: CRC Press.

Turvey, B. (2002). Criminal Profiling: An Introduction to Behavioral Evidence Analysis (2nd ed.). Burlington, MA: Academic Press.

Turvey, B. (2008). Criminal Profiling: An Introduction to Behavioral Evidence Analysis (3rd ed.). Burlington, MA: Academic Press.

CHAPTER 7

Metacognition in Criminal Profiling

Barry Woodhouse and Wayne Petherick

KEY TERMS

Metacognition: The knowledge and awareness one has of his or her own cognitive processes.

Metacognitive monitoring: An individual's ability to reflect and exhibit self-regulation over one's thinking.

The above average effect: When individuals believe themselves to be more competent than they actually are.

Competence: The ability to do something with accuracy, efficiency, and reliability.

CONTENTS

INTRODUCTION

As with many professions, one of the more serious problems that confronts the profiling community is that of the inept examiner. Deliberately unethical behavior is one thing, but ongoing incompetence because of profiler ignorance is something else entirely. In some instances, ignorance is the result of a metacognitive deficit caused by a lack of study, a lack of training, or a general lack of mental dexterity. In such instances, the profiler will continually do the wrong thing, such as using flawed methods and erroneous logic, because he lacks the ability to recognize his own ineptitude; the profiler cannot perceive when his methods and reasoning are wrong or why, let alone that they should be corrected and how.

Although discussed in Turvey (2008), this chapter represents the first comprehensive review of *metacognition* and how it applies to the field of criminal profiling.

145

It is further acknowledgment that the problem exists and it impacts the profession in a negative manner. This chapter first provides a review of the literature and then reports the results of Woodhouse's research on the subject. This chapter closes with basic recommendations on how to overcome metacognitive deficits.

METACOGNITION

The practice of criminal profiling varies significantly from its portrayal in the popular media. Although many unfamiliar with the practice view it as a highly credible source of investigative information, Turvey (2008) notes that the field is replete with examples of incompetent assessment and illogical inferences. Unfortunately, many criminal profilers also display a marked inability to learn from their mistakes and continue to use flawed strategies and methods.

Turvey (2008) notes that although errors within criminal profiling may take a number of forms, such as evidence being misinterpreted or conclusions rendered that do not match the evidence as a result of bias or shoddy work practices, these mistakes are sometimes the result of a common underlying deficit in metacognition. This means that many such mistakes result from an individual examiner's incapacity to know when he is wrong and subsequently fail to correct his course in the face of errors when presented with them.

Metacognition is recognized as an established concept in cognitive psychology. It is defined by Mayer (2003) as one's knowledge and awareness of her cognitive processes, and it can be traced back to Flavell's (1971) early work on metamemory. Alternate definitions describe metacognition as "knowledge and cognition about cognitive phenomena" (Flavell, 1979, p. 906) and "knowledge and regulation of cognition" (Brown, 1978, p. 77). Simply stated, metacognition can be explained as "learning about learning" or, as Turvey (2008) suggests, "thinking about thinking," and it refers to strategies and understanding we apply to our everyday lives—how some of these structures are sound and result in favorable outcomes, whereas others do not and should be disregarded.

Kruger and Dunning (1999) suggest that metacognitive deficits are evident when individuals fail to alter their behavior, even in the face of evidence that their thinking strategies lead to poor reasoning. Not only do these individuals reach erroneous conclusions and make bad decisions from them, but they lack the competence to recognize it. Kruger and Dunning provide a case example to illustrate the concept (p. 1121):

> In 1995, McArthur Wheeler walked into two Pittsburgh banks and robbed them in broad daylight, with no visible attempt at disguise. He was arrested later that night, less than an hour after videotapes of him taken from surveillance cameras were broadcast on the 11 o'clock news. When police later showed him the surveillance tapes, Mr. Wheeler

stared in incredulity. "But I wore the juice," he mumbled. Apparently, Mr. Wheeler was under the impression that rubbing one's face with lemon juice rendered it invisible to videotape cameras (Fuocco, 1996).

This metacognitive deficit has been demonstrated across a number of areas, where participants who scored in the bottom quartile on assessments of humor, logic, and grammar systematically overestimated their own performance and level of ability (Kruger & Dunning, 1999). Individuals who estimated themselves to be in the 62nd percentile rather than the 12th were deficient in metacognitive skill, or ability to distinguish accurate responses from inaccurate ones. It was also shown that by improving participants' skills, there were gains in metacognitive *competence* resulting in improved responses. In essence, Kruger and Dunning showed that incompetent individuals were unable to accurately assess their own level of skill and therefore believed themselves to be performing well, and that some simple instruction about their failures led to an increase in the ability to recognize and subsequently control for them.

METACOGNITIVE MONITORING

The concept of *metacognitive monitoring* (also known as metacognitive competency; see Wang, 1992) posited by Maki, Shields, Easton-Wheeler, and Lowery-Zacchili (2005) can further aid in explaining the ongoing flaws of thinking evidenced in the profiling community. This cognitive process refers to an individual's ability to reflect on and judge his or her own performance and is crucial for overcoming a metacognitive deficit. This is a good place to make clear that the ability to reflect on your own work product (or having others do it for you in the form of honest peer review) is highly underrated and undoubtedly one of the strongest safeguards against metacognitive error.

Metacognitive monitoring (competency) is a crucial aspect of learning. The ability to reflect and exhibit self-regulation over one's thinking has been demonstrated to be one of the prime differences between low-achieving, at-risk students and stronger achievers (Wang, 1992). The inability to appraise oneself robs incompetent individuals of the means to accurately appraise their abilities and usually results in inflated self-assessments. Termed the *above average effect* by Kruger and Dunning (1999), this phenomenon occurs when individuals believe themselves to be more competent than they actually are. This better than average effect may be a factor, in some instances at least, when one overidentifies with an organization one belongs to or works for or in situations in which an individual's assistance is sought because of his employer or celebrity rather than proven work product. Here, the individual will harness himself with the perception that he is better than he actually is, because if he were not good, there would not be so many requests for his assistance. In reality, there may be no link between the individual's ability and being sought out.

The above average effect has not previously been examined within profiling but has been demonstrated across a number of other domains. For example, business managers have been shown to consider themselves more competent than a "typical" manager (Larwood & Wittaker, 1977), football players have been shown to believe they have a greater "football sense" than teammates (Felson, 1981), and high school students have been shown to believe they possess more eloquent written expression and leadership ability than their peers (College Board, 1976–1977, as cited in Kruger & Dunning, 1999). These concerns are at issue in the profiling community when individual profilers fail to understand their own intellectual strengths and weaknesses, as well as to grasp and apply basic principles and practice standards of investigative and forensic examination (Turvey, 2008).

THE ROLE OF COMPETENCE

Competence is the ability to do something, whether it is a simple task or complex analysis, with accuracy, efficiency, and reliability. Competence has an important influence on metacognitive ability. Research in the area of expertise reveals that novices, or those individuals unfamiliar with an area or subject, possess poorer metacognitive skills than their more experienced counterparts.[1]

This suggests that inexperienced individuals tend not to possess the degree or depth of metacognitive ability necessary for accurate self-assessment compared to their more accomplished peers. Inaccurate and subsequently inflated self-assessment in conjunction with the inability to recognize poor performance can lead to an inaccurate assumption of good or competent performance (Kruger & Dunning, 1999). This compounds the metacognitive errors and ensures that more useful and successful strategies are not learned. Kruger and Dunning (p. 1122) explain that not only does incompetence rob individuals of the ability to recognize their poor performance but also it leaves them with the "mistaken impression that they are doing just fine."

Turvey (2008) applies this directly to the context of profiling, stating that based on his casework involving the examination of dozens of profiles and related profiler testimony, the majority of profilers are not aware of their own methodological flaws and inconsistent logic, and this is a direct result of their inability to recognize competence and incompetence alike. Because of the volume and frequency of metacognitive profiling errors discovered, Turvey coined the term *metacognitive dissonance* (p. xxxi):

---

[1]For example, Chi, Glaser, and Rees (1982) demonstrated that novices are less accurate than experts in judging the difficulty of physics problems. McPherson and Thomas (1989) also showed that novices were less able than experienced tennis players to accurately evaluate particular strokes in a tennis match.

Metacognitive dissonance: Believing oneself capable of recognizing one's own errors in thinking, reasoning, and learning, despite either a lack of evidence or overwhelming evidence to the contrary. Examples: Believing oneself to be knowledgeable despite a demonstrable lack of knowledge; believing oneself to be incapable of error despite the human condition; believing oneself to be logical in one's reasoning despite regular entrapment by logical fallacies; believing oneself to be completely objective despite the persistence of observer effects.

The causes of metacognitive dissonance cited by Turvey (2008) are numerous, ranging from examiner bias and observer effects to poor training and a lack of formal education in, or study of, the behavioral sciences by so-called "behavioral analysts" engaged in profiling.

THE WOODHOUSE STUDY

This purpose of this study was to explore faults in metacognition. Specifically, the study investigated whether experts and nonexperts are able to discriminate between two profiles: one that contains a number of structural and logical flaws and one that provides a solid evidentiary basis and sound reasoning.

Method

To critically evaluate either profile, participants had to exercise metacognitive skills such as reflecting upon their own level of knowledge and critically evaluating the assertions put forth by the profile's author. This study took a slightly different tact than previous investigations. By examining these two groups, the goal was to assess the level of metacognitive judgment applied in assessing a problem.

It should be noted that the current study was not an attempt to enter into the existing debate relating to profiling methods or to advocate a particular technique or theoretical orientation. Rather, it was performed to gauge the degree to which metacognition plays a role in discriminating between the bad and the good.

In light of previous research on the nature of expertise and the above average effect, it was hypothesized that

1. Experts would rate their knowledge of criminal profiling higher than nonexperts.
2. Nonexpert participants would not be metacognitively equipped to distinguish between Profile 1 and the evidence-based Profile 2, and they would therefore rate both documents highly, with no significant difference.
3. Experts would rate Profile 2 significantly higher than Profile 1 due to their enhanced metacognitive ability to detect its flaws.

Participants

Participants for the study were divided into either an expert or a nonexpert group based on their experience with profiling.

Respondents in the nonexpert sample were drawn from Bond University undergraduate classes unrelated to the area of criminal profiling and consisted of 32 males and 17 females. Ages ranged from 19 to 50 years, with an average age of 26 years ($SD = 5.1$).

The expert sample consisted of Bond University criminology students enrolled in the criminology subjects Criminal Profiling and/or Behavioral Evidence Analysis (BEA). Criminal Profiling, a subject open to both undergraduate and postgraduate students, is an introductory class that canvasses the theoretical backdrop to profiling as well as covering the major profiling methods and their application. BEA is an advanced profiling subject open to both undergraduate and postgraduate students and focuses specifically on the BEA method, providing in-depth coverage of theory and practice. Postgraduate students undertaking the Master of Psychology (Forensics) program were also included because profiling is included in their curriculum. Students from the profiling and BEA classes were recruited between weeks 10 and 12 of the semester to ensure that they had time to develop a more discriminating set of skills relating to criminal profiling. The expert sample consisted of 20 males and 30 females, age 17 to 38 years, with an average age of 24 years ($SD = 4.5$).

Materials

Materials for the study consisted of two criminal profiles. The first of these was a fictional profile conducted by a fictional profiler on a fictional case. The second was a legitimate profile compiled by Brent Turvey. The fictional profile was used because, on examination, it showed significant flaws in structure and logic and thereby gave a good contrast to the legitimate profile.

Both profiles contained statements informing participants that any identifying information within had been removed or substituted to ensure the anonymity of any parties involved.

Fictitious Profile (Profile 1)

This document was retrieved from the Internet and largely follows a narrative format using inductive logic and intuition, with its conclusions based on a highly idiosyncratic interpretation of the evidence.

This profile is a 3,752-word document detailing the stalking and disappearance of Purity Ariadne Knight, a U.S. college student. The document states the authors are Dr. Maria McManus (retired) and Special Agent Dr. Martin Ballard of the FBI, acting as consultants for the Yoknapatawpha County Sheriff's Department (a fictional department). The profile states that the analysis is based on a thorough review of materials submitted to the PsiCore Consulting Group by Detectives Armstrong and Anderson as well as being a culmination of the education, experience, and intuition of the profilers.

The profile also contains a fairly standard caveat that states "this profile is not a substitute for a thorough investigation, and should not be considered inclusive or wholly accurate." Following this, the evidentiary basis for the profile is noted as "one recording from an answering message and one set of photographs taken by the offender at the victim's residence."

Following the caveat, the profile states that it will "reflect a personality profile type believed responsible for the stalking of victim Knight." The profile then details the subheadings of Victimology, Psycholinguistic Analysis, Voice Stress Analysis, Photographic Evidence Report, Offender Characteristics and Traits, Post Offense Behavior, and Post Offense Victim Behavior, which comprise the majority of the report.

Note that although the fictitious profile provides an opinion relating to both the offender and the victim's state of mind, it is used as a poor example of a profile and contains a number of substantial flaws. A critical evaluation of the document reveals that the authors fail to make clear the full circumstances surrounding the offense and assume the reader has some familiarity with the crime. Furthermore, the conclusions tendered by the report frequently lack any evidentiary basis, relying instead on appeals to the authors' experience and authority.

Finally, the report contains a number of technical errors, such as spelling and grammatical mistakes, as well as confusion relating to the qualifications of McManus, identifying her initially as a psychiatrist and later as a psychologist.

Behavioral Evidence Analysis Profile (Profile 2)
Profile 2 was supplied by Brent Turvey and was compiled as work product for a case already past the trial stage in the United States. By the time this study was conducted, the matter to which the profile relates had been before the courts, meaning that the document was now part of the public record.

Prior to its use in the current study, all identifying information was removed from the document and replaced with generic information about the protagonists. The location of the crime scene, names of investigative staff, and dates relating to the investigation were also altered to control for potential familiarity with the gross details of the crime such that participants might judge the document on its "accuracy" rather than quality. To preserve some continuity, the county where the crime occurred was not changed.

Profile 2 is 2,700 words in length and details a double homicide. The majority of the document relates to examination of the physical evidence and includes clear descriptions relating to the location, position, and injuries sustained by both victims as well as a number of assessments addressing the offender's behavior. It also details the perpetrator's attempt to destroy evidence by setting fires, explanation and analysis of the crime scene location and features, precautions taken by the perpetrator, and an assessment of the offender's level of planning and motivation.

As per the methodology of BEA (Turvey, 2008), Profile 2 contains a detailed reconstruction of the criminal event based on physical evidence. It includes lengthy sections examining the position of each victim within the crime scene and the surrounding environment. The document also assesses the limitations of the available evidence, such as detailing the effects of firefighting efforts at the crime scene.

In contrast to Profile 1, Profile 2 is extremely clear in stating the sources of information that contributed to the final report, where this information was obtained, and specifically identifying the agency or examiner for each piece of evidence.

Profile 2 is also far more conservative in the nature of the conclusions it makes, and it specifically cites the evidentiary basis of each inference made. The profile is also clear in explaining the certainty of any conclusions; it provides a list of possible explanations for behavior for which conclusions are equivocal.

Furthermore, Profile 2 clearly defines any terms used. For example, in the Crime Scene Characteristics section, *location type* is defined with citation to the appropriate textual material.

Measures

Both profiles were rated using a 30-item questionnaire asking participants to evaluate their profile across a number of categories. The questionnaire, titled Metacognition in Criminal Profiling (MCP), asked participants to rate the profile according to its technical aspects (e.g., "How would you rate the profile in terms of its correct use of punctuation and spelling?"), use of logic (e.g., "How would you rate the profile in terms of its use of logic?"), applied use (e.g., "How would you rate the profile in terms of its usefulness to investigators?"), use of evidence (e.g., "How would you rate the profile in terms of making clear the evidence that has been examined?"), level of detail (e.g., "How would you rate the amount of background information included within the profile?"), and examination of perpetrator's behavior (e.g., "How would you rate the profile's examination of the perpetrator's level of planning?"). The full MCP is provided in Appendix A.

Responses to question 1 and questions 3 through 27 were scored across a 5-point Likert scale (1 = very bad, 2 = bad, 3 = neither good nor bad, 4 = good, and 5 = excellent). Question 2 ("How often do you believe criminal profiling is used by the authorities or law enforcement agencies?") was scored using a different 5-point Likert scale (1 = almost never, 2 = on unusual cases, 3 = on serious cases, 4 = most serious cases, 5 = all serious cases).

A total score for the MCP was generated by summing the participant's responses for questions 3 through 27. Higher scores indicated the profile rated higher across the categories outlined previously. The minimum possible score was 24 and the maximum 120.

Cronbach's alpha was calculated to assess the MCP's reliability. For a measure to be considered reliable (i.e., measuring the domain it purports to examine), an alpha of .7 or higher is generally required. Analysis revealed the MCP to be reliable ($\alpha = .969$).

Question 8 ("How would you rate the profile in terms of making the credentials of the author clear?") was excluded from the analysis because the BEA profile did not include the appendices containing the author's curriculum vitae; therefore, it could not be meaningfully assessed across this criterion.

A short demographic section was also included to obtain the respondent's age, gender, and highest level of completed education. Following this, three questions were added to examine the participant's previous experience with profiling; two of these were rated with a forced choice (yes/no), whereas the third asked respondents to list from where they obtained their knowledge of criminal profiling (TV & movies, Books, Academic study, Professional work, and Other).

The MCP was developed from scratch due to the fact that no parallel instrument exists to measure metacognition in this way. The measure was developed in collaboration with Petherick.

Development of the instrument was undertaken through a number of stages, beginning with an extensive review of the literature. This was reviewed to develop an appreciation of common mistakes and inconsistencies exhibited within written profiles as well as the strengths and characteristics of a good profile. From these facets, a number of consistent themes emerged that were then used to generate a list of items. These potential items (in excess of 50) were then refined and revised until items best reflecting the aims of the study remained. The final 30 items that comprised the MCP were selected to broadly reflect the facets elicited by the literature search, as well as to highlight the strengths and weaknesses inherent within the profiles selected for the study.

Procedure

Once agreement to participate in the study had been obtained, respondents were given an explanatory statement, a randomly selected profile, and a copy of the MCP. Prior to reading the document, participants were made aware that the profile contained some graphic descriptions of crime scenes, and that they were free to withdraw from the study should this cause them discomfort. Completed questionnaires were returned either by placement in an envelope or through a drop-box to ensure participant anonymity.

Results
Overview

The data was analyzed using the Statistical Package for the Social Sciences version 15. Initial exploration of the data was done through an examination of descriptive statistics to obtain a more comprehensive understanding of each respondent's familiarity with criminal profiling. Following this, a one-way analysis of variance (ANOVA) was conducted to test if experts and nonexpert participants differ significantly in their perceptions of use by law enforcement agencies. A second one-way ANOVA was used to test hypothesis 1 to determine if experts rated their knowledge of profiling significantly higher than nonexperts.

Prior to examining hypotheses 2 and 3, the assumptions for ANOVA were checked (these are provided later). Once the assumptions had been examined, a 2×2 between-subjects factorial ANOVA was conducted.

Descriptive Statistics

Table 7.1 shows the number of participants who have previously heard of (or read about) criminal profiling, as well as those who have been exposed to a written criminal profile prior to participating in the study.

Of the 100 respondents, 82 stated that they had previously heard of criminal profiling, with 51 stating that they had at some point been exposed to a written criminal profile prior to participating in the study.

Contrary to expectation, a more detailed examination of the data revealed that some participants from the nonexpert sample had been exposed to a written profile (18%) in the past, whereas 16% of respondents from the expert sample claimed to have never encountered a written criminal profile.

Table 7.1 Respondents' Familiarity with Criminal Profiling

	Nonexpert		Expert	
	n	%	*n*	%
Heard of				
No	16	32	2	4
Yes	34	68	48	96
Exposed to				
No	41	82	8	16
Yes	9	18	42	84

One-Way ANOVA

To gain a more comprehensive understanding of the expectancies of participants, a one-way ANOVA was conducted to determine if experts and non-experts differ in their belief as to how often criminal profiling is utilized by law enforcement agencies. This relationship was significant ($F(1, 98) = 16.93$, $p < .001$), revealing that nonexperts believed profiling was used more often ($M = 3.58$, $SD = 0.928$) than did experts ($M = 2.76$, $SD = 1.06$).

Hypothesis 1

A second one-way ANOVA was conducted to examine if experts rated their knowledge of criminal profiling as higher than that of nonexperts. This test was significant ($p < .001$), with an examination of the means revealing that experts tended to rate their knowledge of criminal profiling higher ($M = 3.64$, $SD = 0.8$) than did nonexperts ($M = 2.58$, $SD = 0.91$).

2 × 2 Factorial ANOVA (Assumptions)

As with all statistical tests, the ANOVA technique contains a number of assumptions that must be met for this type of testing to be considered appropriate. The first assumption, termed independence of observations, essentially relates to the requirement that data be collected randomly. In the case of this study, the assumption was satisfied by the research design, which ensured that the allocation of profiles to each participant within the sample groups was random.

As seen in Figures 7.1 and 7.2, the distributions of total profile score for experts and nonexperts were normal, although a slight degree of positive skew was evident within the expert sample.

Total profile scores for both Profile 1 and Profile 2 also showed symmetrical distributions. These are illustrated in Figures 7.3 and 7.4.

The second assumption of ANOVA, termed homogeneity of variance, was not met for this study. Essentially, ANOVA assumes that each of the samples included in the analysis contains an equal amount of variance, or that each sample group will vary to approximately the same degree. This is measured statistically using Levene's test of homogeneity of variance and was found to be significant ($p = .034$). As previously stated, this meant that the assumption was violated; however, ANOVA is considered robust to violations of this assumption, especially when samples are equal in size, as was the case in this study.

If the homogeneity of variance assumption is violated, it is suggested that the level of significance be adjusted from .05 to the more conservative level of .01. This means that it is more difficult to detect relationships within the data, although when detected, these relationships are more likely to be "real" rather than the result of error. This alteration was performed in this study.

FIGURE 7.1

Distribution of Profile Score
for the Expert Sample.

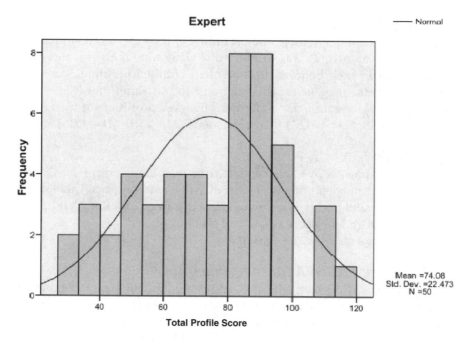

FIGURE 7.2

Distribution of Profile Score
for the Nonexpert Sample.

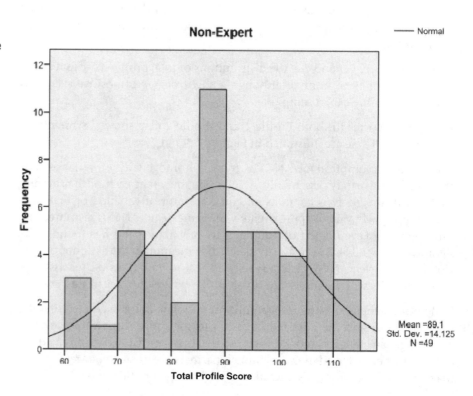

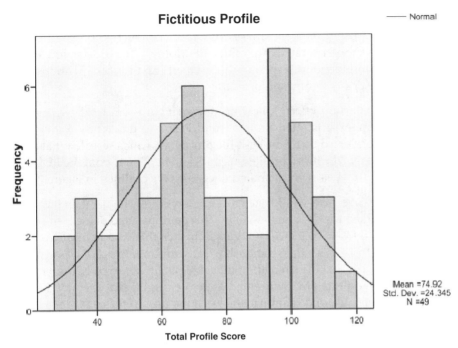

FIGURE 7.3
Distribution of Total Profile
Score for Profile 1.

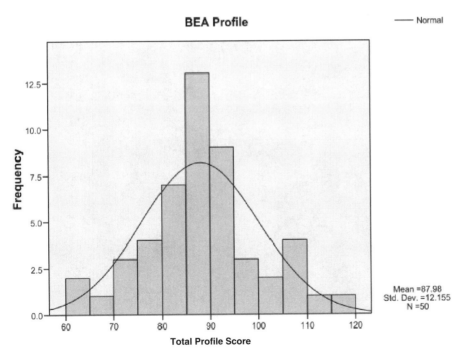

FIGURE 7.4
Distribution of Total Profile
Score for Profile 2.

Hypotheses 2 and 3

A two-way between groups factorial ANOVA was conducted to explore how experts and nonexperts rated two different profiles. The interaction effect between the sample group (expert and nonexpert) and profile (fictitious and BEA) was statistically significant ($p < .001$).

Due to the interaction effect, follow-up univariate analyses were required to determine if nonexperts rated Profile 1 and Profile 2 differently. A one-way ANOVA was conducted using the split-file procedure, which revealed that non-experts did not rate the mock profile as significantly different from the BEA pro-file ($p < .001$). The means and standard deviations are outlined in Figure 7.5.

Hypothesis 2, that experts would rate Profile 2 significantly higher than Profile 1, was also examined with one-way ANOVA. This demonstrated that experts rated the BEA profile ($M = 90.52$, $SD = 12.042$) higher than the fictitious profile ($M = 57.64$, $SD = 17.974$); this relationship was significant ($p < .001$). Essentially what this means is that the strength of the relationship observed is greater than what would be expected by chance and therefore can be explained by the fact that experts were able to discriminate between the two profiles.

FIGURE 7.5

Expert and Nonexpert Ratings of Profiles 1 and 2.

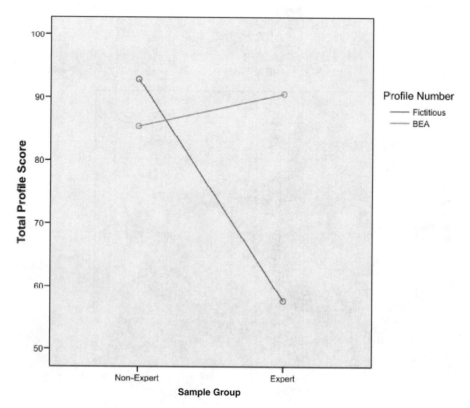

Discussion

Hypothesis 1, that experts would rate their subjective knowledge of profiling higher than nonexperts, was supported. Hypothesis 2, that nonexperts would not distinguish between the profiles, and hypothesis 3, that expert participants would rate Profile 2 higher than Profile 1, were also supported.

The results from this study support the previous findings in the areas of competency, expertise, and metacognition. The fact that nonexperts were not able to distinguish between a low- and a high-quality profile mirrors the findings of Chi, Glaser, and Rees (1982) and McPherson and Thomas (1989), who found that novices were generally less adept at judging difficulty or success within unfamiliar domains.

Kruger and Dunning's (1999) finding that failing to recognize a poor performance will often lead to the assumption of a good performance is also supported by this research. In failing to recognize the discrepancies within Profile 1, participants rated the document highly, indicating that they considered it to be fulfilling the criteria listed in the MCP. In short, by failing to recognize the profile as a poor example, it was assumed to be insightful.

The fact that nonexperts rated the mock profile higher than the BEA profile further supports the previous findings of Kruger and Dunning (1999). In rating Profile 1 higher than its counterpart, nonexperts clearly demonstrated an inability to subject the document to critical evaluation and exercised a general false assumption that the mock profile was correct in its methodology. The fact that experts were clearly able to distinguish between the two profiles and rate them accordingly demonstrates that this assumption is limited to those unfamiliar with the area.

The above average effect (Kruger & Dunning, 1999) is also supported, although in a more limited manner, by the current study. Given that the majority of nonexperts were aware of criminal profiling (65%), with only a small number having been exposed to it (18%), the fact that both profiles were endorsed highly suggests that participants had a great deal of confidence in making evaluations. The fact that no significant difference was noted between the ratings of both profiles indicates that nonexpert participants were not metacognitively equipped to make such judgments accurately.

In addition, the ability of the expert sample to accurately distinguish between the two profiles gives further credence to the idea that some regulation of cognition is being exercised. This in turn supports previous investigations into metacognition and competency that have found robust support for the superior abilities of experts (Chi et al., 1982; McPherson & Thomas, 1989; Kruger & Dunning, 1999).

Overall, the current study provides support for the contention that metacognitive deficits are at least partially responsible for the failure to critically evaluate profiles. It appears that consistent with other areas of metacognition, incompetent (nonexpert) individuals overestimate their own ability and fail to exercise regulation of their cognitive processes. In essence, failing to recognize a bad profile will generally lead to the opposite assumption that it is good.

Although it cannot be ruled out that the difference in ability to rate profiles is a result of experts developing a "profiling-specific" skill base and then applying this when required, this would still require the individual to exercise control and self-monitoring over his or her thoughts and therefore would be considered as metacognition. Furthermore, rating Profile 1 across the criteria included in the MCP instrument required little in the way of profiling-specific skills because respondents were provided the categories with which to assess the document.

The fact that many of the flaws contained within Profile 1 were highly transparent also provides a compelling argument against a profiling-specific skill base, as opposed to any effect from metacognition. None of the questions included within the MCP required participants to utilize a prior knowledge base, nor did they need to have an in-depth understanding of the mechanics underlying criminal profiling. Rather, respondents needed to exercise regulation over their cognition when rating their profile against the provided criteria.

It is also possible that the mock profile was granted additional credibility due to the fact that it resembles many media portrayals of profiling. In reading this document and having an alleged ex-FBI agent as one of its authors, participants unfamiliar with the discipline may have believed that these elements added a degree of authority or accuracy to the conclusions. In contrast, the BEA profile contained no information relating to the author's credentials or experience in the area, and it provided less of a basis for speculation relating to the author's professional experience and ability.

Differences between the expert and nonexpert samples' expectations in how commonly profiling is used also highlight the possibility of the media impacting the attitudes of respondents. Experts and nonexperts differed significantly in their belief regarding how commonly law enforcement agencies utilize the services of criminal profilers, with nonexperts believing it to be far more common. Although this illustrates the lack of applied knowledge relating to the discipline between the two subgroups, it may also be indicative of profiling's popularity within the media, and the popular misconception that it is a commonly used tool of law enforcement.

Methodological Considerations

Although the study is considered to be a good introduction to an area that has not previously been researched, it is by its very nature exploratory and therefore contains a number of methodological factors that could be improved in future investigations.

The MCP questionnaire, used in this study to measure the dependent variable, is the primary methodological consideration within this study. Although the measure demonstrated excellent reliability, the questionnaire's high Cronbach's alpha may indicate that some of the items within the measure are redundant. Future investigations may seek to alter the measure to assess a broader range of domains or to reduce the total number of items to minimize redundancy.

The choice of wording for the Likert scale on the MCP (i.e., very bad, bad, neither good nor bad, good, and excellent) may also have influenced participants' responses due to the scale's labeling. Replication of this research would benefit from rewording the responses on the Likert scale to a more neutral tone, thereby reducing the possibility of response bias.

Finally, the study may have benefited from a more accurate measure relating to how respondents attained their knowledge of criminal profiling. Although a question addressing this was included within the MCP, participants often responded multiple times or in an inconsistent manner. For example, participants listed multiple sources from where they obtained their knowledge of profiling, with no indication as to which contributed the most. Therefore, it was not possible to gain a full understanding of how respondents obtained their knowledge of criminal profiling or what impact the media may have had on their expectations. This is especially important because the media is likely to be the greatest source of knowledge for nonexpert participants, and this presentation of profiling is likely to seriously impact their expectancies.

Implications

Given the nature of the study, it is necessary to be somewhat conservative when expanding on the possible implications of the research. It was, however, convincingly demonstrated that nonexperts were not equipped to draw distinctions between good and bad examples of profiling and therefore should not be placed in a position to evaluate such documents. In short, it seems that any evaluation of profiling should be conducted by subject matter experts rather than by nonexperts, even though they may be well educated in other areas. To be perfectly clear on this issue, it could be argued that the skills of an individual schooled in profiling would be more effective and useful than, for example, those of a psychologist or psychiatrist simply because they are behavioral scientists. In other words, profiling skills are domain specific.

It should also be noted that Kruger and Dunning (1999) suggest a relatively simple solution for incompetence. The authors agree with Miller's (1993, p. 4) assertion that "it is one of the essential features of such incompetence that the person so afflicted is incapable of knowing that he is incompetent. To have such knowledge would already be to remedy a good portion of the offense." In practice, it may be that simply informing an individual of his or her relative lack of experience or competence in a given area will be enough to impart positive change.

The study also has important implications for those individuals who are currently working as profilers. Although Turvey (2008) argues that profiling is replete with examples of incompetent assessments and illogical inferences, this study gives some hope in the finding that experts possessed a good ability to critically evaluate profiling documents. This can be seen as providing support for Turvey's contention that metacognitive deficits are responsible for many of the commonly committed errors within profiling.

Furthermore, Turvey's (2008) concept of metacognitive dissonance, whereby an individual believes himself to be capable of recognizing errors in logic and reasoning despite considerable evidence to the contrary, also has a number of important implications for profiling in general. Although becoming aware of one's own metacognitive deficits is a positive outcome and a partial remedy to future mistakes, this is not enough by itself. Turvey contends that to avoid the continuation of past mistakes, profilers must raise their level of metacognitive competency and fully embrace the scientific method, logic, and critical thinking. By embracing more rigorous methods of thought, profilers will become more competent practitioners and increase standards within the discipline.

This study has demonstrated that nonexperts display a surprising inability to recognize what would be considered by experts to be fairly obvious flaws within a profile. This has serious implications for law enforcement and legal contexts, in which profiling is becoming increasingly popular, yet is likely to be reviewed and utilized by individuals unfamiliar with the area. This study demonstrated that those with some exposure to profiling at a formal level are more discriminating in their assessment of quality than their counterparts. This perhaps calls for a greater level of education among end users of profiling so that they may exercise a similar level of critical assessment. In this way, the quality of work product should improve because consumers will essentially demand it.

Woskett, Coyle, and Lincoln (2007) examined the attitudes of legal practitioners (solicitors, barristers, and crown prosecutors) toward criminal profiling. This research used four vignettes taken from profiles to assess the validity of profiling as expert evidence, with the results showing that on none of the items measured did the opinions reach the positive range. Of interest is the finding that 69% of the lawyers were only partially aware of what is involved in profiling, with 54% stating they are unaware of the different techniques and methods employed by profilers. As such, this study, to determine whether profiling is a valid and probative form of evidence, is putting the proverbial cart before the horse. That is, without a detailed understanding of *what* lawyers know, and *how* they acquired that knowledge, their assessments of profiles may be redundant in light of the findings of the research herein. Having put forward this concern, it should be noted that the legal professionals could likely make a determination as to whether the profile met current legal standards as evidence. However, this would first require the quality of the profile to be assessed, and it is here that metacognition will come into play.

A number of potential remedies arise from the previous discussion that will go some way to addressing the problems of metacognitive impairment. The following list is by no means exhaustive or exclusive, but it is considered a good starting point:

1. Consumers of profiling should do all that they can to inform themselves of the process, and the method that was employed in any given case, rather than relying on uncritical acceptance of the conclusions by virtue of the grandiosity of the profiler or the agency to which the profiler belongs. Profilers should also take time to educate end users in the type of profiling used and in the way the evidence was examined and how the conclusions were formed. To be specific, this means that profiles should contain a full account of the logic and reasoning used in the profile and include a description of the evidence on which the profile is based and how this was factored into the offender characteristics offered.

2. The profiling community as a whole needs to stop engaging in gross levels of intellectual dishonesty. This means that researchers, educators, and practitioners need to be honest and equitable in their accounts of profiling, which is currently not the case. For example, a number of articles and texts that allegedly contain detailed accounts of profiling theory and practice fail to include discussions of any methods other than their own despite extensive literature on them.[2] It is almost as though these authors believe that by not acknowledging other practitioners and approaches, they can deny their existence and/or utility. Conversely, it may be that in acknowledging these other profiling methods, they run the risk of "making them real," thereby validating any claims other authors make against their own paradigms. A short list of research suffering from this includes Dowden, Bennell, and Bloomfield (2007); Godwin (2002); Canter (2000); and Napier and Baker (2005).[3]

---

[2] Or perhaps worse, misinterpret or incorrectly cite the theoretical underpinnings of an approach. Either way, it is a problem of considerable importance.

[3] Again, this is a short list. A critical examination of the literature reveals the problem to be much more systemic than these few references would have us believe. This would be a project worthy of research for any interested graduate student or doctoral candidate.

3. More research needs to be conducted in the area of metacognition in criminal profiling. As discussed previously, said research could address any methodological problems with the current research. For example, restructuring the MCP, using a larger sample, and including profilers and police investigators would help determine the extent to which metacognition is a problem. As discussed by Goldsworthy (2001), many police investigators believe that profiling is investigatively relevant, and so inclusion of this sample would be worthwhile.

4. Because profiling could be considered a subdiscipline of behavioral science, it is also necessary to ensure that profilers are trained in the behavioral sciences. This would actually exclude many in the current profiling community who are typically trained under the law enforcement short course model and who hold, at best in many cases, academic qualifications in education, management, law, chemistry, human physiology, and criminal justice (administration).[4] This would ensure that they are not only better equipped to understand and interpret complex issues surrounding human, and by extension, criminal behavior but also they will be better equipped to understand any impact this may have on their ability to reach rational and logical conclusions from a given set of facts. This is, however, not a given. As stated previously, it appears that profiling knowledge is domain specific. Consequently, formal education in the behavioral sciences should be tempered with more advanced education in criminal profiling.

CONCLUSION

This study demonstrated that nonexperts did not possess the metacognitive ability to discriminate between two alternate criminal profiles, one of which provided a solid evidentiary basis, whereas the other was inherently flawed. Profiling "experts" showed a higher level of metacognitive ability and were able to rate each profile appropriately. The study provides support for the contention that metacognitive skills are responsible for the failure to critically evaluate profiles, and that by failing to evaluate a profile, a nonexpert will assume it to be accurate and insightful.

This is important because the end consumers of profiling are typically detectives with little to no exposure to the finer points of theory and practice in

---

[4] Note that many criminal justice programs are housed within social science departments. However, this does not by extension make them social sciences. Many such programs are more concerned with the administrative or procedural side of criminology—that is, the role, structure, and function of the police, courts, and prisons. They may have little, if any, relevance to the interpretation of actual behavior.

criminal profiling and may thus be inadequately informed to make an educated decision about the quality of any profile. This may be more likely in the case of a serial crime task force, where it is likely a profiler will be called given the repetitive nature of the crime and the greater threat to public safety.

As previously stated, one of the ways to argue for the validity of profiling or specifically the skills of an individual profiler, is to claim that if the profiler were no good, he or she would not get as much work. This thinking is also faulty because, as this research has demonstrated, nonexperts, many of whom are end consumers, are simply not adept at identifying poor work product. Having these metacognitively impaired individuals decide what is good and bad, and by extension, who is good and bad, is wrong and will most likely lead to the increased perception that all profiling is bad and of little use. This is definitely not the case, and we as a community should be doing what we can to educate and illuminate. In this way, we can help overcome metacognitive deficits, thereby assisting end consumers in their discrimination between good and bad criminal profiles.

Questions

1. Define metacognition.
2. Briefly describe the findings of Kruger and Dunning (1999) with regard to metacognition.
3. List the hypotheses of the current study and whether these hypotheses were supported or not.
4. The study found no difference in the ability to rate the profiles between the expert and nonexpert groups. *True or false?*
5. The incongruity between individuals believing themselves to be capable of recognizing their own errors in thinking and reasoning in the face of sufficient evidence to the contrary is known as _____ _____.

REFERENCES

Brown, A. L. (1978). Knowing when, where, and how to remember: A problem of metacognition. Advances in Instructional Psychology, 1, 77–165.

Canter, D. (2000). Offender profiling and criminal differentiation. Legal and Criminological Psychology, 5, 23–46.

Chi, M. T. H., Glaser, R., & Rees, E. (1982). Expertise in problem solving. In R. Sternberg (Ed.), Advances in the Psychology of Human Intelligence (Vol. 1, pp. 17–76). Hillsdale, NJ: Erlbaum.

Dowden, C., Bennell, C., & Bloomfield, S. (2007). Advances in offender profiling: A systematic review of the literature over the past three decades. Journal of Police and Criminal Psychology, 22, 44–56.

Felson, R. B. (1981). Ambiguity and bias in the self-concept. Social Psychology Quarterly, 44, 64–69.

Flavell, J. H. (1971). First discussant's comments: What is memory development the development of? Human Development, 14, 272–278.

Flavell, J. H. (1979). Metacognition and cognitive monitoring: A new area of cognitive developmental inquiry. American Psychologist, 34, 906–911.

Godwin, G. M. (2002). Reliability, validity, and utility of criminal profiling typologies. Journal of Police and Criminal Psychology, 17(1), 1–18.

Goldsworthy, T. (2001). Criminal profiling: Is it investigatively relevant? Journal of Behavioral Profiling, 2(1).

Kruger, J., & Dunning, D. (1999). Unskilled and unaware of it: How difficulties in recognizing one's own incompetence lead to inflated self-assessments. Journal of Personality and Social Psychology, 77(6), 1121–1134.

Larwood, L., & Whittaker, W. (1977). Magerial myopia: Self-serving biases in organizational planning. Journal of Applied Psychology, 15, 73–80.

Maki, R. H., Shields, M., Easton-Wheeler, A., & Lowery-Zacchili, T. (2005). Individual difference in absolute and relative metacomprehension accuracy. Journal of Educational Psychology, 97, 723–731.

Mayer, R. (2003). Learning and Instruction. Upper Saddle River, NJ: Pearson.

McPherson, S. L., & Thomas, J. R. (1989). Relation of knowledge and performance in boys' tennis: Age and expertise. Journal of Experimental Child Psychology, 48, 190–211.

Miller, W. I. (1993). Humiliation. Ithaca, NY: Cornell University Press.

Napier, M. R., & Baker, K. P. (2005). Criminal personality profiling. In S. H. James & J. J. Nordby (Eds.), Forensic Science: An Introduction to Scientific and Investigative Techniques (2nd ed.). Boca Raton, FL: CRC Press.

Turvey, B. (Ed.). (2008). Criminal Profiling: An Introduction to Behavioral Evidence Analysis (3rd ed.). Burlington, MA: Academic Press.

Wang, M. C. (1992). Adaptive Education Strategies: Building on Diversity. Baltimore: Brookes.

Woskett, J., Coyle, I. R., & Lincoln, R. (2007). The probity of profiling: Opinions of Australian lawyers on the utility of profiling. Psychology, Psychiatry and Law, 14(2), 306–314.

Appendix A: Metacognition in Criminal Profiling Questionnaire

Age: _____

Gender *(Please circle)*:   male/female

Profile number   1/2

Highest level of completed education: _____ Primary school
(Please tick)   _____ High school
                                             _____ University degree
                                             _____ Postgraduate university

Occupation   _____

Directions, please read carefully:

The following questions are related to your general knowledge of profiling.

Please circle the most appropriate answer.

1) Have you ever heard of profiling or criminal profiling before?   Yes/No

2) Have you ever been exposed to a written criminal profile   Yes/No
   in the past?

3) Where do you get your knowledge of criminal profiling from?

TV and movies   Professional work
Books
Academic study   Other _____

1) How would you rate your knowledge of criminal profiling?

Very Bad	Bad	Neither Good nor Bad	Good	Excellent
1	2	3	4	5

2) How often do you believe criminal profiling is used by the authorities or law
   enforcement agencies?

Almost never	On unusual cases	On serious cases	Most serious cases	All serious cases
1	2	3	4	5

The following questions will ask you to rate the profile that you just read.

Please circle the most appropriate answer.

3) How would you rate the profile in terms of its layout?

Very Bad	Bad	Neither Good nor Bad	Good	Excellent
1	2	3	4	5

4) How would you rate the profile in terms of its correct use of punctuation and spelling?

Very Bad	Bad	Neither Good nor Bad	Good	Excellent
1	2	3	4	5

5) How would you rate the profile in terms of its use of logic?

Very Bad	Bad	Neither Good nor Bad	Good	Excellent
1	2	3	4	5

6) How would you rate the profile's overall level of clarity?

Very Bad	Bad	Neither Good nor Bad	Good	Excellent
1	2	3	4	5

7) How would you rate the profile's overall level of detail?

Very Bad	Bad	Neither Good nor Bad	Good	Excellent
1	2	3	4	5

8) How would you rate the profile in terms of making the credentials of the author clear?

Very Bad	Bad	Neither Good nor Bad	Good	Excellent
1	2	3	4	5

9) How would you rate the profile in terms of making its reasoning clear?

Very Bad	Bad	Neither Good nor Bad	Good	Excellent
1	2	3	4	5

10) How would you rate the profile in terms of its usefulness to investigators?

Very Bad	Bad	Neither Good nor Bad	Good	Excellent
1	2	3	4	5

11) How would you rate the amount of background information included in the profile?

Very Bad	Bad	Neither Good nor Bad	Good	Excellent
1	2	3	4	5

12) How would you rate the profile in terms of its level of detail?

Very Bad	Bad	Neither Good nor Bad	Good	Excellent
1	2	3	4	5

13) How would you rate the profile in terms of making the details of the crime clear?

Very Bad	Bad	Neither Good nor Bad	Good	Excellent
1	2	3	4	5

14) How would you rate the profile in terms of describing the crime scene?

Very Bad	Bad	Neither Good nor Bad	Good	Excellent
1	2	3	4	5

15) How would you rate the profile in terms of establishing a clear set of facts surrounding the crime?

Very Bad	Bad	Neither Good nor Bad	Good	Excellent
1	2	3	4	5

16) How would you rate the profile in terms of establishing a time line over which the crime occurred?

Very Bad	Bad	Neither Good nor Bad	Good	Excellent
1	2	3	4	5

17) How would you rate the profile in terms of describing the circumstances surrounding the crime?

Very Bad	Bad	Neither Good nor Bad	Good	Excellent
1	2	3	4	5

18) How would you describe the profile in terms of describing the location where the crime occurred?

Very Bad	Bad	Neither Good nor Bad	Good	Excellent
1	2	3	4	5

19) How would you rate the quality of evidence described in the profile?

Very Bad	Bad	Neither Good nor Bad	Good	Excellent
1	2	3	4	5

20) How would you rate the amount of evidence used to justify the conclusions drawn in the profile?

Very Bad	Bad	Neither Good nor Bad	Good	Excellent
1	2	3	4	5

21) How would you rate the profile in terms of making clear the evidence that has been examined?

Very Bad	Bad	Neither Good nor Bad	Good	Excellent
1	2	3	4	5

22) How would you rate the profile in terms of drawing logical conclusions from the evidence?

Very Bad	Bad	Neither Good nor Bad	Good	Excellent
1	2	3	4	5

23) How would you rate the profile in terms of its examination of the victims?

Very Bad	Bad	Neither Good nor Bad	Good	Excellent
1	2	3	4	5

24) How would you rate the profile's examination of the perpetrator's motivation?

Very Bad	Bad	Neither Good nor Bad	Good	Excellent
1	2	3	4	5

25) How would you rate the profile's examination of the perpetrator's prior criminal history?

Very Bad	Bad	Neither Good nor Bad	Good	Excellent
1	2	3	4	5

26) How would you rate the profile in terms of examining the perpetrator's level of planning?

Very Bad	Bad	Neither Good nor Bad	Good	Excellent
1	2	3	4	5

27) How would you rate the profile in terms of describing the perpetrator's state of mind at the time of the crime?

Very Bad	Bad	Neither Good nor Bad	Good	Excellent
1	2	3	4	5

CHAPTER 8

Criminal Profiling as Expert Evidence

Wayne Petherick, David Field, Andrew Lowe, and Elizabeth Fry

KEY TERMS

Probative evidence: Evidence that is court worthy, which should be objective and supported by factual evidence.

State of mind: The psychological state of the offender at the time of the crime, including planning, spontaneity, anger, sadism, remorse, and intent.

Intent: The desire to bring about a certain outcome.

Similar fact evidence: Evidence based on the degree to which the behavior in a crime conforms to the general character of the accused.

Staging: The deliberate alteration of the physical evidence to obscure the facts, mislead investigators, and/or direct the investigation away from the most logical suspect.

Frye **ruling:** Revolves primarily around the general acceptance of expert evidence within the scientific community.

Daubert **ruling:** Proposed that the admissibility of evidence should be based on its reliability and validity, its potential for misrepresentation or falsification, its error rate, and whether it has been subjected to peer review.

Expertise rule: States that an expert must be an expert in his or her respective field, although not necessarily the leading expert.

Area of expertise rule: States that experts cannot testify on areas that are not part of a formal sphere of knowledge or profession.

Factual basis rule: States that the strength of an expert's opinion is related to the factual reliability of the evidence on which the opinion is based.

CONTENTS

171

Common knowledge rule: States that an expert cannot give opinions on matters that may be considered within the general knowledge or common sense.

Ultimate issue rule: States that experts cannot give opinions regarding the ultimate issue of guilt or innocence.

Profiling evidence has been accepted in courts in the United States in both trial and sentencing phases, but other jurisdictions have been more cautious in their acceptance. For example, courts in the United Kingdom and Australia have been reluctant to introduce profilers as experts, even though profiling has been given some exposure in courts operating at the lower end of the justice system. The reasons for this reluctance are varied but include a lack of uniformity in processes and outcomes, fragmentation of methods, and conflict between profiling organizations and practitioners. In short, there are many methods of profiling, and not all practitioners agree on or accept one way as the best or most suitable.

This chapter addresses criminal profiling as expert evidence. First, some of the issues involving profiling as expert evidence are explored, including the induction-centric nature of the literature, the attitude of courts toward profiling evidence, and some common areas of profiling testimony. Next, a detailed overview of the *Frye* and *Daubert rules* of evidence in the United States is provided, followed by a thorough examination of the rules of evidence in Australia. The penultimate section discusses the current status of profiling through a number of cases, and at its conclusion, some recommendations are provided that allow for the maximum benefit from profiling evidence.

CRIMINAL PROFILING AS EXPERT EVIDENCE

It is important to consider the implications that profiling evidence may have in criminal and civil trials, and the rules and regulations that govern its use, because criminal profiling has a role in trial proceedings (Hazelwood, Ressler, Depue, & Douglas, 1999; Turvey, 1999a). In doing so, it must be questioned whether profiling can provide relevant information where the probative outweighs the prejudicial value (Petherick, 2000). *Probative evidence* is court worthy (Turvey, 1999b), and it should be objective and supported by factual evidence. On the other hand, evidence is considered to be prejudicial if it leads to a premature judgment or opinion unwarranted by the evidence. Therefore, it is necessary to consider what information in a profile will most assist the court in its determinations. Ormerod (1996, p. 869) suggests that if we rely on the profile as fact, this will be insufficiently relevant at trial. However, if we rely on it as an opinion, "the court may accept the evidence, but will attach to it such weight as is appropriate given the reliability of the opinion."

Because inductive methods, those relying on correlational or comparative reasoning, dominate discourse in this field, there will be an understandable but often dangerous reliance on these methods as pathways to knowledge in court.[1] It is instructive to discuss several of these works and court decisions and what they have to say about profiling and reliance on statistical databases.

The greater weight of literature on expert evidence covers inductive profiling, and this suggests a lack of awareness that not all profiling methods are equal. First, because psychologists are the professionals most often discussed as giving profiling evidence, it might be assumed that only psychologists can give profiling evidence, an implication that does not augur well for other experts who have made the forensic examination of human behavior their life's work. Second, if only inductive profiling is available for reference in works about expert testimony, does this mean that a deductive model is not likely to be accepted, or is it simply a matter of this method being less prevalent and therefore less well-known? Given this, it would seem that there is a definite training need for legal professionals about the differences among profiling approaches and what each has to offer as evidence.

Bartol and Bartol (1994, p. 329) define profiling in much the same way as other authors and note that "to a large extent, the profiling process is dictated by a database collected on previous offenders who have committed similar crimes." The authors also note, citing Pinizzotto and Finkel (1990), that profiling is of most use in sexual offenses such as serial rape and sexual homicides because we have a more complete understanding of these offenses. In concluding their discussion, they assert that "profiling based on anything but a strong database ... is likely to be plagued by many of the same biases, cognitive distortions, and inaccuracies so characteristic of clinical judgment when predicting dangerousness" (p. 329). In a later work, Bartol (2002, p. 253) again cites Pinizzotto and Finkel (1990) about the use of profiling in sexual offenses and then goes on to state the following:

> This is because we have a more extensive research base on sexual offending than we do on homicide. Furthermore, profiling is largely ineffective at this time in the identification of offenders involved in fraud, burglary, robbery, political crimes, theft, and drug-induced crimes because of the limited research base.

---

[1] Despite what some in the field would have us believe, the prevalence of an approach is not an analogue for utility, nor is it a justification for its continued use.

McCord's (1987) treatise "Syndromes, Profiles and Other Mental Exotica" treats profiles and profiling as analogous to psychological syndromes (e.g., battering parent profiles and sexual abuser of children profiles). The aim of these profiles is to present evidence that the character of the accused is remarkably consistent to the "typical" profile of certain abuser types. The presentation of this type of evidence is more akin to psychological testimony and is not generally consistent with the overall goal of criminal profiling.

In 1999, in *New Jersey v. Fortin*, the appellate division reversed on the admissibility of profile evidence presented by Robert Hazelwood on the grounds that the linkage analysis was not sufficiently reliable (Turvey, 2000). The appeals court found that those elements of modus operandi cited by Hazelwood (and pivotal in his conclusions) did not demonstrate an unusual pattern. In determining the reliability of the evidence, it was noted that (*New Jersey v. Fortin*, 2000)

> if the witness can from a reliable database offer evidence that a combination of bite marks on the breast, bite marks on the chin, and rectal tearing inflicted during a sexual attack is unique in his experience of investigating sexual assault crimes, that evidence could help to establish an "unusual pattern."

In addition,

> The trial court did incorporate Hazelwood's testimony in its 404(b) ruling, stating that Hazelwood's testimony was persuasive in that Hazelwood had not seen in reviewing 4000 cases this combination of bite marks, anal tears, and brutal facial beatings to a victim. If there was such a database of cases, the witness' premise can be fairly tested and the use of the testimony invokes none of the concerns we have expressed about the improper use of expert testimony.

However, such a database of cases did not exist, unless in the minds of the profilers, and so it becomes difficult, if not impossible, to test the reliability of that database and any conclusions reached.

Coming from another school of thought, Alison and Canter (1999, p. 25) state the following:

> In terms of processes of generating profiles, the procedure of Offender Profiling has taken on two rather different meanings. One is as the presentation of the personal opinion of an individual who has some experience of criminals through interviewing them as part of his or her professional activity. The second is as the development of the area of applied, scientific psychology known as "investigative psychology."

Both of these types of profile construction are inductive.

Freckleton and Selby (2002b) include profiling under the rubric of novel psychological evidence and also only discuss inductive profiling.[2] Furthermore, a good deal of the discussion on profiling as expert evidence revolves around the assessment of personality traits of the unknown offender and how these match with a suspect or how they may be suggestive of the predisposition of the accused to act in certain ways (ergo, similar fact or propensity evidence). The overriding thrust of this discussion is on profiling evidence from psychologists, and their discussion on the future of criminal profiling suggests that "the challenge lies ahead for psychiatrists and psychologists who claim to be able to profile particular kinds of offenders ... to show empirically that certain kinds of crimes are ... committed by persons of a particular psychological makeup" (p. 410).

In the United Kingdom, the most substantial analysis on the admissibility of psychological profiling evidence took place in *R. v. Gilfoyle* in 2001 (Freckleton & Selby, 2002b). In this case, Professor David Canter provided evidence as to the likelihood that a deceased person had committed suicide, an analysis referred to as a psychological autopsy (a profile of a deceased person). The evidence put forth by Canter was largely based on an analysis of the suicide note, which he suggested was not penned by Paula Gilfoyle, the deceased.

The court of appeal declined the evidence, noting that although Professor Canter was an expert (Freckleton & Selby, 2002b, p. 403),

> he had never embarked on evaluating suicidality of a deceased person previously and on the basis that "his reports identify no criteria by reference to which the court could test the quality of his opinions: There is no database comparing real and questionable suicides and there is no substantial body of academic writing approving his methodology."

Interestingly, despite Canter's assertion in this case and the degree to which the prosecutors believed that his evidence proved their case was valid, Canter has recently changed tact (Kennedy, 2008).

> The pioneer of criminal profiling in Britain has switched sides to say that a man he helped to jail for life for murdering his wife is innocent.

---

[2]Although not specifically referred to as inductive profiling (most works of this nature do not make the distinction between induction and deduction), you need only consider the nature of the discussion to determine what they are talking about.

Eddie Gilfoyle was prosecuted after David Canter, a psychology professor, told police that his hanged wife's suicide note betrayed signs of having been faked. But research prompted by the case into the difference between genuine and false suicide notes has persuaded Professor Canter that Paula Gilfoyle, 32, was, indeed, the sole author of her final words.

Now campaigners for the jailed husband are hoping to use Professor Canter's analysis of the suicide note as part of a fresh appeal.

On a June evening in 1992, Paula Gilfoyle's body was found hanged in the garage of the home in Upton, Wirral, Merseyside, that she shared with her husband.

Mrs. Gilfoyle, who worked in a local factory, was 8 months pregnant and presented a cheery front to the world. But the long suicide note that she left spoke of a feeling of failure and unhappiness, and hinted at strains in her marriage. She told her husband not to blame himself, and even suggested that the baby was not his. There is an overwhelming feeling of guilt and self-blame in the note.

Friends and relatives refused to believe that she could have killed herself. They insisted that she had no cares and was looking forward to the birth of her first baby. Suspicion soon turned on her husband. Some workmates told police that she had said that her husband, a hospital porter, had persuaded her to write a bogus suicide note as part of a course that he was taking on suicide. No such course existed.

However, Professor Canter points out, in a 10,000-word report on the case, that for the bogus suicide plot to have worked Gilfoyle would have had to persuade his wife to climb a ladder in the garage and allow a noose to be placed around her neck. There were no signs of force on her body.

Gilfoyle has always protested his innocence of what was portrayed as a calculated, evil plot to make his pregnant wife's killing look like suicide.

When Merseyside police began to investigate Mrs. Gilfoyle's death, they consulted Professor Canter, who had been the first psychological profiler to be used by British police and who shared their doubts about the note.

His evidence formed part of the prosecution case, though it was never heard by the jury. He nonetheless believes that it helped to reinforce prosecutors' determination to press ahead against Gilfoyle, who was convicted unanimously of murder in July 1993.

Professor Canter used a technique of linguistic analysis to try to establish whether Mrs. Gilfoyle had composed her note. Police suspected that her husband had dictated it to her. But studies since, including one supervised by Professor Canter, have shown that errors can be produced by using simple word counts as the main basis for deciding authorship.

By chance, a couple of years after the conviction, Professor Canter moved to Merseyside, taking a post at the University of Liverpool. There, he came into contact with Gilfoyle's relatives and eventually met the prisoner himself. "He wasn't that creative an individual," Professor Canter said. The academic then began looking closer into the science of suicide notes.

The most pertinent study was conducted 50 years ago by the founders of the Los Angeles Suicide Prevention Center, Edwin Schneidman and Norman Farberow. The two psychologists, pioneers in suicide prevention, compared genuine suicide notes with artificial ones written by people who had never been suicidal.

Their purpose was to look for ways to stop people taking their own lives. But Professor Canter made a study of those 1950s notes, along with other samples, to seek clues to how a genuine suicide note could be distinguished from an imagined one. It became clear that it is difficult to simulate the elements in a real suicide note. Professor Canter now uses Mrs. Gilfoyle's final handwritten lines, beginning "Dear Eddie" and ending "Goodnight and God bless, love Paula," in his lectures.

"It is my opinion that the suicide note was written, unaided, by Paula Gilfoyle," he said. "That this intention was genuine is difficult to determine, but the way in which the note appears to be the culmination of months of thinking of various possibilities for dealing with her situation, and indicates so directly that Paula could see no other way, is consistent with a very real determination to kill herself."

Gilfoyle's brother-in-law, Paul Caddick, a retired police sergeant who found Mrs. Gilfoyle's body and now runs the miscarriage of justice campaign, praised Professor Canter.

"He is a brave man," Mr. Caddick said. "We are very pleased he has come on to the defense side because he is a man of integrity. Obviously, for a long time, Eddie didn't like him. When he came on to our side he said, 'The bastard, he should've said the right thing in the first place'. But now he realizes it was a dreadful mistake."

Gilfoyle has already lost two appeals against conviction but his new legal team at Birnberg Peirce is preparing evidence to bring before the Criminal Cases Review Commission.

Merseyside Police said: "There was a lot of other evidence heard by the jury and he was convicted on that evidence."

Given the position of Thornton (1997, p. 13) that "induction, not deduction, is the counterpart of hypothesis testing and theory revision," it is of some concern that considerable attention has been given to inductive methods, specifically as this focus relates to the delivery of expert testimony. It is certainly a curious position we find ourselves in when courts that deal in facts prefer a position more aligned to the offering of theories, many of which may not even be supported by the available evidence.

Thus, despite the fact that induction is really the first step in the process of developing a logical argument, it is the dominant style of reasoning in theory, practice, and expert evidence in profiling. Many of the authors discussed previously cite the need for further research and databases on offense types, and although these may have general criminological value, we are also reminded of their frailty and the dangers of using statistical averages when life or liberty may be at issue. If more profilers adopted a deductive approach, then their conclusions would be certain based on known evidence, as opposed to statistical averages, and therefore more suited to forensic practice.

Next, some common areas of expert evidence concerning *state of mind*, *intent*, *similar fact evidence* (also referred to as propensity evidence), and *staging* are discussed.

STATE OF MIND AND INTENT

Perhaps the most beneficial evidence profiling offers to criminal proceedings is the interpretation of the offender's state of mind before, during, and after the commission of a crime (Turvey, 1997). Historically, psychologists or other mental health professionals examined the suspect after his or her arrest using information provided to them by the offender. The problem with this is that information given to the psychologist may not be true and the offender may be in a different state of mind from when the crime was committed—factors that may bias the profiler. According to Turvey (1997), profiling is useful because the only source of information that should be used is the offender's crime scene behavior and interaction with the victim. As a result, the profiler examines what the offender did and has little use for what the offender has to say about what he or she did, providing a more objective measure of the offender's behavior.

From the crime scene, the criminal profiler can observe many behavioral patterns suggestive of the offender's state of mind, including elements of planning, spontaneity, anger, sadism, and lack of remorse (Turvey, 1997). All these elements contribute to an understanding of the offender's state of mind, indicating intent. This is an important consideration because it may influence decisions regarding offender culpability and sentencing. For example, when considering homicide, if the absence of intent can be proven, then an offender may be found guilty of manslaughter. However, if an offender is found to be fully culpable and intent can be proven, the offender may be convicted of the more serious offence of murder and a harsher sentence may be handed down.

The offender's state of mind is directly related to intent. As indicated by Findlay, Odgers, and Yeo (1999, p. 17), a person has intention for a result when he or she means to bring about that result, or when the person is aware it will likely occur in the course of events. Freckleton and Selby (1999a) state that when intent is an issue, the accused may call expert evidence to establish any abnormal characteristics that may have affected the offender's mental functioning. In some cases, criminal acts such as murder may be ancillary and not the primary intent of the offender (Douglas, Ressler, Burgess, & Hartman, 1986), and a crime scene assessment may help to flesh out those intended actions from the unintended and also those acts of criminal behavior from precautionary acts the offender engaged in to escape the attention of the police.

However, in cases in which the mental functioning of the accused is not at issue, evidence on intent may not require the opinion of an expert: "It was said not to be a question of medical science or a question upon which a psychiatrist or any other professionally qualified person has any greater claim to express an opinion than an unqualified person" (Freckleton & Selby, 2002b, p. 179). Readers are cautioned to check local precedent on this issue.

SIMILAR FACT EVIDENCE

Similar fact evidence is often used to suggest that behavior evidenced in a criminal action conforms to the general character of the accused. Attempts have been made in a number of jurisdictions to suggest that because of the character of the accused, he or she is more or less likely to have committed the crime under consideration (Freckleton & Selby, 2002b). It may also describe information from other acts of misconduct by the accused on other occasions, which are similar to the offense currently presented to the court (Field, 2008; McNicol & Mortimer, 1996). Because of its prejudicial nature, similar fact evidence is normally inadmissible unless it is deemed to be directly relevant to the issue before the jury. For similar fact evidence to be allowed, there must be a striking similarity between cases. For example, the fact that in two separate crimes two rapists used a condom is not sufficient grounds on which to link cases. However, two offenders who use exactly the same knot in a ligature and provide an identical script for the victim to read during the assault may be.

In its latest ruling on the subject (*Phillips v R* (2006) 225 CLR 303 at 483), the High Court of Australia reaffirmed that the test of admissibility is that "[similar fact evidence] will be admissible only if its probative value exceeds its prejudicial effect … in other words, that there is no reasonable view of the evidence consistent with the innocence of the accused."

Criminal profiling may assist courts on evidence of similar fact, especially in cases of multicount indictments, by identifying the existence of case linkage based on behavioral information from the crime scene. Links between cases can be either investigative, which serve to dictate the allocation of investigative resources, or probative, which describe connections between cases that are sufficiently distinctive to imply that the same person is responsible (Turvey, 1999b). It is the latter type that could be called upon in court and therefore requires the presence of distinctive and specific modus operandi, signature behaviors, and signature aspects (Turvey, 1999b).

Similar fact evidence is an area also warranting caution because another important consideration is determining exactly when coincidence ceases and clear evidence of case linkage exists. Obviously, this will change depending on the case, and although precedent may provide a guide, it will be up to the individual court to decide if there is a strong nexus of similarity.

STAGING

A staged (also called simulated) crime scene is one in which the offender has deliberately altered the physical evidence to obscure the facts, mislead the investigators, and/or direct the investigation away from the most logical suspect. Staging "involves adding, moving, or removing evidence from a crime scene with the hope that the criminal investigator will not uncover the truth of the events" (Turvey, 2005, p. 1), and it is a conscious criminal action undertaken to thwart the investigation (Geberth, 1996). Some commentators believe staged crimes are a fairly common occurrence (Turvey, 2008), although most others make no statement about their frequency.

The concept of the staged crime scene is not new; it was discussed in Hans Gross's seminal work *Criminal Investigation* in 1924. Gross (1924, p. 439) refers to the "defects of the situation":

So long as one looks only on the scene, it is impossible, whatever the care, time, and attention bestowed, to detect all the details, and especially note the incongruities: but these strike us at once when we set ourselves to describe the picture on paper as exactly and clearly as possible.... The "defects of the situation" are just those contradictions, those improbabilities, which occur when one desires to represent the situation as something quite different from what it really is, and this with the very best intentions and the purest belief that one has worked with all of the forethought, craft, and consideration imaginable.

Gross (1924) touches on two critical points with regard to staging: (1) Staging is a desire on the part of the offender to represent the crime as something other than what it actually is, and (2) no matter what care the offender takes, staging is usually detectable by those who know what to look for. It is because of their experience with a variety of crimes and crime scenes that the profiler may often be called upon to advise the court on aspects of staging (this may not always be a flawless presentation, however, as the case studies discussed later will show).

Although staging is quite well-defined in the literature, even with some uniformity, there is some debate about which specific aspects of an offender's attempt to cover up his or her crime constitute staging. Most authors suggest that the identification of staging be limited to those cases involving criminal intent whereby the staging covers another criminal act. However, Douglas and Munn (1992) include in their discussion the purposeful alteration of physical evidence to protect the victim or the victim's family, as might happen with an autoerotic fatality involving fetishism. This definition is inconsistent with other literature on the topic and is not a suitable way to define the topic.

RULES OF EXPERT EVIDENCE

Profiling does have the potential to serve as useful and important evidence in certain trials. However, as in other fields that fall under the title of expert evidence, it must be subject to rules of admissibility.

In the United States, the first rule of expert evidence was established in *Frye v. United States* (1923) when the results of a lie detector test were offered as evidence (Melton, Petrila, Poythress, & Slobogin, 1997; Moenssens, Inbau, & Starrs, 1986). James Alphonso Frye was charged with second-degree murder, and he argued that the lie detector test would determine whether his protestations of innocence were true (*Frye v. United States*, 1923):

The opinions of experts ... are admissible in evidence in those cases in which the matter of inquiry is such that inexperienced persons are unlikely to prove capable of forming a correct judgment upon it, for the reason that the subject matter so far partakes of a science, art, or trade as to require a previous habit or experience or study in it, in order to acquire a knowledge of it.… When the question involved does not lie within the range of common experience or knowledge, but requires special experience or special knowledge, then the opinions of witnesses skilled in that particular science, art, or trade to which the questions relates are admissible in evidence.

Although the court concurred with the general essence of the rule, it held that the test in question (polygraphy) did not meet the required scientific recognition among physiological and psychological authorities "as would justify the court in admitting expert testimony deduced from the discovery, development, and experiments thus far made" (*Frye v. United States*, 1923).

Essentially, *Frye* revolves around the general acceptance of expert evidence within the scientific community (Freckleton, 1987; Wood, 2003) in that "the thing from which the deduction is made must be sufficiently established to have gained general acceptance in the particular field to which it belongs" (Rudin & Inman, 2002, p. 183). The main problem with *Frye* is that it is too generous with testimony that is generally accepted even if its validity had not been scientifically demonstrated, and it is too restrictive of novel evidence that is the result of excellent scientific verification (Melton et al., 1997). Newer areas of expertise may be excluded regardless of their utility simply because they are not generally accepted (Melton et al., 1997; Moenssens et al., 1986). This may be further complicated by standing practices that may be generally accepted but not necessarily legitimate.

Seventy years later, in 1993, the *Daubert* rule (established in the case of *Daubert v. Merrell Dow Pharmaceuticals, Inc.*, 1993) proposed that the admissibility of evidence should be based on its scientific reliability and validity, its potential for misrepresentation or falsification, its error rate, and whether it has been subject to peer review (Wood, 2003; Wrightsman, Greene, Nietzel, & Fortune, 2002). Underwager and Wakefield (1993) suggest that the unanimous ruling of *Daubert* in effect replaces *Frye* with the Popperian principle of falsification as the key determinant of scientific knowledge. Using *Daubert*, evidence would have to have been proven through testing and examination. The criteria for acceptance of such evidence should include the proof of any theories to be offered as opinion evidence, the scrutiny of peer reviews, and the level of acceptance of scientific methods used to reach a conclusion (Melton et al., 1997). Technically, *Daubert* only applies in federal jurisdictions, but it has also been adopted by many U.S. states, although several still follow the *Frye* ruling (Wrightsman et al., 2002).

Daubert should provide some scope for deductive profiling. This is because the deductive method produces conclusions derived from physical and behavioral evidence such as autopsy and forensic reports, which are themselves valid scientific methods allowed as expert testimony. However, *Daubert* may be less likely to contemplate inductive profiling because the methods used to reach conclusions are based on previous cases and not always on the evidence relating to the case presented in court. This may place too much emphasis on factors outside the boundaries of the case, highlighting the potential for misrepresentation of the facts that may not be valid and reliable.

AUSTRALIAN RULES OF EXPERT EVIDENCE

In Australia, there are essentially five rules of expert evidence that dictate the recognition of expert witnesses and define the scope and limits of their testimony: the *expertise rule, area of expertise rule, factual basis rule, common knowledge rule*, and *ultimate issue rule*. Although these rules specifically relate to the Australian legal climate, they apply in a general way in other legal jurisdictions. For example, in both the United States and the United Kingdom (and most other jurisdictions), an expert must not provide evidence on the guilt of a person and, thus, must not speak to the ultimate issue.

In some way, shape, or form, the following rules apply equally across regions.

Expertise Rule

The expertise rule simply states that an expert must be an expert in his or her respective field but not necessarily the leading expert or authority (Freckleton & Selby, 2002a), although an expert must possess a quantity of knowledge superior to most in his or her given area. Because an expert is allowed to testify to what would be considered hearsay for other witnesses, it must be established that the expert possess sufficient knowledge in an area and that this "hearsay" carries some probative value.

This rule questions whether the witness has knowledge and experience sufficient to entitle him or her to be considered an expert who can assist the court. The witness must "possess some specialized knowledge, skill, training, or possibly experience sufficient to enable them to supply information and opinions" (Freckleton, 1987, p. 18). As a result, counsel must establish the witness's ability and competence to comment on the matter presented.

There is little literature addressing the issue of what education and training one must undertake to be considered a criminal profiler. Turvey (1999a) recommends degrees in the behavioral and forensic sciences, complemented by practical work experience with sex offender treatment programs or law enforcement. However, competency as an expert may also be established through "participation in special courses, membership in professional societies, and any professional articles or books published" (Saferstein, 2004, p. 16), as well as direct occupational experience. Ultimately, whether a person is qualified to give expert opinion is at the discretion of the court after certifying an individual's education and experience is commensurate with the type of analysis to be performed.

Any debate about a person's qualifications to testify as an expert would typically be aired during the voir dire in the absence of the jury or during a pretrial application, when the procedural rules of the relevant criminal jurisdiction provide for such a process. Here, opposing counsel would subject the prospective expert to a grueling examination in which the expert's education, training, and experience would be scrutinized to determine if he should be allowed to present his opinions to the jury.

In a dated but relevant piece, Wiard (1931a, p. 143) discusses the importance of establishing the qualifications of any expert on which decisions may hang:

> The counsel, however, has a certain task which he cannot customarily delegate "in toto" to the expert. This involves eliciting the opinions and conclusions of his technical witness in that form in which they may be most convincing, prior to which, however, he must establish, to the satisfaction of the court and jury, the gentleman's ability and integrity. This of course would be very simple were it necessary only to introduce him as witness, call upon him to present his opinions, and allow him to depart without having to offer either any background for his conclusions or to substantiate them by withstanding a cross-examination. However, court procedure does not recognize the capability of a so-called expert merely because his name may be such and such, and the opposing side, of course, will refuse to grant his qualifications under any conditions.

Area of Expertise Rule

Experts cannot testify on areas that are not a part of a formal sphere of knowledge or profession (Freckleton & Selby, 2002b), whereby others of similar experience and knowledge are able to evaluate their theoretical and operational applications. A profession is "defined by its ability to regularize, criticize, to restrain vagaries, to set a standard of workmanship and to compel others to conform to it" (Turvey, 1999a, p. xxvii), and until recently, such things did not exist among individuals referring to themselves as criminal profilers.

The establishment of the Academy of Behavioral Profiling indicates efforts to change this, laying down a professional code of ethics, criminal profiling guidelines, and allowing peer review for further research (Academy of Behavioral Profiling, 2001), encouraging this field to become a "formal sphere of knowledge." However, few professional groups of profilers exist to validate this function.

Factual Basis Rule

The strength of an expert's opinion is related to the factual reliability of the evidence on which the opinion is based. The court will allow expert opinion evidence if the factual basis of that opinion has not yet been established, provided that after further evidence is admitted, the facts on which the evidence is based will be highlighted (Australian Law Reform Commission, 1994). If not, the testimony is still admissible, but the weight of the evidence will decline on direction of the judge (Australian Law Reform Commission, 1994). If the facts on which the expert testimony is based are not established at all, then of course the expert evidence will be worthless see *R. v. Ryan* (2002) VSCA 176.

This rule affects criminal profiling in a similar, if not identical, manner to any other expert testimony. The base information of a criminal profile includes, but is not limited to, crime scene photographs, investigator's reports, autopsy documentation, evidence logs, and witness statements (Geberth, 1996; Turvey, 1999a). As such, the weight of profiling testimony is only as strong as the underlying evidentiary value of the information provided to the profiler in the case before the court. Testimony may be weighed by the degree to which an opinion is based on evidence or supposition and also on the quality of the interpretation. In addition, the closer the expert is to the facts of the case, whether conducting the crime scene reconstruction himself if qualified, or indeed whether he even visited the scene, the more authoritative the opinion. In particular, it should be noted that expert witnesses frequently give their opinions on the basis of assumed facts given to them by the party commissioning them. The easiest way to neutralize expert opinion is therefore to cast doubt on or disprove the facts on which that opinion is based. Because of this, the profiler is cautioned to independently establish the basic facts on which his or her opinion is based.

In arriving at a profile, the expert witness may be called upon to utilize reports prepared by others, such as autopsy reports, psychiatric assessments, physical examinations, or records from family services department files. From the prosecutor's point of view, it will be essential to ensure that every document is "spoken to" by an appropriate witness to lay a factual basis for the profiler's assessment. From the profiler's perspective, he or she may occasionally need to admit that the final opinion is based on the facts regarding the accused that are being "assumed," in that the contents of the files and reports on which the opinion is based have been treated as accurate records of the facts.

If the expert witness is prepared to "adopt" previous literature on which her report is based, so as to incorporate it within the report, then that previous literature becomes "evidence" as part of her final conclusion; see *PQ v. Australian Red Cross Society* (1992) 1 VR 19.

Common Knowledge Rule

This rule precludes the offering of expert evidence on matters that may be considered within the general knowledge or common sense (Freckleton & Selby, 1999b, p. 2; Freckleton & Selby, 2002b). For example, an expert would not be allowed to testify that roads are slippery when wet because this is within common knowledge, but the expert could testify after the mechanical examination of a particular vehicle that it would behave in a particular way on a wet road.

Criminal profilers have "expert knowledge about domains of interrelated procedures" (Bekerian & Jackson, 1997, p. 221), including forensic science, behavioral science, and medicolegal death investigation. In the course of their analysis, profilers examine many areas, such as modus operandi, signature, and motivation (Turvey, 1999a), and these procedures are not considered part of general knowledge and common sense of the lay person or practitioners of the law. However, a profiler could not testify to the fact the offender in a given case was a male if it had previously been established that the victim was raped before she was murdered, that there was semen found on the body that did not belong to anyone known to her, and that she was not in a relationship at the time of the offense. These conclusions could be reached without specialist knowledge.

The reasoning behind this rule can be traced back to an opinion expressed by Lord Mansfield in the 18th century (*Folkes v. Chadd*, 1782):

> The fact that an expert witness has impressive scientific qualifications does not by that fact alone make his opinion on matters of human nature and behavior within the limits of normality any more helpful than that of the jurors themselves; but there is a danger that they may think it does.

The theme has been adopted and built upon considerably in *R. v. Turner* (1975). Although accepting that it was permissible to expose eyewitness identification to the challenge of psychiatric analysis of how the human identification process works, Lawton LJ emphasized the general caveat that "psychiatry has not yet become a satisfactory substitute for the common sense of juries or magistrates on matters within their experience of life."

Note, however, that objections of this genre are predicated on the belief that somehow the evidence of behavioralists is being substituted for the "everyday common sense" of the jury as to how people, in their experience, behave in a given situation. As such, it is seen as a challenge to the process whereby the actions of "ordinary" humans are judged by other ordinary humans who make up the jury. This, of course, is not what profiling is about.

The work of a profiler, in the main, is conducted in the context of abnormal behavior. What he or she seeks to bring to the attention of the jury are salient facts that may be adduced about the perpetrator of the particular offense through the perpetrator's behavior. It is sometimes no different from the subconscious process employed by a jury when they are told that an accused battered his wife to death when she confessed to being unfaithful to him. In both cases, the reference is to "known" behavioral characteristics—the difference is that the jury in the case of the wife killer is dealing with a common situation to which they can all relate, if necessary with the application of a little imagination. In a case in which the profiler is offering assistance, on the other hand, the behavior is not that with which one could expect a jury to be familiar.

Very few jurors, from everyday experience, could form a mental picture of someone who rapes and murders in a ritualistic way, any more than they could conclude from the fact that the hyoid bone of the deceased was fractured or that he or she had been manually asphyxiated. Both are areas of scientific conclusion based on observable facts, in respect to which the jury requires assistance from someone who can interpret those facts by means of an acceptable and accredited scientific process.

Ultimate Issue Rule

It is still generally regarded as the basic rule that an expert witness must not seek to decide the ultimate issue before the court (i.e., guilt or innocence) and is usually concerned with whether an expert's contribution will supplant the function of the jury by deciding on this issue for them (Freckleton & Selby, 1999a).

However, note that in Australian jurisdictions covered by the Uniform Evidence Law (principally New South Wales, the Australian Capital Territory, and Tasmania and all cases involving federal laws being tried in federal courts), this "ultimate issue" rule has been relaxed to the point of abrogation; see, for example, Evidence Act 1995 (Cth), s. 80.

It is impossible for behavioral evidence from the crime scene to suggest that an accused is guilty or innocent of a crime, although several cases show how some profilers have erroneously tried just that (some of which are discussed later). Criminal profiling "will not implicate a specific individual in a specific crime. It can be used, however, to suggest a specific type of individual, with specific psychological and emotional characteristics" (Turvey, 1999a, p. 228).

In summary, these five rules of expert evidence serve to promote the reliability of the information being provided to the court by the expert. This is achieved by certifying that the individual has the appropriate education and experience in a "formal sphere of knowledge" to perform examinations that the court cannot do itself. It also ensures the validity of the information forming the basis of the expert's opinion.

THE LATEST INDICATIONS ON THE STATUS OF PROFILING

R. v. Ranger

Many of the issues raised in this chapter were most recently considered by the Court of Appeal for Ontario in *R. v. Ranger* (2003). The accused was convicted of the first-degree murder of a former girlfriend and the manslaughter of her younger sister. The accused was said to have been unable to accept the termination of the relationship. Both deaths occurred at approximately the same time, and the two bodies were found in the house they shared with their mother. The victims were knifed to death (allegedly by the accused and his cousin), and a curious feature of the case was that although the house gave the appearance of having been ransacked, only three items had been taken. All of these related to the accused's former girlfriend, one of which was a necklace the accused had given to her.

Profile evidence offered by the Crown at trial related specifically to a suggestion that whoever had committed the crimes had "staged" a break and enter to divert attention from his or her connection to the victims. Following a voir dire, the trial judge ruled as follows (*R. v. Ranger*, 2003):

> I am satisfied that opinion evidence is needed in this case in the sense that it will likely provide information that is outside the experience and knowledge of the jury. The factual issue of whether a break and entry is authentic or staged is not likely to be a subject within the common knowledge of the jurors. This, of course, is subject to the Crown qualifying the proposed expert as an expert in this particular area.

In short, the proposed evidence satisfied the first test of relating to an issue outside the likely experience of the average juror and could be admitted provided that (1) the Crown could demonstrate the evidence of the expert was one proceeding from an established and recognized field of specialist study, and (2) the proposed witness was an expert in that field.

The witness offered by the Crown was Detective Inspector Kathryn Lines from the Behavioral Sciences Section of the Ontario Provincial Police, who claimed that criminal profiling was "a behavioral approach to criminal investigation," in which she had considerable experience. Crown counsel confirmed (in answer to a question from the trial judge) that the detective inspector was being offered as "an expert witness in the area of staged crimes," who would confirm that the crime scene had indeed been staged.

Neither counsel made submissions regarding the detective inspector's qualifications as an expert in this area, and the trial judge ruled that she was qualified "to give expert opinion as to staged crimes." Of note, this decision was arrived at despite the fact that the witness conceded during voir dire that there was no independent or objective process in existence against which to test the hypothesis of a "staged crime scene."

Defense counsel expressed concern that the witness's evidence might wander into the area of the alleged motive for the murder and was assured by Crown counsel that this was not his intention. As it transpired, the witness went much further than that.

On three occasions during her examination in chief, Crown counsel was allowed to elicit the witness's opinions regarding the motivations of the likely perpetrator and his or her characteristics. On each occasion, defense counsel objected on the ground that such a question was beyond the scope of what was deemed admissible during the voir dire, and on each occasion he was overruled.

The first occasion concerned the suggestion that the perpetrator of the crime was more interested in the former girlfriend of the accused than her younger sister. Despite the objection that this issue had more to do with the perpetrator's psychology than the staging of the crime scene, the question was allowed and answered in the affirmative. The second objectionable question related to the type of person likely to stage a crime scene, and the witness was allowed to incorporate into her answer a quotation from a crime scene manual which stated that "it is almost always someone who had some kind of association or relationship with the victim." This despite the predictable objection from the defense that the question and answer amounted to "dime store psychology" that sought to make the accused fit within the class of person likely to commit the offense "through the mouth of an expert witness." The trial judge seemed content to admit the question on the basis that if the break and enter was staged, it rendered it likely that the perpetrator knew the victim. Third, the witness was allowed to testify to the fact that only items belonging to the accused's former girlfriend were missing from the crime scene, and because of this it was concluded that the perpetrator had "a particular interest in the possessions or things related to" her.

When defense counsel began cross-examination, he asked a series of questions designed to suggest that the witness's final opinion was fatally contaminated because she knew what the police investigation team was hoping to conclude. The trial judge brought this line of questioning to a close by reminding the jury that it was their opinion that mattered and not that of either the witness or the police. The Court of Appeal held that defense counsel should have been allowed to continue down that avenue of inquiry, quoting in support one of the caveats of Kaufman (Report of the Kaufman Commission on Proceedings involving Guy Paul Morin, 2003): "Profiling, once a suspect has been identified, can be misleading and dangerous, as the investigators' summary of relevant facts may be colored by their suspicions."

This case clearly demonstrates the danger of allowing the expert to wander outside her alleged area of expertise, down the perilous avenue toward the "ultimate issue." It also illustrates how easy it is to allow this to happen.

The initial agreement was that the expert witness would deal only with the issue of whether or not the crime scene had been staged. It was never suggested by the Crown (or contemplated by the trial judge) that she would be allowed to drift into the area of why the crime scene had been staged, even less that she would be allowed to offer an opinion on whether or not the accused met the profile of the likely perpetrator.

Yet this is, according to Ormerod (1996, p. 865), the very work of a profiler, who begins by reconstructing how the crime occurred, on which is based an inference as to why the crime happened, and culminates in an educated guess about the characteristics of the offender. This "what" to "why" to "who" is seen as the nucleus of a criminal profile.

Indeed, it is difficult to imagine any other logical reason for admitting the "what," other than its relevance to the "who." This is the very reason we have criminal trials, and it should have been within everyone's contemplation that the evidence skirted the issue of whether or not the accused was the perpetrator of the crime.

The error committed by the trial judge was that of allowing someone whose expertise was the "what" to answer the "why" and "who" questions. Despite the fact that she had not been deemed qualified to make those extended conclusions, there was a distinct risk that the jury would believe that she was qualified and would not be able to define the moment at which she stepped outside the boundary of what she was qualified to give opinions on. This was all the more dangerous given that (*R. v. Ranger*, 2003) "expert opinion testimony about 'why' or 'who' usually raises more concerns. These concerns relate to … the requirement that the evidence be sufficiently reliable to warrant its admission and the requirement that its probative value exceed its prejudicial effect."

In illustrating the distinctions to be made, the trial judge Charron J gave, as examples of the "what," the opinion in an arson that the fire was deliberate rather than accidental and a pathologist's opinion on the likely cause of death. She added that (*R. v. Ranger*, 2003)

> the scientific basis for this kind of evidence is usually not contentious. By contrast, attempts to adduce expert opinion evidence and WHY an offense was committed in a particular manner and, more particularly, about WHO is more likely to have committed the offense, that is, the kinds of evidence that I have labeled more particularly as criminal profiling, have generally not met with success, either in this jurisdiction or elsewhere.

In support of this assertion, Her Honour quoted the Supreme Court of Canada's observation in *R. v. Mohan* (1994) that "the closer the evidence approaches an opinion on an ultimate issue, the stricter the application of this principle." Charron J adopted the rule that she took to have emerged from *Mohan*, to the effect that before evidence relating to the disposition of an accused might be admitted via an expert witness, "There must first be something distinctive about the behavioral characteristics of either the accused or the perpetrator that makes a comparison of the two sets of characteristics helpful in determining innocence or guilt."

This confirms some observations that lawyers become very nervous when "disposition" evidence is offered against an accused without proof that he or she has in the past exhibited the characteristics identified in the profile. Even when there is such proof, the Court will be required to be convinced of the scientific reliability of the profile characteristics. As per Sopinka J in *Mohan*, the trial judge should consider the opinion of the expert and whether the expert is merely expressing a personal opinion or whether the behavioral profile the expert is putting forward is in common use as a reliable indicator of membership of a distinctive group. In other words, has the scientific community developed a standard profile for the offender who commits this type of crime?[3] An affirmative finding on this basis will satisfy the criteria of relevance and necessity.

In *Mohan*, the Court went on to hold that the expert evidence being offered for the defense did not satisfy that test, and therefore,

> in the absence of these indicia of reliability, it cannot be said that the evidence would be necessary in the sense of usefully clarifying a matter otherwise inaccessible, or that any value it may have had would not be outweighed by its potential for misleading or diverting the jury.

In a subsequent case involving criminal profiling, the Supreme Court of Canada again rejected psychiatric evidence for the defense to the effect that the accused did not exhibit the allegedly distinctive personality traits of the perpetrator. This was on the grounds that the profile in question was not sufficiently "standardized." The Court explained that "the requirement of a standard profile is to ensure that the profile of distinctive features is not put together on an ad hoc basis for the purpose of the particular case."[4]

The court in *Ranger* then reminded itself that the testimony of the expert witness had not been restricted to the simple question of whether or not the crime scene had been staged (the "what" question) but, rather, had drifted

---

[3]Again, one can see the fairly ubiquitous reference to inductive profiles despite all of their fallibilities discussed throughout this work and others.

[4]Here is another reference to "standard profiles." Ironically, criminal profiles should be constructed on a specific case with a specific set of evidence to make them valid for that case and its individual context.

into "why" (to redirect the suspicion away from the most obvious suspect) and then "who" ("almost always someone who has some kind of association or relationship with the victim"). The Crown had supported this extension with the argument that this type of profiling had been accepted in both the United States and Canada, an assertion that was rejected by the Court of Appeal.

Also considered was a recent English authority in *R. v. Gilfoyle* (2001), in which the defense at a murder trial had sought to admit expert evidence from David Canter (this case was discussed previously) of a psychological autopsy of the deceased. Canter's opinion was that the deceased had committed suicide, but this was rejected by the Court of Appeal on the basis that

> there is no data base comparing real and questionable suicides
> and there is no substantial body of academic writing approving his
> methodology.... If evidence of this kind were admissible in relation to
> the deceased, there could be no difference in principle in relation to
> evidence psychologically profiling a defendant. In our judgment, the
> roads of enquiry thus opened up would be unending and of little or
> no help to a jury. The use of psychological profiling as an aid to police
> investigation is one thing, but its use as a means of proof in court is
> another.

Putting together all these strands of authority, the Ontario Court of Appeal in *Ranger* rejected the evidence of the expert witness because

> criminal profiling is a novel field of scientific evidence, the reliability of
> which was not demonstrated at trial.... Her opinions amounted to no
> more than educated guesses. As such, her criminal profiling evidence
> was inadmissible. The criminal profiling evidence also approached the
> ultimate issue in this case and, hence, was highly prejudicial.

New Jersey v. Fortin

In *New Jersey v. Fortin* (2000), profiling evidence was utilized to link an unsolved homicide to a solved sexual assault and abduction, for which an offender was located. The facts in relation to the unsolved homicide are as follows (*New Jersey v. Fortin*, 2000):

> On the 11th of August 1994, the body of Melissa Padilla was located
> half inside a drainage conduit in Woodbridge, New Jersey. She was
> found wearing a shirt, no bra, and naked from the waist down. Her
> shorts, with her underpants rolled inside, were located in a nearby
> bush. She had been beaten around her face, leaving her with a bruised
> and swollen face and fractured nose. She had been manually strangled,
> anally penetrated, and had bite marks on her left breast, left nipple and
> left chin.

The matter went unsolved for a considerable time with no apparent leads.

On April 3, 1995, Maine State Trooper Vicki Gardner intercepted a vehicle driven by Steven Fortin. After calling for assistance from other state troopers, Gardner began to administer a field sobriety test, before Fortin seized her by the throat and dragged her into the car. Gardner was strangled into semiconsciousness, sexually assaulted both anally and vaginally, and had been bitten on her left breast, left nipple, and left chin. Her bra had been removed, and her underpants were found rolled up inside her pants. Fortin sped off with Gardner in the vehicle when other state troopers approached the location. Fortin's vehicle overturned a short time later and he was apprehended.

Fortin entered into a plea bargain agreement with regard to the assault, abduction, and sexual assault on Gardner. The New Jersey police were contacted in relation to Fortin's previous activities in New Jersey. Subsequent inquires resulted in Fortin being charged in relation to the murder of Melissa Padilla.

During Fortin's trial, evidence was sought from a criminal profiler regarding the similar modus operandi and signature behaviors that connected the homicide of Padilla and the assault on Gardner. During testimony, Robert Hazelwood from the FBI noted 15 consistent modus operandi aspects linking the crime:

- High-risk crimes
- Crimes committed impulsively
- Victims are female
- Age of victims generally the same
- Victims crossed the path of the offender
- Victims were alone
- Assaults occurred at the confrontation point
- Adjacent to or on well-traveled highway
- Occurred during darkness
- No weapons involved in assaults
- Blunt force injuries inflicted with fists, with nose of victims broken
- Trauma primarily to upper face, no teeth damaged
- Lower garments totally removed, with panties found inside the shorts or pants of the victims
- Shirt left on victims and breasts free
- No seminal fluid found in/on victims

Hazelwood concluded that both crimes were the result of anger that was manifested in the following "ritualistic" or "signature" behaviors:

- Bites to the lower chin
- Bites to the lateral left breast

- Injurious anal penetration
- Brutal facial beating
- Manual frontal strangulation

Hazelwood then concluded the following (*New Jersey v. Fortin*, 2000):

> In my 35 years of experience with a variety of violent crimes...
> I have never observed this combination of behaviors in a single
> crime of violence. The likelihood of different offenders committing
> two such extremely unique crimes is highly improbable. Based on
> a comparison of the M.O. and the ritualistic behaviors of the two
> crimes, it is my opinion that the same person was responsible for the
> murder of Ms. Melissa Padilla and the subsequent assault of
> Ms. Vicki Gardner.

In considering the rules of expert evidence, the appellate court identified two areas of concern with the testimony of the criminal profiler. First, it encroached on issues related to the ultimate issue. The thrust of the profiler's testimony was that "if Fortin committed the Maine attack (a known fact) and Hazelwood were to testify that the same person who assaulted the Maine trooper committed the New Jersey homicide, then he has essentially testified that Fortin committed the New Jersey crime" (*New Jersey v. Fortin*, 2000). Second, the appellate court evaluated the testimony of the profiler under the provisions of *Daubert* and noted concern with its scientific reliability. The appellate court indicated that the linkage analysis performed by the profiler was a field that lacked peer review and the validation of study results. The court stated that the testimony and its foundational research were not at a level of maturity to ensure that the expert's testimony will be sufficiently reliable (McGrath, 2001) because the profiler in this matter was substituting defensible scientific fact and research with his alleged case experience (Turvey, 2000).

These issues were again revisited by the court in 2007. This time, rather than recalling an expert whom the court was skeptical of, the prosecution instead opted for a Violent Criminal Apprehension Program (ViCAP) assessment of case linkage (Turvey, 2008). This time, a new profiler was asked to review the crimes in light of the ViCAP linkage and to opine on the unique signature nature of the offenses. This new request was problematic if for no other reason than the problem of bias: The linkage was rendered for the purpose of the new trial, with full knowledge of the previous court's decisions. As stated in *New Jersey v Fortin* (2007),

> It is noteworthy that only through the importuning of the Middlesex
> County Prosecutor's Office, which was preparing for defendant's
> murder trial, did Agent Safarik input a ViCAP form for the 9-year

old Gardner sexual assault. Thus, the Gardner ViCAP form was not submitted in the course of an ordinary investigative routine by the Maine State Police, but rather for litigation purposes—to find a match with the Padilla murder. Although the State maintains that the description of the Gardner crime on the ViCAP form is unassailable, it cannot be known in hindsight how the information would have been entered into the system for normal record keeping and investigative purposes. That is why the motion judge concluded that the State could not show that Agent Safarik's searches were based on "an unbiased generation of data."

The Estate of Samuel Sheppard v. The State of Ohio

In *The Estate of Samuel H Sheppard v. The State of Ohio*, the state hired retired FBI Supervisory Special Agent Gregg O. McCrary to testify that the crime scene of the homicide of Marilyn Sheppard in 1954 was staged (McCrary, 1999; Turvey, 2002). According to the report, staging is the "purposeful alteration of the crime and the crime scene by the offender. Staging is a conscious effort by the offender to mask the true motive for the crime by altering the crime scene to suggest false motives" (McCrary, 1999, p. 2).

In his report, McCrary (1999) concludes that Dr. Sheppard staged the crime scene to look like a profit- and drug-related burglary with a sexually motivated homicide.

The principal aspects of the case and McCrary's conclusions are as follows. The victim was murdered on approximately July 4, 1954, and her body was found in her bedroom having been severely beaten around the head approximately 25–35 times. Marilyn Sheppard was discovered with her pajama top pushed up to expose her breasts and one trouser leg pulled off. The victim's legs were hanging off the end of the bed, with one on either side of the bedpost. From this evidence, McCrary concluded that the crime scene had been staged to give the appearance of a sexually motivated homicide. He based these conclusions on the evidence of overkill, which is generally thought to occur only in crimes in which the offender and victim know each other. Also, there was no physical evidence of sexual activity, and the rage in which the offender killed the victim is inconsistent with the careful removal of the pajamas without ripping them, indicating a stark difference between the two behaviors. McCrary therefore concluded that there is no physical, forensic, or behavioral evidence that this was a sexually motivated homicide, but that it had been staged to give the appearance of one.

Parts of the house had been ransacked, including the drawers of a desk and Dr. Sheppard's medical bag and trophies; however, the damage was minor. The fact that there was a minimal amount of damage to property and that nothing of great value was taken led to the conclusion that the burglary was also staged. The only items taken were money from Dr. Sheppard's wallet and morphine from his bag, although this was based purely on Dr. Sheppard's previous evidence alone. McCrary (1999, p. 2) determined that "in this case it was the victim, not money or goods that were the primary focus of the attack." There were inconsistencies between the homicide and the burglary in that there was evidence of overkill, yet the offender took much care with the property. This suggested to McCrary that the offender had an interest in the condition of the property.

Forensic inconsistencies are apparent when considering the lack of blood found on Dr. Sheppard and the testimony that he did not clean himself at all. According to his testimony, the killer, who would have been covered in blood, touched him after the murder on two occasions. During one of these contacts, the killer took his wrist watch and ring, yet there was absolutely no blood found on Dr. Sheppard beyond a few blood spatters on the watch, later found outside the house. This raised questions not only because the killer would have been covered in blood after such a brutal attack but also because McCrary concluded that the blood spatters on the watch were consistent with impact spatter. This would only have been transferred onto the watch if it was in close proximity to the body of the victim during the attack. Dr. Sheppard also testified that he felt for his wife's pulse, which also means that he should have had a secondary transfer of blood, which then should have been transferred again to the telephone he used to call his neighbors. Dr. Sheppard testified that the killer took his wallet from his trouser pocket, yet there was no blood on his trousers.

The report also argued that this crime would have taken a considerable amount of time to commit. According to McCrary (1999, p. 5), "offenders who spend a great deal of time at a crime scene often have a legitimate reason for being at the scene and therefore are not worried about being interrupted or found at the scene."

This indicated that the offender felt comfortable and familiar at the crime scene. McCrary (1999, p. 8) then goes on to match every aspect of the homicide to the *Crime Classification Manual*'s definition of a staged domestic homicide, before concluding that

> the totality of the physical, forensic, and behavioral evidence allows for only one logical conclusion and that is that the homicide of Marilyn Reese Sheppard on July 4, 1954, was a staged domestic homicide committed by Dr. Sheppard. The known indicators for criminal staging as well as the known crime scene indicators consistent with a staged homicide are abundantly present. This evidence not only supports no other logical conclusion, but also significantly contradicts Dr. Samuel Sheppard's testimony and statements.

After a lengthy voir dire from Dr. Sheppard's attorney, McCrary's evidence was limited only to staging in general and not the Sheppard case, largely because of an affidavit prepared by Turvey (2000). Turvey came to the conclusion that McCrary's evidence should not be admitted for several reasons, including the fact that his determinations were drawn from the definition of staged domestic homicide in the *Crime Classification Manual*. Although this manual may be considered by some as a useful investigative guide, it is not an adequate base from which to draw conclusions and facts in a court of law. McCrary identified all characteristics of the accused and named the accused as the offender, which violates the ultimate issue rule. McCrary also admitted that he had no experience investigating domestic homicides or blood spatter analysis, rendering those aspects of the evidence outside his area of expertise. Furthermore, McCrary based his opinions on behavioral evidence alone and did not question or discuss other possible scenarios of what may have occurred (Turvey, 2000).

There are also some notable assumptions and inconsistencies in McCrary's report. For example, he stated that Dr. Sheppard testified he was rendered unconscious on the beach but then regained consciousness in the bedroom where the victim was found. This supports Turvey's concern that McCrary did not question or confirm the evidence his conclusions were based on.

R. v. Klymchuk

Maria Klymchuck was murdered on Easter Sunday, 1998 (unless otherwise stated, all information is taken from *R. v. Klymchuk*, 2005). The murder occurred in the drive shed located on their property near Bolton, Ontario, where the deceased used to train her dogs. On this particular evening, she had gone out to the shed at approximately 10 p.m. with one of her dogs. At approximately 11 p.m., her husband, Kirk Klymchuk, called 911 reporting that he had found his wife in their driveway with head injuries. He was told to perform cardiopulmonary resuscitation until emergency services arrived. Upon arrival, they were to find Maria Klymchuk dead.

Kirk Klymchuk was interviewed about the matter three times between Easter Sunday and June. In December 1998, he was arrested and charged with his wife's murder.

The Crown's case rested primarily on opportunity, that the accused was home on the night and had access to his wife, and motive, that he was under pressure from his girlfriend, Robin Mays, to leave his wife and children, aged 5 and 2 years.

Mays announced that she was returning to her de facto husband and wanted to end their relationship. Klymchuk called Mays a few days later and stated that his wife agreed to a divorce and that she would announce this to her parents on Good Friday. Klymchuk then called Mays on Friday claiming that there was a delay as his wife was ill. The relationship between Klymchuk and Mays continued after Maria's death, and Mays informed police of their relationship. Telephone conversations between the two were subsequently intercepted. In August 1998, Mays ended their relationship.

It was to become the prosecution's contention that the crime scene was staged, given the appearance that someone had broken into the shed through the window. To assist in this argument, the Crown called Special Agent Allan Brantley of the FBI.

The following is from *R. v. Klymchuk* (2005):

> [22] Special Agent Brantley had worked for the FBI for 17 years. He had been trained in and become an expert in what he described as criminal investigation analysis. Agent Brantley testified that criminal investigation analysis is an umbrella designation referring to a number of investigative services offered to police agencies to assist them in their investigations and sometimes offered to the courts as expert evidence. These investigative services included profiling and crime scene analysis. Agent Brantley testified that when performing a crime scene analysis, he was always concerned with whether the scene had been staged or manipulated to create a misleading impression. He defined staging as:
>
> The intentional alteration or manipulation of the crime scene by the offender to divert attention away from that individual as a logical suspect and/or to divert attention away from the most logical motive.
>
> [23] In response to a long hypothetical, that was rooted in the evidence, Agent Brantley opined that the scene in the drive shed had been staged to make it appear as though there had been a break-in. He emphasized that his opinion was based on the combined consideration of many circumstances and not on any one factor. He testified that there were many "behavioral, forensic, and investigative contradictions" that told him there had not been a real break-in, but rather an attempt to make it appear as though there had been a break-in.
>
> [24] The factors referred to by Agent Brantley can be grouped into five categories. First, he opined that the drive shed was a "high-risk" target for a break-in (in the sense that the risk to a burglar of being caught was substantial), and not one likely to be selected by a burglar. This statement of the risk posed to a burglar was based on many considerations, including the ample lighting around the drive shed, the locks on the doors, the alarm system, the presence of dogs in the home, the activity in the area of the home on that evening, the Klymchuks'

presence in the home that evening, the close proximity of neighbors, the relative unlikelihood that there would be valuable, easily portable property in the drive shed, and the availability of easier targets in the vicinity.

[25] Second, Agent Brantley described Mrs. Klymchuk as at a very low risk to be the victim of crime. She was security conscious, lived in a good neighborhood, and did not engage in any activities, such as drug dealing, that would make it more likely that she would become a victim of crime.

[26] Third, based on a statistical review of break and enters in the United States and in the 5 years between June 1995 and October 2000 in the area of the Klymchuks' home, Agent Brantley concluded that confrontations between the burglar and the victim were rare, and that in those rare cases where a confrontation occurred, there was seldom any violence directed at the victim. The burglar preferred to flee the scene. Brantley said:

> When you consider the incidents where contact is made between a burglar and the resident, when that happens for there to be a confrontation or the offender remains in the area and does not flee immediately, that is very rare. Even more rare is when a confrontation does occur and it turns violent. It is even more rare when that violent confrontation is also murder or homicide.

[27] Brantley testified that his review of the 5 years for which he had statistics of break and enters in the area of the Klymchuk home revealed no other case where a break and enter had resulted in a homicide.

[28] Fourth, Brantley considered the nature of the violence inflicted on Mrs. Klymchuk, the absence of any evidence of sexual assault, or theft from her person, and the indication that the perpetrator had quickly gained control over Mrs. Klymchuk in a confined area as contraindicative of homicide by an unknown intruder.

[29] Fifth, Agent Brantley focused on the window which was the apparent point of entry by the burglar. In Brantley's view, a burglar would not have entered the drive shed through that window. The window was in plain view and there were other, less exposed windows in the drive shed. The cutting of the screen on the window also, according to Agent Brantley, seemed unnecessary to gain entry through the window since the screen could be easily removed. The location of the cut on the screen and the manner in which the cut was made were viewed by Agent Brantley as inconsistent with the screen having been cut by someone who was trying to gain entry through the window. He

also noted that the area around the window where the screen had been cut did not show any indications of entry through that window (i.e., fingerprints). Finally, Brantley found it significant that the window had been left open. In his opinion, a burglar would close the window after the burglar gained entry to avoid the risk that the open window could attract someone's attention.

[30] While I will have more to say about parts of this evidence later in these reasons, for the moment I observe that this evidence was all directed at the WHAT question and Brantley's opinion that this was not a break-in, but an attempt to make it appear as though there had been a break-in.

[31] At the end of his examination-in-chief, Brantley gave a series of answers which Mr. Gold contends went beyond the permissible limits of expert evidence of staging. I will quote those questions and answers in full:

> Q. Sir, you indicated in this case that one of the factors that you considered as one of the more highlighted ones, and you pointed it out initially, was the apparent maximum human injury or human loss to the minimal property loss, did I understand that as being your evidence?
>
> A. That's correct.
>
> Q. What, if any significance, does that have to do from a crime scene analysis point of view?
>
> A. It is important in terms of what was the focus of the offender. *Was the focus of the offender assault and killing of the victim and was there more time spent accomplishing those acts than any other acts that we assessed at the scene.*
>
> Certainly we consider what was done to the victim. The numerous forms of trauma and the length of time that that process took. You compare that with the rather minimal movement of that snow blower. *Clearly, that the focus in this particular situation was on her and not on that piece of equipment.*
>
> Q. Is there a name for that sort of focus?
>
> A. Well, we would refer to this, because there was no indication of sexual activity or that the sexual parts of the body were traumatized or any semen or sperm or body fluids present and the fact that there was nothing taken from the scene we *would describe this or classify this as a "personal cause homicide."*

Q. And what does a personal cause homicide mean?

A. Well, the victim is killed, *because of who that victim is, he or she and not necessarily because of what that victim possesses. This generally includes reasons of revenge, anger, elimination of an obstacle to a goal. Those kinds of things are part and parcel to the personal cause homicide.*

Q. *Agent Brantley are you aware of any homicide case that you have been involved with in which staging was found to exist wherein the victim and the offender were strangers?*

A. *I'm aware of none* [italics added].

[32] The answers quoted above provide Brantley's opinion as to the possible motives for the murder and offer his opinion that there was a prior relationship between Mrs. Klymchuk and her killer. These answers are directed at the WHY and the WHO questions and not the WHAT question. They offer Agent Brantley's opinion that the killer was someone who knew Mrs. Klymchuk and had a personal motive for killing her. That profile of the killer fit the appellant.

In addressing the expert evidence, the Court applied the decisions of both *R. v. Clark* and *R. v Ranger* (*Ranger* was discussed previously). From *R. v. Klymchuk* (2005):

[33] In *Ranger*, the expert was allowed to offer an opinion as to the killer's motive, the existence of a prior relationship between the killer and the victims, and which of the victims was the true target of the killer. This court held that none of that evidence was properly admitted stating at para. 82:

Detective Inspector Lines' [the expert] *opinions about the perpetrator's likely motivation for staging the crime scene and his characteristics as a person associated with the victims and having a particular interest in Marsha [one of the victims] constituted evidence of criminal profiling. Criminal profiling is a novel field of scientific evidence, the reliability of which was not demonstrated at trial. To the contrary, it would appear from her limited testimony about the available verification of opinions in her field of work that her opinions amounted to no more than educated guesses* [italics added]. As such, her criminal profiling evidence was inadmissible. The criminal profiling evidence also approached the ultimate issue in the case and, hence, was highly prejudicial.

[34] In *Clark*, the expert (the same expert who testified in *Ranger*) was allowed to advance the opinion that the killer knew the victims and

was familiar with the residence in which the homicides occurred. In holding that this evidence went beyond the pale of permissible expert evidence of staging, this court said at para. 87:

> To the extent that the Detective Inspector's evidence about the phone and the lighting may have conveyed the impression that the offender was someone familiar with the layout of the Tweeds' [the victims] apartment, it was offensive. *She was not entitled to testify about the characteristics of the likely offender, characteristics which in this case comfortably fit with the appellant. That constituted criminal profiling evidence* [italics added]. As such, for reasons stated earlier, it was inadmissible and should not have been received.

[35] No meaningful distinction can be drawn between Agent Brantley's answers quoted above and the evidence found to be inadmissible in *Ranger* and *Clark*. In all three cases, the evidence was offered to identify the killer by reference to the killer's motive and his prior association with the victim(s). In each case, the accused fit the profile of the killer provided by the expert.

[36] There is nothing in the basis of Agent Brantley's opinion that renders it inherently more reliable as expert evidence than the similar opinions rejected in *Ranger* and *Clark*. The Crown did not offer any evidence that Agent Brantley's opinions as to the motives and prior connection between the killer and victim of those who stage a break-in in the course of committing a homicide had been or could be tested according to the generally accepted scientific methodology identified in *Daubert v. Merrell Dow Pharmaceuticals, Inc.* 509 U.S. 579 (1993) and quoted with approval in *R. v. J. (J.L.), supra*, at 501-502.

[37] Agent Brantley's opinions as to the killer's motive and prior relationship with the victim were not founded on any scientific process of inquiry, but on his own experience as augmented by his review of similar case files and interviews with incarcerated felons. Agent Brantley's experience and review of the other sources led him to conclude that those who staged break-ins as part of a homicide probably had a personal motive for the homicide and probably had a prior association with the victim. Even if those opinions accurately reflect the statistical probabilities that a killer who stages a break-in as part of a homicide has a personal motive for the homicide and a prior relationship with the victim, conclusions based on statistical probabilities can offer no insight as to what happened in a specific case. For example, evidence from a homicide investigator that in his experience, his review of similar cases, and his interviews of killers, 85 percent of spousal homicides (a hypothetical figure) not involving a sexual assault or theft from the

victim were committed by the surviving partner, could not be offered as evidence (expert or otherwise) that a specific spousal homicide was committed by the surviving partner. To borrow the words of Charron J.A. in *Ranger*, Agent Brantley's opinion as to the killer's motive and prior relationship with the deceased were "educated guesses" and not scientifically based opinions. As Charron J.A. indicated, those "educated guesses" can play a valuable role in the investigation of crime by directing the police to fruitful areas of investigation. They cannot, however, be admitted as evidence under the guise of expert opinion.

[38] The trial judge erred in law in allowing Agent Brantley to give opinion evidence as to the killer's prior relationship with Mrs. Klymchuk and the possible motives for her killing. These errors were compounded by the failure to limit Agent Brantley's opinions as to the WHAT question to evidence based on his examination and reconstruction of the crime scene.

The court took issue with the basis of Agent Brantley's conclusions, specifically citing the probabilistic nature of the opinions and the inherently unreliable nature of discussing average or typical victims and crimes. The following were noted as points of concern:

- There were essentially five factors guiding the conclusion that the crime was staged. These were (1) the drive shed was a high-risk burglary target; (2) the victim was considered a low risk for being the victim of crime; (3) statistics relating to break and enters and the incidence of associated violence; (4) observations of the victim's body and the surrounding areas; and (5) observations of the cut shed window. The first two, it was concluded, are essentially profiling conclusions revolving around whether the victim and the shed were typical targets of a burglary gone wrong. Furthermore, the last two are properly viewed as reconstruction evidence on which an expert could base an assessment of staging.

- There was nothing in Brantley's evidence to suggest that his profile of burglary locations or victims was any more scientific than his profile of those who stage break-ins. The court noted the range of offenders who engage in burglaries, from "drug addled teenagers" to the sophisticated "second story" man. The court further noted that given the differences in offenders, it was their targets that would have much in common.

- Brantley's assessment of the shed as high risk relied on an assumption of the type of offender who would usually commit this type of crime. If the assumption of offender type was removed from the argument, the argument has no validity.

- Brantley's assumption of Maria Klymchuk as a low-risk victim suffered from the same problems as his assumption of the shed being high risk.

- Brantley's assessment required little to no expert knowledge in that the average person could assess the shed as a potential high-risk burglary target (well lit, with dogs in the home, and a burglar alarm).

- The court also noted the problems with applying general information or knowledge to a specific case under consideration: "Statistical evidence of probabilities based on prior similar events, while useful in many disciplines, offers no admissible evidence as to what happened on a specific occasion in a criminal trial."

Given the issues presented by the evidence, the court saw fit to quash the conviction and grant a new trial. In 2008, Klymchuk was convicted of the crime, although it is alleged that questions remain. Makin (2008) reported the following:

> A fatigued jury convicted Ontario chiropractor Kirk Klymchuk of second-degree murder yesterday after deliberating for 5 days over whether he had bludgeoned his 27-year-old wife, Maria, to death with an axe on Easter Sunday, 1998.
>
> The verdict ended a legal drama that included three trials—one that resulted in a conviction that was overturned on appeal, one that resulted in a hung jury, and the proceedings that concluded yesterday—over 8 years.
>
> Yesterday's verdict may have reflected a divided jury since the Crown pressed hard for a first-degree conviction on the basis that Mr. Klymchuk stage-managed the crime scene to make it look as if a burglar had killed his wife.
>
> "In my view, this was a miscarriage of justice," defense counsel Tim Breen said shortly after the verdict. "There are many unresolved questions that point to the innocence of my client, and that made this a very suspect case."
>
> Second-degree murder carries a sentence of life imprisonment, with parole eligibility of between 10 and 25 years. Mr. Klymchuk is to be sentenced May 30.
>
> Eight of the jurors made no parole recommendation yesterday. One proposed 10 years, one suggested 12 years, and one recommended 20 years. The 12th juror was discharged for medical reasons early in the deliberations.
>
> The verdict was a particular triumph for prosecutor Eric Taylor and Ontario Provincial Police homicide officers who investigated the case. An acquittal or hung jury would likely have meant the end of Mr. Klymchuk's legal troubles, since it is virtually unheard of for the Crown to attempt to procure a fourth trial.

Should Mr. Klymchuk launch an appeal, it would likely center on defense allegations that investigators failed to convey evidence honestly or falsified it.

In his charge to the jury, Mr. Justice Fletcher Dawson of the Ontario Superior Court specified that were the jury to accept that police dealt with a portion of the evidence dishonestly, the entire investigation could be in doubt.

Ms. Klymchuk, a teacher, was killed in a drive shed behind the couple's suburban home as their children slept nearby. Mr. Klymchuk told police that he went out to check on her before going to bed, and found her bleeding profusely.

In apparent panic, he called 911 and attempted to provide CPR to his blood-drenched wife.

Soon after the killing, police discovered that Mr. Klymchuk had been involved in a torrid, 5-month love affair with Robin Mays, who had moved from Alberta to Brampton to be near him. Just days before Ms. Klymchuk was killed, Ms. Mays had broken off the relationship because Mr. Klymchuk had not left his wife.

Mr. Taylor alleged that the defendant's staging included ripping a window screen in the drive shed, opening the window behind it, and pressing a shoe print onto the window sill.

He said that Mr. Klymchuk also put a snow blower outside the drive shed, as if to suggest that a thief had been in the process of stealing it.

Mr. Breen dismissed the Crown theory as fanciful and full of holes. He said investigators fixed their sights on Mr. Klymchuk almost from the moment he called 911 on the day of his wife's violent death. He also said they paid no attention to hunting down other suspects and even tried to hide evidence that would corroborate Mr. Klymchuk's story of giving the dying woman CPR in an effort to save her life—irrefutable proof of his innocence.

RECOMMENDATIONS

Although it may seem as though this chapter has provided more support for excluding profiling evidence than including it, this was not the aim. In fact, it is our belief that profiling can bring a considerable level of expertise to court proceedings. On this note, and as these recommendations will suggest, we do recommend caution in the way that profiling evidence is applied. If for no other reason, there is nothing more damaging than experts who build their careers as people who speak on demand, doing immeasurable harm to the field in which they are speaking.

The following recommendations are by no means exhaustive but do cover some of the major considerations for experts presenting evidence in court. They are based on the rules of evidence, on legal precedent, and on the past behavior of experts who have given evidence on profiling.

First, although the development of inductive profiles is likely to be more readily understood, and although they may yield results on the odd occasion, it is probable in the long term that they will have a negative impact on the case for profiling in court. Deductive profiling, on the other hand, will be more likely to elicit productive information as long as the profiler explains his or her analysis and conclusions in a clear and concise manner. Furthermore, the profile is a direct extension of the physical evidence, which has been established either by some other expert or by the profiler giving evidence if so qualified. This ensures that the basis of the testimony has also been established and can be accepted by the court.

Second, in line with the expertise rule, it is not unreasonable to expect that experts be just that. Although there are no universal standards for profilers in terms of education, training, and experience, it is imperative that, given the nature of profiling, those providing the service have an adequate level of education and experience in the behavioral sciences, particularly psychology and criminology. As noted by Hans Gross in his seminal work *Criminal Psychology* (1968, p. 1), "Of all disciplines necessary to the criminal justice in addition to the knowledge of law, the most important are those derived from psychology. For such sciences teach him to know the type of man it is his business to deal with."

This should extend beyond coverage of the fundamental principles of psychology (history, application, etc.) and should ideally involve more advanced coursework in this field. Postgraduate study in related areas would ensure that the individual's education is well rounded. This is not to say that the acceptance of an expert rests solely on his or her education, or that this alone should dictate the weight given to an expert's testimony, but it must surely play a considerable role. The general warning given by Kirk (1974, p. 16) is relevant here: "When the liberty of an individual may depend in part on physical evidence it is not unreasonable to ask that the expert witnesses who are called upon to testify, either against the defendant or on his behalf, know what they are doing."

Of utmost importance is the requirement that experts realize the limitations of their own skills. The best expert is not one who continually oversteps the boundaries of his trade but one who realizes its limitations and endeavors to operate within these. If something is not discernible from the evidence or the behavior, then one cannot draw conclusions from it. In addition, if something is unknown, experts should refrain from simply filling in the gaps based on what they assume to be the case or what their experience suggests. In the witness box, the expert must not be tempted to stray from the basis on which her expertise was deemed to be of assistance to the court: The closer her expertise comes to offering an answer to the ultimate issue, the greater the need for constraint.

Next, in accordance with the area of expertise rule, there should be some theoretical basis on which an opinion is formed. For example, a conclusion that an offender rapes elderly women because of a hatred of elderly women formed during his teenage years should be based on more than a "gut feeling" or the simple issue that the victims are elderly. In short, an expert should be able to articulate his or her conclusions and the reasoning behind them. Anyone who cannot articulate an opinion, or provide detailed information on the method used to arrive at one, should be treated with the utmost skepticism and excluded from giving expert testimony.

As discussed by Wiard (1931b, p. 539), caution should be exercised when employing the testimony of experts, with particular care taken to ensure that they adopt the impartiality incumbent upon them as an advisor to the court:

> If the witness makes statements which are too dogmatic and too general, he thereby lays himself open to more or less successful attack by the opposition and may soon find himself in an unenviable position. The other side should, therefore, note carefully the general complexion of the comments of the witness, in an endeavor to determine whether or not he is making an honest effort to be fair and impartial and offer the benefit of his experience for the general good of the case, or whether he is merely saying certain things, presenting testimony which is colored to suit his employers. Unfortunately, there are so-called expert witnesses who are credited at least, if not actually proven, to be able to take either side of a question and discourse quite learnedly upon it. Such men are usually most dangerous, because they are ordinarily acquainted with the procedure of the courts and can deal in half truths, equivocations, and evasions, to such an extent that it is almost impossible to pin them down to bold misstatements, perjury, or the like.

The essence of Wiard's cautions should be no different today, and his last concerns are echoed and reinterpreted in a critical discussion by Thornton (1997, pp. 16–17), who notes that occasionally experts may deliberately seek to mislead the court. In Table 8.1, Thornton poses common questions asked of experts, their responses, and the occasionally hidden meanings behind these.[5]

Although it stands to reason that the expert's credentials should be established, regardless of the level of the court, this is not done in all cases. In a bail hearing

---

[5]Although most experts testify openly and honestly, there can be no doubt that the expertise offered in some instances is questionable, in either its integrity or its purpose.

Table 8.1 Question–Answer–Translation for Cross-Examination

Question	Answer	Translation
Is this situation unusual?	I have never seen a similar situation.	You don't know what I have seen and what I haven't, so I can say this and get away with it.
What is the basis of your opinion?	My 26 years of experience in the field.	It's really a surmise on my part. I believe it to be true, but I can't really tell you why I think that. It's really more of an impression that I have than anything else but I can't say that it's a surmise or a vague impression, could I?
Can you tell us how many cases of this type you have examined?	Many hundreds.	I don't know, and I certainly don't know how many of them would support my current position, and I might not be able to tell even if I went back and pulled the files.
Can you supply us with a list of those cases?	Oh, no, I don't think so. They go back many years.	No way. You don't have any way of smoking those cases out of me, and even if I was ordered to do so, I could come up with plenty of reasons not to comply.
Can you supply us with the raw data on all those cases?	I don't think so. Some of them were when I was employed in my previous job. And some could be on microfilm. And it would take weeks or months to locate all of them.	Not a chance.
Were those cases subjected to independent scrutiny for technical correctness?	All of them were reviewed by my supervisors. I don't have any reason to believe that their review wasn't adequate.	No. And also, now you are going to have to argue with those nameless, faceless supervisors that I have alluded to but haven't identified.

From Thornton (1997).

at the Coroner's Court level, a "behavioral consultant" testified as to the continued danger posed by the applicant. As noted by Crispin J,

> I have no doubt that he gave his opinion honestly but, in my opinion, he was plainly not qualified to express the opinions that he did.... The bulk of this evidence was clearly inadmissible and whilst no objection was taken to it ... I was obliged to conclude that it could be given no real weight.

As a result, some experts are allowed to offer their opinions in a relatively unfettered manner, occasionally doing incalculable damage to the defendant or his or her case.

Even in cases in which the guilt of the accused may not be an issue, the role of the expert in the initial trial may be such that it provides the defense with grounds for appeal at a later date, whereas if not for the expert giving his or her own tainted view of events, the trial would have proceeded within legal constraints, ultimately seeing justice best served. The outcome here may be to see guilty defendants walk free on technicalities raised at appeal. This is also clearly not desirable.

As a final point and observation of those legal professionals who employ consultants to provide an exam of their case, it is similarly not unreasonable to expect they be at least conversant in the language of the area the expert will testify in, and that they possess some working knowledge of how the testimony may relate to or affect their case. Again, Wiard (1931b, p. 540) provides some poignant commentary:

> It is almost hopeless for a lawyer lacking a scientific education to oppose technical testimony by apparently searching interrogations upon the minutiae of the matters involved. Needless to say, both counsels may be in the same boat in this respect, as was evinced in a recent case in which the writer appeared. This was in connection with a shooting, and the counsel employing the expert witness believed, and practically so stated in court, that all bullets were flaming as they passed through the air. The opposing counsel, on the other hand, believed that automatic pistols were loaded in a manner similar to that employed for the muzzle loading cap-and-ball arms which went out of existence at the end of the Civil War days. One can well imagine that under these conditions the witness, although amused at the continual misstatements of facts, was not in a very enviable position, for most of the questions propounded by both attorneys were based on utter misconceptions of the facts, so that he was in the position of having to disagree with practically everyone concerned.

CONCLUSION

Some jurisdictions in the United States have been more receptive in their adoption of profiling than others, whereas Australian and English courts have been more reluctant. The rules of expert evidence in Australia allow for profiling as expert testimony, even if only in a limited manner, perhaps in some lower levels of the criminal justice system. As profiling receives more attention through practical application and academic literature, it stands to reason that it will receive a greater chance of being accepted in court.

It is unlikely that any acceptance will come in a flood, but legal commentators of recent times also scoffed at the acceptance of other forms of evidence that are now commonplace in the courtroom. Providing that courts are suitably judicious in their use of this evidence, and that they ensure that experts are just that, profiling may help clarify behavioral evidence for a judge and jury in the same way that experts have begun clarifying other technical areas such as DNA probabilities.

Questions

1. What is perhaps the most beneficial evidence that profiling offers to criminal proceedings?
   a. Motive and intent to commit the criminal act
   b. Offender state of mind before, during, and after the commission of a crime
   c. Offender modus operandi
   d. Signature analysis and case linkage
   e. Offender residential status
2. List and briefly discuss the areas in which profiling may be used in court.
3. Courts in Australia and the United Kingdom have been very open and receptive to profiling evidence. *True or false?*
4. The rules of expert evidence presented in the chapter are unique to Australia and not utilized in other countries. *True or false?*
5. Gross argued that of all the disciplines necessary to criminal justice, in addition to the law, the most important is psychology. *True or false?*

REFERENCES

Academy of Behavioral Profiling. (2001). Academy of Behavioral Profiling criminal profiling guidelines. Available at http://www.profiling.org. Accessed January 14, 2004.

Alison, L., & Canter, D. (1999). Professional, legal and ethical issues in offender profiling. In D. Canter & L. Alison (Eds.), Profiling in Policy and Practice. Aldershot, UK: Ashgate Dartmouth.

Australian Law Reform Commission. (1994). Compliance with the Trade Practices Act 1974: Issues related to court procedure. Available at http://www.austlii.edu.au. Accessed November 12, 2004.

Bartol, C. R. (2002). Criminal Behavior: A Psychosocial Approach (6th ed.). Upper Saddle River. NJ: Prentice Hall.

Bartol, C. R., & Bartol, A. M. (1994). Psychology and Law: Research and Practice (2nd ed.). Pacific Grove, CA: Brooks/Cole.

Bekerian, D. A., & Jackson, J. L. (1997). Critical issues in offender profiling. In J. L. Jackson & D. A. Bekerian (Eds.), Offender Profiling: Theory, Research and Practice. Chichester, UK: Wiley.

Daubert v. Merrell Dow Pharmaceuticals, Inc., 113 S. Ct. 2786 (1993).

Douglas, J. E., & Munn, C. (1992, February). Violent crime scene staging: Modus operandi, signature and staging. FBI Law Enforcement Bulletin.

Douglas, J. E., Ressler, R. K., Burgess, A. W., & Hartman, C. R. (1986). Criminal profiling from crime scene analysis. Behavioral Sciences and the Law, 4(4), 410–421.

Field, D. (2008). Queensland Evidence Law. Sydney: Butterworths/NexisLexis.

Findlay, M., Odgers, S., & Yeo, S. (1999). Australian Criminal Justice (2nd ed.). Melbourne: Oxford University Press.

Folkes v. Chadd, 3 Doug. K. B. 157 (1782).

Freckleton, I. R. (1987). The Trial of the Expert: A Study of Expert Evidence and Forensic Experts. Melbourne: Oxford University Press.

Freckleton, I. R., & Selby, H. (1999a). Australian Judicial Attitudes toward Expert Evidence. Melbourne: Australasian Institute of Judicial Administration.

Freckleton, I. R., & Selby, H. (1999b). The Law of Expert Evidence. Pyrmont, Australia: LBC Information Services.

Freckleton, I. R., & Selby, H. (2002a). The Law of Expert Evidence. Pyrmont, Australia: Law Book Company.

Freckleton, I. R., & Selby, H. (2002b). Expert Evidence: Law, Practice, Procedure and Advocacy. Pyrmont, Australia: Law Book Company.

Frye v. United States, 293 Fed. 1013 (1923).

Geberth, V. J. (1996). Practical Homicide Investigation: Tactics, Procedures and Forensic Techniques (3rd ed.). Boca Raton, FL: CRC Press.

Gross, H. (1924). Criminal Investigation (3rd ed.). London: Sweet & Maxwell.

Gross, H. (1968). Criminal Psychology: A Manual for Judges, Practitioners and Students. Montclair, NJ: Patterson Smith.

Hazelwood, R. R., Ressler, R. K., Depue, R. L., & Douglas, J. E. (1999). Criminal investigative analysis: An overview. In R. R. Hazelwood & A. W. Burgess (Eds.), Practical Aspects of Rape Investigation: A Multidisciplinary Approach. Boca Raton, FL: CRC Press.

Kennedy, D. (2008, February 25). Hope for prisoner as expert recants on wife's suicide letter. The Times.

Kirk, P. (1974). Crime Investigation (2nd ed.). New York: Wiley.

Makin, K. (2008, May 17). Man's 3rd murder trial ends with verdict of guilty. Globe and Mail.

McCord, E. (1987). Syndromes, profiles and other mental exotica: A new approach to the admissibility of nontraditional psychological evidence in criminal cases. Oregon Law Review, 66, 19–108.

McCrary, G. (1999). Criminal investigative analysis in The Estate of Samuel Sheppard v. The State of Ohio. Available at http://www.courttv.com. Accessed November 22, 2004.

McGrath, M. (2001). Signature in the courtroom: Whose crime is it anyway? Journal of Behavioral Profiling, 2(2). Available at http://www.profiling.org.

McNicol, S. B., & Mortimer, D. (1996). Evidence. Chatswood, Australia: Butterworths.

Melton, G. B., Petrila, J., Poythress, N. G., & Slobogin, C. (1997). Psychological Evaluations for the Court: A Handbook for the Mental Health Professionals and Lawyers (2nd ed.). New York: Guilford.

Moenssens, A. A., Inbau, F. E., & Starrs, J. E. (1986). Scientific Evidence in Criminal Cases (3rd ed.). New York: Foundation Press.

New Jersey v. Fortin, 162 N.J. 517, 745 A.2d 509 (2000).

New Jersey v. Fortin, 189 N.J. 579, 917 A.2d 746 (2007).

Ormerod, D. (1996). The evidential implications of psychological profiling. Criminal Law Review, 717, 863–877.

Petherick, W. (2000). Criminal profiling in the Australia legal system. Paper presented at the Academy of Behavioral Profiling General Meeting, Las Vegas, Nevada, October 6–8.

Pinizzotto, A. J., & Finkel, N. (1990). Criminal personality profiling: An outcome and process study. Law and Human Behavior, 14, 215–233.

R. v. Gilfoyle, 2 Cr. App. Rep. 57 (2001).

R. v. Klymchuk, 203 C.C.C. (3d) 341, 205 O.A.C. 57 (2005).

R. v. Mohan, 2 SCR 9, 89 C.C.C. (3d) 402 (1994).

R. v. Ranger, 178 C.C.C. (3d) 375 (Ont. CA) (2003).

R. v. Turner, QB 834 (1975).

Report of the Kaufman Commission on proceedings involving Guy Paul Morin. (2003). Toronto: Queen's Printer for Ontario. Available at http://www.attorneygeneral.jus .gov.on.ca/english/about/pubs/morin. Accessed June 20, 2005.

Rudin, K., & Inman, N. (2002). An Introduction to Forensic DNA Analysis (2nd ed.). Boca Raton, FL: CRC Press.

Saferstein, R. (2004). Criminalistics: An Introduction to Forensic Science (8th ed.). Upper Saddle River, NJ: Prentice Hall.

Thornton, J. I. (1997). The general assumptions and rationale of forensic identification. In D. L. Faigman, D. H. Kaye, M. J. Saks, & J. Sanders (Eds.), Modern Scientific Evidence: The Law and Science of Expert Evidence. St. Paul, MN: West.

Turvey, B. E. (1997). The role of criminal profiling in the development of trial strategy. Available at http://www.corpus-delicti.com/Trial_Strategy.html. Accessed January 14, 2004.

Turvey, B. E. (1999a). Criminal Profiling: An Introduction to Behavioral Evidence Analysis. San Diego: Academic Press.

Turvey, B. E. (1999b). Offender modus operandi, signature, and the law. Available at http://www.corpus-delicti.com/signature_law.html. Accessed January 15, 2004.

Turvey, B. E. (2000). Criminal profiling and the problem of forensic individuation. Journal of Behavioral Profiling, 1(2), 1–15. Available at http://www.profiling.org.

Turvey, B. E. (2005). Staged burglary: Technical note and civics lesson. Journal of Behavioral Profiling, 5(1).

Turvey, B. E. (2008). Criminal Profiling: An Introduction to Behavioral Evidence Analysis (3rd ed.). Burlington, MA: Academic Press.

Underwager, R., & Wakefield, H. (1993). A paradigm shift for expert witnesses. Institute for Psychological Therapies Journal, 5, 1–18. Available at http://www.ipt-forensics. com/journal/volume5/j5_3_2.htm. Accessed October 21, 2004.

Wiard, S. (1931a). The preparation and presentation of expert testimony. American Journal of Police Science, 2, 143–147.

Wiard, S. (1931b). The cross examination of expert witnesses. American Journal of Police Science, 2, 538–542.

Wood, J. (2003). Forensic sciences from the judicial perspective. Australian Journal of Forensic Sciences, 35(1), 115–132.

Wrightsman, L. S., Greene, E., Nietzel, M. T., & Fortune, W. H. (2002). Psychology in the Legal System (5th ed.). Belmont, CA: Wadsworth.

Where to from Here?

Wayne Petherick

KEY TERMS

Academy of Behavioral Profiling: A professional organization dedicated to the advancement of evidence-based deductive profiling techniques.

The scientific method: A systematic way to investigate how or why something works through observation, theorizing, and experimentation.

Ethics: The rules or standards that govern the conduct of members of a profession.

INTRODUCTION

The history of profiling is easy to trace—after all, it has already been recorded and is available for review (see Chapter 1; Petherick, 2003; Turvey, 2008). The future of profiling is another story entirely. Given the nature of the craft and the advances made in recent years, it stands to reason that only further improvements will be made. At least, this should be our hope.

An increase in use in the real world is matched by an increase in the number of scholarly works dedicated to the field. Most provide a general overview of profiling (Ainsworth, 2001; Jackson & Bekerian, 1997), with others providing a more in-depth examination of particular methods (Rossmo, 2000; Turvey, 2008). Apart from a few peripheral discussions on practical issues, few dedicate much time to the more pragmatic issues of professionalization, the *scientific method*, research, *ethics*, accountability, and education and training.

None of the issues in the following discussion should be considered in isolation. Indeed, the degree of interreliance many of these topics share often

213

makes their discussion difficult to separate. For example, one cannot argue for ethical standards without professionalization, and one cannot argue professionalization without having standards for education and training.

Bekerian and Jackson (1997) provide a decent overview that considers the future of profiling. They note that (p. 209)

> all profiling techniques focus on behavior; and there is a good deal of diversity in the techniques that are employed. Variation in an area of research is important for scientific progress. However, too much diversity can result in the field becoming fragmented theoretically, and therefore less accessible to application. There are at least three ways in which fragmentation might occur in the area of offender profiling: differences in frameworks, individual differences between profilers, and differences in culture.

Differences in frameworks, they explain, refers to the debate regarding the appropriate methodological framework. Perhaps nowhere is this more profound in profiling than in the debate between those who adhere to a deductive model and those who would prefer an inductive model (see Chapter 2; Turvey, 2008). These differences will not be easily overcome.

Further fragmentation is created when profilers vehemently pronounce the utility of their own method while at the same time denouncing that of their counterparts. This is not in itself a problem, but when practitioners do not understand the shortcomings of the methods they employ, this does suggest a fundamental and overall flaw in practice. Healthy competition does foster progress, but it also affects overall harmony in the community. This in-fighting may be seen by potential consumers as evidence of profiling's lack of value.

Individual differences between profilers suggest that no two profilers will produce the same profile (this is possible, even likely). They argue that this is because of differing levels of education, training, and experience, and each can bring something different to the table. Whereas one profiler may have keen insight into what motivates a particular offender, another may have similarly keen insight into precautionary acts and staging. In essence, a profile will be the result of a person's experiences, or as Bekerian and Jackson (1997, p. 211) state, "the act of profiling is personal."

With regard to differences in culture, it is noted that although contemporary approaches to profiling started in the United States, it must be questioned how and if these methods may be culturally juxtaposed. Note that the differences in offending between countries are distinct in many areas, and this is well documented in the criminological literature (e.g., the homicide rates of the United States and Australia, weapon availability, and victimological differences). Caution should be exercised when using a statistical model in which research is applied in a culture other than the one in which it was developed. (See Canter, 2004, for a discussion of one particular method.)

The following is one such example among many (Medicolegal Society of New South Wales, undated):

> The particular problem with some statistical methodologies is that they are also often built around a localized database and localized demographic situations, and it is very difficult to transfer this information from one group or one country to another. In the past we have had experiences where FBI profilers have come up with the view that the perpetrator of a New South Wales crime was a 26-year-old black American negro on the basis of the statistical analysis they have done, which is not very likely.

PROFESSIONALIZATION

One way to improve on a product such as profiling is to increase the standards of those who practice it. This would involve establishing standards of practice and accountability. To provide context for any future approach at professionalization, we must examine what has been done in the past. Commenting on the formation of the *Academy of Behavioral Profiling* (ABP), McGrath (as cited in Turvey, 2002, p. 573) notes that "we struggle with what has been done in the past, what we are doing now, how we are doing it and why."

Given the multiplicity of profiling approaches and the fragmented and often ad hoc approach to profiling that many take, it is unreasonable to suggest that we settle all of our differences, form one professional organization, and develop a unified theory of criminal profiling. Although much of the theory and practice involved in criminal profiling is consistent across methods, as are its goals, subtle differences prohibit such an aggregation. Such unification may on its face seem advantageous, but the differences in individual approaches are beneficial and will help to elevate standards (as discussed by Bekerian & Jackson, 1997).

Professionalization is one of the greatest obstacles to profiling's advance, in which education and training undoubtedly play a role. Essentially anyone can call himself a criminal profiler, regardless of education, training, and experience. This leads to a lack of uniformity in training and education standards, which subsequently affects the work product of those in the community (which may in turn taint the perception of profilers in the investigative community they serve and academic communities that research them).

One exception to this is in the United Kingdom, where a register of profilers is kept with the National Crime Faculty as part of the Association of Chief Police Officers. Part of their function is to act as a regulatory agency for criminal profilers. This is a commendable endeavor and goes a long way toward providing a common standard by which to ensure a profiler's skills. Either a person meets these requirements and can profile, or that person does not and therefore cannot. Although this demands certain standards, it is still a considerable way from a professional organization that serves not only to set such requirements but also to further the field through continued training, education, and the dissemination of information.

Thus far, only the ABP has put forward this goal. The goal of the ABP is not to bring all practitioners together under one banner but, rather, to provide a forum for the discussion and distribution of information concerning evidence-based criminal profiling and its application. The ABP also has a code of ethics that regulates the conduct of its members, who are subject to varying levels of penalties should they behave unethically.

THE SCIENTIFIC METHOD

There can be no doubt that the scientific method should be the cornerstone of any inquiry made from a scientific standpoint, but this is unfortunately not the case in many instances. Some may argue that because criminal profiling is not a science, the scientific method simply does not apply. Given that one can apply the scientific method to many forms of inquiry, and one need not be a scientist to apply the scientific method, this argument does not stand up to scrutiny.

According to Turvey (2008, p. 47),

> The scientific method is a way to investigate how or why something works, or how something happened, through the development of hypotheses and subsequent attempts at falsification through testing and other accepted means. It is a structured process designed to build scientific knowledge by way of answering specific questions about observations through careful analysis and critical thinking. Observations are used to form testable hypotheses, and with sufficient testing hypotheses can become scientific theories. Eventually, over much time, with precise testing marked by a failure to falsify, scientific theories can become scientific principles. The scientific method is the particular approach to knowledge building and problem solving employed by scientists of every kind.

Inman and Rudin (2001) agree, stating that the scientific method provides a framework for hypothesis testing, whereby a theory is formulated and measured against the evidence, and support or lack thereof confirms or refutes the hypothesis. If the process is repeatedly applied, conclusions should be complete, well informed, and able to stand up to a great deal of scrutiny. Without relying on a process of falsification, one cannot be sure that one's conclusions are sound or that one conclusion is more likely than any others. As such, it is necessary to falsify all theories regarding offender behavior; only in this way can we be certain that our conclusions are reflective of the available evidence and not some a priori bias.

However, just because one makes meager attempts to falsify one's theories does not mean that one is applying a scientific method. For example, one theory in a profile may be that the victim was high risk, so we should look for evidence that disproves this, such as safety and security procedures taken by the victim or a cautious personality. In the absence of such signs, this theory seems more likely, but this still does not mean it is necessarily correct. One must also develop other theories and try to disprove these by measuring them against the evidence. At the end of the day, if all theories are tested rigorously and the theory remains that the victim was high risk, then this hypothesis is most likely correct and could be posited with a high degree of confidence. In short, to "prove"[1] a theory, a vigorous attempt must be made to disprove it.

RESEARCH

One of the ways to improve a product such as profiling, and one that is sorely lacking, is to conduct research into its effectiveness and the features that have been helpful or detrimental. More research on profiling and the ways it can assist police in their inquiries is definitely warranted.

Note, however, that there are many problems in researching a field such as profiling, and these are outlined in detail elsewhere (Ainsworth, 2001; Petherick, 2003). Research to date has been somewhat repetitive, unhelpful, or confusing. Perhaps the most common form of research stems from questions about the accuracy of profilers (Gudjonsson & Copson, 1997; Pinizzotto, 1984; Pinizzotto & Finkel, 1990). The latest variation of this is aimed at not only determining how accurate profilers are but also how accurate profilers are compared to other groups, such as students, psychologists, police, and detectives (Kocsis, 2001, 2003; Kocsis, Hayes, & Irwin, 2002; Kocsis, Irwin, Hayes, & Nunn, 2000). Goldsworthy (2001) has also examined a number of features of consumer attitudes toward profiling.

Although it may be useful to examine the differences between such groups, it would be more useful to examine the abilities of practitioners from the different approaches. This would possibly help clarify much of the confusion that exists regarding the differences between the methods, such as how they approach a case and how they develop their insights. This research approach may also help to answer some lingering questions about which methodology provides the most fruitful profiles.

---

[1] I am well aware that we can never truly prove a theory, only consistently fail to disprove it.

This may sound like an easy task, but such examinations carry many potential flaws. First, laboratory settings lack the same pressures as operational police environments. The dynamics created by the involvement of the media, the victim, families and friends of the victim, and other contributors are near impossible to introduce in a controlled environment. Second, it is difficult to decide whether to use a "freestyle" approach in which profilers provide all of their opinions based on the supplied information or an approach involving simply ticking a box corresponding to a predefined template of answers. The first scenario would provide detailed information but may present problems in tabulating such data. In the second scenario, some advice that would otherwise be useful may not be accommodated because it would fall outside the limits of the template. This would restrict the flow of information and data available on which to base an assessment. Also, a template approach, although trying to capture the essence of profiling, may ask unrealistic questions about the offender.

Research on the content and processes involved in profiling (Petherick, 2007) shows that there are a number of significant shortcomings in terms of explaining the reasoning behind the conclusions in the profile, as well as in the background documentation regarding its construction. For example, the background to the case was provided less than half of the time, definitions for any terms used occurred slightly less than one-third of the time, and most methods (with the exception of behavioral evidence analysis [BEA]) gave little information regarding the documents examined or specific analysis of the evidence. In addition, few of the profiles examined provided any basis for the conclusions. With BEA profiles, 89% of the characteristics in the profiles used physical evidence as justification; criminal investigative analysis profiles offered no justification 65.7% of the time; investigative psychology profiles, despite a research backdrop, used statistics as justification only 27% of the time; and diagnostic evaluations used statistics 60% of the time and personal belief 25% of the time.

A similar research project (Almond, Alison, & Porter, 2007) examined the reports of behavioral investigative advisors in the United Kingdom. The study found that of the sample of 47 reports, there were 805 claims with 96% containing grounds for the claim, although only 34% had any formal support. Furthermore, whereas 70% were verifiable, only 43% were falsifiable in terms of objective measurement postconviction. Both pieces of research have illustrated the vast variability in both gross profiling approaches and within and between individual reports.

This research is of vital importance in understanding how profiles are constructed and argued, but it is by no means the final word. More research into these areas needs to be done to best understand what each method has to offer and how one particular approach may assist in case resolution. Further development of this understanding will lead to more informed decisions among consumers.

ETHICS

Due to the fact that profilers come from a variety of backgrounds, one of the areas in which there is definite room for improvement is in the development of ethical standards. Although profiling was originally sired by those in the mental health profession, and although many of its protagonists are still a part of that fraternity, it is often a practice undertaken by them (and others) outside of their normal duties. In other words, there are few full-time criminal profilers. As a result, some may argue that the ethical guidelines of a practitioner's professional organization do not apply to any work undertaken as a profiler. This is problematic because it may tempt the practitioner to step outside acceptable boundaries and engage in practices that would otherwise be unacceptable in other areas of his or her trade.

Ethics are not often at the forefront of individual practice—that is, they do not always guide what an individual does and how he or she does it. Instead, they come into play once an individual has done something wrong and must attempt to mitigate it. Rarely are ethics seen for what they are—a set of principles that guide a whole approach. To use the definition employed by Turvey (2008, p. 717), ethics are "rules or standards which have been established to govern the conduct of members of a profession." A profiling approach itself cannot be unethical, nor can conclusions, but the behavior of the individual using the approach or drawing the conclusion most certainly can be. Dempsey (1996, p. 17) highlights the importance of the behavioral component in his definition, which states that "ethics can be defined as the practical normative study of the rightness and wrongness of human conduct."

Unfortunately, such rules or standards have been absent from the field of profiling for too long, and the behavior of many practitioners within the field has been deplorable because of this absence. Too often, unethical practitioners will fall back on this lack of standards as an excuse for their misconduct. This behavior should not be tolerated, nor does it have to be. In addition, some may simply argue that profiling is an inexact tool, nothing more than educated guesswork. As long as this is the prevailing attitude, we can expect little in terms of advancement.

One notable example of this is of Richard Walter, a prison therapist who perjured himself while testifying in the trial of Robie J. Drake for two counts of second-degree murder. The facts of the case are as follows (*Drake v. Portuondo*, 2003a):

> In 1982, Drake was convicted by a jury in New York State Supreme
> Court, Niagara County, on two counts of second-degree murder for the
> shooting of a young couple in a parked car in an isolated area near a

junkyard. The defense theory was that Drake often used abandoned cars for target practice, that he shot up the victim's car without realizing it was occupied, and afterward in panic stabbed the young man (who was dying), and drove the car to a nearby dump. To aid the prosecution of a crime that was seemingly without motive, the prosecutor at the last minute called to the witness stand a putative expert who testified about a particular syndrome of sexual dysfunction that appeared to account for the particular, gruesome circumstances of the crime.

The *Daily Record* (2003) also included the following facts:

He fired 19 rounds of ammunition from the semi-automatic rifle. The petitioner claimed he did not intend to kill the victims and only found out they were in the car when he heard a groan from the car. He opened the car door and discovered the two bodies.... He then stabbed Rosenthal in a fit of panic because he thought Rosenthal was still alive. The petitioner then drove the car to a secluded spot down the road from the parking lot and he was discovered by two police officers on routine patrol.

The prosecution conceded that the expert testimony was designed to plug a large hole in their case, namely the issue of intent. The defense was given one weekend to find a psychologist to rebut the prosecution's expert, although they informed the trial judge that try as they might, they were unable to find an expert who had heard of piquerism (a psychological condition ascribed to the accused in which one receives sexual stimulation from cutting, stabbing, slashing, or shooting). Given the time frame and the time of the week, this was probably not unreasonable.

In outlining his qualifications, it was stated of the expert, Mr. Richard Walter, that (*Daily Record*, 2003)[2]

he had extensive experience in the field of psychological profiling. This included working on 5,000 to 7,500[3] cases over a number of years in the Los Angeles County Medical Examiner's Office; an adjunct professorship at Northern Michigan University; and 4 years as a prison psychologist with the Michigan Department of Corrections. He also stated that he had given expert testimony in hundreds of criminal trials in Los Angeles and Michigan.

With regard to this testimony, it was noted by the presiding judge, "It is now clear that the expert's qualifications were largely perjured, and that the syndrome, dubbed 'piquerism,' is referenced nowhere but in true crime paperbacks" (*Drake*

---

[2] This information has been verified with the trial transcript and is an accurate reflection of the testimony given.

[3] Even using a conservative estimate of 5,000 cases during 4½ years, this equates to approximately 3.04 cases profiled each and every day for the full 4½-year period.

v. Portuondo, 2003b). If experts were taken to task over such opinions more often, they would be less likely to bound haphazardly over the rules and regulations.

This case was again revisited in 2006 at the federal level (*Drake v. Portuondo*, 2006) and is discussed at length in Turvey (2008). Here it is noted that (p. 734)

> federal judge John T. Elfvin ultimately concluded, based on the profiler's testimony and its context, that it was reasonable to presume that he had indeed given false testimony with regards to his qualifications. Moreover, Judge Elfvin found that the profiler had made additional false and misleading statements about his credentials while under oath that could not be conclusively referred to as perjury, which is a specific legal charge.

To address the issue of ethics, the ABP has constructed a set of ethical guidelines covering many of these issues in detail, providing a useful overview of those things profilers should heed in their own practice. These ethical guidelines are as follows (Academy of Behavioral Profiling, 1999):

Applicants, students, affiliates, and members of the ABP shall:

- Maintain an attitude of professionalism and integrity
- Conduct all research in a generally accepted scientific manner
- Assign appropriate credit for the ideas of others that are used
- Treat all information (not in the public domain) from a client or agency in a confidential manner, unless specific permission to disseminate the information is obtained
- Maintain an attitude of independence and impartiality in order to ensure an unbiased analysis and interpretation of the evidence
- Strive to avoid preconceived ideas or biases regarding potential suspects or offenders from influencing a final profile or crime analysis when appropriate
- Render opinions and conclusions strictly in accordance with the evidence in the case
- Not exaggerate, embellish, or otherwise misrepresent qualifications when testifying, or at any other time, in any form
- Testify in an honest, straightforward manner and refuse to extend their opinion beyond their field of competence, phrasing testimony in a manner intended to avoid misrepresentation of their opinion
- Not use a profile or crime analysis (the inference of Offender or Crime Scene Characteristics) for the purpose of suggesting the guilt or innocence of a particular individual for a particular crime
- Make efforts to inform the court of the nature and implications of pertinent evidence if reasonably assured that this information will not be disclosed in court
- Maintain the quality and standards of the professional community by reporting unethical conduct to the appropriate authorities or professional organizations

To hold only those few wrongdoers responsible for the lack of standards in the field as a whole is also irresponsible. In fields such as profiling, people often choose to do wrong because we as a community or profession allow it. If our tolerance for such behavior declines, so too should the misfeasance. Inman and Rudin (2007) suggest that peer pressure may be the most effective means for ensuring ethical conduct, but that peers must be willing to challenge each other for this to be effective. I could not agree more.

ACCOUNTABILITY

Inherent within any discussion of ethics is the notion of accountability. Although related, it is of sufficient importance to warrant its own discussion. One can be held accountable for one's conclusions, regardless of ethics, just as one can behave ethically but still fail to be held accountable for one's conclusions.

Unlike ethics, however, where one can unwittingly breach an ethical guideline, one cannot mistakenly fail to be responsible for one's opinions. Such a failure arises from conscious thought, and this accountability is currently lacking.

Accountability is the requirement to justify actions or decisions, and it may by extension involve a continued responsibility toward one's opinions, thoughts, and conclusions. As such, even the most responsible and ethical of people may refuse to be held accountable for their actions. One may also adopt the position that their lack of accountability stems from the fact that they were only allowed access to a limited amount of the evidence. In such a case, it is incumbent on the profiler, not the client, to point out the limitations of the profiler's analysis and not to blaze ahead despite it, only to cry foul at some later date. The bottom line is that your conclusions are just that, and you should have a continuing commitment to them.

One way to make an end run around accountability is to provide a caveat to the effect that the information provided is based on a "best guess" or is not to be taken as accurate and/or reliable. Although caveats are not an enemy to a good profile, and one should be provided if some part of the information was not provided for assessment, one that highlights the profile's flaws from the onset may be a sign of things to come. For example, the following profile states (Prodan, 1995),

> The following crime scene analysis was prepared by Special Agent Supervisor/Criminal Investigative Profiler Michael Prodan in consultation with FBI Supervisory Special Agent James Wright and other members of the National Center for the Analysis of Violent Crime (NCAVC), FBI Academy, Quantico, Virginia. This analysis is based upon a thorough review of the materials submitted by your agency and the conclusions are the result of the knowledge drawn from the personal investigative experience, educational background, and research conducted by these crime analysts. It is not a substitute for a thorough,

well-planned investigation and should not be considered all inclusive. Any information provided is based upon reviewing, analyzing, and researching criminal cases similar to the case submitted by your agency. The following analysis is based upon probabilities, noting, that no two criminal acts or criminal personalities are exactly alike. Therefore, the offender at times may not always fit the analysis in every category.

One of the ways that we may assist in upholding accountability in the profession is to insist, as Turvey (2008) does, that all profiles be written documents. In this way, the contents of the profile are irrefutable and accessible. This opens one up for scrutiny in a number of ways, although perhaps most important, it allows for peer review. Inman and Rudin (2001, p. 259) also highlight the importance of providing documentation when they warn, "If you did not write it down, you did not do it." Although this comment relates specifically to laboratory examination, it applies equally to profiling.

Again, Turvey (2002, pp. 573–574) provides commentary on this issue:

> Responsibility is the key.... If criminal profilers perceive no duty to actually assist an investigation, and see themselves only as academics with a higher scientific or academic goal in mind, then this absolves them of any [ethical] responsibility to a case. That means having no moral obligation to opinions rendered in a given case.

An interesting discussion on this issue dates back to 1998 between private forensic scientist Brent Turvey and retired FBI profiler Gregg McCrary. In an e-mail exchange between Turvey and McCrary, Turvey (personal communication with Gregg McCrary, May 14–15, 1998) suggested that

> if you do not write reports you will have trouble getting a profile or elements of it into court. Even a neophyte detective understands this. And in many jurisdictions LEOs [law enforcement officers] aren't able to move forward with a lead or idea from outside unless it gets put in writing.

In a curious response to this position, McCrary (personal communication with Brent Turvey, May 14–15, 1998) claims that "most current and past FBI profiles, including many of the detailed and in-depth works prepared by Hazelwood, myself, and other FBI profilers, consisted of absolutely no pages. There is sound legal reasoning for minimizing written documents." Furthermore, McCrary insists "any detective who 'is dying to have things in writing' is a neophyte and will learn a painful lesson along the way if he does so. A written analysis tends to create many more problems than it solves."

However, what legal reasoning may there be to preclude a written analysis in toto? Perhaps, it is as I have heard a number of times, that to put one's conclusions in writing does little more than generate *Brady* material. According to *Brady v. Maryland* (1963), a U.S. legal precedent dictating the disclosure of evidence,

After the petitioner had been convicted in a Maryland state court on a charge of murder in the first degree (committed in the course of a robbery) and had been sentenced to death, he learned of an extrajudicial confession of his accomplice, tried separately, admitting the actual homicide. This confession had been suppressed by the prosecution notwithstanding a request by the petitioner's counsel to allow him to examine the accomplice's extrajudicial statements. Upon appeal from the trial court's dismissal of his petition for postconviction relief, the Maryland Court of Appeals held that suppression of the evidence by the prosecution denied petitioner due process of law, and remanded the case for a retrial of the question of punishment only.

In short, a *Brady* violation is one in which the prosecution withholds potentially exculpatory evidence that, if it had been made available to the defense, may have affected the outcome of the trial. In case of a *Brady* violation, the court may order a retrial.

According to *Strickler v. Greene* (1999),

There are three essential components of a true *Brady* violation: The evidence at issue must be favorable to the accused, either because it is exculpatory, or because it is impeaching; that evidence must have been suppressed by the State, either willfully or inadvertently; and prejudice must have ensued.

Regarding the first, if the profile was constructed using valid methodology and consists of conclusions resulting from a careful and meticulous examination of the physical evidence that point away from the accused, it could be argued that the profile may be favorable to the accused. Regarding the second, regardless of the intent, if the state is aware that the profile is potentially exculpatory and fails to turn it over, then it could be considered to have been suppressed. Regarding the last, prejudice may ensue when in the absence of information regarding the mismatch between the profile and the characteristics of the accused, the jury may be more inclined to accept the prosecution's contention that the accused is guilty.[4]

This becomes relevant to profiling when, for instance, the prosecution requests a profile of a suspect who has already been arrested and charged and is due to stand trial (or perhaps when the profile is done during the investigation). Should the profile provide characteristics that do not match the defendant, it

---

[4]It could perhaps be argued that such a profile would be more prejudicial than probative, but this would be a matter for the presiding judge to decide.

may be argued by the defense that the mismatch is evidence of the defendant's innocence. As such, the profile may not be surrendered to the defense because this would be seen to "help" its case. Withholding this information, however, may constitute a *Brady* violation.

If this is in fact the legal reasoning for not writing a profile down, then it would seem that many in the community do not like the idea of accountability, especially where having it may be seen to assist "the enemy" with its case. This speaks of a notion of sides when working as an expert, a position that is the antithesis of scientific expert opinion, where the first responsibility is to the evidence, not for whatever side the expert believes he or she is on.

As a final point, note that accountability extends to the report and to the utilization of the information contained therein. It is not up to the end users to demonstrate the utility and/or the application of the information to their investigation. Rather, it is up to the profiler to demonstrate its application. As Inman and Rudin (2001, p. 274) note,

> The scientist must take responsibility for communicating his results and conclusions, using thoughtful wording that clearly conveys the intended meaning of the data. The report should be organized, easy to read, and written in grammatically correct English. In other words, the burden should be on the scientist, not the reader, to ensure that written communication is effective in disseminating the scientist's opinion.

EDUCATION AND TRAINING

Another topic that has not been addressed at any length in the literature, and perhaps it is more deserving of detailed analysis, is the problem with the governance of profiling and the lack of universal training or education standards. This means that virtually anyone can go forth and call him- or herself a profiler, even without formal training (university or otherwise). This is problematic because profiling is an area in which the behavior of one individual can tarnish the work of others very easily.[5] In addition, anyone can call him- or herself a profiler after having done little more than read a number of books on the topic.

---

[5]I conducted a training session attended by several detectives from state police services. I was approached after the session by a detective who remarked that there was a lot more to the area than they had been shown previously. In a session run by their police service, a consultant forensic psychologist presented his particular approach to profiling without informing them that his was not the only approach. After the presentation, all 25 detectives questioned the utility of profiling and viewed the process as useless and of little value to their investigations. They believed all profilers used the same approach and therefore it was not worth considering as an investigative tool. This highlights a training need.

The lack of standardized education is evident and widely demonstrated in a number of sources. All one has to do is search the Internet for any number of web sites dedicated to the topic, and exactly how poorly defined this issue is becomes clear. Some even set a standard and admit that they do not meet this standard. The following information is taken from the Sexual Homicide Exchange (http://www.she-dc.com) in answer to the question of education and training standards:

> There aren't any and by that I mean there are really no established rules and regulations that have been followed with any consensus. Obviously, it is always nice to have as much traditional education as possible. Employers like degrees and if you can get a PhD, more power to you. However, a master's may be perfectly acceptable and a bachelor's will at least give you the ability to say you are college educated. There are very few actual criminal profiling programs around, although they are starting to surface. Most people chose forensics, psychology, or criminal justice as their degree programs. Some double major along the way and some focus on one aspect like psychology in their undergraduate program and then go on to get a forensics degree for their master's. Some students take police investigative courses or death investigation courses at community college and then go on to a 4-year university.

> Others who want to become profilers join the FBI or the police. Either one of these organizations may offer the possibility of becoming a profiler in the very distant future and neither one can promise you will get the opportunity to actually profile. If you go this route, you need to be willing and interested in other aspects of these jobs in case you never get the opportunity to become involved in profiling.

> There are a few of us who did not study profiling in college nor do we have law enforcement backgrounds. We accumulated our knowledge through self-study and research, seminars, and experience.

> Regardless of how you gain your knowledge in the field, it is up to your employer or client to determine the suitability of your skills to handle the job.

The extract notes that a PhD is desirable or that a master's degree is perfectly acceptable, but it fails to note what areas might be most useful. For example, whereas a master's in business administration might be useful in running a family business, or a PhD in accounting would be useful for an accountant, neither of these programs do anything for profilers in their ruminations of human behavior. In addition, simply possessing a university degree so one can say one is educated offers little and is misleading. Again, a bachelor's program may be in an unrelated area (e.g., environmental science or liberal arts), and whereas these are useful in their respective trades, they offer little for the development of theoretical and practical skills as a profiler.

So this begs the question: What is an acceptable level of training and education for one to possess to call oneself a profiler? As a general rule, university-level training in the social sciences is a must, and some higher degree training in a relevant area is not just desirable but recommended. This would include higher degrees (e.g., a master's degree) in areas including but not limited to psychology, criminology, and forensic science. Knowledge of the investigative procedures used by police may also assist profilers in keeping their information relevant. Turvey (2008) identifies, very importantly, that profiling is a multidisciplinary skill one develops after an individual becomes proficient in other disciplines.

However, developing this proficiency is about more than reading a few books, taking a few courses, and being able to "talk the talk." Unfortunately, this is exactly what a large amount of profiler education has become, with the short course model being front and center.

Short courses, as the name implies, are compacted forums usually designed for working professionals who typically cannot take large amounts of time away from their work commitments. They may range from hours to days, and in some cases they may be as long as months.

In profiling, a number of short courses may be taken over a long period of time, which collectively are suggested to impart proficiency in one or a number of areas (crime reconstruction, bloodstain pattern analysis, bomb damage assessment, etc.). The problem is that although these short courses may help one communicate with other professionals in a meaningful way, they do not alone give expert status.[6] For example, a course on the interpretation of human behavior will be less meaningful if the individual has no behavioral science background. A course on bloodstain patterns will be less meaningful without a substantive understanding of forensic science. This has been discussed by Chisum (2007, pp. 314–317), who also notes a number of problems inherent in short courses[7]:

> In addition to reading the recommended publications, it is advised
> that anyone interested in crime reconstruction take a course in
> bloodstain analysis from a qualified forensic scientist. These courses
> can be useful for providing certain basic overviews of fundamental
> concepts. However, depending on the scientific background of the
> instructor, they may be lacking in certain crucial areas. A true scientist

[6] I run a number of short courses on profiling and am an advocate of their use given the right conditions, and given the appropriate warnings are made to protagonists. The number of times I have been asked "what can I now call myself" or "what am I now qualified to do" after a 2- or 3-day course is a cause of great concern.

[7] Although the courses discussed are related to bloodstain patterns, the same general problems apply in many short courses.

will find that a majority of the short bloodstain classes are lacking with regard to a discussion of accuracy, precision, and significant numbers. Appreciating these deficiencies is the difference between the technician's pedantic understanding of bloodstains and the forensic scientist's interpretive role in the reconstruction of the crime.

A great deal of time in these classes will be spent on single drop analyses and the review of basic bloodstain types and terms.

These terms will allow you to communicate with other bloodstain analysts and are important for that reason. However, there are mathematics and physics components necessary to make certain bloodstain interpretations. Without this background, the reconstructionist is insufficiently prepared to perform bloodstain pattern analysis. The mathematics are seldom included in short bloodstain classes, and this should be noted by all concerned.

For example, seldom does anyone but a scientist question the measuring devices used. It is well-known that all measuring devices have limitations. The accuracy of any instrument used should be determined and accounted for in all interpretations. For example, a reticule in a hand lens cannot be used to measure micrometer distances. It is at best ±0.2 mm, yet there have been cases in which the second decimal place or 0.01 mm was claimed. In teaching classes and enlarging the drops to five times their size we enlarged photo copies of the drops to 5 times their size. Thirty students measured the drops using stereomicroscopes and reticules. There was considerable variation in the measurements. Yet drops at a scene are measured one time, and the results are used to calculate the angle at which the drop strikes a surface. The variation in measuring is not calculated. There is a range associated with all measurements, and accounting for it is a significant but seldom discussed interpretive limitation.

Another issue is significant numbers. When using the formula for calculating the angle, which involves taking the arc sine or arc cosine, a calculator will give the answer to 12 or more places. These numbers are not meaningful. The concept of significant figures is not normally taught. The result cannot have more figures (or places past the decimal) than the lowest number of figures. That is, if a measurement is 2.2×0.5 cm, then the result can only be one significant figure: $80 \pm 5°$, not $79.863°$.

More important, in actual casework, bloodstains are very seldom limited to a single drop. Consequently, the reconstructionist is concerned not with individual drops but, rather, their overall pattern.

The short courses that exist do tend to cover general patterns, and this is perhaps their greatest value. But the approach to interpretation tends to be parochial as opposed to holistic, and it betrays a misunderstanding of the variation that can exist in actual casework. Analysts who are trained to look at and interpret single drops in a rote and technical fashion tend to miss the forest for concentrating on the individual trees with respect to their conclusions.

This issue has also been canvassed by Cooley (2007, pp. 532–535) and is reproduced in its entirety[8]:

> The CSI-reconstructionist model is too often premised on completing a series of short courses. For instance, many investigators attend 5-day (40-hour) workshops or courses on bloodstain pattern analysis, trajectory analysis, or crime scene reconstruction. Some may even attend advanced 2-week (80-hour) courses in these subjects. Attending these courses does not automatically transform an investigator into a bloodstain or trajectory analysis expert.... As Stephen Bright, director of the Southern Center for Human Rights and forensic watchdog, explains (as quoted in Wrolstad, 2002, p. 1A):
>
>> [W]hat you have in many laboratories are police officers who have been sent up to the FBI training facility in Quantico, Va., and come back after 2 weeks claiming to be experts.... They tend to embellish, to make statements not supported by science, that often go unchallenged because defendants are poor and don't have the resources to hire independent experts.
>
> Using the short course model rationale, I could justifiably claim expertise in forensic pathology. Not only have I attended various 40-hour (5-day) seminars on forensic pathology and medicolegal death investigation but also I participated in a 3-month forensic pathology/medicolegal death investigation course in graduate school at the University of New Haven. Moreover, considering my area of criminal defense (i.e., death penalty cases), I have also viewed and read innumerable autopsy reports, autopsy photos, crime scene photos, and crime scene reports.
>
> However, I am fully aware that such a claim of expertise is ridiculous because there is more to developing ability than acquiring knowledge. There is refinement through application and error, there is

---

[8]To be absolutely clear, the discussions by Chisum and Cooley relate specifically to forensic issues, but the problem is no different in other short courses for profilers. In addition, many short course profiling models also include those specific courses discussed here.

experimentation, there is proficiency at following established practice standards when engaging in analysis, there is keeping current with trends within the relevant disciplines, and much, much more.

In their crime laboratory management treatise, Kirk and Bradford (1965, p. 58) scoffed at the notion that examiners or reconstructionists can acquire expert levels of knowledge simply by attending only short or "correspondence" courses:

> A degree in science from a college or university ordinarily falls far short of meeting the minimum requirements. Except in the most unusual instances, such a college degree must be considered an *essential*, [italics added] but not sufficient in itself. Directed laboratory and theoretical work in the field of criminalistics itself is the other essential requirement for the absolute minimum training.
>
> Correspondence and extension courses are occasionally helpful, but generally totally inadequate except as a supplement to sounder training. The student does not learn the subject—he learns a little about it. It does not truly become part of him, either technically or philosophically. For the same reasons, reading of books, however helpful and relevant they may be, is likewise inadequate by itself to meet minimum requirements. The reading and supplementary study should accompany, not replace, the laboratory training. All of this, including the laboratory training, is still inadequate without sound groundwork in basic sciences, such as can be obtained in the colleges and universities.

Again, mastering the many scientific and technical skills needed to properly carry out a reconstructive analysis cannot be acquired in a 2- or 3-week time span. An undergraduate or graduate science degree, combined with broad-based knowledge of the forensic sciences, and a demonstrated proficiency in reconstructing crimes using analytical logic, critical thinking, and the scientific method are essential.

The short course model is just one example of the how the law enforcement community has "oversimplified" a process, which by its very nature is scientifically complex, to serve its own self-interests. As one of the cocontributors to this text (Casey) has said on quite a few occasions, "The less you know about something the simpler it seems." Unfortunately, this is how generations of CSI-reconstructionists have been educated or trained. They are taught superficial kernels of truth regarding the professed principles and practices of forensic science. Then they are told that these principles and practices are so simple that anyone can apply them to forensic or criminal investigations. James W. Osterburg and Charles E. O'Hare (1949, p. x) expressed their frustration with law enforcement's desire to oversimplify complex forensic concepts and procedures more than a half century ago:

> The student entering the field of scientific crime detection finds himself confronted by an odd assortment of texts. Most of these are popularizations which explain away the difficulties of subject matter in terms of facile analogies. The most serious works are optimistically written with a view to making a scientist out of a detective; but here again, the road to a true understanding of the principles of criminalistics is blocked by the necessity for oversimplification. A few texts meet squarely the major problem: To make a detective out of a science student, i.e., to develop from the scientist the scientific investigator of crime, by showing how the principles and techniques which he has studied can be applied to the peculiar problems of examiner clue materials.

With all of the confusion among both practitioners and authors in the area, it is no wonder that there are many confused students and prospective profilers out there. For this reason, if for no other, the subject of education and training needs to be addressed in a more detailed manner. Only then might we develop a more critical eye for those who are qualified to carry out the work and those who are not.

CONCLUSION

As noted in this chapter, there are many areas that will plague the future of profiling and stifle its future development. The answers to many of the questions posed by the foregoing discussion will not be easily come by, and only continued application will see a resolution to many of these issues. One thing that may assist in this process is for end users of criminal profiling to become more educated, and this text and others like it will, it is hoped, go a long way to ensure that this goal is met. Perhaps when consumers better understand these issues and the problems thus far, they will start to question approaches and take those they have previously called upon to task in their conclusions.

Questions

1. Ethical standards could be discussed without regard to professionalization. *True or false?*
2. To apply the scientific method, one must be a scientist. *True or false?*
3. The requirements to justify actions or decisions is called _____.

4. There is an established standard for education and training in criminal profiling. *True or false?*

5. List and discuss the issues in the chapter that must be addressed for profiling to advance.

6. What are some of the general problems with short courses?

REFERENCES

Academy of Behavioral Profiling. (1999). Ethical guidelines for professional conduct. Available at http://www.profiling.org/abp_conduct.html. Accessed June 21, 2005.

Ainsworth, P. B. (2001). Offender Profiling and Crime Analysis. Devon, UK: Willan.

Almond, L., Alison, L., & Porter, L. (2007). An evaluation and comparison of claims made in behavioural investigative advice reports compiled by the National Policing Improvements Agency in the United Kingdom. Journal of Investigative Psychology & Offender Profiling, 4, 71–83.

Bekerian, D. A., & Jackson, J. L. (1997). Critical issues in offender profiling. In J. L. Jackson & D. A. Bekerian (Eds.), Offender Profiling: Theory, Research and Practice. Chichester, UK: Wiley.

Brady v. Maryland, 373 U.S. 83 (1963).

Canter, D. (2004). The organized/disorganized typology of serial murder. Psychology, Public Policy, and Law, 10, 293–320.

Chisum, W. J. (2007). Reconstruction using bloodstain evidence. In W. J. Chisum & B. E. Turvey (Eds.), Crime Reconstruction. Burlington, MA: Academic Press.

Cooley, C. (2007). Reconstruction in a post-Daubert and post-DNA courtroom. In W. J. Chisum & B. E. Turvey (Eds.), Crime Reconstruction. Burlington, MA: Academic Press.

Daily Record. (2003, February 5). More discovery needed to review expert's statements. Available at http://www.corpus-delicti.com/miller_020503.html. Accessed January 27, 2004.

Dempsey, J. S. (1996). An Introduction to Public and Private Investigations. Minneapolis: West.

Drake v. Portuondo. (2003a). United States Court of Appeals for the Second Circuit. August Term. Available at http://www.corpus-delicti.com/forensic_fraud.html#cases. Accessed January 27, 2004.

Drake v. Portuondo. (2003b) Docket No. 01-2217, January 31 (321 F.3d 338); argued: September 9, 2002; decided: January 31, 2003.

Drake v. Portuondo. (2006) United States District Court, Western District of New York, 99-CV-0681E(Sr), Memorandum and Order, March 16.

Goldsworthy, T. (2001). Criminal profiling: Is it investigatively relevant. Journal of Behavioral Profiling, 2(1).

Gudjonsson, G. H., & Copson, G. (1997). The role of the expert in criminal investigation. In J. L. Jackson & D. A. Bekerian (Eds.), Offender Profiling: Theory, Research and Practice. Chichester, UK: Wiley.

Inman, K., & Rudin, N. (2001). Principles and Practice of Criminalistics: The Profession of Forensic Science. Boca Raton, FL: CRC Press.

Jackson, J. A., & Bekerian, D. A. (Eds.). (1997). Offender Profiling and Crime Analysis: Theory, Research and Practice. Chichester, UK: Wiley.

Kocsis, R. N. (2001). Psychological profiling in murder investigations. Australasian Science, 22(1), 26–27.

Kocsis, R. N. (2003). Criminal psychological profiling: Validities and abilities. International Journal of Offender Therapy and Comparative Criminology, 47(2), 126–144.

Kocsis, R. N., Hayes, A. F., & Irwin, H. J. (2002). Investigative experience and accuracy in psychological profiling of a violent crime. Journal of Interpersonal Violence, 17(8), 811–824.

Kocsis, R. N., Irwin, H. J., Hayes, A. F., & Nunn, R. (2000). Expertise in psychological profiling: A comparative assessment. Journal of Interpersonal Violence, 15(3), 311–331.

Medicolegal Society of New South Wales. (undated). Criminal profiling—A psychiatric confession. Available at http://www.medicolegal.org.au/index2.php?option=com_content&do_pdf=1&id=133. Accessed June 16, 2008.

Petherick, W. A. (2003, June). What's in a name? Comparing applied profiling methodologies. Journal of Law and Social Challenges.

Petherick, W. A. (2007). Criminal profiling: A qualitative and quantitative analysis of methods and content. Unpublished doctoral dissertation, Bond University, Robina, Queensland, Australia.

Pinizzotto, A. J. (1984). Forensic psychology: Criminal personality profiling. Journal of Police Science and Administration, 12(1), 32–40.

Pinizzotto, A. J., & Finkel, N. J. (1990). Criminal personality profiling: An outcome and process study. Law and Human Behavior, 14, 215–233.

Prodan, M. (1995, February 27). Criminal investigative analysis of unknown subject.

Rossmo, K. (2000). Geographic Profiling. Boca Raton, FL: CRC Press.

Strickler v. Greene (98-5864) 527 U.S. 263 (1999) 149 F.3d 1170.

Turvey, B. (2002). Criminal Profiling: An Introduction to Behavioral Evidence Analysis (2nd ed.). Burlington, MA: Academic Press.

Turvey, B. E. (2008). Criminal Profiling: An Introduction to Behavioral Evidence Analysis (3rd ed.). Burlington, MA: Academic Press.

CHAPTER 10

Criminal Profilers and the Media: Profiling the Beltway Snipers[1]

Brent E. Turvey and Michael McGrath

KEY TERMS

Sniper: A skilled rifleman who is usually tasked to targets of military value from a concealed position. Snipers are far more skilled than sharpshooters or marksmen.

Media: A channel of communication that serves a variety of functions, such as entertainment or news and information.

Hybrid killer: A type of multiple killer who is a combination of a serial, spree, and mass murderer.

Cumulative anger motivation: An anger motivation that develops and builds over time.

Geoprofiler: A profiler who focuses on the probable spatial behavior of the offender as a function of the locations of various crime sites.

Criminal profilers are regularly enlisted as the pundit of choice by *media* agencies reporting on developments related to unsolved crimes in the public eye. In fact, a review of the Criminal Profiling Archives (located at http://www.corpus-delicti .com/prof_archives_media.html) shows that rarely has a sensational crime occurred in the past 5 years where a criminal profiler has not been solicited for public comment. Given the profit-oriented nature of the media, it is not difficult to surmise that their demand for criminal profilers must be a function of audience

---

[1] This article was first published as Turvey, B., & McGrath, M. (2003). Criminal profilers and the media: Profiling the Beltway Snipers. Journal of Behavioral Profiling, 4(1). It is reprinted with permission.

share. In other words, the media knows that the public wants to hear what criminal profilers have to say. The ratings speak for themselves (Neuman, 2002): "The reign of terror is boosting ratings for cable news networks. At the end of last week, Fox News Channel's average daily audience was up 27 percent from the previous month, CNN was up 29 percent, and MSNBC up 24 percent."

The public fascination with criminal profilers and what they know, or claim to know, reached a never-before-seen apex in the fall of 2002 when a series of related *sniper* attacks began during the first days of October. What occurred as part of the intense, wall-to-wall coverage of the investigation that ensued, which lasted at least 4 weeks, was a threefold watershed event in the history of criminal profiling:

- First, the public was exposed to more criminal profilers and their divergent methods and opinions, on the same case, at the same time, than ever before. This media saturation by profilers was made all the more unusual by the fact that it was available around the clock through almost every major news outlet around the globe.
- Second, criminal profilers (and the authorities) were commenting and opining about criminal behavior in real time, as events unfolded, and the offenders were responding.
- Finally, the global public was exposed to the very real fallibility of criminal profilers and their opinions.

The purpose of this chapter is to discuss the relationship between criminal profilers and the media during the so-called "Beltway Sniper" shootings in October of 2002; examine the nature, value, and implications of their public statements; and discuss what the end result of that relationship has been with an eye to navigating its future.

THE FIRST 45 HOURS

The first five killings in the shooting spree took place within a 2-mile radius inside of Montgomery County, Maryland, over a period of only 16 hours. Forty-five hours into the spree, six people were dead. A seventh victim was left critically wounded.

The first killing occurred on Wednesday, October 2nd, at 6:04 p.m. when 55-year-old James D. Martin, a program analyst at the National Oceanic and Atmospheric Administration, was shot and killed in the Shoppers Food Warehouse parking lot across the street from a police station in Wheaton, Maryland.

On Thursday, October 3rd, four more people are killed in a 2-hour shooting spree starting at 7:41 a.m.: 39-year-old James L. "Sonny" Buchanan, a landscaper, was shot in the back and killed while cutting grass at an auto dealership in Bethesda, Maryland; 54-year-old taxi driver Prenkumar Walekar was shot in the upper chest and killed as he pumped gas at a station in Aspen Hill, Maryland; 34-year-old Sarah Ramos, an emigrant from El Salvador, was shot in the head and killed while sitting on a park bench outside a post office in Silver Spring, Maryland; 25-year-old Lori Ann Lewis-Rivera, a nanny, was shot in the back and killed while she vacuumed her minivan at a gas station in Kensington, Maryland.

Thursday ended with a sixth victim, 72-year-old Pascal Charlot, a father of five who cared for his wife with Alzheimer's disease. He was shot below the neck and killed while crossing the street at the intersection of Georgia Avenue and Kalmia Road in Washington, DC, at 9:20 p.m.

These first six attacks all occurred within a 10-mile radius in Montgomery County, Maryland.

On Friday, October 4th, at 2:30 p.m., a 43-year-old woman was shot in the back in the parking lot of a Michaels craft store in Fredericksburg, Virginia, 70 miles southwest of the epicenter of the other attacks. The sniper had moved south. But this time the victim survived.

THE SYNERGY OF POOR JUDGMENT

During the weekend of October 5th and 6th, no new sniper-related shootings were reported. Responding to public anxiety and fear, criminal profilers were enlisted to start making sense of press conferences held by law enforcement that provided little or no new information about the case. Profilers of all kinds, and from all fields, hit the airwaves to fill the information void. In an unwitting collaboration of poor judgment, at least three events occurred that arguably synergized the course of events, incensing the snipers and drawing them into a dialog with authorities. They included name-calling from media pundits, the public announcement of a *geoprofiler's* involvement, and a perceived challenge to the snipers by authorities.

THE PUNDITS

Over the weekend of October 5th and 6th, criminal profilers and investigators such as Clint Van Zandt, Gregg McCrary, and Bo Dietl appeared in newspapers and on cable news networks characterizing the sniper as a powerless loser, whose actions were those of an attention-seeking coward. They further suggested that he was likely getting a kind of emotional high from playing God. These comments were picked up and republished globally in the print media (Neuman, 2002; Wapshott, 2002). Because the use of this kind of language was so widespread and came even from those in positions of authority, some speculated that this was done intentionally, to provoke the snipers and get them to make a mistake.

However, emotionally charged judgments that might provoke the snipers were advised against by some, including the authors of this paper (Leinwand, 2002):

> "I would be concerned about egging the individual on," says Michael McGrath, a forensic psychiatrist and associate clinical professor at the University of Rochester. "Just take anyone. To call them a coward is inviting a response. If this is part of some larger scheme that they have, and certainly I'm not privy to it, I wouldn't recommend such a tactic."

> Brent Turvey, a forensic scientist from Sitka, Alaska, says taunting won't help the investigation and may actually spur the killer to kill again. "They are making very emotional political statements that are not related to the criminal investigation at all," he says. "I think it's completely irresponsible to provoke an offender to act."

PROFILERS ON THE CASE

On Sunday, October 6th, it was announced at one of the law enforcement press conferences that a geographic profiler had been brought in to examine the shootings at the recommendation of the Bureau of Alcohol, Tobacco, and Firearms. Rather than pursuing a low-key, behind-the-scenes strategy, the geoprofiler spoke at the press conference to discuss his role in the case and fielded questions (Police Appeal to Public to Help Catch Sniper, 2002):

> D. Kim Rossmo, a former Vancouver, Canada, detective working with investigators, said geographic profiling compares the location of the crimes with other information collected by police to give investigators "some idea of the likely base or residence of the offender responsible."

Rossmo explained the full tactical capability and theoretical basis of his geoprofiling method to a concerned nation during the press conference, describing it as an "optimal search strategy" (Legon, 2002):

> Rossmo said he relies on what psychologists term the "least-effort" theory. Crimes typically happen "fairly close to an offender's home but not too close," he said.

> "At some point, for a given offender, their desire for anonymity balances their desire to operate in their comfort zone," he said.

The basic idea is that where an offender strikes tells something about where the offender lives, works, and/or regularly visits. Of course, once an offender is made aware that investigators are examining this particular feature of a crime, the likelihood that they may change their pattern to confuse search efforts increases dramatically. This is something that the authorities may not have entirely understood when announcing Rossmo's involvement in the case.[2]

In tandem with the announcement of Rossmo's involvement, Chief Charles Moose of the Montgomery County Police also announced the involvement of FBI profilers, and gave the first suggestion into their profile of the snipers (Police Appeal to Public, 2002):

> Montgomery County Police Chief Charles Moose said the FBI was also trying to develop a psychological profile of the killer or killers.

> Moose urged residents to be vigilant. "We remain convinced that someone in our community knows who's engaged in this," he told reporters.

> He urged residents to heighten their suspicions of people who appear unusual. "[Someone] is aware that they haven't been around, is aware that they have been acting differently, that they have altered their schedule, that they may be gloating," he said.

ANNOUNCING THE "SAFE HAVENS"

In a misguided attempt to assuage increasingly concerned parents, Montgomery County Executive Douglas Duncan and Chief Charles Moose of the Montgomery County Police declared public schools to be "safe havens" for area children. According to reports:

> [Montgomery County Executive Douglas Duncan] appeared on several national networks, assuring nervous parents. "We feel children will be safe inside schools with us," he said on CNN (Sefton, 2002).

> [Chief] Moose and County Executive Doug Duncan had promised Sunday [October 6th] that the schools would be safe, vowing a massive police presence and noting the killer did not appear to have targeted children (Kennedy, 2002).

They went on to advise that there was no need for parents to keep their children from attending school. The message was repeated in the print media, and a flyer of similar content was circulated to parents.

---

[2]It should be noted that key assumptions of geoprofiling include that multiple offenders are not involved, and that a serial offender most often lives or works near the locations where the offenses are committed. If multiple offenders are involved, or the offender has no base in the area, geographic profiling is at best useless and at worst misleading in that it can suggest nonexistent anchor points (anchor points being the likely "base or residence" of the offender).

THE RESPONSE

Apparently, the snipers were listening. On Monday, October 7th, at 8:08 a.m., a 13-year-old boy was shot and wounded in the abdomen. He had just been dropped off in front of Benjamin Tasker Middle School in Bowie, Maryland, by his aunt, who heard the shot as she drove away and looked back to see him on the ground.

At the scene of this shooting, some important evidence was found. This included a matted area of brush just opposite the school and a spent .223 shell casing, showing where the snipers had lain in wait for their next target. This also included a tarot card, pictured in Figure 10.1.

Information about the tarot card and the message left behind by the snipers was leaked from inside the investigation.[3] As pictured on the next page, the actual message had been worded a bit differently than first reported.

The media picked up on the connection between what was being said by their pundits, what was being said by authorities, and the sniper's actions. This became its own story within the constant news coverage:

> On October 7, one day after Montgomery County Executive Douglas Duncan declared schools safe havens, a 13-year-old boy was shot as he walked toward class. The boy survived, but was in critical condition for nine days until Thursday, when he was upgraded to serious. A tarot card found near the shooting scene said "Dear Policeman, I am God." (News Media Playing a Role in the D.C. Sniper Case, 2002).

---

[3]An infuriated Chief Moose of the Montgomery County Police appeared on national TV chastising those in law enforcement that were responsible for leaking the information to the media, promising to fire them once their identities were discovered. It was reported that (Man Shot in D.C. Suburb, 2002):

> Moose said he has investigated the leak of the information and has put the release of the tarot card incident behind him. He said he was angry because his investigators had requested that the card information not be released to the public.

It was further reported of Chief Moose that (Wilbur, 2002):

> While requesting continued help, Moose also lashed out at those he believes are hindering his investigation.
>
> He strongly criticized former FBI profilers who have been omnipresent commentators on television and in other media reports, saying they might prevent people from calling in tips because they do not think suspicious activity fits with experts' opinions of the shooter.
>
> "Unfortunately, we have any number of talking heads in the media, retired police professionals and you know, as a police professional, it is very insulting when they are retired police professional because we know that they have not been briefed. They have not seen the evidence. They've not talked to any investigators."

This was not the last emotional outburst by Chief Moose, which telegraphed the growing dissent within the investigation about how new and useful case information was being withheld from the public by those in charge.

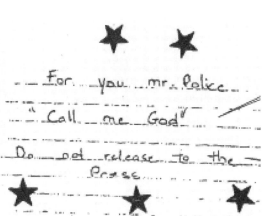

FIGURE 10.1
Tarot Card and Message
Left by the Snipers.

[Retired FBI Profiler Clint] Van Zandt discovered at first hand how profilers can inspire the sniper. Shortly after he was reported on television saying, "It gives this shooter a tremendous hit to be able to play God," the sniper killed again and left a message saying: "Dear Mr. Policeman, I am God" (Wapshott, 2002).

Gregg McCrary, a former FBI psychological profiler, tells CBS News the sniper has "a God complex, killing these people at random and from a long distance."

Three days later, a 13-year-old boy is wounded after being dropped off at school. The sniper reportedly leaves behind a Tarot card inscribed with the message: "Mister Policeman, I am God" (Neuman, 2002).

The snipers had backtracked to the north (east of the original spree), had shot a child in front of a school, and were feeling the need to declare their omnipotence to authorities in a written message left at the crime scene. Their actions appeared to be a response to the highly publicized statements of media pundits, public officials, and the authorities investigating the case. This type of near-real-time interaction among sideline profilers, authorities, and offenders, combined with this scale of media coverage, was something entirely new.

CATCHING A "HYBRID"

Spree killers tend to be motivated by *cumulative anger*, whether it is rational or not. They desire to correct perceived injustices with murder, to punish those who they believe have wronged them, and to satisfy their ever-building rage. Spree killing is about regaining lost power and control. Ironically, killing sprees often end with a violent confrontation between the offender and the authorities in which the offender is killed or takes his own life.

But something happened this time that had never happened before, at least not on this scale. On October 4th the killing spree ended, and on the morning of October 7th, something else had begun. As one report put it (Cannon & Duffy, 2002):

> The snipers killed their first six victims … in just over 24 hours.
> This seemed to fit the classic pattern of a spree killer. But having
> embarked on the spree, then witnessed the overwhelming reaction
> of the public and the news media, the snipers may have had other
> thoughts.

Victims were no longer killed five in a day, but rather one victim was hit every two to four days. The offenders began allowing themselves a period of time between shootings. The anger and intensity had burned off, and the snipers wanted something else—money. And they were still listening to the pundits.

On October 9th at 8:15 p.m., 53-year-old Dean Meyers, a design engineer, was fatally shot in the head at a Sunoco gas station in Manassas, Virginia; on October 11 at 9:30 a.m., 53-year-old Kenneth Bridges, an MBA on a business trip, was fatally shot in the back at an Exxon gas station in Fredericksburg, Virginia; on October 14th at 9:15 p.m., 47-year-old Linda Franklin, an FBI analyst, was fatally shot in the head as she and her husband loaded packages into their car in a crowded Home Depot parking lot in Falls Church, Virginia.

On Tuesday, October 15, *The Washington Post* ran a story with the headline "Weekend Lulls in Shootings Could Offer Clue on Lifestyle," because the shootings had all occurred on weekdays. On Friday, October 18th, retired FBI profiler Robert Ressler appeared on CNN. He stated: "I could see, he could keep going on down to Ashland, possibly all the way to Richmond" (Sefton, 2002).

On Saturday, October 19th at 8 p.m., an unidentified 37-year-old male was shot in the abdomen outside of the Ponderosa Steak House in Ashland, Virginia, as he walked to his car with his wife. This was the first victim to be killed on a weekend. On October 22 at 6 a.m., 35-year-old Conrad Johnson, a bus driver, was fatally shot in the abdomen as he was preparing for his morning bus route in Aspen Hill, Maryland.

During this period of time, the snipers made numerous attempts to make contact with authorities, calling the hotline four times on one occasion. In one of their failed attempts to contact authorities, they called the Rockville, Maryland Police Department (Tape Reveals Sniper's Call to Police, 2002):

> In a tape recording obtained by ABC News, the caller can be heard telling the dispatcher:
>
> "Good morning. Don't say anything, just listen."
>
> "We are the people that are causing the killing in your area. Look on the tarot card. It says, 'Call me God.' Do not release the threat."
>
> "We have called you three times before trying to set up negotiations."
>
> "We've gotten no response. People have died."
>
> At that point, the dispatcher tells the caller there is nothing she can do and tells him to call the hotline set up by the multistate task force investigating the shootings. Then the caller hangs up.
>
> Neil Greenberger, spokesman for the city of Rockville, said the tape sounds like a call received by a police dispatcher Oct. 15. Greenberger said police gave the tape to the sniper task force, but he did not know if investigators were able to trace it.

On October 17th, a man called the sniper hotline and shouted "Don't you know who you are dealing with? Just check out the murder–robbery in Montgomery" (Cannon & Duffy, 2002). Still failing to get through, on October 18th the snipers contacted a priest in Ashland, Virginia, and left a similar message on his answering machine. Authorities would not respond to this tip until Sunday, October 20th (Thomas, 2002).

The snipers, angered by their numerous failed attempts to make contact with law enforcement, left another shell casing and written letter behind at the crime scene on Saturday, October 19th (see Figure 10.2). The letter was tacked to a tree. It documented their failed attempts to get various dispatchers and hotline staffers to take them seriously. It also demanded $10 million with instructions that the money be transferred to a stolen credit card account number. The letter further explained that the failure of hotline operators to take the snipers seriously had cost lives. It also worked to exacerbate public fear by threatening the lives of children in a postscript. A contact number was provided with a deadline for law enforcement's response—Sunday, October 20th, at 6 a.m. Unfortunately, the letter was not read by investigators until several hours after the 6 a.m. deadline (Arena & Frieden, 2002):

> The note, wrapped in plastic, was retrieved near the Ponderosa restaurant. It included a section in which the writer rambles on about how law enforcement officials have messed up the sniper investigation. Some of the letter focuses on criticizing the performance of those officials.

FIGURE 10.2A
Letter Demanding Money
from the Snipers.

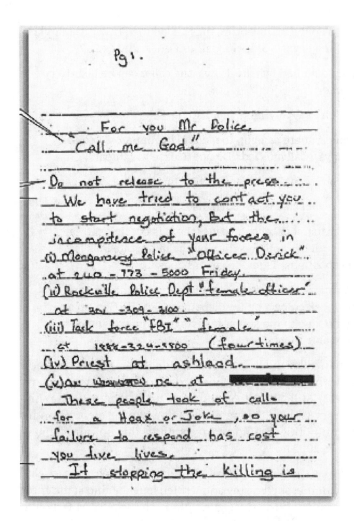

The writer of the letter documents six incidents in which he alleges that officials whom he called hung up on him when he was attempting to convey a message to authorities.

On Sunday, October 20th, Chief Moose held a press conference and pleaded with the sniper, asking for more time and directing them to call authorities, stating "The message that needs to be delivered is that we are going to respond to a message that we have received. We are preparing our response at this time" (Manning, 2002).

That same day, the FBI visited a priest in Ashland, Virginia, to follow up the tip he had provided to the task force. According to Thomas (2002):

The pastor, Msgr. William Sullivan, told the investigators that he had indeed received a call from a man who reportedly introduced himself,

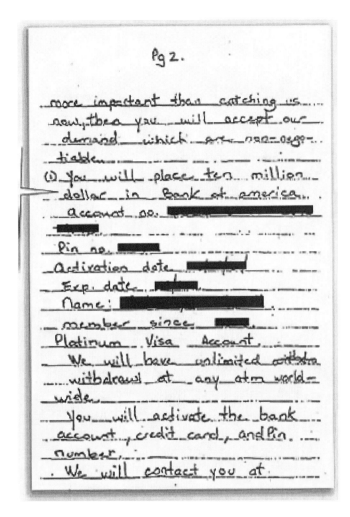

FIGURE 10.2B
Letter Demanding Money from the Snipers.

"I am God." According to the priest, the caller complained that the woman at the Home Depot (FBI cyber-analyst Linda Franklin, slain on October 14) would not have died if police had not ignored his calls. It took two visits from the FBI to surface the key detail. The caller had instructed the priest to write down a message for police to "look into Montgomery, Alabama." The caller wanted the police to know about the slaying at the liquor store.

Although this information was clearly intended to identify the caller as the sniper by suggesting details from an unpublicized crime committed with the same weapon, it was not likely intended to reveal the identity of the sniper. The identity of the person responsible for the robbery–homicide in Montgomery, Alabama, was unknown, and there was no reason to expect that existing evidence could be used to identify the offender, because it hadn't already. But it did.

FIGURE 10.2C

Letter Demanding Money from the Snipers.

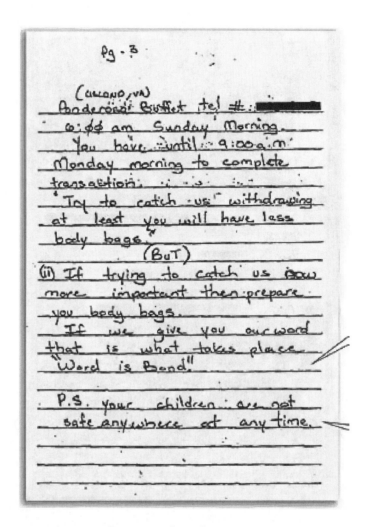

The sniper task force contacted the police in Montgomery, Alabama, and confirmed that an unsolved robbery–homicide had occurred there at a liquor store on September 21, 2002. A local FBI agent took the evidence from that case and flew with it to Washington, D.C.

On Monday, October 21st, the snipers called authorities, but the connection was too garbled for the authorities to understand. They again held a press conference in which Chief Moose pleaded with the sniper to call back (Manning, 2002): "The person you called could not hear everything you said. The audio was unclear and we want to get it right. Call us back so that we can clearly understand," Moose said.

That night, the task force ran an unknown fingerprint from the Montgomery, Alabama, robbery–homicide against the INS database and found a match—

17-year-old Lee Boyd Malvo, a juvenile facing immigration charges in Bellingham, Washington. According to reports (Cannon & Duffy, 2002):

> The most important piece in the pile, it turned out, was the fingerprints pulled off a copy of a gun magazine, an ArmaLite catalog, apparently dropped near the scene of the liquor-store killing. No match had ever been found in state records. But the fingerprints had never been entered into the federal database (Alabama does not belong to a service that provides it).

Shortly, the connection between Lee Malvo and 41-year-old John Muhammad became known. The two had been spending a great deal of time together in the past year, to the point where Malvo's mother had to intervene with the assistance of authorities. Muhammad, presenting himself to others as Malvo's stepfather in their cross-country journey, was also connected to a blue 1990 Chevrolet Caprice. According to Duffy (2002):

> The U.S. Marshals—part of the sniper task force—found another stunning detail: Muhammad had been stopped in northwest Baltimore on October 8, one day after the sniper critically wounded a 13-year-old boy outside a middle school. The vehicle he was in was a 1990 Chevy Caprice with New Jersey tags.

After a heated discussion and much disagreement, law enforcement held a press conference on Wednesday, October 23. Chief Moose announced that John Muhammad was wanted for questioning, releasing his physical description and vehicle details. It was also explained that John Malvo, Muhammad's stepson, was traveling with him. A federal arrest warrant for firearms violations was issued for Muhammad (Sniper Probe Issues Warrant, Message, 2002).

> By Wednesday, the Marshals connected Muhammad to the 1990 Caprice with New Jersey license plate NDA 21Z as a result of the Baltimore stop, and the noose was tightening on the suspects. The license plate and vehicle description was released to the news media.

> Later Wednesday, Montgomery County, Maryland Police Chief Charles Moose ... announced Muhammad might have information related to the sniper investigation and said an arrest warrant had been issued for unrelated firearms violations.

> Truck driver Ron Lantz recognized the car as that being sought in the sniper case and notified police, who relayed the tip to the sniper task force, which immediately dispatched officers to the scene some 50 miles northwest of Washington, D.C., where the arrests were made (Duffy, 2002).

During that same press conference, Chief Moose again pleaded with the snipers to make contact with the task force, and delivered a message to the public on their behalf (Sniper Probe Issues, 2002):

> Moose also issued a new plea to the letter writer authorities believe is the sniper, asking the person to contact the task force directly—either by phone or at a post office box.

> "You have indicated that you want us to do and say certain things. You asked us to say, 'We have caught the sniper like a duck in a noose.'

> "We understand that hearing us say this is important to you. However, we want you to know how difficult it has been to understand what you want because you have chosen to use only notes, indirect messages, and calls to other jurisdictions," Moose said.

The phrase "like a duck in a noose," it has been widely reported, may be a reference to an old fable in which an overconfident rabbit snares an unsuspecting duck in a noose. In most of the versions of the fable, the tables are turned on the rabbit in some way, the duck escapes, and the rabbit is reduced to eating his own fur in order to survive. Having Chief Moose repeat this during one of his press conferences may have been part of the snipers' agenda to control and humiliate authorities (Anderson, 2002).

As a direct result of information provided to the public through the media, Lee Malvo and John Muhammad were found in Muhammad's Caprice at a rest stop off I-70, near the Pennsylvania border. An alert truck driver recognized the vehicle and license plate after hearing a radio news bulletin and contacted the police. Muhammad and Malvo were both asleep when authorities approached the vehicle to apprehend them in the early morning hours of Thursday, October 24th, 2002.

FIGURE 10.3
The Caprice's Modified Shooting Platform.

Muhammad's Caprice, it was soon learned, had been modified to serve as a clandestine shooting platform. (See Figure 10.3)

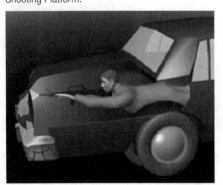

The two holes were there so that shots could be fired without opening the trunk, this source said, adding that the back seat could fold down, enabling a potential shooter to stretch out in the back without setting foot outside (Duffy, 2002).

A Bushmaster .223-caliber rifle, a scope, and a tripod were recovered from Muhammad's Caprice. The BATF soon found a ballistics match between this weapon and bullets recovered from all but three of the sniper shootings. After 22 days, despite all of its failings, the task force had captured and identified the snipers.

THE "SNIPERS"

John Muhammad had four children by two marriages that ended in divorce. Both involved bitter custody battles. He converted to Islam after he divorced his first wife, around the same time he joined the U.S. Army. He served in the Army from 1985 to 1995, in engineering units in Germany, California, and Washington State and in the Gulf War. He also served in the National Guard in Louisiana and Washington State (Muhammad a Gulf War Vet, Islam Convert, 2002):

> His military record shows that he received a summary court-martial on August 2, 1982, in the Louisiana National Guard.
>
> He was tried on one count of failing to report to his duty station on time, three counts of willfully disobeying an order, one count of striking another noncommissioned officer, one count of wrongfully taking property, and one count of being absent without leave. He was demoted one grade and served seven days confinement.

John Muhammad's military background also shows that he had some advanced familiarity with an M-16 rifle (the Bushmaster is a civilian version of the M-16), but he was not trained as a sniper (Ballistics Match Rifle to Sniper Attacks, 2002):

> Muhammad qualified as an expert marksman with the M-16 during his service in the Army, the highest of three levels of expertise in weapons for the typical soldier. That means he had to hit 36 out of 40 targets at a range of about 50 to 300 meters.
>
> Military officials also said Muhammad was not trained as a sniper; nor was he in Special Forces. He served in combat support missions as a mechanic or water truck driver.

Muhammad also had a documented history of domestic violence that included allegations of threats and abuse (Muhammad a Gulf War Vet, Islam Convert, 2002):

> After his discharge, Muhammad moved to Tacoma with his second wife, Mildred Green, whom he had married in 1988 at Fort Lewis. The couple had three children, John Jr., Salena and Taalibah, and operated a car mechanic business in Tacoma. Muhammad's second marriage also fell apart, and Mildred Muhammad was granted a divorce in 2001 based on a finding of domestic violence by the courts.
>
> In court documents obtained by CNN, Muhammad's second wife wrote that her ex-husband was an irrational man who repeatedly threatened to "destroy my life" and told her he would "not let me raise our children."
>
> At one point, John Allen Muhammad picked up the couple's three children from school and disappeared with them. Mildred Muhammad

eventually got her children back and got a restraining order against him, one that was made permanent. She moved to Clinton, Maryland, just outside Washington.

Lee Malvo was a 17-year-old immigrant from Jamaica.

Malvo was allegedly in the country illegally and had a deportation hearing scheduled for November 20, federal law enforcement sources told CNN.

Jamaican authorities said he moved to the United States at age 4, but the State Department said it had no record of issuing a visa to Malvo.

The immigration status of Malvo and his mother, Una James, came into question when authorities were called to the house they shared with Muhammad in December 2001 during an unspecified dispute. Malvo and his mother were taken into custody and fingerprinted before being released on bond.

According to friends and relatives, Malvo was polite, respectful, and brilliant at school when he attended. Little else is known about him, and more is certain to be learned as his case goes to trial.

THE MOTIVE

According to statements made to police by Lee Malvo, he and John Muhammad took turns shooting victims. For example, Malvo claimed that he shot both the 13-year-old boy and FBI analyst Linda Franklin, while Muhammad was responsible for the death of Dean Meyers. Furthermore, the victims were shot in the head for "horrific effect" when possible. The shootings, he explained, were intended to make a point to the police, to terrorize the community and force the authorities to pay them to stop. As reported in Horwitz and White (2002):

According to the documents, Malvo bragged about his shooting prowess and laughed while pointing to parts of the body where the bullets hit. He said that, given the chance, he would do it all again.

The objective was to "terrorise" the community and to force police to pay them to stop. He believed he would get the $10 million the snipers asked for. There was no political or personal reasons for the shootings. It did not matter who walked into his sights when he was ready to shoot.

Malvo stated that on several occasions he waited around after the shootings, observing police and the media. At some of the scenes, he approached police officers to ask what had happened. He explained that he was smarter than those in law enforcement, and believed that he would not have been caught but for his own mistakes (Horwitz & White, 2002).

Mildred Muhammad, John Muhammad's ex-wife, is certain that she and her children were the ultimate targets of the shooting spree (Sniper Suspect's Ex-Wife Links Killings to Custody Fight, 2002):

> "I'm sure he had me in his scope," Mildred Muhammad, 42, said in an interview published in Friday's editions of *The Washington Post.* "This was an elaborate plan to make this look like I was a victim so he could come in as the grieving father and take the children."

> She sees messages she thinks may have been meant for her. Several of the shootings took place at stores, including Michaels and Home Depot, where she had frequently shopped in Tacoma, Washington. She also views the sniper's warning in a letter left near a shooting scene—"Your children are not safe anywhere at any time"—as a message to her.

THE PROFILERS

It is fair to say that federal criminal profilers consulting with the sniper task force, ex-FBI profilers consulting with the media, and others who ascribe to FBI profiling methodology used essentially the same reasoning when it came to the Beltway sniper: Offender characteristics from solved cases in the past can predict offender characteristics in similar unsolved cases today. According to one report (Sperry, 2002): "The task force's operating assumption that the sniper was a lone, unstable white male came from the FBI's stock profile developed from the Timothy McVeigh and Ted Kaczynski cases, sources close to the investigation say."

Everyone was working on the same assumption: The Beltway sniper was an angry white male in his twenties or thirties, a pathetic loner, and lived in Montgomery County, Maryland, where most of the attacks had occurred. This was reflected in the fact that Muhammad had been identified by authorities in the area no fewer than 10 times during the investigation, but was ignored as a suspect because he didn't fit the profile (White & Whitlock, 2002):

> Authorities in the Washington region spotted the same faded blue 1990 Chevrolet Caprice and recorded its New Jersey plates on at least 10 different occasions this month, but saw no reason to link it to the sniper attacks until this week, law enforcement sources said Friday.

> Ten times, authorities thought the car warranted enough suspicion that they ran its license-plate number through a national police database, sources said. Each time, however, they let the driver go ....

> "We were looking for a white van with white people, and we ended up with a blue car with black people," said Washington, D.C., Police Chief Charles Ramsey, whose department ran the Caprice's license October 3, just hours before a fatal shooting in Washington that has been tied to the sniper suspects, John Allen Muhammad, 41, and John Lee Malvo, 17.

This profile was the result of inductive reasoning,[4] both inside and outside of the sniper task force. Inductive reasoning is not itself flawed, but it is limited. When the limitations of inductive reasoning are not explained or even understood by those wielding it in an investigative or forensic context, misunderstandings come more often, and errors are more likely to occur.

The inductive thinking in the sniper investigation was officially buttressed by the involvement of geographic profiler Kim Rossmo. His methodology, while appearing scientific, is merely statistical, being derived from studies of past serial crimes that he himself describes as inadequate. Additionally, the "least effort" theory that he explained to the world media as one of the core tenets of geographical profiling is also inductively derived. It was used to suggest an offender living in or near the area of the attacks.

There are other notable examples of flawed inductive profiling throughout the sniper investigation.

Former New York Police Department detective Richard "Bo" Dietl, who retired in 1985 to start his own security consulting firm, was one of the most commonly featured experts on cable news channels during the sniper investigation. He was regularly critical of the criminal profilers speaking in the media, and adamantly defended his own harsh personal deprecation of the snipers (Huff, 2002):

> "I don't want to talk to these profilers and clairvoyants," said Dietl, who has appeared on such outlets as CNN, Fox and radio's "Imus in the Morning" since the first shooting. "Not once has there ever been a profiler who profiled and arrested and put handcuffs on a person."

> "I watch these profilers saying the same crap over and over," said Dietl, who has used his airtime to call the sniper a psychopath, homicidal maniac and parasite.

> "I know he watches, this creep," Dietl said. "I'm trying to instill into him that he's not this scary person that's got people paralyzed."

Though not a criminal profiler, Dietl regularly offered his own profile of the snipers. He felt strongly that there were two offenders, but this is essentially where his profiling insight ended. He went on to state with confidence that the

---

[4]Inductive reasoning is best illustrated when contrasted with deductive reasoning. According to Hurley (2000, p. 6):

When the arguer claims that it is impossible for the conclusion to be false given that the premises are true, then the argument is best considered a deductive argument. When the arguer merely claims that it is best considered improbable that the conclusion be false given that the premises are true, then the argument is best considered an inductive argument.

Inductive reasoning is identified by the use of qualifiers such as "generally," "likely," and "probably," as well as the use of statistical or so-called "scientific" probability.

killings were the work of "two skinny kids out there who have made a pact with each other," that they were unpopular at school, and that they had no practical firearms training. Rather, he felt strongly that they had gotten the idea to go on a shooting spree from video games (Farhi & Weeks, 2002; Koerner, 2002). Dietl was quoted as saying (Garland & Mitchell, 2002):

> "I think the motive comes out of these sick video games. It's a couple of young adolescents that are not very popular, and now they have everybody in the world looking at them. It's a game to them. They may even have a death pact together."

These conclusions would prove to be almost entirely inaccurate on every level.

Another commonly featured media pundit was retired FBI profiler Clinton Van Zandt. He concluded early on that the sniper was someone who lived in the area, was married, and had a steady job (Wapshott, 2002):

> The fact that the sniper has never killed at the weekend might suggest he has a family or a weekend activity that keeps him occupied. "One has to think he has a job," van Zandt says. "Should he be employed Monday through Friday, it could be a job where he's not accountable for his hours every day. He may be a repair person, a painter, some type of job where he's out and about. At weekends he may be responsible either to a job where he has to be there, to a significant other, or to some purpose where, if he was absent, people would notice."

This profile suggests someone who is not antisocial at all, but rather a person living two lives. These conclusions were entirely false.

Maurice Godwin, a geographical profiler like Rossmo, offered yet another profile of the sniper that was just as flawed. He, like Rossmo, felt the sniper was someone who lived or was anchored in the area. He also concluded that the shootings were in no way motivated by rage (Ashburn, 2002):

> "This is not thrill killing," Godwin said in an interview Tuesday. "I don't think it's anger or rage."

> Godwin said the places the killer has chosen to strike not only make weeks of planning necessary for a hit but require a high level of familiarity with the area likely to be had only by a resident of northern Virginia. "The general theory behind (geographic profiling) is that the way in which criminals travel when they commit crimes reflects where they travel when they aren't committing crimes."

> The suspect's home base likely is nearer the border of Virginia and Washington than that of Maryland and the district, Godwin said.

He attributed the initial killings in Montgomery County, Maryland, to a day trip outside the killer's home zone. "I would suggest he was actually up there on some other business."

Not only were the snipers from out of state and homeless, often sleeping in their car, but rage was cited as a factor by both Lee Malvo and John Mohammad's second ex-wife, as previously discussed.

On October 16th, after Linda Franklin was killed in Falls Church, Virginia, Godwin also incorrectly predicted that the sniper would move east and hit a sensitive target, like a school (Ashburn, 2002): "'They need to watch to the east,' he said, adding that the killer, who is growing increasingly bold, likely will strike a more sensitive target next time. 'They need to be watching out for schools.'"

This was not so much profiling as it was guessing that the snipers' pattern would repeat. In any case, the snipers' next hit was quite some distance south of Falls Church in Ashland. Furthermore, the snipers did not hit a school or other similar type of target again.

All things tolled, the sniper case represents one of the most spectacular public failures of geographic profiling to date. In the aftermath of the coverage, confronted by the blatant and all-too-public inaccuracies of their expert opinions, criminal profilers scrambled to save face.

Retired FBI profiler Candace DeLong admitted that her profile was off by quite a bit, but tried to emphasize that she made some apparently accurate statements (Gettlemen, 2002):

> "A black sniper?" said Candice DeLong, a former FBI agent. "That was the last thing I was thinking."
>
> ... DeLong says she was wrong about the shooter being a firefighter or construction worker. But she was vindicated, she said, on her assessment of the sniper as a "macho guy, all into this stealth ninja stuff."
>
> "Just look at him," DeLong said, referring to a mug shot of Muhammad. "You know he is."

Professor Jack Levin, director of the Brudnick Center on Violence and Conflict at Northeastern University and author of several works on the subject of criminal profiling, came out with a profile similar to that offered by Van Zandt (Farhi & Weeks, 2002):

> "The truth is he has other responsibilities in his life," criminologist Jack Levin said on Larry King's program on CNN last week. "He may be married. He may be playing with his children, watching football on Sunday, or he may have a part-time job."

When the snipers were captured and his profile proved to be inaccurate, he came clean. He also argued that even though inaccurate, his opinions were a public service that were intended to comfort (Gettlemen, 2002): "'My predictions were not that close. But the average American was hungry for information,' he said. 'People wanted a story of who this guy was. What we did, by providing it, comforted them.'"

So everyone of real influence on the task force was working from the same page. Moreover, when they tuned in to watch media coverage, which included criminal profilers speculating from the stands, their reasoning was parroted and by extension endorsed. Certainly this reinforced the official profile.

One of the great advantages of inductive profiles is that they are ready made, requiring little or no work to render. The statistical probabilities and/or experiences of the profiler are easily summoned for dispersal. This makes inductive conclusions available and easy to use for anyone. However, this is also one of its great weaknesses, as discussed in Turvey (2002, p. 28): "Inductive profiling methods are very easy tools to use, for which no specialized forensic knowledge, education, or training in the study of criminal behavior or criminal investigation is required."

Without some kind of education, training, or experience, inductive conclusions may be presented inappropriately, or with too much confidence. They may even be confused by the untrained profiler as deductive conclusions. In the case of the Beltway sniper, the widespread inductive reasoning suffered from what logicians refer to as a fallacy of presumption. Fallacies of presumption are those that overlook the facts, evade the facts, or distort the facts. Most commonly, the fallacy of presumption that snared criminal profilers was the aptly named Sweeping Generalization, in which generalizations that are usually true are applied to an exceptional case by ignoring its peculiarities.

Questions

1. What are the three reasons the Washington Sniper case was a watershed event in the history of profiling?
2. Little harm was done by profilers in the Washington Sniper case. *True or false?*
3. In the Sniper case, profilers were generally accurate in their determinations. *True or false?*
4. Explain how the snipers ended up being apprehended.
5. John Muhammad was a trained sniper. *True or false?*

REFERENCES

Anderson, H. (2002, October 24). Sniper's odd "duck in noose" from fable? UPI.

Arena, K., & Frieden, T. (2002, October 23). Sources: Sniper's note shows frustration with police. CNN.

Ashburn, E. (2002, October 16). Profiler predicts D.C. sniper. The Daily Tarheel.

Ballistics match rifle to sniper attacks. (2002, October 25). CNN.

Cannon, A., & Duffy, B. (2002, November 4). The end of the road. U.S. News & World Report.

Duffy, S. (2002, October 25). Closing the net: How they cracked the case. CNN.

Farhi, P., & Weeks, L. (2002, October 25). With the sniper, TV profilers missed their mark. Washington Post.

Garland, G., & Mitchell, J. (2002, October 12). Killer's low profile frustrates police. Maryland Sunspot.

Gettlemen, J. (2002, October 26). Profilers proven wrong. New York Times.

Horwitz, S., & White, J. (2002, April 7). Shootings planned with military precision, Washington sniper tells police. Sydney Morning Herald.

Huff, R. (2002, October 24). Do analysts help or hurt? New York Daily News.

Hurley, P. (2000). A Concise Introduction to Logic (8th ed.). Belmont, CA: Wadsworth.

Kennedy, H. (2002, October 8). Sniper kills for the thrill. New York Daily News.

Koerner, B. (2002, October 25). Did criminal profilers blow it in the sniper case? MSN.

Legon, J. (2002, October 9). Computer profiler aids in sniper hunt. CNN.

Legon, J. (2003, April 28). Teen sniper suspect remains a mystery. CNN.

Leinwand, D. (2002, October 8). Experts: Accusing shooter of being a "coward" is risky. USA Today.

Man shot in D.C. suburb, police investigating. (2002, October 9). WRAL News.

Manning, S. (2002, October 25). Police ask sniper: "Call us back." Associated Press.

Muhammad a Gulf War vet, Islam convert. (2002, October 24). CNN.

Neuman, J. (2002, October 24). Media face criticism in D.C. sniper coverage. Los Angeles Times.

News media playing a role in D.C. sniper case. (2002, October 18). Associated Press.

Police appeal to public to help catch sniper. (2002, October 7). CNN.

Profiler's clues on Maryland killer. (2002, October 4). CNN.

Sefton, D. (2002, October 22). Media may have unwittingly foreshadowed sniper's moves. Newhouse News.

Sniper probe issues warrant, message. (2002, October 24). CNN.

Sniper suspect's ex-wife links killings to custody fight. (2002, November 8). Fox News.

Sperry, P. (2002, October 25). Cops "wasted time" hunting white guy. Worldnet Daily.

Subramanya, M. (2002, October 15). Indiscriminate murder shocks, unsettles county. The Gazette.

Tape reveals sniper's call to police. (2002, November 2). Fox News.

Thomas, E. (2002, November 4). Descent into evil. Newsweek.

Turvey, B. (2002). Criminal Profiling: An Introduction to Behavioral Evidence Analysis (2nd ed.). London: Academic Press.

Wapshott, N. (2002, October 19). Inside a sniper's mind. The Times of London.

White, J., & Whitlock, C. (2002, October 26). Police spotted suspects' car 10 times during sniper spree. San Jose Mercury News.

Wilbur, D. Q. (2002, October 10). Man killed at Va. gas station. Baltimore Sun.

CHAPTER 11

Serial Stalking: Looking for Love in All the Wrong Places?

Wayne Petherick

KEY TERMS

Stalking: A repeated pattern of intrusion and harassment involving various forms of communication and physical contact.

Typology: A clustering or grouping of types based on shared or similar characteristics.

Incidence: The extent or frequency of a particular occurrence.

Prevalence: The total number of cases of a disease or occurrence in a population at a given time.

Consecutive stalker: A stalker who pursues two or more victims in generally different time frames.

Concurrent stalker: A stalker who pursues two or more victims at the same time.

Investigative phase: Where a profile is used during the operational phase of an investigation to narrow a suspect pool: a profile of an unknown offender for a known crime.

Trial phase: Where a profile is used during the trial of a suspect: a profile of a known offender for a known crime.

Threat management: A targeted approach utilizing the 25 techniques of situational crime prevention to reduce or prevent crime.

CONTENTS

With the recent drafting of *stalking* legislation in most Western jurisdictions, our exposure to this crime is still relatively new. Although our contact with stalkers and their behavior is new in many ways, according to Sheridan, Blauuw, and Davies (2003, p. 148), "It may no longer be the case that stalking

257

research is in its infancy and that we are feeling our way in the dark."[1] With our general knowledge increasing exponentially, so too does our understanding of different types of stalking and stalkers.

For some time, the perception of the typical stalking victim was tainted by a number of high-profile cases involving Hollywood celebrities, who were relentlessly pursued by obsessive and sometimes mentally ill fans. Although we have gone a long way in shedding these images, they are still reinforced in media coverage, where reference is made to pathological attachments held by the stalkers toward celebrities such as Steven Spielberg, Madonna, Pamela Anderson, David Letterman, or George Harrison (Fremouw, Westrup, & Pennypacker, 1997; "Natalie's Nightmare," 2003; "Objects of Obsession," 2000; Pearce & Easteal, 1999).

As our knowledge of this crime increases, so too does recognition of the average person as the most likely victim. With increasing access to, and use of, communications technologies, other types of stalking have come to the fore. With stalkers turning to the Internet and other electronic means in "cyberstalking," and due to a number of recent cases, our knowledge of this crime has been updated yet again. Other examples have introduced yet another variant of the same stalking behavior: the serial stalker, where one offender has a number of victims.

It may seem out of place to talk about a stalking as a serial crime; after all, it is by its very nature a crime prone to repetition. That is, in most definitions and legal terms it is a behavior that must occur on more than one occasion before an offender can be classified as a stalker. This very feature separates stalking from other crimes, such as murder and arson, and related offenses such as sexual assault, which may be perpetrated on only one occasion.

This chapter focuses on a number of features of serial stalking. First, general definitions of stalking are provided before discussing its *incidence* and *prevalence*. Then, the features that constitute a serial crime are presented, such as victim numbers and dynamics, followed by a discussion of the utility of profiling in stalking matters. Finally, two case studies are provided as an overview of selected features of serial stalking.

WHAT IS STALKING?

Before any attempt is made to examine stalking, it is necessary to consider what we mean by stalking, how it is defined, and what behaviors may constitute stalking. According to Sheridan, Davies, and Boon (2001), the following

---

[1]Although the literature on stalking has seen considerable growth, there is still much we do not know or completely understand. As noted later in this chapter, serial stalking is one of these areas.

is one of the most prominent questions to arise out of the criminalization of stalking: What exactly constitutes stalking? As with many areas of social inquiry, stalking is defined in a number of ways. Of particular importance are legal definitions, which draw on the ways that legislatures have defined the behavior, and social science definitions, which rely to some degree on regional legislation to identify the criteria or behavior being examined, as well as provide some understanding of psychopathology.

Stocker and Nielssen (2000, paragraph 5) claim that the "psychiatric literature on stalking has been hampered by the difficulty in arriving at an agreed definition of stalking," further noting that because of this, most commentators borrow from legal discourse in defining stalking. In legal terms, some provide comprehensive descriptions of behaviors, whereas others apply only broad terms (Sheridan et al., 2003), although the definitions of stalking remain fairly uniform regardless of the jurisdiction. It is mainly in specific legal requirements, such as the number of individual acts, that they differ. For example, the Protection from Harassment Act (1997) in the United Kingdom simply cites a course of conduct requirement; Section 646.9 of the Californian Penal Code cites "any person who willfully, maliciously, and repeatedly follows or willfully and maliciously harasses another person"; and the Queensland legislation (Section 359 of the Queensland Criminal Code Act 1899) cites behavior "engaged in on any one occasion if the conduct is protracted or on more than one occasion."

Meloy (1998) identifies three common provisions in stalking legislation: a pattern (course of conduct) of behavioral intrusion upon another that is unwanted; an implicit or explicit threat evidenced in the pattern of behavioral intrusion; and that as a result of these intrusions, the threatened person experiences reasonable fear. Holmes (2001) suggests that from many definitions, there are four components of stalking: (1) a deliberate course of action; (2) a repeated course of action; (3) this action causes a reasonable person to feel threatened, terrorized, harassed, or intimidated; and (4) this action actually causes the victims to feel threatened, terrorized, harassed, or intimidated.

According to Mullen, Pathé, and Purcell (2000), the term *stalking* has come to describe persistent attempts to impose on another various forms of communication or contact. Behaviors associated with stalking include the sending of unsolicited gifts, the ordering or canceling of services on the victim's behalf (pizza, taxi, etc.), threats, loitering near, following, surveilling, and in some cases assault or homicide. Communications include letters, telephone, e-mail, and graffiti. The range of stalking behaviors and communications is limited only by the motivation, innovation, and imagination of the stalker.

Although the behaviors are limitless, what we consider stalking may also include those innocuous behaviors encountered in typical courting scenarios, such as persistent calling, letter writing, or the giving of gifts. Because of this, there is some concern that "the liberty of people to pursue everyday activities or sincerely seek to initiate a relationship may be compromised" (Sheridan et al., 2003, p. 150). Although stalking behavior may manifest as benign gestures meant to represent the stalker's affection, the victim may react with fear. In some countries, legislators have found it difficult to frame stalking laws because many of the behaviors that constitute stalking are routine, mundane, or harmless (Sheridan & Davies, 2001). This is perhaps one reason why "legislatures have experienced great difficulty in framing legal sanctions to effectively outlaw stalking activities" (Sheridan & Davies, 2001, p. 3). In the United Kingdom, it was not deemed appropriate to tightly define stalking because the clustering of a number of seemingly innocuous behaviors when taken together constitute stalking harassment (Sheridan, 2001).

Stalking behaviors may also extend into assault, masturbatory fantasies, theft of the victim's belongings (especially underwear and other intimate or personal items), and property damage. Although there is some concordance between courting and stalking, stalking is typically characterized by its duration and persistence. "In the spectrum of actions that lie between surveillance and physical harm, it is probably repeated harassment that defines the difference between stalking and unwanted courtship by a stranger, rejected suitor, or former lover" (Miller, 2001, p. 5).

Miller (2001, p. 5) provides a definition of stalking that is more reflective of legal considerations in that "stalking is obsessional pursuit, harassment, and intimidation by a person who has or believes he has a significant relationship with the object of his unwanted attention." Not all stalkers have, or believe they have, a relationship with the victim, and although this may be the intended goal of a number of stalkers, this definition potentially excludes cases of stranger stalking.

Sheridan (2001, p. 2) defines stalking as a "series of actions directed at one individual by another that taken as a whole amount to unwanted persistent personal harassment," whereas Wright, Burgess, Laszlo, McCrary, and Douglas (1996, p. 487) define stalking as "the act of following, viewing, communicating with, or moving threateningly or menacingly toward another person." Given that much stalking is covert in nature, such a "movement criterion" would seem obsolete.

When viewing the component behaviors in isolation, stalking is perceptually nonthreatening, although when one considers the universe of behaviors in a given case, and then factors in duration, it is reasonable to see how it constitutes an intrusive and deleterious invasion of private life. To account for this, a definition is put forward in this work that sees stalking as "a constellation of behaviors that may, when considered in isolation, seem innocuous, but when viewed collectively and in the context in which they occurred, constitute a maladaptive and proscribed course of conduct." This definition is useful for a number of reasons. First, it not only acknowledges the broad range of behaviors that constitute stalking but also identifies their possible innocence when viewed individually. Second, it makes no attempt to explain motive because any definition would by necessity have to encompass cases borne of desperation, revenge, and sexual stimulation. Last, it emphasizes the maladaptive nature of stalking behaviors when viewed collectively and in the context in which they occurred.

INCIDENCE AND PREVALENCE

As also discussed by Goldsworthy with regard to rape (see Chapter 12), it is difficult to disaggregate the number of serial stalkers from the overall number of stalkers represented by various studies on the prevalence of this crime. Serial stalking has not received any significant coverage in the literature to date; in fact, a review of several hundred pieces of academic literature on stalking revealed only a handful of articles in which the topic was discussed and data was presented.

In developing a stalking *typology* of use to law enforcement, Boon and Sheridan (2001) examined 124 cases. Their findings indicate that more than one-third of the victims (48) claimed that their stalker had also targeted at least one other person. Twelve of the 48 serial stalkers had a previous relationship with the victim, and all of these had previously stalked another former partner. Of the 48, the vast majority (44) had stalked others before the victims taking part in the study, with another 3 stalking others at the same time as those taking part in the study. Although this study does not purport to represent the general population of serial stalkers, the issue is considerably more problematic than we may possibly know if even a fraction of this applies to the larger population of stalkers.

Beyond this, it would be difficult to try to determine the number of cases that are serial in nature for a variety of reasons. This would include the inability of investigators, researchers, and victims to link offenses; the fact that stalking is a covert crime and may not be recognized; the perceptions of victims themselves (e.g., "nothing can be done about it," "it is a private matter," "it is embarrassing," and "I don't want to get him in trouble"); and underreporting. The following is a general discussion of how widespread stalking is in a number of countries.

In Australia, the first extensive community study, titled Women's Safety, was undertaken by the Australian Bureau of Statistics (ABS) in 1996 (McLennan, 1996).[2] This study found that 2.4% of women older than age 18 years had

---

[2]This study also explored other aspects of women's safety and did not focus exclusively on stalking. It has also been criticized for its findings because of its narrow scope; see Mullen et al. (2000).

been stalked by a man in the past 12 months, with 15% having been stalked by a man at least once in their lifetime. Of those polled, 7.5% were still undergoing victimization at the time of the survey. This study showed that women were more likely to be stalked by strangers than by men they knew (this survey only considered stalking cases in which females were the victims and males were the offenders). Purcell, Pathé, and Mullen (2000) conducted a smaller scale study of their own involving a random selection of 3,700 men and women in Victoria. For those who responded positively to the defined forms of harassment, further information was sought about the frequency and presence of fear. Results indicated that 23.4% of the respondents had been stalked at some point in their lives, with 5.8% being stalked in the 12 months prior to the survey. Approximately 10% were subjected to prolonged harassment involving multiple intrusions that lasted at least 4 weeks. Females were far more likely to be a victim of stalking in their lifetimes. Those who were younger were more likely to be stalked, with those aged 18 to 35 years making up 31.8% of the sample, whereas the 36- to 55-year age group comprised 27.6% of the participants, and only 14.6% of those older than 56 years reported being stalked.

In the largest and most widely cited study in the United States, the National Institute of Justice noted that "survey findings indicate that stalking is a bigger problem than previously thought, affecting about 1.4 million victims annually" (Tjaden, 1997, p. 1). Other reports indicate that 8% of women and 2% of men have been stalked at some time in their lives, which is more than 1 million women and more than 250,000 men (Tjaden & Thoennes, 1998). This study (of 8,000 men and 8,000 women) also found that most victims are female, that 52% of all victims are aged between 18 and 29 years, and that women are significantly more likely than men (59% versus 30%) to be stalked by someone with whom they had a prior relationship.

Basile, Swahn, Chen, and Saltzman (2006) conducted further research into the stalking problem in the United States. Their research yielded 9,684 interviews (4,877 women and 4,807 men). Participants were first asked a question about stalking:

> Have you ever had someone besides bill collectors or salespeople follow or spy on you, try to communicate with you against your will, or otherwise stalk you for more than one month?

If they answered in the affirmative, they were then asked:

> The last time this happened to you, how serious would you say the stalking was?

Participants were limited in their responses to "nothing to be concerned about," "annoying," "somewhat dangerous," or "life threatening."

The results of this survey show that for those aged 18 years or older, "4.5% reported that they have been stalked in their lifetime in a way that they perceived to be somewhat dangerous or life threatening" (Basile et al., 2006, p. 173). Women had a significantly higher rate of victimization than men (7% and 2%, respectively). Those respondents who were never married, separated, widowed, or divorced were at higher risk of being stalked than those who were married or lived as a couple. Those aged 55 years or older or who were retired had a much lower chance of being stalked. Note that the rate of stalking is different in this study compared to other rates reported throughout this chapter. This may be because of the relatively narrow definition of stalking used or because the 4.5% figure was limited to those who perceived the stalking to be somewhat dangerous or life threatening (and thus at the extreme end of the spectrum). It may also be due to the specific use of the term "stalking," which may of itself evoke a particular type of response.

In the United Kingdom, the picture is similar. The British Home Office produced a report on the nature of stalking from the British Crime Survey, which showed that 11.8% of adults aged 16 to 59 years were the subject of unwanted and persistent attention at least once since age 16 years (Budd, Mattinson, & Myhill, 2000). It further found that, like their Australian and U.S. counterparts, victims were more likely to be female (73%). Another similarity is that youth tends to elevate one's risk of victimization, with almost one-fourth of women aged 16 to 19 years and one-fifth of women aged 20 to 29 years reporting stalking harassment. This is compared with only one-tenth of women aged 55 to 59 years.

University students have also been widely studied as a population to determine their victimization from stalkers. There are a number of reasons why this group may be particularly prone to the attention of persistent harassers. First, the age at which one leaves for university is generally the age at which many people experience their first "adult" relationship, making for a volatile mix of love and love lost on the dissolution of a relationship (some studies have indicated that younger females, typically between 18 and 35 years old [Purcell et al., 2000; Tjaden & Thoennes, 1998] are the most common victims of stalking). Second, for many people, this is their first time away from home, leading to a change in social and familial support networks that may have been relied on in previous periods of crisis. This may also mark the first serious period of experimentation with alcohol and/or drugs.

In an undergraduate sample from West Virginia, Fremouw et al. (1997) examined the prevalence of stalking on campus. This study explored two facets of stalking, with the first assessing the behaviors of those who stalk and the second assessing the victims, also taking into account the relationship of the victim to the stalker. Two actual studies were conducted, with the second using a sample of 299 participants and a revised questionnaire, the goal of which was to replicate the first study. Their findings suggest that stalking among this college population is higher than that indicated by other community samples (indicating a general increase in victimization among this age group). In this study, 44 of the 165 female respondents (26.6%) and 17 of 129 male respondents (14.7%) reported that they had been stalked. In the second study, the rate was somewhat higher, with 35.2% of females and 18.4% of males reporting victimization. A large proportion of females (47% in the first study and 40% in the second) were stalked by someone they had "seriously dated." Males were stalked by someone they had "seriously dated" in 24% of the reported instances. Interestingly, this study also inquired as to the number of respondents who had themselves stalked another. Only 3 of 129 males responded in the positive, meaning that either the participants underreported their own stalking behaviors or that those individuals responsible for the victimization were outside of the study sample.

Fisher, Cullen, and Turner (2000) also conducted a national survey of stalking among college women in the United States. Their sample was considerably larger than that of the previous study, with 4,446 respondents completing the survey with a response rate of 85%. Of this sample, 13.1% of females had been stalked at least once since the beginning of the academic year. Of those who had been stalked, 12.7% had been stalked twice, and 2.3% were stalked on three or more occasions. This rate is again higher than that of some community samples. Nearly all of the stalkers were male. In a similar study on student victimization, Coleman (1997) used a sample of 141 undergraduates, with 29.1% responding positively to being stalked. Furthermore, 9.2% of the students stated that this repeated attention was malicious, physically threatening, or fear inducing.

All of these studies tend to suggest that the picture of stalking in English-speaking countries is fairly universal: Young females tend to be victimized more often by typically male offenders they know or with whom they have had a former relationship. Overall, and depending on the study, rates of victimization range from approximately 8% to 23%. This suggests that stalking constitutes a considerable social problem.

WHAT MAKES SOMETHING SERIAL?

This question has a great deal of practical impact on the examination of serial behavior and in the allocation of investigative resources. It is argued herein that once a case has been identified as the work of a serial offender, the approach taken to case resolution should then undergo a fundamental change, such as the formation of a task force in an extreme case and considerations of public safety. Although much of the literature defining serial crime relates specifically to serial homicide, the same issues apply across the board: victim numbers, dynamics, and investigative difficulties. Thus, although the following discussion relies heavily on research on serial homicide, the same general caveats and considerations apply equally to serial stalking, serial rape, serial arson, or any other crime committed by the serial offender.

Kocsis (2000) suggests that of the issues plaguing the examination of serial murder, foremost is a lack of consensus on the basic definition of what is a serial murderer. This becomes apparent even if only a cursory examination of the literature is undertaken. Definitions of serial murder typically encompass three areas:

- A defined number of victims
- A period of time between each offense
- Offenses occurring in different geographic locations from each other

By definition alone, it is the inclusion of a "cooling-off" period and the commission of the offense in different geographic locations that distinguishes among serial, spree, and mass murder. Spree killings are "a series of murders connected to one event committed over a time period of hours or days without a break or cooling-off period" (Busch & Cavanaugh, 1986, p. 5) and are characterized by a single murder event over a number of different geographic areas. They murder at least two victims, and the reason for the offense is said to be primarily for the enjoyment of it (Helsham, 2001; Power, 1996). Blackburn (1993, p. 214) claims that "in mass murders, several victims are killed on one occasion, while in serial murders, killings are repeated over an extended period," with mass murder being defined primarily by the length of time over which the murders take place (usually a single temporal event), occurring in the same geographic location (Gresswell & Hollin, 1994). Mass killers are identified elsewhere (Fox & Levin, 1997) as those who kill their victims in one event, who tend to target people they know, often for the purpose of revenge, and use weapons of mass destruction such as high-powered firearms.

The number of victims is typically between two and four, but higher requirements are also identified. Egger's (1984, 1990) definition states that a serial murder has occurred when a second or subsequent murder is committed. Hickey (1991) and Ressler, Burgess, and Douglas (1988) believe a serial murderer claims three or more victims over a period of time. Dietz (1986), however, believes that the victim count should be at least five. Whereas most authors adopt a numerical system, Kocsis & Irwin (1998, p. 194) is critical of defining serial murder from the perspective of victim numbers:

> The heart of the problem of definition has been the development of an entrenched association of a minimum victim tally as a criterion for serial murder. Indeed, this apparently simple issue of a minimum victim number to identify the crime as serial murder shows a remarkable

diversity within the literature on the topic.... Unfortunately researchers have become absorbed in this debate on minimum victim tally and have overlooked several conceptual problems that exist in defining serial murder on this criterion.

Kocsis and Irwin (1998) suggest these victim tally definitions be abandoned in favor of definitions that encompass the propensity to reoffend. Note that this too would be problematic due to a variety of factors outside of the offender's control, such as the intention but not the ability to reoffend (he might be apprehended before his second offense; future offenses might be disrupted; and the reasons for the offending, called criminogenic needs, may be addressed). It may further be argued that we consider the motivation and the dynamics of the offense while disregarding the number of victims. Given that motivations are poorly understood and the dynamics of the offense may not become known until some time later, such an approach could leave some serial offenders uncategorized and undetected. This is clearly not a favorable outcome from a policing or public safety perspective.

With all this talk of utility and futility, a decision must still be made on how to define a serial crime so that it can be accurately identified once committed (an excellent discussion is provided in Turvey, 2008). Whereas some have argued that it is too arbitrary to simply attach a numerical value, others prefer to consider the case dynamics and motivations of the offense. All of these considerations will dictate how we view, identify, and treat the serial criminal. Although not a perfect approach, I argue that victim numbers are likely the best yardstick we have to define the point at which a criminal becomes a serial offender. Admittedly, although the distinction of serial offending based solely on numerical value is problematic, it is currently the best starting point and is useful in allocating resources, dictating investigative strategies, and identifying other deficiencies in the investigative process that must be overcome (e.g., motivations and dynamics).

Based on these definitions and the preceding discussion on serial crime, a serial stalker is one who pursues multiple victims over time and location, with this chapter distinguishing between two manifestations of pursuit style. First, the *consecutive stalker* pursues two or more victims in generally different time frames—that is, the stalker moves from one victim to another. This may occur when a pursuit is thwarted for some reason (the victim moves away or seeks assistance with *threat management* or from the police, or someone else "catches the stalker's fancy") and the stalker moves on to another victim. Second, the *concurrent stalker* pursues two or more victims at the same time. Neither type is mutually exclusive, but each describes an overall victim targeting strategy. For example, one stalker may identify and pursue a new target before moving on from a current victim.

In one of the few pieces written on serial stalking, Lloyd-Goldstein (2000) defines serial stalking as the sequential stalking of different victims at different times (those that are consecutive in nature as discussed). He also notes that any subsequent victims should not be linked to the original victim to whom the stalker became attached because in such cases additional victims may simply be friends, family, or coworkers who become entwined in the stalking while assisting the primary target of the stalking. However, in identifying the difference between consecutive and concurrent stalkers, it is noted that "stalkers with multiple love objects on a concurrent basis should be distinguished from true serial stalkers" (p. 178). From this, it is not clear whether a stalker who harasses multiple victims at the same time is considered less of a serial offender than someone who moves from victim to victim.

Although the two case studies presented later represent both consecutive and concurrent pursuit styles, the following example highlights purely consecutive stalking to contextualize the difference (Petherick, 2001):

> A 34-year-old female was being stalked by a former intimate. She claims they met while working as volunteers in a community project, and that they had dated for approximately 1 year. It later turned out that he had joined the project simply to get close to her, a modus operandi he had repeated on three previous occasions. She sought help from a number of sources, but all were unable to assist with her situation for a number of reasons. One evening, after stealing a key to her apartment during a previous visit, he let himself in and was found crawling down the hallway of her house with her dog's muzzle clamped in his hand. She called the police and they asserted that, given their prior relationship, a conviction would be problematic at best. It was only after more time elapsed, her physical and psychological functioning continued to decline, and neighbors reported seeing him outside her bedroom window, that she sought other help. At this point she contacted this author, who assisted with threat management. In a fortuitous telephone conversation and subsequent meeting, she found out that this person had done similar things to others who had shown him any form of care and attention. He was not known to stalk a number of people at once, but instead moved from victim to victim at the dissolution of relationships, or when victims sought outside help.

WHAT CAN BE DONE ABOUT IT?

It should be acknowledged that much can be done about serial stalking, from counseling of offenders once they are identified to educating potential victims about individual characteristics that predispose someone to stalking behaviors (as discussed in Michele Pathé's book, *Surviving Stalking*, 2003). Only two things are discussed here, however: criminal profiling and threat management.

Due to the repetitive nature of stalking behavior, it is argued that profiling may be suited to the investigation of many stalking scenarios. Profiling is "an inferential process that involves an analysis of offender behavior including their interactions with the victim and crime scene, their choice of weapon and their use of language, among other things" (Petherick, 2003, p. 173). Pinizzotto (1984), Geberth (1996), and Holmes and Holmes (2003) argue that profiling is most suited to those crimes involving psychopathology, and with many stalking scenarios exhibiting signs of pathological behavior, this further reinforces the utility of profiling for this crime.

There is both conformity and contention in the literature about what information a criminal profiler can provide. Geberth (1996) provides a fairly exhaustive list that will not be replicated in full but includes age, sex, race, marital status, scholastic achievement, lifestyle, personality style, emotional adjustment, demeanor, evidence of mental decomposition, and work habits. In discussing the FBI's approach, O'Toole (1999) cites a number of features discernible through a criminal profile, including a range of characteristics of the offender and his or her lifestyle, emotional age, level of formal education or training, the offender's ability to relate and communicate with others, prior criminal activity, and feelings of remorse and/or guilt concerning the crime or the victim. Although some authors suggest a broad range of offender characteristics that can be derived from the offender's behavior, others are more conservative in their approach, suggesting that less is directly inferable from offender behavior.

So exactly what use can profiling be in the assessment of stalking cases? To begin, an examination of the general applications of profiling from Turvey (2008) is provided, followed by a cursory discussion of motive and concluding with applications of threat management outlined by Petherick (2002). These are by no means the only applications, but they are the ones with which I have found most success.

Generally, there are two main phases in which criminal profiling may be applied: the *investigative phase* and the *trial phase*. These are best characterized as profiling the unknown criminal for the known crime and the known criminal for the known crime. Profiling in the investigative phase is perhaps the one with which most people will be familiar, and it is this one that has been the focus of most media and movie attention.

In the investigative phase, there are five primary goals (Turvey, 2008) aimed at reducing the suspect pool: helping prioritize suspects, assisting in the linkage of related crimes, assessing the escalation of nuisance behaviors, providing investigators with investigatively relevant leads and strategies, and keeping the overall investigation on track (these were also discussed in Chapter 6).

Essentially, it is the profiler's job to help investigators determine the value of the available evidence and what it means with regard to the offender in an effort to ensure the best use of manpower and resources. This may greatly enhance the utility of the investigative effort by preventing already over-stretched resources from becoming strained to the breaking point. In cases of serial stalking, a profile may assist in developing suspect pools by identifying the motive or depth of knowledge the offender has about the victim and the various locations in which the behaviors are perpetrated. Due to the repetitive nature of serial stalking, a profiler may also assist in determinations of case linkage by identifying connections between modus operandi and signature behaviors, thereby allowing for the identification of serial offenders and the allocation of relevant investigative resources. Although many stalking scenarios are characterized more as psychologically intrusive, many cases will culminate in physical contact or other attempts at harm. Here, the profiler may provide insight into the potential for an offender's escalation; this may indicate the likelihood that someone engaging in "peeping Tom" activities will escalate to stalking focusing on one or more of their victims, or perhaps go even further into crimes of violence. As per the fourth and fifth goals given previously, further general assistance may be in the form of leads and strategies for advancing the investigation or by weeding through irrelevant or distracting information that is obtained during the investigative phase (see Chapter 6).

In the trial phase, there are also five primary goals (Turvey, 2008): evaluating the nature of forensic evidence, developing interview and interrogative strategy, developing insight into fantasy and motivation, developing insight into state of mind, and highlighting crime linkage issues. In this stage, the profiler's main task is to assist with the determination of issues that relate to developing a case brief, planning, intent, offender motivation, and any other evidentiary considerations (e.g., the nature or meaning of physical evidence). The idea is that the opinion of the profiler helps the court to understand complex behavioral issues that manifest in stalking.

Because the main purpose of a criminal profile is to define and identify suspect pools, and the suspect pool can be defined in some cases by the motive, assessing what drives an offender in a given case can be a useful tool assisting in case resolution. Motive is described by Turvey (2008) as the emotional, psychological, or material needs that impel and may be satisfied by behavior. Determining motive can provide the following benefits to an investigative effort (Turvey, 2008, p. 274):

- It reduces the suspect pool to those individuals with that particular motive.
- It assists in the investigative linkage of unsolved crime with a similar motive.
- Along with other class evidence (i.e., means, opportunity, and associative evidence), motive can provide circumstantial bearing on offender identity.

- Along with other contextual evidence, motive can provide circumstantial bearing on offender state of mind.
- Along with circumstantial evidence, motive can provide circumstantial bearing on whether a crime has actually occurred.

Understanding motive can also assist with the development of a threat management approach (discussed later).

Where public safety may be an issue, a criminal profile may help identify aspects of the offender's behavior that constitute a clear threat to individual safety. For example, a profile may provide a picture of the offender's victim selection and aspects of an offender's modus operandi, and it may commentate on future risk suggested by current behavior. Identifying precursor behaviors may assist in identifying crimes that are potentially the work of the same offender but that are not currently regarded as part of a series. For example, "peeping Tom" or surveillance activities of a stalker may help to build an overall picture of an offender's geographic behavior or some other aspect, such as victim selection and planning.

As discussed in Petherick (2008), a profile may also be useful in providing threat management services to victims. Here, a profile is utilized to fill knowledge voids by providing an understanding of aspects of the case such as the motive and intent of the unknown stalker. If the case should require criminal justice system intervention, a profile may also help the police identify a suspect pool and reduce the time to apprehension. As practiced by this author, it involves an adaptation of the techniques of situational crime prevention as discussed by Clarke (1997), Clarke and Homel (1997), and Cornish and Clarke (2003). This approach involves identifying intrusive and harassing behaviors of the stalker, antecedent and consequent behaviors of the victim, and the environment in which they occurred. Following this, an approach is developed in which aspects of the 25 techniques of situational crime prevention are applied. For example, repeated attempts by the stalker to contact the victim may be addressed by Rule Setting under the broad category of Removing Excuses. Here, the victim should issue what is commonly referred to as a "letter of noncontact" outlining the invasive and harassing nature of her pursuit (Pathé, 2003). Another example concerns addressing repeated telephone contacts where the stalker calls simply to hear the victim's voice on her answering machine. A successful approach might be to have the victim replace her current answering machine message with a generic store-bought one or have a female friend record a plain message for her,[3] which would fall under Denying Benefits within the general category of Reducing Rewards.

---

[3] This strategy has been used successfully in a number of cases.

A deductive profile can also help to fill a number of voids in what is currently known to be true, and on which further action must be based. Motive and intent are just two areas that may be unknown at the time of case intake, and not only do they narrow the suspect pool but also their assessment may become an instructive part of any threat management undertaken to assist the victim. In one case (Petherick, 2000), a determination of motive guided the entire threat management process to a successful conclusion by focusing solely on manipulating specific motive-oriented behaviors.

CASE STUDIES

This section briefly examines two case studies involving serial stalking. The first is from Queensland, Australia, and the second is from New York. They both involve a large number of victims over a considerable period of time. For the sake of brevity, only selected features of each case are discussed, including the number of victims, the duration, victim selection, motivation, and the effect on the victim. The chosen cases are not necessarily representative of the general nature of serial stalkers, but they have been selected because of their high number of victims and the amount of information available about them.[4]

Robert Zeljko Vidovich

Investigators first identified a link between victims on Queensland's Gold Coast when new complainants began to recount similar details to detectives (Wilson, 2002a). The crimes of Vidovich spanned 3½ years, with his total known victim count at 52 (there are potentially other victims who never made the connection or who, for one reason or another, did not receive further harassment and did not reveal their victimization to police). The victims ranged in age from 16 to 83 years.

The victims reported receiving nuisance and harassing telephone calls during which the caller would first make a generally innocuous claim (e.g., he accidentally received some of their mail). Following this, the caller would propose various forms of sexual activity, such as rape or bondage, or he would make comments suggestive of voyeurism. Lingerie also played a significant role in the interactions he had with his victims. The following précis from the Supreme Court of Queensland Court of Appeals summarizes the offenses (*R. v. Vidovich*, 2002):

> The applicant had pleaded guilty to an ex officio indictment charging
> him with 52 counts on the 9th of May 2002 at the Southport District
> Court.... The applicant ... was aged between 38 and 42 years over

---

[4]A note of acknowledgment should go out to investigators involved with these and similar cases. They are, by nature, difficult crimes to investigate, and it is often only through dogged detective work that they can be solved.

the various times of the offences. The stalking offences to which he pleaded guilty were committed over a period of approximately three and a half years from April 1998 to September 2001. There were 52 complainants ranging in age from 16 years to 83 years, most of them being aged between 35 and 50. The offences ... generally they involve the applicant telephoning women, most often at their home, but also at work. The phone calls were made from public phones and motel rooms.... In the calls, he proposed various forms of sexual activity in explicit and demeaning language. He threatened to rape the women the subject of three counts, and impliedly threatened to rape, or indecently assault many of the others. He sent pornographic photographs to eight of the women depicting various sexual acts. The women in the photos looked like the recipients and captions accompanied the photos describing what the applicant wanted to do to the recipient. From the conversations he had with some five of the women it was clear that he had been spying on them. In one instance he first made contact with the complainant during her pregnancy. At the time of his last call five months later she was breast-feeding at the time but not in public. During the call he made reference to her nipples being full of milk.... The applicant attempted to conceal his identity by adopting accents when speaking to the complainants, using gloves when preparing the obscene materials, disguising his handwriting, using an alias when booking into the motels in which he made calls and calling from public phones. He was arrested by police on the 28th of September 2001. In the course of their search the police found 800 pornographic files on his computer, some of which contained captions referring to some of the complainants and a phone list with 23 names on it. With the exception of two complainants the applicant said the women were not known to him and that he'd selected them randomly from the phone book.

Vidovich was fairly random in his victim selection, and they did not represent significant others in his life, nor someone he harbored particular grudges against (an often-touted motivation for many stalking scenarios). Nor did his victims exhibit similarity to one another; in fact, there appeared to be little, if anything, connecting his victims at all. Their ages and appearances were generally inconsistent, and no links could be found between them or any facilities or services they used. It would seem that most of them were just unfortunate to cross his path.

This randomness begs the following questions: How did these victims come to be chosen? and What features of victimology may have been enticing to their harasser? In reference to the summary from the Court of Appeal, the women in the pornographic images bore striking resemblance to some of his victims, and in "doctoring" these images, he would often use their name and provide some commentary of what he was doing (behavioral evidence suggests he saw himself as the male portrayed in the images) or what he would like to do to them. Others still provided some insight into his perceptions of their "relationship." One manipulated image in which the victim's hair had been computer edited contained the caption "Oh yes ... so you are a friend of Paul's ... well he won't be home until later tonight." The sentiment of this action was further verbalized by another of his victims in that "he saw each one of us as someone he was having a relationship with" (Margen, 2003). As another example of his misguided perceptions of a relationship, he offered to assist one victim in removing her clothes—specifically, "he was offering to help me get undressed out of my work uniform" (Margen, 2003). So it seems then, at least in some of the cases, that his behavior was *reassurance oriented* whereby he wanted, or at least fantasized about, some form of relationship he perceived he was having.

Beyond the pornography and letters, it was obvious from an early stage that the offender had also engaged in detailed surveillance of the victims and their homes. It has been suggested that some of their telephone details had been secured by stealing mail from their letter boxes, although this could never be proven by police. One of the victims described a letter in which Vidovich wrote about her liking for long dresses, specifically citing colors of dresses she owned (Wilson, 2002a). In yet another case, a victim came home from work to find underwear from her washing line neatly folded on her doorstep along with a letter; other victims received similar treatment. For example, in one telephone conversation he recounted details of underwear hanging on her washing line (which was not visible from the street). Others had underwear stolen. During a break-in, one victim had some of her underwear stolen from inside her home, which was subsequently referred to during a later telephone call (Wilson, 2002a).

The effect this intrusion had on the victims is obvious, and the reactions of these victims are typical. The breach of their privacy had a distinct impact on their personal, professional, and social lives, and the enduring effects of this victimization will be akin to those of other stalking victims (Brewster, 1997; Collins & Wilkas, 2000; Hall, 1998; Hills & Taplin, 1998; Meloy, 1996; Pathé & Mullen, 1997). One victim's consternation at being selected can be seen in the comment, "To think that it could happen to anyone, just purely by having your name in a phone book." The loss of security and trust they have experienced is echoed in the following statements: "You still look over your shoulder, hate answering the phone, and don't like being by yourself" and "You certainly don't trust people, you think they are capable of just about anything" (Margen, 2003). One businesswoman claimed, "I had my partner ring me at work during the day to check on things and he would come in and help me lock up my Burleigh business" (Wilson, 2002b). One of Vidovich's victims, who received telephone harassment and letters from him for more than 2 years, told the author, "You don't trust anyone. You treat everyone who walks past like a potential criminal. You just don't know who it is, or who it could be. It might be the mailman, the delivery man, or the guy you buy your food from. You just don't know." This is not an uncommon sentiment among stalking victims.

On apprehension, there was a distinct failure on the part of Vidovich to appreciate the seriousness of the charges. Detective Lithgow recounts, "The day we arrived at his house, he was surprised that it was such an issue," and "This is a person who thought that as a punishment for what he had done, it would be adequate for him to clean out police vans on a weekend rather than go to court" (Margen, 2003). Also noted by prosecutor Mark Whitbread, Vidovich's naïveté about his offenses was almost disturbing. In court, Whitbread claimed Vidovich had asked police, "Why do I have to go to court? I mean, I'll apologize. I'll help you with your cases or something" (Stolz, 2002).

The Vidovich case likely represents the worst stalking case in Queensland, and possibly in Australia, and this was factored into the judge's considerations, where it was noted, "It is a case where the protection of the community takes precedence over your rehabilitation" (Wilson, 2002b). Furthermore, the custodial penalty imposed on Vidovich was 4 years for 13 of the cases (at the time, 5 years was the maximum penalty allowable), whereas for the remaining cases he was sentenced to 7 years, the new maximum allowable under Queensland law. These sentences were to be served concurrently. In addition to his custodial sentence, he was ordered not to have contact with his victims for the next 10 years and was made liable for damage claims that may escalate into the millions.

Robert D. King

Dating back to 1996, Robert D. King of Yorkshire, New York, harassed and terrorized 28 women in a stalking campaign that involved numerous instances of harassing telephony during which he would threaten to kill or harm them, usually with a knife. The women lived in different geographic locations, including Concord, Sardinia, Holland, Yorkshire, Delevan, Machias, and Arcade (Porter, 1998).

King, age 45 years, made his calls from a variety of phone booths in the towns where his victims lived. Once the call was answered, he would establish the identity of the person he was talking to, often using the person's first name. As one victim noted, "Once he established that it was me on the phone, he would lower his voice to a whisper and say things like, 'I'm going to stab you with a knife.... Tonight is the night.... I'm going to rape your dead body'" (Marciano, 1998).

For his crimes, King was sentenced to 18 months for aggravated harassment and menacing ("King Sentenced to Additional Jail Time," 1998), with another

11 months added (to be served consecutively) by Concord Town Court ("King Sentenced," 1998). In addition, he was ordered to undergo a variety of counseling regimes, electronic monitoring, and financial penalties, and many of the victims were issued orders of protection.

As noted previously, one of the most interesting aspects of both cases is the apparent randomness of the victim selection. With regard to King (Porter, 1998),

> "He had no personal connection to most of the people he called," said Erie County Sheriff's Department Detective Ronald Kenyon, the arresting officer in Concord and Sardinia.... "He got their names from going into a business and looking at name tags or by going through the papers."

The haphazard selection of victims is perhaps one of the things that makes serial stalking so difficult to identify and investigate. Without links between victims, it is difficult to know when and in what context they were encountered, or indeed whether there are any links at all. In an effort to overcome this, investigators in the case asked complainants to complete a list of places they frequent, places they shop, and any gym or club memberships.

Regarding his victim selection in New York, King stated the following (T. Whitcomb, personal communication, July 20, 2004):

> The women that I called were selected for different reasons, some of them I knew personally, others I selected from public newspapers, and occasionally I would run into them while they were working in a store and remember their name and call them later. All of the women I called were listed in the public phone book, either under their name or their husband's. The women that I remember calling include:
>
> A woman who is blonde and works at the [deleted] Department store in Yorkshire. She was chosen when I noticed her working.
>
> [Deleted] who lives in Delevan, and she was chosen because I know her personally.
>
> I selected [Deleted] from her being in the newspaper.
>
> [Deleted] was chosen because I knew of her and she crossed my mind.
>
> I do not know how I selected [Deleted], I think I just ran into her and remembered her name.
>
> I selected [Deleted] from the newspaper and I also selected [name] at the same time because they were in it together.
>
> [Deleted] was chosen from me knowing her from her employment.
>
> [Deleted] was selected because I knew her husband and I would see her on the road now and then.

This is just a small number of the victims identified by King. Some were unfortunate enough to know him, and others were unfortunate to be known to him by association, whereas still others appear simply to have been in the wrong place at the wrong time.

When detectives searched his premises, a collection of individual pieces of paper were found containing the names and details of a number of other females. Some of these were the complainants in the case leading to the investigation; others reported receiving no phone calls, and still others reported receiving calls prior to the inception of the investigation when no suspect was identified. There can be little doubt that the harassment would have continued if King was not apprehended.

Another interesting feature of both cases is the failure of the offender to accept responsibility for what he had done. Vidovich pleaded with detectives to allow him to make reparations to the victims and the police by washing police vehicles and doing menial chores around the victims' homes. King also failed to appreciate the gravity of his situation. According to prosecutor Joseph E. Dietrich III, "His lack of remorse is disturbing.... It's disturbing that he doesn't think what he did was so very wrong" (Marciano, 1998). However, in a later interview with police, King claimed (T. Whitcomb, personal communication, July 20, 2004):

> Yes, I know that there were a couple of times where circumstances may have triggered me to do this that I actually did not carry it out because I know that this is wrong, I am actually glad in some ways that I was caught because now I know for sure that I will never do this again. It has also been brought to my attention the impact that I had on these women and their families, and although I knew what I was doing was wrong, I never realized how much pain I was causing them.... I take full responsibility for what happened, and would like to bear the shame alone.

The context in which this act of contrition occurred must be kept in mind, and it is not known whether King would have experienced a similar form of remorse outside of an arrest scenario or whether he fought with these feelings during his offending.

Although these two offenders are a veritable geographic world apart, their offenses are remarkably similar. Both offenders employed similar modi operandi in contacting their victims. Vidovich and King would first establish the identities of their victims before talking, and both made use of the anonymity afforded by public pay phones. Neither seemed to appreciate the seriousness of their offenses, with Vidovich believing his crimes could be mitigated by offering menial services as restitution to the victims and police. Another commonality between each was their sheer number of victims, all being victimized over a similar period of time. This would understandably be a time-consuming activity and speaks to the motivation of each in continuation of the harassment.

CONCLUSION

Stalking is a new crime but an old behavior that has received increasing scholarly attention during the past decade. With more research and more exposure to cases, we are provided with a deeper and more substantial understanding of many aspects, including victim and offender relationships, motivation, dynamics, treatment outcomes, and classifications. With communication technologies providing the stalker with a new medium through which to carry out harassment, the number of victims and the exact sequence and nature of their harassment, it is argued, provide another variant that is the subject of this chapter: serial stalking. In one pursuit type, the consecutive stalker will pursue one victim after another, whereas in concurrent cases the offender will pursue multiple victims during the same approximate time period. This type of stalking has not been the subject of much academic study, which would be understandably difficult given the inability to link the crimes of the one offender, its covert nature, victim perceptions, reporting styles, and the inability to keep track of an offender once attentions subside. Repeat victimization from one stalker poses a significant obstacle to law enforcement charged with the investigation of such offenses, and only through a deeper understanding of the dynamics of these offenses will our appreciation of individual offenses improve.

Questions

1. One reason why legislators have had trouble framing legal sanctions is because
   a. The identity of stalkers is never known before they are apprehended.
   b. Most stalkers know the law and operate within the bounds of the law.
   c. Most of the behaviors constituting stalking are routine, mundane, or harmless.
   d. Stalkers never leave evidence that they could be prosecuted for.
   e. None of the above.
2. The Australian Bureau of Statistics found what percentage of respondents in its study would be stalked at some time in their life?
   a. 7%
   b. 9%
   c. 15%
   d. 16%
   e. 24%

3. Which of the following is not one of the goals of the investigative phase of criminal profiling?
   a. Assist in the linkage of related crimes
   b. Assess the escalation of nuisance behaviors
   c. Provide investigators with relevant leads and strategies
   d. Keep the overall investigation on track
   e. Develop insight into offender motive and intent before, during, and after the crime
4. Generally, there are two main ways in which profiling might assist an investigation. *True or false?*
5. What are the three common provisions of stalking legislation according to Meloy (1998)?

REFERENCES

Basile, K. C., Swahn, M. H., Chen, J., & Saltzman, L. E. (2006). Stalking in the United States: Recent national prevalence estimates. American Journal of Preventative Medicine, 31(2), 172–175.

Blackburn, R. (1993). The Psychology of Criminal Conduct. Chichester, UK: Wiley.

Boon, J. C. W., & Sheridan, L. (2001). Stalker typologies: A law enforcement perspective. Journal of Threat Assessment, 1(2), 75–97.

Brewster, M. P. (1997). An exploration of the experiences and needs of former intimate stalking victims (Proposal No. 5-8432-PA-IJ). West Chester, PA: West Chester University of Pennsylvania.

Budd, T., Mattinson, J., & Myhill, A. (2000, October). The extent and nature of stalking: Findings from the 1998 British Crime Survey (Research Study No. 110). London: Home Office Research, Development and Statistics Directorate.

Busch, K. A., & Cavanaugh, J. L. (1986). The study of multiple murder: Preliminary examination of the interface between epistemology and methodology. Journal of Interpersonal Violence, 1(1), 5–23.

Clarke, R. V. (1997). Situational Crime Prevention: Successful Case Studies (2nd ed.). New York: Harrow & Heston.

Clarke, R. V., & Homel, R. (1997). A revised classification of situational crime prevention techniques. In S. P. Lab (Ed.), Crime Prevention at a Crossroads. Cincinnati, OH: Anderson.

Coleman, F. L. (1997). Stalking behavior and the cycle of domestic violence. Journal of Interpersonal Violence, 12(3), 420–432.

Collins, M. J., & Wilkas, M. B. (2000). Stalking trauma syndrome and the traumatized victim. In J. A. Davis (Ed.), Stalking Crimes and Victim Protection: Prevention, Intervention, Threat Assessment and Case Management. Boca Raton, FL: CRC Press.

Cornish, D. B., & Clarke, R. V. (2003). Opportunities, precipitators and criminal decisions: A reply to Wortley's critique of situational crime prevention. In M. Smith & D. B. Cornish (Eds.), Crime Prevention Studies, Vol. 16: Theory for Situational Crime Prevention. New York: Criminal Justice Press.

Dietz, P. (1986). Mass, serial and sensational homicides. Bulletin of the New York Academy of Medicine, 62, 477–491.

Egger, S. A. (1984). A working definition of serial murder and the reduction of linkage blindness. Journal of Police Science and Administration, 12(3), 348–357.

Egger, S. A. (1990). Serial Murder: An Elusive Phenomenon. New York: Praeger.

Fisher, B. S., Cullen, F. T., & Turner, M. G. (2000, December). The sexual victimization of college women [research report]. Washington, DC: U.S. Department of Justice, National Institute of Justice, Bureau of Justice Statistics.

Fox, J. A., & Levin, J. (1997). Serial murder: Popular myths and empirical realities. In A. Thio & T. C. Calhoun (Eds.), Readings in Deviant Behavior (3rd ed.). Boston: Pearson.

Fremouw, W. J., Westrup, D., & Pennypacker, J. (1997). Stalking on campus: The prevalence and strategies for coping with stalking. Journal of Forensic Sciences, 42(4), 666.

Geberth, V. J. (1996). Practical Homicide Investigation: Tactics, Procedures and Forensic Techniques (3rd ed.). Boca Raton, FL: CRC Press.

Gresswell, D. M., & Hollin, C. R. (1994). Multiple murder. British Journal of Criminology, 34(1), 1–15.

Hall, D. (1998). The victims of stalking. In J. R. Meloy (Ed.), The Psychology of Stalking: Clinical and Forensic Perspectives. London: Academic Press.

Helsham, S. (2001). The profane and the insane: An inquiry into the psychopathology of serial murder. Alternative Law Journal, 26(6), 269–273.

Hickey, E. (1991). Serial Murderers and Their Victims. Pacific Grove, CA: Brooks/Cole.

Hills, A. M., & Taplin, J. L. (1998). Anticipated responses to stalking: Effect of threat and target–stalker relationship. Psychiatry, Psychology and Law, 5(1), 139–146.

Holmes, R. R. (2001). Criminal stalking: An analysis of the various typologies of stalkers. In J. A. Davis (Ed.), Stalking Crime and Victim Protection: Prevention, Intervention, Threat Assessment, and Case Management. Boca Raton, FL: CRC Press.

Holmes, R. R., & Holmes, S. (2003). Profiling Violent Crimes: An Investigative Tool (2nd ed.). Thousand Oaks, CA: Sage.

King sentenced to additional jail time, counseling, probation. (1998, August 27). Arcade Herald.

Kocsis, R. N. (2000, January/February). The motives of the serial murderer. Queensland Police Journal.

Kocsis, R. N., & Irwin, H. (1998). The psychological profile of serial offenders and a redefinition of the misnomer of serial crime. Psychiatry, Psychology and Law, 5(2), 1–10.

Lloyd-Goldstein, R. (2000). Serial stalking: Recent clinical findings. In L. Schlesinger (Ed.), Serial Offenders: Current Thoughts, Recent Findings. San Diego: Academic Press.

Marciano, J. (1998, August 6). Man jailed for making threatening calls. Buffalo News.

Margen, D. (2003). A Current Affair. Nine Network, Australia.

McLennan, W. (1996). Women's Safety Australia (ABS Catalogue No. 4128.0). Canberra: Australian Bureau of Statistics.

Meloy, J. R. (1996). Stalking (obsessional following): A review of some preliminary studies. Aggression and Violent Behavior, 1, 147–162.

Meloy, J. R. (1998). The psychology of stalking. In J. R. Meloy (Ed.), The Psychology of Stalking: Clinical and Forensic Perspectives. London: Academic Press.

Miller, M. C. (2001, March). Stalking. The Harvard Mental Health Letter.

Mullen, P. E., Pathé, M., & Purcell, R. (2000). Stalking. The Psychologist, 13(9), 454–459.

Natalie's nightmare. (2003, March 14). Gold Coast Bulletin.

Objects of obsession. (2000, 20 November). Who Magazine.

O'Toole, M. E. (1999). Criminal profiling: The FBI used criminal investigative analysis to solve violent crimes. Corrections Today, 61(1), 44–47.

Pathé, M. (2003). Surviving Stalking. Cambridge, UK: Cambridge University Press.

Pathé, M., & Mullen, P. E. (1997). The impact of stalkers on their victims. British Journal of Psychiatry, 170, 12–17.

Pearce, A., & Easteal, P. (1999). The "domestic" in stalking: Policing domestic stalking in the Australian Capital Territory. Alternative Law Journal, 24(4), 165–167.

Petherick, W. A. (2000). Case number 0700.

Petherick, W. A. (2001). Case number 0601.

Petherick, W. A. (2002). Stalking. In B. E. Turvey (Ed.), Criminal Profiling: An Introduction to Behavioral Evidence Analysis. London: Academic Press.

Petherick, W. A. (2003, June). What's in a name? Comparing applied profiling methodologies. Journal of Law and Social Challenges, 173–188.

Pinizzotto, A. J. (1984). Forensic psychology: Criminal personality profiling. Journal of Police Science and Administration, 12(1), 32–40.

Porter, D. (1998, March 26). Local man arrested for threatening phone calls made to over 28 women. Springville Journal.

Power, D. (1996). Serial killers. The Criminologist, 20(2), 94–102.

Purcell, R., Pathé, M., & Mullen, P. E. (2000). The incidence and nature of stalking victimization. Paper presented at the Australian Institute of Criminology Stalking: Criminal Justice System Responses Conference, Sydney, December 7–8.

R. v. Vidovich. (2002). QCA 422 (10 October 2002).

Ressler, R. K., Burgess, A. W., & Douglas, J. E. (1988). Sexual Homicides: Patterns and Motives. Lexington, MA: Lexington Books.

Sheridan, L. (2001). Stalking. Journal of Interpersonal Violence, 16(2), 151–158.

Sheridan, L., & Davies, G. M. (2001). What is stalking? The match between legislation and public perception. Legal and Criminological Psychology, 6(3), 3–17.

Sheridan, L., Davies, G., & Boon, J. (2001). The course and nature of stalking: A victim perspective. Howard Journal of Criminal Justice, 40(3), 215–234.

Sheridan, L. P., Blauuw, E., & Davies, G. M. (2003). Stalking: Knowns and unknowns. Trauma, Violence and Abuse, 4(2), 148–162.

Stocker, M., & Nielssen, O. (2000). Apprehended violence orders and stalking. Paper presented at the Australian Institute of Criminology Stalking: Criminal Justice System Responses Conference, Sydney, December 7–8.

Stolz, G. (2002, May 10). Porno stalker jailed for seven years. The Courier Mail.

Tjaden, P. (1997, November). The crime of stalking: How big is the problem? National Institute of Justice Research Preview.

Tjaden, P., & Thoennes, N. (1998, April). Stalking in America: Findings from the National Violence against Women survey (Research in Brief). Washington, DC: National Institute of Justice and the Centers for Disease Control and Prevention.

Turvey, B. E. (2002). Criminal Profiling: An Introduction to Behavioral Evidence Analysis. London: Academic Press.

Turvey, B. E. (2008). Criminal Profiling: An Introduction to Behavioral Evidence Analysis (3rd ed.). Burlington, MA: Academic Press.

Wilson, T. (2002a, May 10). Saved from sex stalker. Gold Coast Bulletin.

Wilson, T. (2002b, May 10). Evil stalker can count the years. Gold Coast Bulletin.

Wright, J. A., Burgess, A. G., Laszlo, A. T., McCrary, G. O., & Douglas, J. E. (1996). A typology of interpersonal stalking. Journal of Interpersonal Violence, 11(4), 487–503.

CHAPTER 12

Serial Rape: An Investigative Approach

Terry Goldsworthy[1]

KEY TERMS

Serial rape: Two or more rape offenses committed by the same offender.

Rape: Nonconsensual sexual intercourse, including penetration by both digital and foreign objects.

Power assertive: A motivation where the offense is an expression of virility, mastery, and/or dominance.

Power reassurance: A motivation where the offense is an effort to resolve disturbing doubts about the offender's masculinity.

Anger retaliatory: A motivation where the offense is an expression of hostility and rage.

Anger excitation: A motivation where the offender finds sexual pleasure, thrill, and excitation in the suffering of the victim.

Crime scene stage: The first stage of the investigative model that deals with the initial response of police to the report of an alleged crime.

Initial assessment stage: The second stage of the investigative model in which investigators should have control of the investigation and begin to identify possible witnesses and suspects.

Investigation stage: The third stage of the investigative model in which investigators must attempt to establish a motive for the crime.

CONTENTS

[1]The views presented in this paper are those of the author and do not necessarily reflect the views of the Queensland Police Service.

283

Target stage: The fourth stage of the investigative model in which investigators generate potential suspects from evidence available during the target stage.

Arrest stage: The fifth stage of the investigative model in which investigators need to make a decision regarding whether to take affirmative action against the potential suspect.

Linkage blindness: Occurs when there is an inability on the part of investigators to recognize connections and confusion regarding which crimes are part of a particular series of crimes.

INTRODUCTION

Laura Showalter … Dorcas Callen? These names mean nothing to me.
— Harvey Louis Carignan as quoted in Berry-Dee (1998, p. 87)

This comment reflects the attitude of serial rapist and murderer Harvey Louis Carignan toward the victims he brutalized. Carignan, known as Harv the Hammer for his use of a hammer in his crimes, murdered and raped a number of women in the United States beginning in the 1940s. Callen escaped Carignan when he attempted to *rape* her; however, another victim, Showalter, was not so fortunate, and she was killed during the rape. He "smashed her head causing terrible brain injuries. The victim's face had been virtually destroyed from chin to forehead, bone and tissue crushed to a pulp" (Berry-Dee, 1998, p. 87). His total number of victims is unknown, but when arrested, investigators found a map with approximately 180 locations circled in red, some of which matched other offenses.

What is the motivation that drives these offenders to commit such crimes? What are the characteristics that make these individuals take a path to crime? The crimes of serial rapists such as Carignan can have a number of effects on society, including revulsion, fear, fascination, and disbelief. But what is it about this kind of rape that generates this kind of reaction? After all, rapes occur every day, and some barely rate a mention in the press. Are we drawn to these rapes because of their extremely violent nature or because they are part of a series? Or is it that the rapes are more expressive, fulfilling some inner need of the offender, rather than instrumental, having some function or purpose?

Perhaps because of the media attention these crimes receive, they have come to the fore in the past few decades. There has been an increase in awareness of the predators among us, who seemingly rape and kill for no other reason than the pleasure of such acts. Public imagination and fear have been captured by press monikers such as "the Boston Strangler" and "the Night Stalker" to describe serial rapists and murderers. *Serial rape* has also been brought to the fore by the ability of police to better link serial offenses.

Hazelwood and Burgess (1987, p. 16) suggest that the serial rapist can "create a climate of fear in the entire community, who then pressure law enforcement to identify, locate, and apprehend the responsible individual in the shortest possible time." Because of the "seriousness of serial rape and havoc that such attacks cause," it is often the case that all available law enforcement resources are used to address the issue (Carney, 2004, p. 149).

This chapter examines the characteristics of the rape offense and defines serial rape and how it differs from the "normal" rape offense. Motivational typologies of rapists are briefly examined to assist in developing an understanding of why offenders commit rape, followed by an analysis of various studies on serial rapists and their characteristics. An investigative model is explained with a view to assisting in the investigation of serial rape offenses. Lastly, a variety of investigative issues that investigators should be aware of are discussed.

RAPE: CHARACTERISTICS OF THE CRIME

In Queensland,[2] there were 2,163 rapes and attempted rapes reported for the year 2006/2007,[3] although it should be noted that rape is a crime that suffers from chronic underreporting. In a national survey of victims, it was revealed that 80% of respondents did not report the offense to police (Easteal, 1992). This survey also showed that reporting occurs most often in cases in which the offender is a stranger to the victim, which represented 43% of cases reported. Of the offenses reported in Queensland for 2006/2007, 57% were cleared or solved.

Females made up 82% of the victims, whereas males accounted for 18% of reported offenses in Queensland. The number of female victims has declined in recent years (91% of victims reported in the first edition of this book correlates with a national survey of 2,762 rape cases that were examined, in which 96%

---

[2]Queensland is one of the states of Australia. It has a population of approximately 4 million people, with a state police service of approximately 9,600 sworn officers responsible for all law enforcement activities. Note that these numbers are similar to those in other countries and jurisdictions and are suitable for illustrative purposes.

[3]These and other data are available from the Queensland Police Statistical Review at the Queensland Police Service web site at http://www.police.qld.gov.au/Resources/Internet/services/reportsPublications/statisticalReview/0607/documents/ASR-0607-EntireDocument.pdf. The total number of reported crimes does not necessarily relate to the total number of committed offenses due to reports made from crimes committed in previous years.

of victims were female [Easteal, 1992]). Queensland data reveals that females age 10 to 19 years were the most at-risk female group, comprising 47% of the total number of victims. Of note is the number of male rape victims of all ages—6% of victims. In her analysis of the national survey conducted in 1992, Easteal (1992) noted that the risk for young males was particularly high, with 70.1% of the male victimizations prior to the age of 17 years.

Unfortunately, there appears to be little statistical information gathered in relation to serial offenses committed. This paucity of readily available data has been acknowledged in the United Kingdom, where it was noted that "there is no way of knowing what proportion of the sexual attacks reported to the police are in fact the work of serial rapists" (Gregory & Lees, 1999, p. 109). The limited research on this offense is likely plagued by many of the same issues facing law enforcement in its investigation: the failure to link offenses, the prevalence of serial offenses in unreported offenses, and the offenses only being identified or acknowledged when an offender is arrested.

Let us now discuss the typical locations where these offenses are committed. The majority of offenses took place in residential areas (1,777 offenses or 82%), which includes dwelling houses and outbuildings. Approximately 18% were committed in community areas such as educational, health, religious, and transport facilities. Approximately 3% of this 18% were committed on the street or footpath. In their study of serial rapists, Hazelwood and Warren (1989) found that 50% of rape offenses were committed in the victim's home, with 6% occurring in other public places (e.g., the street).

OFFENDER AND VICTIM RELATIONSHIPS AND CHARACTERISTICS

From the data, it can be seen that males are most likely to be the offenders (Queensland Police Service, 2007, p. 11):

> In total, 125 females committed sexual offences in 2006/07. Thus, 96% of offenders were male. The age distribution of male offenders is unique for this offence type in that the distribution is almost uniform across all age groups with the exception of fifteen to nineteen year olds. The number of offenders is only slightly lower in the older age groups, with males aged fifty years and over responsible for 17% of all sexual offences. For those proceeded against, 57% were arrested and 16% were served with a notice to appear.

A number of studies (Australian Bureau of Statistics, 2005; Moran, 1993) have shown that approximately three-fourths of the time there is some relationship between the victim and the offender, with data from many other Australian states confirming this relationship.

Regarding the Queensland data, one must remember that 43% of offenses remained unsolved, and an unknown proportion of these may have been the crimes committed by strangers; hence the difficulty in solving such crimes. Various research has shown that "a large number of sex crimes against strangers are committed by a relatively small number of serial offenders" (Warren et al., 1998, p. 35). In Hazelwood and Warren's (1989) study of serial rapists, it was found that 85% of victims were unknown to the offender. The main reasons nominated by the offenders for victim selection were availability and gender, with age, location, and race also being determinants (Hazelwood & Warren, 1989). Consideration of all of these factors can allow an offender to determine the vulnerability of the potential victim, which directly affects the chances of success. Serial rapes present significant difficulties, as noted by Homant and Kennedy (1998, p. 319), "because of the chance connection between perpetrator and victim in these kinds of crime, and because a perpetrator frequently commits crimes across jurisdictions, such cases are especially troublesome to local law enforcement."

Whereas single rape offenses are most often committed by someone known to the victim, the serial rapist is more likely to target strangers except in certain circumstances. The relatively recent attention to "date rape" may well indicate that the offender who commits such offenses does indeed know the victim. It has also been noted that with the advance of DNA technology, it is increasingly difficult for offenders to deny their role in the offense once DNA has been identified. As a result, serial rapists may change and adapt their tactics in that "they may well have realized that a defense of consent where they mimic the stereotypical date rape scenario is far more likely to lead to successful acquittals" (Gregory & Lees, 1999, p. 100).

A DEFINITION OF SERIAL RAPE

What is the difference between rape and serial rape? For the purpose of this discussion, the term *serial rape* refers to two or more offenses committed by the same offender with a cooling-off period between the offenses (see Chapters 11 and 13 for other definitions and variations). In recent times, the term *rape* has been expanded from its traditional meaning of nonconsensual sexual intercourse to include penetration by both digital and foreign objects and also oral sexual acts. Due to the variety of statutory definitions in effect, a definition of rape is not provided except to say in general terms that it is a sexual attack of a nonconsensual nature including a variety of acts. Note that both serial rape and murder are offenses that overlap and are not mutually exclusive. It is for this reason that techniques used in response to serial killers are also of use in the investigation of serial rape offenses.

TYPOLOGIES OF RAPE OFFENDERS

A typology is a grouping of items based on shared similarities, with a rapist typology grouping rapists by some shared characteristics such as motivation. Groth, Burgess, and Holmstrom (1977) studied 133 rape offenders and 92 rape victims, from which they determined that three factors play a dominant role in any rape offense: power, anger, and sexuality. They suggested that the sexual act of rape was in fact primarily a display of anger or power. To expand upon this, they developed four motivational typologies of rape offenders: *power assertive, power reassurance, anger retaliatory,* and *anger excitation* (Table 12.1).

Of the rape offenses studied by Groth et al. (1977), they found that approximately 65% were classified as power rapes, whereas approximately 35% were anger rapes. Anger retaliation was the most common type of offense in the sample examined. However, in the victim sample it was only the third most prevalent, with power assertive being the most common. These typologies are useful in helping the investigator understand what drives the offender to commit the crime. It is of interest that anger retaliation is the most common category for offenders because serial rapist studies have shown that victim resistance will increase the duration of the attack and the pleasure levels of the offender (Hazelwood & Warren, 1990).

The utility of these classifications has been noted by certain judiciaries, with particular attention paid to the assistance they can give in the investigation of serial rapists. It has also been suggested that police should receive some training in relation to them. Gilbert Atwell, a serial rapist who attacked and/ or raped 11 elderly women in the southern suburbs of Brisbane, Australia, in the late 1990s, was sentenced to life imprisonment by District Court Judge Pratt. Judge Pratt stated that Atwell was a power reassurance rapist who feigned concern for his victims and assured them he would not hurt them. Atwell

Table 12.1 Rapist Classifications

Rapist Type	Characteristics
Power assertive	Rape as an expression of his virility and mastery and dominance
Power reassurance	Commits the offense in an effort to resolve disturbing doubts about his masculinity
Anger retaliatory	Commits rape as an expression of his hostility and rage toward women
Anger excitation	Finds pleasure, thrills, and excitation in the suffering of the victim

committed his crimes on elderly females usually older than 60 years and living alone. The following commentary on the case makes Judge Pratt's view clear (Oberhardt, 2000):

> Police might have earlier arrested serial rapist Gilbert Atwell, who terrorized elderly women, had they been trained in new profiling techniques, according to the sentencing judge. Judge Eric Pratt was high in his praise of the investigation and officers involved in capturing Atwell. He said, however, if in 1997 police had been able to use profiling techniques now available, Atwell might have been caught sooner. Judge Pratt has been a major advocate of police training and the use of profiling in solving serial crimes. He said serial offenders often felt immunity because they believed authorities could not link their crimes nor their methods.

The judiciary are not alone in the call for training of this type. In a survey of police officers, it was found that 93% believed that police should receive some sort of training in relation to the psychological traits of offenders (Goldsworthy, 2001).

CHARACTERISTICS OF THE SERIAL RAPIST

Warren et al. (1998) conducted a study of 108 serial rapists who were responsible for 565 rape offenses. They found that the offenders on average carried out 5.3 rapes, with a range of 2–17 rapes. They also found that older rapists tended to travel farther than younger rapists, and that 98% of the serial rapists younger than the age of 20 years committed their offenses an average of 2.75 miles from their homes (Warren et al., 1998). A study of UK serial rapists also supports the proposition that younger men will offend closer to home, and that in general the serial rapists studied committed offenses close to their homes (Davies & Dale, 1995). In their study of 45 serial rapists in the United Kingdom, Canter and Larkin (1993) found that the offenders on average committed 5.6 offenses, with a range of 2–14 offenses, and the average age of the offender was 26.6 years.

Perhaps the most relevant information can be drawn from Hazelwood and Warren (1989, 1990), in which 41 serial rape offenders were studied (the offenders had to have committed at least 10 offenses). These offenders committed approximately 837 sexual offenses and approximately 400 attempted rapes. The average age of the offenders at the time of committing their offenses was 25 years; this is consistent with the previous data discussed for Queensland and the United Kingdom. Approximately 92% of the offenders were employed to some degree, with 71% of offenders having been married once and 34% having been married more than once (Hazelwood & Warren, 1989).

The statistics in relation to marriage are of interest because they dispel the perception that most serial rapists are sex-starved animals; many do in fact have consensual sexual relations, although slightly more than one-third of the offenders in the Hazelwood and Warren (1990) study experienced some kind of sexual dysfunction. This concurs with the study of sexually sadistic criminals by Dietz, Hazelwood, and Warren (1990), which showed that 43% of offenders were dysfunctional. The most common sexual acts performed during the serial rape offenses were vaginal rape and forced oral sex (Hazelwood & Warren, 1990).

Indeed, the presence of consensual sexual relations is not a determinant in deciding whether an offender will rape, with the following example given (Hazelwood & Warren, 1989): An offender was on his way home for an intimate dinner with his wife where he had already discussed the likelihood of sex; he stopped a woman by impersonating a police officer and raped her in his car.

ACQUIRING THE VICTIM AND COMMITTING THE OFFENSE

Hazelwood and Warren (1990) outlined three main methods of approach that applied to serial rapists: the con approach, the blitz approach, and the surprise approach. The blitz style of approach involves the use of direct and injurious force to the victim to gain control; this was used in 17–23% of cases.[4]

The con approach was used in 24–35% of cases studied by Hazelwood and Warren (1990). An example of the con approach is the method used by a serial rapist in Milan, in which he would target women coming home to apartment blocks late at night. He would then enter the lobby behind the victim, and when she entered the lift he would yell out "I'm coming up too," at which point the victim would allow the offender to enter the lift, where he would then attack (Santtila, Zappala, Laukkanen, & Picozzi, 2003, p. 45).

The surprise approach involves the offender waiting for an opportunity to approach the victim and presupposes that the offender may well have targeted or stalked the victim. This was used in 44–54% of cases and was the most common method of approach used by the serial rapists studied (Hazelwood & Warren, 1990). Serial rapist Gilbert Atwell used the surprise approach by gaining entry to his victims' homes, usually in the early hours of the morning when they were asleep. After gaining entry, he would use his physical presence to control the victim.

---

[4]Turvey (2008) argues against the use of the term *blitz* as a form of approach, but it will be used herein for illustrative purposes.

Having acquired the victim, this physical presence was the most common form of control and the knife was the weapon of choice in controlling the victims (Hazelwood & Warren, 1990). Approximately 75–84% of the offenders studied by Hazelwood and Warren used minimal or no physical violence in their offenses.

IMPORTANT ASPECTS FOR INVESTIGATORS IN SERIAL RAPE OFFENSES

The serial rapist differs from the offender who may commit a single offense as a result of impulsivity. The serial rapist could be termed a professional because of the fact that he often prepares in detail the way he will commit his offenses. As Turvey (1996, p. 1) explains, "The serial rapist knows how to position himself for rape activity, engage in rape activity, and continue to rape successfully, without any concern that law enforcement will understand, identify, and apprehend him."

One study showed that "it is probable that the premeditation involved in these crimes is particularly characteristic of these serial rapists" (Hazelwood & Warren, 1990, p. 11). George Kaufman, the South Eastern Suburbs rapist, was wanted for a series of rapes carried out in Melbourne in the 1980s. He often prepared for the offenses by burgling the house of his victim prior to the offense and in some cases stalked them (Miller, 1996). During a study of sexually sadistic criminals, it was revealed that 93% showed evidence of careful planning in their offenses (Dietz et al., 1990; Homant & Kennedy, 1998). This is perhaps a function of their intellect because serial rapists "demonstrate an unusually high level of general intelligence" (Hazelwood & Warren, 1989, p. 13).

Furthermore, many serial rapists are evidence aware. Numerous offenders have a history of other minor offenses prior to committing their rape offenses, with most consisting of minor sexual offenses such as peeping or willful exposure and other crimes such as burglary or stealing. This can also go some way toward explaining why so many serial rape offenses happen in the victim's home: The offender feels comfortable in gaining access to the crime scenes. Hazelwood and Warren (1989) noted that only one of the serial rapists whom they studied did not have a criminal history, and 68% had a history of window peeping.

Joseph Steven Thompson was convicted of more than 40 sexual attacks on females in New Zealand. It was noted during the investigation that Thompson (then an unknown offender) would go to considerable lengths to avoid identification and detection (Manning, 1997). Kaufman was also evidence aware to the extent that after having committed the rape he would wash both himself and the victim in an effort to destroy vital evidence. This caution among offenders was also found by Kocsis (2000) as a common behavior trait of the serial rapists he studied.

The following example highlights the lengths that some offenders will go to (Hazelwood & Warren, 1989, p. 14):

> Ted was steadily employed ... and considered himself to be socioeconomically advantaged.... In preparing for a series of rapes, he would drive a great distance from where he resided or worked and select a residential area into which he would easily blend. Through peeping activities, he would select a minimum of six females who lived alone and would begin observing their homes in order to ascertain their patterns of behavior. He explained that he always maintained a minimum of six potential victims and after raping one, he would select another to replace her.... On some occasions, after successfully attempting a rape, he would subdue an alternative victim and rape her while the police were responding to the first victim's complaint. Ted was a very ritualistic rapist. Prior to entering the victim's residence he would dress in his "going in clothes," which consisted of work gloves, loose fitting coveralls and oversized sneakers, and a ski mask. Using a glasscutter and a suction cup, he would noiselessly make entry through a patio door or window. After ensuring that the victim was asleep and alone he would disconnect the telephone and light emitting devices in her bedroom. He would then leave the residence, but prior to doing so, he would raise a window or leave the door ajar. Returning to his vehicle he would change into his "rape clothes."... Upon approaching the home he would check to see if the window or door had been closed. If it had, he would realize that the victim had awakened, and he would leave and go to another victim's home.

Some important features can be drawn from the Canter and Larkin (1993) study of 45 serial rapists who had committed approximately 257 offenses in the United Kingdom. They suggested that the area around an offender's home was the home range and the area within which the offender committed his crimes was the criminal range. They put forward the hypothesis that the rapists were either commuters or marauders. The commuter theory suggests that there is little or no overlap between these two areas and the offender moves to an area typically outside his home range to commit offenses. The marauder theory argues that there is a much closer relationship between the crimes and the home of the offender and that there is a large overlap of the home range and the criminal range areas (Canter & Larkin, 1993). In addition, they suggested the circle hypothesis, which argues that (p. 66)

> the offenses of a single offender will be encompassed within a circle that is drawn with its diameter as the two offenses that are furthest from each other ... the residence of the offender at the time of the offenses will be within the same circle.

Canter and Larkin's (1993) study revealed that for the cases they examined, 91% of the offenders had all their offenses contained within such a circle and 87% had their home base within such a circle and thus fell into the marauder model. Of note is that the offenders, although operating close to their base, would ensure that there was a small buffer zone between their offenses and this base. This allowed the offenders to carry on normal day-to-day activities with some confidence of not being discovered.

In his study of serial rapists, Kocsis (1997) applied Canter's circle theory to 24 Australian serial rape cases, and it revealed that in 79% of the cases the "criminal range encompassed all of the offenses" (p. 252). Furthermore, in 71% of the serial rape cases examined, the offender's home base was found to be inside the criminal range, and the majority of serial rapists examined behaved in the marauder model as put forward by Canter (Kocsis, 1997). Conversely, 29% of serial rape offenders were not marauders; instead, they commuted to commit their offenses. This is a warning flag for investigators not to become narrow focused in their search for the offender. In addition, although some studies have highlighted certain facets of geographic behavior, the application of geographic models to ongoing police investigations is questionable.

THE INVESTIGATIVE PROCESS: A MODEL FOR SERIAL OFFENSES

Bennett and Hess (2000, p. 3) state that an investigation is "the process of discovering, collecting, preparing, identifying, and presenting evidence to determine what happened and who is responsible." When any crime has been committed, investigators are usually faced with the task of determining who is responsible for the crime because in many cases the identity of the perpetrator is unknown. Law enforcement agencies are called upon to investigate the crime with a view to bringing the offender to justice by successfully identifying and prosecuting that offender. The investigator becomes a collector of evidence, as well as the central figure in giving the investigation direction, which will ultimately determine the success or otherwise of the investigation.

Swanson, Chamelin, and Territo (2000) and Bennett and Hess (2000) suggest that when a crime is committed, the investigator is charged with the following responsibilities: to establish that a crime has been committed, to identify and apprehend the suspect, and to assist in prosecuting the suspect. There is considerable overlap between these and basic investigative principles that the investigator needs to consider during the course of the investigation:

- Determining whether a crime has been committed (e.g., is the death a murder or an accidental death? Consensual sex or rape?)

- Identifying the offender
- Locating the offender
- Identifying and showing a nexus between the offender and the victim (this can be achieved in a number of ways, such as physical evidence, admissions, or witness statements)

How should the investigator approach a series of sex-related crimes? Certainly, an amount of basic knowledge and practical experience dictates how such investigations are usually approached. Swanson et al. (2000) argue that much of the success of an investigation depends on the investigator being self-disciplined and professional and paying attention to detail. They go further to liken an investigation to a series of gates, at each of which certain evaluations and judgments must be made before proceeding to the next gate (Swanson et al., 2000, p. 23). The following attributes contribute to what makes a good investigator (Peak, Evans, Adams, & Ashby, 1998, p. 165):

> In addition to performing the usual investigative functions, investigators must be able to think logically, comprehend and understand complex masses of data, communicate and relate well with other members of the agency, and understand the concepts of organized crime, intelligence collecting, and civil liberties. They must also have self-discipline, patience, attention to detail, knowledge of the law, and some understanding of scientific techniques. Deductive and inductive reasoning and decision-making abilities are also assets.

Gross (1924, p. 1), in his seminal work on criminal investigation, also provides a list of qualities a good investigator should possess:

> An investigating officer should possess the vigor of youth, energy ever on the alert, robust health, and extensive acquaintance with all branches of the law. He ought to know men, proceed skillfully, and possess liveliness and vigilance. Tact is indispensable, true courage is required in many situations.... He has to solve problems relating to every branch of human knowledge ... he should know what the medical man can tell him and what to ask the medical man; he must be as conversant with the dodges of the poacher as with all the wiles of the stock jobber, as well as acquainted with the method of fabricating a will as with the cause of the railway accident; he must know the tricks of card sharpers, why boilers explode, how a horse-coper can turn an old screw into a young hunter. He should be able to pick his way through account books, to understand slang, to read ciphers, and be familiar with the processes and tools of all classes of workmen.

If an officer does not possess sufficient experience to know how to approach an investigation in relation to a sexual offense, then an investigative model would clearly be of use to illustrate a basic investigative approach (Figure 12.1). To produce a model that allows for, and deals with, any eventuality would make the model too cumbersome and difficult to apply, so this model is generic and can be adapted to meet the differing requirements of various investigations (e.g., there will be elements in a rape investigation that do not apply to a break-and-enter investigation, such as a medical examination of the victim and possible locations of evidentiary specimens). The approach detailed here is designed to be simple to use and to provide investigators with an easy-to-understand series of stages that can be adapted to the crime under investigation.

Using this model allows the investigator to follow a clear and logical series of steps or stages that can assist in bringing the investigation to a successful

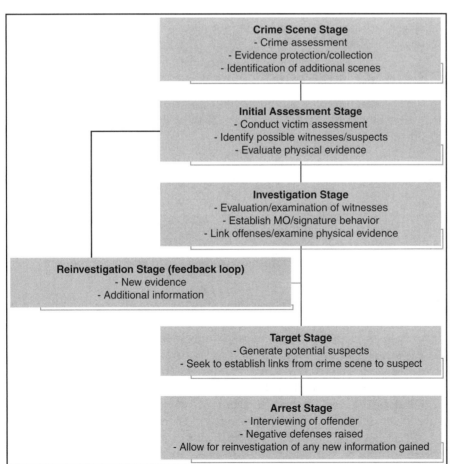

FIGURE 12.1
Generic Investigative Model.

conclusion. Bennett and Hess (2000) argue that it is essential that an investigation be conducted in a logical sequence and that all actions undertaken are legally defensible. Bowker (1999) states that an investigative plan can be used to focus the investigation to ensure all offense elements are addressed. Carney (2004, p. 149) also promotes the use of an investigative plan to ensure that there is a "collaborative climate in which the investigators, patrol personnel, and the support units work in tandem to attack the threat posed by the rapist." It can also assist by ensuring that investigators avoid duplication, coordinate activities, and provide stability and communication, and, finally, it can also be a training aid to inexperienced staff. The use of a model allows investigators to focus on the overall goals of the investigation by clearly setting out the path they should follow to achieve these goals. Both Bennett and Hess (2000) and Swanson et al. (2000) support the idea of a preliminary investigation and a subsequent follow-up investigation. In the proposed model, the preliminary investigation would include the *crime scene stage* and the *initial assessment stage*. The follow-up investigation would consist of the *investigation stage, target stage,* and *arrest stage*. An examination of each stage is now undertaken.

CRIME SCENE STAGE

In any investigation of serial offenses, the crime scene is of prime importance: It is often the only common thread that links the various acts of the rapist together.

Rapes, murders, ritualistic crimes, and sadistic torture, among others, are crimes that usually involve high levels of psychopathology (Geberth, 1996) and greater offender–victim interaction. This results in a greater amount of evidence being left at the scene for investigators to draw information from (this interaction includes physical evidence with regard to Locard's exchange principle, and it also encompasses nonverbal and verbal activity). The initial preservation, collection, and recording of physical evidence are important to the success of any investigation.

The crime scene stage deals with the initial response of police to the report of an alleged crime. Rossmo (1997) states that the focus of any police investigation is the crime scene and its evidentiary contents. Often, the first few minutes or hours will be crucial in ensuring that the scene and evidence are protected or collected and in determining the success (or otherwise) of the investigation. In many cases, the first officers to the scene will not be trained investigators but patrol officers with limited exposure to serious crimes and their associated crime scenes. Saferstein (1998, p. 38) argues that "it is the responsibility of the first officer arriving on the scene of a crime to take steps to preserve and protect the area to the greatest extent possible," because as Turco (1990) suggests, the final outcome of an investigation rests on thorough police work being conducted at the crime scene.

Upon arrival, trained investigators need to make an initial assessment. Does the situation need to be treated as a crime scene or is it a noncriminal event (e.g., suicide versus homicide)? Having decided that the event should be treated as a crime scene, investigators should conduct a thorough examination of the crime scene and ensure that all evidence is protected and collected. The importance of this was illustrated during the Granny Killer serial murderer investigation in Sydney, where at one major crime scene (Hagan, 1992, p. 136) "persons acting in good faith, washed blood and other forensic material away from crime scenes prior to notification and arrival of police, so as to alleviate the anxiety that could be caused to other elderly people."

Geberth (1996) states that upon arrival at the scene it is important that investigators implement crime scene procedures, supervise uniform personnel, and provide direction to the investigation. Saferstein (1998, p. 38) discusses the pressure involved with the crime scene:

> Investigators will have only a limited amount of time to work a crime site in its untouched state. The opportunity to permanently record the scene in its original state must not be lost. Such records will not only prove useful during an investigation but are also required for presentation at trial.

To facilitate this, an investigative team should be nominated. This team should consist of an arresting officer, a corroborating officer, and an exhibit officer. The exhibit officer is responsible for the protection and collection of exhibits through to the examination of exhibits and their final production in court cases. There also needs to be an overall team leader or operations manager who can assess the investigation from a more complete viewpoint than can the investigative team. The purpose of this is to ensure that someone is responsible for the conduct of the investigations. Careless or incompetent investigations are often the result of a failure of a senior investigator to assume control and responsibility and direct the investigation.

Particular attention should be paid to determining if this is the only crime scene or whether there are secondary crime scenes that need to be located. For example, the point of contact may be where the offender acquired the victim, but the victim was subsequently moved to a primary crime scene to carry out the offense. Because serial rapists are more likely to keep records or mementos from their crimes (Homant & Kennedy, 1998), this may well indicate that the home or other locations where the offender spends time should also be treated as a potential crime scene even if the offense did not occur there.

INITIAL ASSESSMENT STAGE

At this point, trained investigators should have control of the investigation and begin to identify possible witnesses and suspects. They should begin the initial assessment stage by evaluating physical evidence located with a view to assisting with suspect generation by prioritizing the most important evidence (e.g., DNA located at a scene is powerful evidence compared to an unidentified item of clothing).

It is also at this point that the investigators should familiarize themselves with the victim by conducting a victimology. This is important because the characteristics of a victim can provide links to possible suspects and particular inferences may be able to be drawn about the offender's motive, modus operandi, and signature behaviors (Turvey, 2008). It should be remembered that "investigations of rape would arguably be one of the most sensitive areas of crime detection" (Richardson, 1994, p. 16); therefore, when dealing with the victim, investigators need to ensure that they communicate effectively and appreciate the impact the offense has had on the victim. Of the victims in the national survey conducted by Easteal (1992), 37% stated that they did not think that the police were supportive. It is essential to the success of the investigation to establish a positive relationship between the victim and the investigators.

The head of the Victorian[5] rape squad recognized the importance of the victim when he stated, "In all modern investigation, you look at your crime scene and the environment around it to identify suspects. You also look at the victim and everything that is around that person" (Miller, 1996, p. 15). Indeed, when investigating serial rape offenses "it is hoped the victim can reconstruct all interactions with the rapist, especially including all the verbal and nonverbal techniques used by the offender to gain control" (Homant & Kennedy, 1998, p. 320). The investigators should then begin the process of suspect generation having regard to the evidence available to them and the information known about the victim.

INVESTIGATION STAGE

It is at the investigation stage that the most challenging work is undertaken. At this point, investigators must attempt to establish a motive for the crime. If this can be done accurately, it will greatly assist in reducing the suspect pool. In addition, signature behaviors also need to be identified because these may also assist in narrowing the suspect pool. These signature behaviors are acts

---

[5]Victoria is a state of Australia with a population of more than 5 million people.

committed by an offender that are not necessary to successfully complete the offense (Turvey, 2008) and can be related to the offender's personality, specifically the unique fantasies of the offender (Homant & Kennedy, 1998; Keppel, 2000). The actions of one Italian serial rapist may help highlight this point. The offender had committed more than 50 rapes over a period of approximately 23 years around Milan. In a large number of the assaults, the offender would lick and suck the right foot of the victim (Santtila et al., 2003).

Conversely, modus operandi (MO) refers to those acts that the offender had to complete to successfully carry out the crime (Homant & Kennedy, 1998; Keppel, 2000; Turvey, 2008). It has been suggested that over time the MO of most serial rapists changes little from one rape to another (Hazelwood, Reboussin, & Warren, 1989). There is little discernible difference in the levels of force used, the pleasure experienced by the offender, the number of victim injuries incurred, or the time devoted to the assault. Others argue against this and suggest that MO will change over time as the criminal's ability develops (Turvey, 1996). Although the basic MO may not dramatically change, parts of it can be modified as the offender may become more forensically aware, or alternatively, the offender may change certain aspects to allow the offense to be completed more successfully (Goldsworthy, 2000). An offender's MO may also change as a result of opportunity. Again, Atwell provides an example. He initially attempted to control his victims by placing his hand over the victim's mouth, but in his later offenses he resorted to placing a pillow over the head of the victims to prevent them from screaming. The aim of the act is the same—to prevent the victim from screaming; however, the use of the pillow could be seen as a more effective way to achieve this aim, thereby representing an evolution in MO.

Witness accounts will also need to be closely examined at this stage and evaluated with regard to the assistance they can provide in generating a suspect. During Operation Lynx, the hunt for UK serial rapist Clive Barwell, the investigating officer "broke the victim's statements down into what terminology was used, actions practiced before the abduction, action after the abduction, the descriptions of the attacker, accents used and also sexual behavior and put them up on the wall" (Bratby, 1999, p. 1).

When dealing with a serial rapist, it is important that police compare and identify any offenses committed by the offender (or exclude those that were not). To achieve this, a table of all the offenses should be prepared so that they can be compared with ease. This chart should include features such as the date, time, location of offense, method of control, method of approach, and signature. The identification of signature behaviors will allow investigators to link offenses that are being committed by the same offender. Table 12.2 provides

Table 12.2 Offense Summary of Serial Rapist Gilbert Atwell

Date	01/26/1998	02/04/1998	02/25/1998	03/06/1998	07/15/1998
Time	0100	0330	0100–0330	1200–1230	1155
Victim	Female, 76 years	Female, 59 years	Female, 46 years	Female, 65 years	Female, 82 years
Offense type	Burglary and attempted rape	Rape	Suspected	Attempted rape	Attempted rape
Offense location	Victim's residence	Victim's residence	Victim's residence	Victim's residence	Victim's residence
Method of approach	Surprise	Surprise	Surprise	Surprise	Surprise
Method of control	Hand placed over mouth, body weight	Body weight, pillow placed over victim's head	Unknown item placed over head	Unknown item over mouth and face	Body weight and hand over mouth
Modus operandi	Offender came in through an unlocked door and put his hand over her mouth. He ran off when she screamed.	Offender laid on top of the victim and held a pillow over her head before completing rape offense.	Offender placed something over the victim's head. She blacked out and woke up 2 hours later. She believed she had been raped.	Offender gained entry and approached the victim where he placed something over her mouth and face. The incident lasted 5 minutes.	Offender gained entry into premises and used his body weight to pin the victim to her bed. He placed a hand over her mouth.
Signature	Nil	Nil	Nil	Nil	Nil
Sexual contact	Attempted vaginal intercourse	Rape	Suspected rape	Attempted rape	Attempted rape

an example of this type of investigative aid and chronicles some of the offenses of serial rapist Gilbert Atwell.[6]

During this stage, investigators should also ensure that trained experts are evaluating all available physical evidence. Furthermore, consideration also needs to be given to any matter that might require reinvestigation as a result of information obtained during this stage. These matters would be dealt with by the feedback loop, which allows for reinvestigation of any new leads.

TARGET STAGE

Having carried out a thorough examination of the crime scene, investigators need to generate potential suspects from evidence available during the target stage. The investigators should then test the veracity of this evidence by seeking to establish links between the suspect and the crime. It is at this point that investigators need to be fully conversant with the investigation as a whole, and they should be evaluating the importance of information gathered by the investigation with regard to generating potential suspects.

The investigators should then begin the process of suspect generation, having regard to the evidence available to them and the information known about the victim. Serial rapists often target a group of victims, and these may be persons who are easily acquired, such as prostitutes, or easily overpowered, such as young children or old women. Alternatively, the offender may seek out a group as integral to his fantasy. For example, an *anger retaliatory* offender may seek out women who resemble an ex-wife on whom the offender wishes to express his anger.

ARREST STAGE

Having generated a suspect during the target stage, the investigators will need to make a decision as to whether they take affirmative action against the potential suspect. This could be in the form of search warrants, surveillance, or bringing the suspect in for questioning. The investigator will have to make a decision regarding what action to take depending on the nature and strength of evidence against the suspect. By this stage, the investigator should have sufficient evidence to link the offender to the crime. However, it is often the case that in speaking to the suspect new evidence or information is gathered. This may

---

[6] For the sake of confidentiality, this information was drawn from information in the public domain (taken from the *Courier Mail* article outlining the offenses and also the judgment against the offender). Not all information on these offenses was available from these sources, but the general idea will not be lost without this information.

also require reinvestigation. For example, the suspect indicates that on the day of the offense he was driving a vehicle the investigators were unaware of. This vehicle would have to be seized and examined.

A key facet of the aforementioned stages is that they are aimed at gathering and utilizing information that is relevant to the investigation. But how should investigators determine what information is relevant to the investigation and what is not?

THE ISSUE OF INVESTIGATIVE RELEVANCE

All investigations depend on information to proceed to a successful conclusion, but not all information received during an investigation is of use. When police undertake an investigation, the principal feature of the initial investigation into a crime is usually a widespread search for information. For example, during Operation Lynx the task force was inundated with 1,847 phone calls in response to an appeal for information in June 1997 (Bratby, 1999). Research has shown that 64% of police suffer from information overload during an investigation; this rate increased to 90% for criminal investigation personnel (Goldsworthy, 2001). For instance, during Operation Park, the hunt for New Zealand serial rapist Joseph Thompson, approximately 560,000 initial suspects were identified (Manning, 1997).

Investigators have to determine what information is relevant to an investigation. To assist in this process, many investigators are taught that when approaching an inquiry, they should be able to answer the following questions at its conclusion: Who? What? Where? When? Why? and How? These can be referred to as the six basic investigative questions.

These can be expanded to the following (or any variation thereof): Who did it? What did they do? Where did they do it? When did they do it? Why did they do it? and How did they do it? In general, most investigators are able to answer what, when, where, and how at an early stage. The factors that are usually unanswered are who did it and why they did it. This is partly because the information available to investigators is constrained by the fact that the investigators have access to "only an account of what has happened, who the victim is, where it took place and when" (Canter, 1997, p. 486).

It could be suggested that any information or input that assists in answering one of the foregoing investigative questions is investigatively relevant and could be useful to investigators. Pinizzotto and Finkel (1990) state that upon examination of a crime scene, including the victim, the profiler may be able to provide information as to what kind of person committed the offense. They go further and suggest the following (p. 216):

Once the material has been collected, referred to as the "WHAT" of the crime, the profiler attempts to determine the "WHY" of the crime: that is, the motivation behind each crime scene detail and for the crime itself. A basic premise of profiling is that if the WHAT and the WHY of the crime can be determined then the WHO will follow.

In its most basic form, information can be said to be of investigative relevance if it assists in the identification and/or apprehension of an offender.

ISSUES FOR INVESTIGATORS

There are a number of issues that investigators need to be mindful of when conducting an investigation into serial offenses. When any serial rape has been committed, investigators are usually faced with the task of determining who is responsible for the crime because in most cases the identity of the perpetrator is unknown. Wilson and Pinto (1990) state that serial offenders present a serious challenge for investigators. As indicated by Turvey (1996, p. 1), the serial rapist is a "successful criminal because law enforcement fails to connect his crimes, fails to understand his motives, and subsequently fails to identify and apprehend him." An examination of many serial offenses reveals that the offender is often interviewed at some point but is then left alone to continue his offenses. Examples include Peter Sutcliffe (the Yorkshire Ripper), who was interviewed, but not pursued, and who subsequently killed eight more times (Wilson & Pinto, 1990). Serial killer Dennis Nilsen was interviewed about various assaults on homosexual males (in fact bungled murder attempts) several times by police, with no action being taken. This was due to complainants not wishing to proceed or alternatively police not pursuing the matter. He continued to kill until caught (Smith, 1995). Andrei Chikatilo was also interviewed about his offenses approximately four times but was left alone because of pressure from the Communist Party. A number of issues pertinent to the investigation of serial rape offenses are discussed next.

Dedicated Task Force

When faced with a potential serial rapist, authorities should be quick to implement a dedicated task force with the sole purpose of linking offenses and locating the offender. However, supplying investigators is just one part of the response; there also needs to be sufficient intelligence support to assist in the investigative effort by providing direction and dealing with information that will inevitably flow into the task force. Furthermore, investigators from a number of areas should be seconded to the task force because they each bring a different skill set to the investigation dependent on the features of the offense.

This may include property crimes or robbery officers if the offender displays some skill at breaking into premises, and it may include the homicide squad if a rape offender also murders his victims. However, investigators also need to ensure that information flows out from the investigation to assist its momentum, without releasing details that could adversely affect it. This is a delicate balance.

This outward flow of information needs to be not only external to the public but also internal to fellow police officers. During the investigation of the Granny Killer in Sydney, two parallel investigations were taking place—the first in relation to the killings and the second in relation to a series of sexual assaults—yet the same offender was responsible for both. These parallel investigations were not linked until late in the investigation. A better information flow may have allowed these to be linked earlier. Essential to the success of any such task force is the ability of senior officers to efficiently and effectively manage the resources dedicated to the task force and to ensure that the direction of the investigation is maintained.

Criminal Profiling

When investigating serial rapes, the investigator must rely on a number of investigative techniques and aids, some of which are well established, such as fingerprints, whereas others are relatively new, such as criminal profiling and DNA identification. Investigative techniques available to police now extend beyond the once traditional investigative and forensic tools that police relied on in the past. We now discuss one of the newer investigative tools available to police, the criminal profile, which is the process of inferring distinctive personality characteristics of offenders (Turvey, 2008). Holmes (1989) argues that the criminal profile should be used as a starting point in an investigation rather than the sole forensic tool.

This explanation of criminal profiling can be expanded further to describe it as a process designed to assist criminal investigative efforts (McGrath, 2000, p. 315). Douglas, Ressler, Burgess, and Hartman (1986, p. 402) state that "profiling does not provide the specific identity of the offender. Rather it indicates the kind of person most likely to have committed a crime by focusing on certain behavioral and personality characteristics." This in turn will allow investigators to reduce the suspect pool. The following gives some insight into the process of criminal profiling in a general way (Pinizzotto & Finkel, 1990, p. 216):

> Through close examination of the crime scene one is able to extrapolate certain relevant psychological material that leads to a profile. Said another way, the forensic investigator will let the entire crime scene, including the victim, tell, in effect, what kind of person committed this act.

A criminal profile should examine "behavioral evidence at a crime scene, in the witness statements, or in autopsy protocols anything we can get that might lead us to helping the police in their hunting down the unknown subject" (Douglas & Olshaker, 1999, p. 81). Criminal profiling is not a suitable forensic tool for use in all types of crimes; those involving some form of psychopathology are most suited. This includes rape offenses (Pinizzotto, 1984; Wilson, Lincoln, & Kocsis, 1997). Turvey (2008) suggests that it is the responsibility of the profiler to provide suggestions to the investigators that are investigatively relevant in an effort to assist the investigation. In relation to criminal profiling, it is important that the information provided to investigators can be acted upon. Furthermore, the information should provide suggestions that are generally discriminating for a given case. One of the advantages that criminal profiling provides to police is that it has the potential to reduce suspect pools and thus assist in limiting information overload.

Linkage Blindness

Rossmo (1997) proposes that *linkage blindness* occurs when there is an inability on the part of investigators to recognize connections and there is confusion regarding which crimes are part of a particular series of crimes. Barwell committed a variety of offenses in the United Kingdom in the 1990s, and during the course of the investigation into his acts five police authorities became involved in the operation. The ability to link the offenses from various jurisdictions or areas is evidence of effective management of cross-border investigations that "is regarded by the National Crime Faculty as a model of good practice for future linked series of crimes" (Bratby, 1999, p. 1).

Unfortunately, it is often the case that serial offenders will rely on these jurisdictional boundaries to hamper investigations and cause linkage blindness in relation to their offenses. The serial killer Ted Bundy was adroit at utilizing jurisdictional boundaries to impede investigations (Goldsworthy, 2002). Indeed, during a review of sexual assault investigation procedures, the Victorian Police identified "that serious repeat sex offenders existed, and more alarmingly, they had not been identified nor the serial activity linked" (Richardson, 1994, p. 16). It was a direct result of this linkage blindness that led to the forming of the Victorian Rape Squad (Miller, 1996). The failure to link offenses and subsequent failure to detect the offender can result in "a high number of victims and a great deal of behavioral evidence that has not been collected or investigated" (Turvey, 1996, p. 3).

This linkage blindness is often caused by a lack of confidence to link serial offenses due to the possibility that the series has not been recognized by investigators and because there is a lack of forensic evidence to connect the offenses (Canter, Missen, & Hodge, 1996). With an increasing reliance on DNA evidence and the growth of a criminal DNA database, the latter issue should be addressed to some degree because it will allow for the comparison of forensic evidence left at the scene with records of offenders held on file. Turvey (2008) supports the use of criminal profiling as a guard against linkage blindness, which he argues is caused by the tendency of investigators to rely too heavily on MO behaviors, the use of jurisdictional boundaries by the offender to confuse investigators, and a breakdown in communication between agencies and a lack of information sharing.

The identification of signature behaviors will also allow investigators to link offenses that are being committed by the same offender in serial offenses. The importance of linking these offenses is twofold in that it enables "investigators to pursue one subject instead of operating without the knowledge that particular cases are linked" and it also allows prosecutors to deal with the offender on multiple charges at one trial (Keppel, 2000, p. 122).

CONCLUSION

Serial rapists constitute only a small proportion of the overall total of rape offenders, although the exact incidence of this crime will never be known. A note of caution should be added, however, because there might well be unreported or undetected serial rape offenders who authorities are not yet aware of. The overall number of unreported or unsolved rapes could well include offenses committed by unknown serial rapists.

It is clear that serial rapists do have distinct characteristics that differentiate them from other offenders. For law enforcement, the serial rapist presents an unusual challenge. The occurrence is so rare that it would be difficult to justify a permanent task force to investigate these matters on a regular basis. Thus, when called upon to investigate matters such as these, authorities will need to be aware of new and unique investigative techniques such as criminal profiling to assist them where possible. In approaching an investigation into serial rape offenses, investigators need to ensure that they have a clear direction and methodical process for working through the information received during the course of the investigation.

It is also vital for police to receive training in relation to psychological traits of these types of offenders so that they at least have some basic understanding of the offender and his behavior. The important issues of offense linkage and signature behaviors should also be kept in mind and will require the investigator to approach the investigation with an open mind. The investigator needs to accept the possibility that the single offense he or she is investigating could well be part of a series of offenses.

Questions

1. List and briefly describe the phases of the investigative model developed by Goldsworthy.
2. What are the six investigative questions?
3. Why is it important to form a task force during a serial crime investigation?
4. There is little statistical information available in relation to serial rape offenses. *True or false?*
5. The inability to recognize connections between offenses and realize that one offender is responsible for a series of crimes is called _____ _____.
6. It could be suggested that any information that assists in addressing the six investigative questions is investigatively relevant. *True or false?*

REFERENCES

Australian Bureau of Statistics. (2005). Annual report 2005–2006. Available at http://www.abs.gov.au/AUSSTATS/abs@.nsf/DetailsPage/1001.02005-06?OpenDocument. Accessed June 11, 2008.

Bennett, W., & Hess, K. (2000). Criminal Investigation. Sydney: Wadsworth.

Berry-Dee, C. (1998). Psychopathic self-denial in serial rape and multiple homicide. The Criminologist, 22(2), 85–94.

Bowker, A. (1999). Investigative planning: Creating a strong foundation of white collar crimes cases. FBI Law Enforcement Bulletin, 68(6), 22–25.

Bratby, L. (1999). Operation Lynx. Jane's Police Review, 107(5545).

Canter, D. (1997). Psychology of offender profiling. In D. Canter & L. Alison (Eds.), Criminal Detection and Psychology of Crime. London: Ashgate.

Canter, D., & Larkin, P. (1993). The environmental range of serial rapists. Journal of Environmental Psychology, 13(6), 63–69.

Canter, D., Missen, C., & Hodge, S. (1996). Are serial killers special? Policing Today, 2(1), 2–11.

Carney, T. P. (2004). Practical Investigation of Sex Crimes: A Strategic and Operational Approach. London: CRC Press.

Davies, A., & Dale, A. (1995). Locating the stranger rapist (Special Interest Series Paper 3). London: Home Office Police Department.

Dietz, P. E., Hazelwood, R., & Warren, J. (1990). The sexually sadistic criminal and his offences. Bulletin of the American Academy of Psychiatry, 18, 163–178.

Douglas, J., & Olshaker, M. (1999). The Anatomy of Motive. New York: Scribner.

Douglas, J., Ressler, R., Burgess, A., & Hartman, C. (1986). Criminal profiling from crime scene analysis. Behavioral Sciences and the Law, 4, 401–421.

Easteal, P. W. (1992). Survivors of sexual assault: A national survey. In P. W. Easteal (Ed.), Without Consent: Confronting Adult Sexual Violence. Proceedings of a Conference Held 27–29 October, 1992. Canberra: Australian Institute of Criminology.

Geberth, J. (1996). Practical Homicide Investigation: Tactics, Procedures and Forensic Techniques. Boca Raton, FL: CRC Press.

Goldsworthy, T. (2000, December). How important is modus operandi and signature behavior? Queensland Police Union Journal, 30–32.

Goldsworthy, T. (2001). Criminal profiling: Is it investigatively relevant? Journal of Behavioral Profiling, 2(1).

Goldsworthy, T. (2002). The hunters amongst us: Serial killers. Australian Police Journal, 56(4), 274–284.

Gregory, J., & Lees, S. (1999). Policing Sexual Assault. London: Routledge.

Gross, H. (1924). Criminal Investigation. London: Sweet & Maxwell.

Groth, N., Burgess, A. W., & Holmstrom, L. L. (1977). Rape: Power, Anger and Sexuality. American Journal of Psychiatry, 134(11), 1239–1243.

Hagan, M. (1992). Special issues in serial murder. Paper presented at The Police Perspective, May 12–14, Canberra, Australia.

Hazelwood, R., & Burgess, A. (1987, September). An introduction to the serial rapist: Research by the FBI. FBI Law Enforcement Bulletin, 16–24.

Hazelwood, R., Reboussin, R., & Warren, J. (1989). Serial rape: Correlates of increased aggression and the relationship of offender pleasure to victim resistance. Journal of Interpersonal Violence, 4(1), 65–78.

Hazelwood, R., & Warren, J. (1989, February). The serial rapist: His characteristics and victims. FBI Law Enforcement Bulletin, 18–25.

Hazelwood, R., & Warren, J. (1990, February). Rape: The criminal behavior of the serial rapist. FBI Law Enforcement Bulletin, 11–15.

Holmes, R. M., & Holmes, S. T. (2008). Profiling violent crimes: An investigative tool. (4th ed.). Thousand Oaks, CA: Sage.

Homant, R. J., & Kennedy, D. B. (1998). Psychological aspects of crime scene profiling. Criminal Justice and Behavior, 25(3), 319–344.

Keppel, R. D. (2000). Investigation of the serial offender: Linking cases through modus operandi and signature. In L. Schlesinger (Ed.), Serial Offenders: Current Thought, Recent Findings. Boca Raton, FL: CRC Press.

Kocsis, R. (1997). Criminal profiling the residence location of serial rape and arson offenders. Australian Police Journal, 51, 250–253.

Kocsis, R. (2000). Psychological profiling of Australian serial rapists. Policing Issues and Practice Journal, 8(3), 6–10.

Manning, J. (1997). Serial rape: Offender profiling. Paper presented at the Second National Outlook Symposium: Violent Crime, Property Crime and Public Policy, Canberra, Australia, March, 3–4.

McGrath, M. (2000). Criminal profiling: Is there a role for the forensic psychologist. Journal of the American Academy of Psychiatry and the Law, 28(3), 315–323.

Miller, M. (1996). Anatomy of a rape. Police Life (Victorian Police Monthly Journal), 14–17.

Moran, A. (1993). Patterns of rape: A preliminary Queensland perspective. Proceedings of Without Consent: Confronting Adult Sexual Violence, Australian Institute of Criminology, October 27–29, 1992.

Oberhardt, M. (2000, March 18). Judge tips profiling to help solve crimes earlier. Courier Mail.

Peak, K., Evans, S., Adams, F., & Ashby, H. (1998). Recruiting and testing criminal investigators: A job related approach. The Police Chief, 65(4), 165–168.

Pinizzotto, A. (1984). Forensic psychology: Criminal personality profiling. Journal of Police Science and Administration, 12(1), 32–40.

Pinizzotto, A., & Finkel, N. (1990). Criminal personality profiling: An outcome and process study. Law and Human Behavior, 14(3), 215–232.

Queensland Police Service. (2007). Queensland police service: Annual statistical review 2006/07. Available at http://www.police.qld.gov.au/Resources/Internet/services/reportsPublications/statisticalReview/0607/documents/ASR-0607-EntireDocument.pdf. Accessed June 10, 2008.

Richardson, T. (1994). Stalking the stalkers. Police Life (Victorian Police Monthly Journal), 16–17.

Rossmo, D. (1997). Geographic profiling. In J. Jackson & D. Bekerian (Eds.), Offender Profiling: Theory, Research and Practice. Chichester, UK: Wiley.

Saferstein, R. (1998). Criminalistics: An Introduction to Forensic Science. Upper Saddle River, NJ: Prentice Hall.

Santtila, P., Zappala, A., Laukkanen, M., & Picozzi, M. (2003). Testing the validity of a geographical profiling approach in three rape series of a single offender: A case study. Forensic Science International, 131, 42–52.

Smith, C. (1995). Dennis Nilsen: Serial killer. The Criminologist, 19(4), 201–209.

Swanson, C., Chamelin, N., & Territo, L. (2000). Criminal Investigation. Boston: McGraw-Hill.

Turco, R. (1990). Psychological profiling. International Journal of Offender Therapy and Comparative Criminology, 34, 147–154.

Turvey, B. E. (1996). Behavior evidence: Understanding motives and developing suspects in unsolved serial rapes through behavioral profiling techniques. Available at http://www.corpus-delicti.com/rape.html. Accessed June 11, 2008.

Turvey, B. E. (2008). Criminal Profiling: An Introduction to Behavioral Evidence Analysis (3rd ed.). Burlington, MA: Academic Press.

Warren, J., Reboussin, R., Hazelwood, R., Cummings, A., Gibbs, N., & Trumbetta, S. (1998). Crime scene and distance correlates of serial rape. Journal of Quantitative Criminology, 14(1), 35–59.

Wilson, P., Lincoln, R., & Kocsis, R. (1997). Validity, utility and ethics of profiling for serial violent and sexual offenders. Psychiatry, Psychology and Law, 4(1), 1–12.

Wilson, P., & Pinto, S. (1990). Trends and Issues in Crime and Criminal Justice, No. 25: Serial Murder. Canberra: Australian Institute of Criminology.

CHAPTER 13

Understanding Serial Sexual Murder: A Biopsychosocial Approach

Robert J. Homant and Daniel B. Kennedy

KEY TERMS

Serial killing/murder: The killing of two or more people by an individual or a group acting in concert.

Organized offender: An offender who may be psychopathic and is literally organized in his or her offense behavior, cleaning up the crime scene, removing weapons and evidence, and attempting to hide the body, among others.

Disorganized offender: An offender who may be psychotic and makes no attempt to clean up the crime scene, remove evidence, hide the body, among others.

Psychopath: An individual with a personality disorder characterized by a pervasive disregard for the welfare of others, a callous lack of remorse, and a grandiose sense of self-worth.

PCL-R: The Psychopathy Checklist–Revised, which measures a number of personality and background factors of the individual to assess the presence or degree of psychopathy.

Trauma control model: A theory of serial killing where traumatizations coupled with predispositions provide the developmental context for serial homicide.

Motivational model: A theory of sexual homicide that attempts to explain the developmental progression of a serial murderer.

CONTENTS

311

Serial killers are not exclusively a product of the 20th century. In fact, history suggests that they have always been with us. From the 15th-century castle of horrors of Gilles de Rais and the 19th-century London streets of Jack the Ripper to the depredations of Green River Killer Gary Ridgway in the United States, profoundly flawed individuals have visited awful fates on innocent human beings (Newton, 2000; Schechter, 2003). Of the many types of serial killers, nothing challenges our view of human nature so much as the behavior of the serial sexual sadistic killer. This individual kills not out of necessity or for convenience but for the very satisfaction of killing. Furthermore, he or she gains satisfaction from the pain and terror of the victim, a satisfaction that arouses, enhances, or even consummates the killer's sexual pleasure. One test of our knowledge of human behavior—indeed of ourselves—is our ability to put ourselves in the place of others and, by empathizing with their feelings, to understand their thoughts and behavior. Serial sexual sadistic killers, then, raise a special challenge to understand what went wrong. Is it possible that "there but for the grace of God go I?" Could anyone develop into a serial sexual killer—given enough time and the "right" circumstances?

We agree with the point raised by Levin and Fox (2008) that most serial killers actually appear to be quite normal. That is, many of their traits fall well within the normal range of behaviors: the ability to dehumanize others, to compartmentalize behavior, to act friendly and charming, to adopt normal social roles, and to take satisfaction in having power over others. Nevertheless, there are some critical differences that place serial sexual killers beyond the pale. Although they may well be able to empathize with their victims, this empathy is devoid of any inhibiting sympathy that would interfere with their enjoyment of a victim's utter humiliation and terror. Furthermore, this lack of sympathy is not a mere blocking of all feeling because it is accompanied by positive sexual arousal that seems to be directly fueled by the victim's pain.

In this chapter, we explore the phenomenon of *serial killing* in general before focusing specifically on the serial sexual sadistic killer. We review the main theories that have been offered to explain such behavior and the evidence that has been put forth to support these theories. Finally, we suggest some new directions for theory and research in the area of serial sexual killing.

DEFINING SERIAL KILLING

There is fairly good consensus that serial killing is one of three main types of multiple homicide, which may be simply defined as the killing of three or more people, by either an individual or a group acting in concert. Multiple homicides are generally classified as mass, spree, or serial. With mass murder there are three or more homicides occurring at the same time. In spree killing, the homicides are spread out as to time and/or location but form a more or less continuous series of actions: There is no appreciable "cooling-off period." With serial killing, the same person (or persons) commits three or more murders with a cooling-off period intervening.

Our definition of a serial killer raises two minor issues that should be dealt with here. The first concerns the cooling-off period. Holmes and Holmes (1998) suggest 30 days as the minimum period for distinguishing spree from serial killing. There is sometimes a gray area here, such as, for example, when a serial killer such as Ted Bundy starts to decompensate and kills with increasing frequency, perhaps with only a few hours separating events. Researchers, however, are free to designate some arbitrary period, such as 24 hours, to separate spree from serial killing. The main point is that the first killing has temporarily satisfied whatever motives are driving the killer, and the subsequent killings are part of a separate sequence of behaviors. The second issue concerns the number of killings required for someone to be considered a serial killer. It should be noted that multiple and serial killing are not legal terms; thus, Egger (1984) requires only two killings, whereas other authors have required as many as four (Hickey, 2002; Hodge, 2000) or even five (Dietz, 1986; Myers, 2004). Three killings seem to be required in the most popular operational definition of serial killing since they are enough to provide a pattern within the killings without being overly restrictive. This is not to say that someone who has "only" killed twice does not "qualify" as a serial killer. Indeed, someone who has only killed once may well be a serial killer, psychologically speaking, who simply has not yet acted on his impulses or has lacked the opportunity (perhaps being arrested after the first homicide). Insisting on three separate homicides simply lends more assurance that a given person is a suitable example of a serial killer, and we follow that approach in this chapter.[1]

TYPES OF SERIAL KILLERS

Various researchers have proposed typologies of the serial killer. In general, these typologies try to identify the dominant motive of the killer. For example, those who kill three or more times for purely practical or instrumental reasons, such as witness execution, might be expected to have certain traits in common that would distinguish them from those serial killers who kill for revenge or out of anger and, in turn, from those who kill "for the fun of it."

As early as 1886, Krafft-Ebing (1886/1965) distinguished three types of homicide that occurred in connection with rape and could include serialists: accidental (the unintended consequences of use of force), witness elimination, and

---

[1]The debate concerning numerosity continues. Myers (2004) cites a variety of authors who propose definitions of serial murder that would include two, three, four, or even five victims. See other discussions on the issue throughout this book.

lust murder (or sexual sadism). A century later, another typology was proposed by Dietz (1986), based primarily on his clinical experiences and requiring five separate killing incidents to be considered a serial killer. Dietz's types are:

1. Psychopathic sexual sadists (enjoy killing; not psychotic)
2. Crime spree killers (using "spree" more in the sense of a criminal career as exemplified by Bonnie and Clyde)
3. Functionaries of organized criminal operations (contract killers)
4. Custodial poisoners and asphyxiators (e.g., caretakers of the disabled)
5. Supposed psychotics (who may be mentally ill/hallucinating or just malingering)

Holmes and DeBerger (1988) proposed four basic types of serial killer:

1. Visionary ("God wants me to eliminate some evil")
2. Mission oriented ("I want to rid the world of prostitutes," etc.)
3. Hedonistic (for pleasure in the killing itself)
4. Power control (for a sense of dominance)

In a revision of this typology, Holmes and Holmes (1998) describe six categories of serial killer. Three of these—vision, mission, and comfort—seek to accomplish nonsexual goals. The main difference between the visionary and the mission killer appears to be that the visionary is psychotic (voices tell him to rid the world of prostitutes), whereas the mission killer acts on an ego-syntonic belief ("I want to make the world a better place by ridding the world of prostitutes"). The comfort killer, on the other hand, is more rational, killing because of reasonably anticipated gains, the payoff to a contract killer being an extreme example. The remaining three types all combine sexual and aggressive motives.

Lust and thrill killers seem to differ mainly in how fantasy is used and whether or not they need a live victim. The power/control type, although described as non-sexually motivated by Holmes and Holmes (1988), still uses sex as one of the means of obtaining dominance. Because lust, thrill, and power/control all involve rape and other forms of sexual assault combined with torture, mutilation, etc., they all appear to be subtypes of sexual sadistic killing. We later return to the issue of distinguishing sadistic from nonsadistic serial sexual killing.

Some observers, however, believe that the Holmes and DeBerger typology suffers from conceptual overlap in certain areas and have suggested minor revisions.[2] Using the Holmes and DeBerger typology as a basis, Levin and Fox (2008) suggested three main types, each with two subtypes:

---

[2]In an empirical study of serial killers' crime scenes, Canter and Wentink (2004) found some support for Holmes and Holmes' (1988) broad categories but were unable to distinguish "power or control" from lust and thrill killings.

1. Thrill, subdivided into sexual sadism and dominance (depending on how directly sexual arousal is linked to victim pain)
2. Mission, subdivided into reformist and visionary (depending on whether auditory hallucinations are present)
3. Expedience, subdivided into profit and protection. Both profit and protection reflect basic criminal activity: In profit, the criminal gains directly from the murder, as in a professional hit man or someone taking over assets or an inheritance. Protection refers more to a criminal killing someone in order to eliminate a potential witness.

In a separate publication, Fox and Levin (1998) offer yet another typology based even more closely on the motivation of the offender. Five motives are specifically mentioned: power (including sadism), revenge, loyalty, profit, and terror. These motives may also underlie mass murder and presumably spree killing as well. In short, it seems that serial homicide may occur for any of the diverse motives that have fueled murder throughout human history.

Furthermore, there is certainly nothing in theory that would preclude a person from killing one time out of revenge, following this up with killing a witness to a crime, and then evolving into a hit man. Fox and Levin (1999) maintain, however, that the sexual sadist is the most common of all types of serial killer. Whether or not this is the case, it is the serial sexual sadist that has certainly generated the most attention.

Besides distinguishing among serial killers based on their motivation, several other distinctions have been noted, including travel patterns, victim acquisition techniques, and attack strategies. For example, some serial killers are "place specific" and kill in their homes or other special places (e.g., Brudos, Gacy, and Dahmer), others kill in a general area or region (e.g., Bianchi and Buono, and Williams), whereas still others travel widely to murder (e.g., Bundy and Lucas). Serial killers may also stay in their immediate neighborhoods as marauders or travel some distance as commuters to forage for victims (Canter & Larkin, 1993; Godwin & Canter, 1997; Hickey, 2002; Holmes & Holmes, 2002).

Rossmo (1997) uses hunting analogies to explain victim acquisition: hunter (searches from home), poacher (searches from another location), troller (any opportunity), and trapper (careful plan). He further identifies three attack methods as raptor, stalker, and ambusher. Beauregard, Proulx, Rossmo, LeClerc, and Allaire (2007) further refine this into three scripts, which are in turn subdivided into five tracks. Hazelwood and Burgess (1999) described three attack modes as blitz, con, and surprise. The blitz is a sudden attack similar to Rossmo's raptor method. The con is a trick or involves a lure and corresponds roughly to Rossmo's ambusher. Finally, surprise involves sneaking or stealth, such as when a victim wakes up to find a rape murderer in her bedroom.

ORGANIZED VERSUS DISORGANIZED SERIAL KILLERS

Although all of the foregoing distinctions may prove important for pursuing and understanding the serial killer, the distinction that has received the most attention is that of the organized versus the disorganized serial killer (Ressler, Burgess, Douglas, Hartman, & D'Agostino, 1986).

Ressler et al. (1986) compiled extensive data on 36 sexual killers, 25 of whom qualified as serial killers. Based on the offender's background and personality, his behavior during the crime, victim characteristics, and the various crime scenes, each offender was classified on approximately 357 variables.[3] Using these variables, Ressler et al. described two types of offenders and their crime scenes. The *organized offender* is intelligent and socially competent. His criminal behavior is more likely to be precipitated by stress, and he is likely to show significant planning prior to the offense, as shown by traveling to the crime scene, bringing a weapon or other instruments, careful victim selection, and so on. In contrast, the *disorganized offender* is of relatively low intelligence and poor social adjustment. His crime seems to take himself as well as his victim by surprise. He frequently must kill the victim prior to his sexual release to maintain control over the victim. The crime is likely to be committed close to the offender's home, the weapon is something usually acquired on site, and the scene is in disarray. The body is left exposed at the scene or only poorly hidden. The crime is unlikely to have been planned or rehearsed through fantasy.

Originally intended to apply only to serial sexual killers, the distinction between organized and disorganized crime scenes and offenders has been enthusiastically embraced by many in law enforcement and has been extended to other forms of serial criminal behavior, such as arson (Kocsis, Irwin, & Hayes, 1998), as well as to single, or nonlinked, crime scenes (Canter, Alison, Alison, & Wentink, 2004).

The distinction between organized and disorganized crime scenes made good intuitive sense, and one study found adequate reliability among profilers in

---

[3]All of the serial sexual killers studied by Ressler et al. (1986) were males, as is the case with all of the studies cited here. The female serial killer, however, has not been neglected in case studies and typologies (Hickey, 2002; Holmes & Holmes, 1998; Keeney & Heide, 1994; Silvio, McCloskey, & Ramos-Grenier, 2006). Serial killing is unusual for female serialists. When it does occur, it is typically a matter of killing husbands or lovers for money or revenge rather than in connection with sexual arousal. An exception might be the case of Carol Bundy, who allegedly used trophies from her murders in subsequent sexual rituals (Holmes & Holmes, 2002, p. 152). Kelleher and Kelleher (1998) classify Aileen Wuornos as a "sexual predator." An active prostitute, Wuornos used sex to lure seven men to their deaths, but it is debated as to whether she experienced sexual arousal in doing so (Myers, Gooch, & Meloy, 2005). Cases of females who act as partners to male sexual sadists are more common (Cooper, 2000).

classifying crime scenes as organized, disorganized, or mixed (Ressler et al., 1985). One criticism of this early work, however, was that there was no independent test of whether the disorganized elements in the crime scene were correlated with any general (non-crime scene) behavioral characteristics of the offender (Homant & Kennedy, 1998). Ressler et al. (1986) had originally derived their concepts of what constituted organized and disorganized by examining offenders and crime scenes more or less simultaneously (i.e., the offenders and their characteristics were known to those classifying the crime scene characteristics). Thus, there was never any clear evidence that crime scenes tended to cluster as organized versus disorganized, or that the individual elements that make up the operational definition of organized were more likely to co-occur.

To subject the organized/disorganized distinction to a cross-validating test, Canter et al. (2004) analyzed data on 100 crime scenes involving sexual homicide that were linked to 100 different serial killers. Canter et al. found that features indicating an organized crime scene were highly common and found in all 100 crime scenes. As these authors point out, this makes sense in that the killers in their sample were at least able to perpetrate three sexual killings before being caught; thus, some planning and organization must have occurred.

More important, Canter et al. (2004) found that the presence of one disorganized element did not affect the probability of other disorganized elements occurring. Rather, certain elements of disorganization tended to occur together. Canter et al. therefore proposed that all crime scenes involving serial sexual homicide involve both organized and disorganized elements, with the disorganized elements clustering into one of four subtypes, which they labeled mutilation, sexual control, plunder, and execution. These four subtypes represent different ways that the perpetrator is motivated to exploit the victim. Perpetrators who do not need a live victim, for example, behave differently from those who do. Offenders driven to mutilate the victim are going to show the highest frequency of so-called disorganized factors. Although this means that the offender's personality does in some sense determine the nature of the crime scene, the data did not suggest clear patterns. Rather, Canter et al. concluded that contextual factors in the interaction between offender and victim, rather than individual traits, play an important role in determining the nature of the crime or crime scene. Such a model is much more in keeping with the general social psychological finding that traits are at best loose clusters of behavior that do not lead to highly consistent, predictable patterns (Alison, Bennell, Ormerod, & Mokros, 2002; Homant & Kennedy, 1998).

In summary, although we do not believe that the research of Canter et al. (2004) requires the immediate abandonment of the organized/disorganized distinction, it does mean that much more attention needs to be paid to the checklist of elements thought to make up this dichotomy and to whether there are meaningful correlations between the occurrences of elements said to indicate one type or the other.[4] Only when the concepts are more clearly operationalized will it make sense to search for the more important correlation between crime scene type and an offender's noncriminal (lifestyle) behaviors and characteristics.

INCIDENCE OF SERIAL KILLING

Two issues arise concerning the frequency of serial killing. One issue is how common it is. If serial killing is fairly common, then this suggests that relatively normal personalities are quite capable of committing serial homicide. Conversely, to the extent that it is a rare phenomenon, one would look for highly unique factors that result in someone becoming a serial killer. A second issue concerns changes in the frequency of serial killing, over either time or place. Changes over time, especially relatively short periods of time such as a few decades, suggest the importance of social factors, at least for understanding the changing rates, whereas differences based on location suggest cultural or subcultural forces at work.

Studies of incidence rates for serial killing are complicated by whether one takes into account all forms of serial killing, such as a criminal having committed two or three instrumental homicides over a long career, or whether one is focused more narrowly on sex- or thrill-related homicides. Authors also vary in terms of the amount of evidence they require for considering a homicide the work of a serial killer, with some requiring specific evidence of linkage (if not evidence linking the homicides to a specific killer) and others seeming to attribute not just unknown perpetrator killings but also missing persons to the work of hidden serial killers. One of the more extreme estimates of serial killing in the United States in modern times was approximately 5,000 people per year, which could amount to more than 20% of homicides during the 1980s.

Most authors, however, derive much more conservative figures. Hickey (2002) suggests the figure could be as low as 49–70 per year, whereas Fox and Levin (2005) suggest that approximately 120–180 Americans were slain annually during the serial murder peak years of the 1980s. Quinet (2007), after adjusting for the possible victimization of reported and unreported missing persons,

---

[4]Turvey (2002) was an early critic of the organized versus disorganized dichotomy. Most crime scenes are mixed, for example. Also, disorganized crime scenes can be staged or they can be drug or anger induced. Organized characteristics do not automatically suggest a psychopathic offender. For these and other reasons, Turvey suggests that investigators and profilers purge themselves of any oversimplified expectations before entering a crime scene.

and of the identified and misidentified dead, has revised upward the Fox and Levin estimate of serial murder victims each year. Her series of elaborate calculations suggests a minimum of 362 annual serial murder deaths and an upper limit of approximately 2,012 such victims.

The foregoing frequency estimates generally attempted to identify the number of known and unknown serial sexual killers operating at a given time and then estimated the number of victims these killers were likely to have. Holmes and Holmes (2002) argued that there are approximately 100 serial murderers active in the United States, down from an earlier estimate of 200 (Ferguson, White, Cherry, Lorenz, & Bhimani, 2003). McNamara and Morton (2004) examined every known killing in Virginia during a 10-year period. Multiple sources were examined to try to establish linkages among approximately 5,183 homicides. Twenty-eight homicides—one-half of 1%—were found to be the work of six serial sexual killers.[5] If this rate should prove generalizable to the entire country, it would indicate approximately 75 victims per year of serial sexual homicide. Out of a population of approximately 300 million, this is certainly rare enough to suggest that it may take a quite unusual combination of variables to produce a serial sexual killer.

Regardless of how many serial sexual killers there are, is their number increasing relative to the population? Are some areas and times more likely to produce serial killers? Hard data are extremely difficult to come by, but certainly cases of serial killing can be found throughout the world and from various historical periods. Capp (1996, p. 21) finds evidence that "serial murders were just as common in 17th-century England as they are today," although his examples are not sexual homicides. Krafft-Ebing (1886/1965) found numerous cases of lust murder in 19th-century Germany, and Peter Lorre came to fame as a movie actor in the (silent) German film *M* portraying a serial murderer of children in 1920s Berlin. Newton (2000) lists numerous cases of a variety of types of serial killers throughout the world during the past two centuries.

Missen (2000) finds a general increase in serial killing over time (1860 to 1995) that is more or less consistent with industrialization/urbanization. Fox, Levin, and Quinet (2008) show that the number of known serial killers active in the United States from 1900 onward closely parallels the total homicide rate. In other words, serial killing increases at approximately the same rate as crime in general, especially violent crime. More significantly, however, when known cases of serial killing are examined, *sexual* serial killers are found to make up an increased percentage of U.S. serial killers. This suggests to Missen that some

---

[5]Pallone (2000) and Meloy (2000) both cite evidence that fewer than 1% of murders reported each year in the United States are sexual homicides, let alone the result of serial sexual killers.

contributing factors can be found in current social trends (e.g., increased child abuse of all types).[6] Missen found the distribution of serial killing across states to be largely consistent with population and crime rates. However, Missen did point out some significant exceptions that he believed needed to be explained. DeFronzo, Ditta, Hannon, and Prochnow (2007) found that California had a rate of 18.6 male serial killers per 10 million residents, whereas Pennsylvania had a rate of 3.4. DeFronzo et al. identified various cultural factors that may account for differences in the rates of serial killing among the states. We return to this point later.

SERIAL SEXUAL SADISTIC KILLING

Although we do not mean to dismiss visionary, mission, and comfort serial killers, to use the Holmes and Holmes (1998) typology, it seems that main-stream theories of crime can easily account for comfort killers, and theories of psychopathology can account for visionary and mission killers.[7] At this point, then, we focus on understanding the serial sexual sadistic killer. First, a few definitional points are in order.

When we previously reviewed the hedonistic subtypes proposed by Holmes and Holmes (1998), we noted that the lust, thrill, and power/control types all combine sexual assault with physical and/or psychological torture of the victim. In this sense, at least, all three might be considered sadistic killers. In the Holmes and Holmes model, however, the link between torture of the victim and sexual arousal for the perpetrator is most clearly spelled out in the lust murderer. Although it may be important to draw distinctions based on the way that sadists torture their victims and whether sexual arousal precedes torture (perhaps in anticipation), accompanies torture, or follows afterward, we are satisfied that all three subcategories qualify for the term *sexual sadist*.

This raises the issue, however, of whether all serial sexual killing has a sadistic element. We believe that sexual killing should be understood in the context of rape and other assaultive sexual offenses, and thus typologies of rape become very relevant for understanding sexual killing. One of the most prominent rape

---

[6]Whether there is truly an increase in the per capita rate of serial sexual killing is arguable. Better communications and forensics greatly affect law enforcement's ability to detect the work of a serial killer, especially one who is mobile. The point is more than academic: A stable rate supports the theory that causes are rooted in basic human nature—biology—whereas a variable rate implicates social psychological factors.

[7]It is important to distinguish the terms psychopathology and psychopathy. A psychopath may be said to possess psychopathy (extreme antisocial tendencies), whereas a mentally ill person has psychopathology (e.g., a severe mood disorder). See Lykken (1995) and Schlesinger (1980) for a discussion of the often confusing and inconsistent use of terms such as sociopath, psychopath, and antisocial personality disorder.

typologies was originally proposed by Groth, Burgess, and Holmstrom (1977). In a widely cited application of this original typology, Hazelwood (1999) distinguished four main types of rape: power assertive, power reassurance, anger retaliatory, and anger excitation. Using this system, Keppel and Walter (1999) examined the frequency with which each category accounted for the 2,476 sexual murderers they found in the Michigan prison system. In anger excitation rape, a planned sexual assault and homicide are designed to inflict pain on the victim and thereby bring satisfaction to the perpetrator. Whether or not the actual death of the victim is intended, the infliction of pain is integral to the offender's ego and sexual satisfaction. By their analysis, only 7% of the cases fit this category. The major difference in anger retaliatory rape–homicide is that there is a more specific anger-arousing stimulus; the victim is seen as responsible, in reality or symbolically, for some more or less specific affront to the perpetrator. This, too, could be considered a sadistic rape in that the acting out of the anger leads directly to the perpetrator's sexual satisfaction. Keppel and Walter found anger retaliatory to account for 34% of Michigan sexual murderers. With power reassurance rape–murder, the rapist killer is seen as acting out a conquest fantasy. The victim's lack of compliance is seen as both angering and panicking the offender. The resulting homicide is seen as overkill (unintended). However, Keppel and Walter continue: "Because the incomplete sexual assault does not validate his sexual competency, he will often explore … sex … postmortem….Consequently, there is sometimes mutilation of the body….The postmortem activities and ritualisms can satisfy and reinforce him" (p. 425). In other words, sexual failure leads to anger arousal, which leads to homicide and mutilation, which leads to postmortem arousal. Perhaps this is not sadism in a technical sense, but there is still a fusion of sex and aggression. Power reassurance accounted for 21% of the Michigan sexual murderers. Finally, the power assertive rapist rapes to reassure himself of his masculinity. He does not have the conscious intent to traumatize the victim, but when his power and control are challenged, he may become violent. "Although violence … may have been severe, there is generally no mutilation of the body; that would be perverse in his mind" (p. 421). This type, which seems to show the least evidence of sadism, was found to account for 38% of Michigan sexual murderers.[8]

In summary, if one holds to a strict construction of the concept of sexual sadism—deliberate pain to the victim as a necessary and anticipated part of the

---

[8]Myers, Husted, Safarik, and O'Toole (2006) argue that the sexual sadist is not "angry" at his victim because anger is an unpleasant feeling and the sadist enjoys acting out his or her extreme aggression against the victim. They further explain that although aggression arousal may enhance sexual feeling, the biology of anger arousal is such that it diminishes or even eliminates sexual arousal. We agree that the uninhibited acting out of hostile aggressive impulses is affectively different than normal anger, which has an aspect of inhibited aggression to it and in that sense is usually negative affect (Homant, 1980).

offender's sexual arousal—then serial sexual sadistic rape–murder becomes an even more rare phenomenon. However, if the term may be used for all of those cases in which harm to the victim appears to contribute to the offender's satisfaction, then most sexual murders seem to involve sexual sadism. Could one have a serial sexual murderer who is not sadistic? Perhaps, but if rape–murder is repeated three times, we suspect that the homicide is part of the attraction and not simply some instrumental elimination of a witness.

A related consideration is whether all sadists are sexual sadists. One of the authors had an inmate client with a history of spanking young children. Although the client readily admitted to sadistic tendencies—that is, taking pleasure in spanking the children—he denied any sexual implications. After significant probing, however, he admitted to masturbating soon after a few of the spanking episodes. The point is that much behavior that may seem "merely sadistic" probably has an underlying sexual element, although we concede the possibility of a nonsexual sadism.[9]

AN ILLUSTRATIVE CASE

Numerous authors have presented detailed case histories of some of the more infamous serial sexual killers, such as Ed Gein (loosely the model for *Psycho's* Norman Bates as well as Hannibal Lecter), Ted Bundy, John Wayne Gacy, and Kenneth Bianchi. Newton (2000) and Schechter (2003) present case summaries outlining the basic facts known about hundreds of serial killers, most of them sexual killers. Rather than repeat details of cases that can be found elsewhere, we introduce here a case that has not been covered in the academic literature, although it is described to some extent on Internet web sites devoted to serial killers. Our information comes from police reports, mental health reports, and court depositions that were generated in connection with an ensuing lawsuit. We call our subject "Robert." Names and places have been altered to avoid possible distress to victims' families. As in all such case histories, our confidence in the accuracy of various facts varies greatly from one to the other, but we are confident that the following reconstruction is essentially accurate.

---

[9]We do not wish to raise a semantic argument here. By definition, sadism can mean either "the association of sexual satisfaction with the infliction of pain on others" or, more simply, "delight in cruelty" (Morris, 1969). Obviously, if the first meaning is adopted, the term sexual sadist is a redundancy. In its sexual meaning, sadism is a paraphilia (Abel & Osborn, 1992)—a linking of the sex drive to an object or activity not normally considered sexual. In labeling various sexual deviations, sadistic killing has sometimes been referred to as erotophonophilia (Money, 1990). The *Diagnostic and Statistical Manual of Mental Disorders* (*DSM–IV–TR*; American Psychiatric Association, 2000) only refers to sexual sadism, which it describes as sexual excitement linked to a victim's pain or humiliation, or simply to dominance over the victim (consenting or nonconsenting).

Robert committed a series of five sexual assaults during a 14-month period. Three of the victims were killed and two were raped but escaped death. Robert committed his first sexual assault/murder when he was 17 years old, which is young for a serial sexual killer.[10] Robert was born and raised in a midsized city of a mid-Atlantic state. He was biracial, normally taken for white. His black–Hispanic father and white mother quarreled frequently, with his father occasionally assaulting his mother and possibly Robert as well. The father had a history of alcohol abuse and had served a 7-year prison term for manslaughter a few years before the start of his relationship with Robert's mother. Robert described his mother as the disciplinarian of the family, who would occasionally give him a whipping with a belt. His parents divorced when he was 3 years old, after which he was raised by his mother. He saw his father only occasionally and came to idealize him. Robert had an older brother who also served prison time. This brother converted to Islam while in prison, as Robert also did after his own eventual incarceration.

Robert's school record indicates that he was in trouble at the age of 6 years. Impulsiveness, mood swings, and fighting are specifically noted. A juvenile arrest record begins at age 9 years. During an 8-year period, Robert is arrested 13 times and adjudicated delinquent on six occasions. Three times he is placed in a juvenile home, where fighting with teachers is noted. Most of the arrests were for property crimes, and as a teenager he has a reputation as a burglar. Robert says that he started drinking at age 9 years, and during one juvenile home intake he says that he had been high almost every night during the previous 2 years. His intelligence was variously noted as average and above average. All in all, Robert's childhood would qualify him as a "life-course persistent" delinquent, which is thought to have genetic predispositions (Moffitt, 1993).

When Robert is 17 years old, he has still another burglary charge lodged against him and is awaiting a juvenile court hearing. Probably, he is angry at the prospect of being institutionalized again; perhaps he feels that he might as well do something noteworthy while still a juvenile. It is probable that he begins stalking some women in his neighborhood. The stalking is not overt. It amounts mostly to taking note of their behavior and where they live. The women have in common that they are white and overweight, and probably they are all older than Robert. It is probable that they remind Robert of his mother in various ways, at least subconsciously.

One night, Robert follows one of the women, Jane, to her apartment. Jane is approximately 29 years old and has a history of mild mental illness. She

---

[10]Myers (2004) details six case histories of serial sexual murderers who committed at least two of their homicides before they were 18 years old; the cases are of interest precisely because they are rare.

is staying in an assisted living complex approximately four or five blocks from Robert's home. Looking through a window, Robert observes her getting ready for bed. Impulsively, he tears a screen out of the front window and enters the apartment. He confronts Jane in the back of the apartment, but Jane escapes into a different room where she begins pounding on the wall and screaming. An upstairs neighbor hears the commotion but does not get involved. Robert turns the television up very loud to cover the noise of the continuing assault but succeeds mainly in calling more attention to the noise. Nevertheless, the upstairs neighbor does nothing, and Jane receives approximately 37 blows to the head, the first few of which would have killed her. It was unclear whether Robert had carried some sort of club with him, or grabbed some convenient object from the apartment; in any event, the murder weapon, thought to be something like a baseball bat, was never found. After Jane dies, Robert rifles through her bedroom dresser and retrieves a pair of her shorts. He returns to the dead body and proceeds to masturbate over it, ejaculating into the shorts as the television continues to blare loudly. Finally, he leaves through the back door and walks, while still covered with Jane's blood, across a field.

Robert's behavior fits the pattern of a disorganized killer, specifically a plunderer in the Canter et al. (2004) reformulation. He engaged in a blitz attack, showed "overkill," had poor control of the victim, and literally got blood all over the room as well as all over himself. His sexual release was after the victim died, and he (carelessly) left ejaculate behind. There was, however, some planning because he apparently stalked his victim, picked a location where people were unlikely to come to each other's aid, probably brought a weapon with him, and carried it away. Perhaps he might be classified as a "mixed" rather than a disorganized offender. In terms of Ressler, Burgess, and Douglas's (1988) rape classification system, we think he best illustrates the anger retaliatory rapist. We believe that Jane represented some hated aspect of his mother, whom Robert blamed for the loss of his idealized father.

Despite the trail of evidence that might have pointed to Robert and ended his career after one killing, the police focused their attention on a fiancé who had recently broken up with Jane. Meanwhile, Robert was again adjudicated delinquent based on the pending burglary charge and sent to a juvenile institution where he stayed for approximately 8 months. His record in the institution was fairly good—a trend that has been noted of other serial sexual killers.

A few weeks after release from the juvenile institution, now age 18 years, Robert returns to the site of his first killing. It is now approximately 6:30 on a midsummer morning, not a time he is ordinarily up and about. He is driving his mother's blue Tempo. Cruising the neighborhood, he notices a 13-year-old girl on a bicycle delivering newspapers. He stops by the curb, waiting. As she approaches, he releases the trunk latch, jumps out of the car, overpowers the girl, and forces her into the trunk of the car. Although this is still a high-risk blitz attack that could easily have been noticed by any number of people, Robert has shown some development in his technique. He is able to spirit the girl out of the neighborhood before anyone realizes anything is amiss. It is several hours later before the girl's parents are aware that she did not report to school that day, and a search is begun. Her abandoned bicycle is found close to the abduction site, someone reports having seen a blue car drive off down a road to a nearby park, and the park is searched. A trail of blood leads from a parking area down a hillside. The body is quickly found, carelessly covered by last year's leaves. The girl has been raped and then stabbed 22 times. Although a killing is a rare event in this area, the police do not connect the killing with Jane's unsolved murder from approximately 8 months previous and only a few blocks away. Robert, in the meantime, proceeds to live a reasonably normal teenage life in that he has a girlfriend and hangs out with friends. He continues to drink heavily and uses drugs occasionally.

Approximately 6 weeks later, Robert selects his third victim. He follows a woman to her house, which is within a few blocks of his own residence, slightly closer to his home than the locations of the two killings. After dark, Robert breaks into the house and proceeds quietly to the upstairs bedroom. He is surprised to see that the woman is sleeping with her boyfriend. He decides he had better not confront two people. Back downstairs, he pokes around to see if there is anything worth stealing. He encounters the woman's 5-year-old daughter and hesitates only briefly. Grabbing some towels and dirty clothing from the floor of the laundry room, he jumps on the sleeping girl, smothering her with the clothes as he proceeds to vaginally rape her. She is able to put up only minimal resistance before passing out and perhaps this saves her life. The next morning, she is found unconscious but still alive. She was unable to tell anything of what happened to her, but it was determined that she had been raped. With three sexual assault victims, two of them dead and the third almost having been killed, within approximately eight blocks of each other and within less than 1 year, police and community now begin to think in terms of a serial killer.[11]

---

[11]Robert's crimes were eventually linked by DNA evidence. Other than DNA and geographic proximity, there was little to link Robert's first three crimes. Two involved breaking and entering the victim's home, but one was a street abduction. Two victims were described as heavy set, but one was a small child. One victim was bludgeoned, one was stabbed, and one was strangled. In short, there was little consistency in terms of modus operandi, signature, or victimology. This is consistent with the finding of Bateman and Salfati (2007) that any behaviors that were consistent across crime scenes were too common to be discriminatory among serial killers.

Approximately 1 month later, Robert selects his fourth victim, again a large (possibly overweight) white woman whom he follows home. She is having trouble sleeping that night and hears someone moving about in the house. Concerned about a possible serial killer in the area, she decides to exit the house quickly. Robert has picked up a knife from the kitchen, but he is surprised when she quickly exits the bedroom, and he drops the knife. He catches her trying to get out the front door and tries to trap her inside. Nevertheless, she escapes to the front yard. It is approximately 4 a.m. Robert follows her to the front yard and pins her to the ground while proceeding to rape and simultaneously strangle her. She manages to bite him and to cry out just before passing out. A light comes on next door and Robert breaks off the assault and flees, possibly thinking that the victim is dead. He learns from the paper the next day that there is a living adult victim who can potentially identify him.

Either because he is afraid of being identified or because he is enraged that his victim survived, Robert feels compelled to return and finish the job. On at least two different occasions, he stakes out the house but does not get the opportunity to assault the victim. On one of these occasions, he is actually in the house again when he sets off a newly installed burglar alarm. Frustrated by his failure, Robert stakes out a new territory approximately 2 miles from his home and the sites of his first four victims but within a few blocks of where he once lived as a child. Again, he follows an overweight white woman home and breaks into her house. The woman's adult children and a grandchild are sleeping upstairs while Robert assaults the woman in her downstairs bedroom. Some loud fans help muffle the sounds during the warm late summer night. This time, Robert is successful in raping and then strangling the woman to death. He has clearly progressed to a more organized killer, leaving a much neater crime scene, methodically strangling his victim during or after intercourse, and slipping away without anyone knowing there had been an intruder—although this was still a highly risky rape–murder.

Encouraged by this success—or still not able to accept his previous failure—Robert decides to try one more time to kill his fourth victim. During the middle of the night, he breaks a window and enters her house. He is surprised to find a police officer waiting for him. The officer has been staying in the house for the past several days, expecting one more attempt. Even now, Robert's luck holds. He succeeds in running past the officer, is missed by two pistol shots, and exits the back of the house, setting off the burglar alarm but getting away successfully. However, Robert has cut himself breaking the window and the officer calls the local hospitals and tells them to be on the alert for someone seeking treatment for a cut. Robert does go to a hospital and is finally caught.

Robert consistently maintained his innocence while sitting calmly through two trials. He refused to follow his lawyers' advice that he testify in his own defense. He showed no emotion when he was found guilty and sentenced to death on all three murder counts. Several years later, an appellate judge threw out two of the death penalties because the jurors had not been properly instructed during the penalty phase of the trial. The third death penalty remains in effect and Robert is on death row with a stay of execution while federal court appeals continue.

In summary, Robert engaged in five sexual assaults during a 14-month period, 8 months of which he spent in a juvenile institution. In addition, there were three other attempts to return and kill the victim of the fourth assault. His victims were all female and white, but they varied in age from 5 to almost 50 years; the youngest girl was no doubt a secondary target. In the first assault, his sexual release was postmortem, but in the remaining assaults he completed vaginal rape while the victim was still alive. All of the assaults took place on the offender's (and victim's) home turf. Several methods were used: a club, a knife, smothering, and manual strangulation. His control of the victims and the crime scenes was minimal: He left hair, semen, or blood at every site; he was noticed by someone other than the victim during three crimes (first, second, and fourth crimes) and was at risk of detection during the other two crimes.

Why did Robert commit his crimes? Does the fact that he had the presence of mind to break off his fourth assault when a neighbor turned on a light or that he knew enough to return to kill that possible victim–witness mean that he had "control" of his behavior and should be held legally responsible? Unfortunately, Robert continues to maintain his innocence and has no interest in psychotherapy. His conversion to Islam apparently has satisfied any need for redemption that he may have felt. Hints at possible causes, however, abound. His father was a killer—perhaps there was a genetic predisposition to aggression. There is a hint of physical child abuse—perhaps there was frontal lobe damage, although his above normal IQ suggests more of a bottling up of some sort of rage. Perhaps the early separation from his father left him feeling abandoned and angry. Perhaps his early exposure to alcohol and drugs weakened whatever cognitive restraints he may have had. Perhaps his mixed racial identity played a role, as he identified with his (partly) African American father and felt rejected by his peer group (if, for example, they disparaged blacks in his presence, thinking of him as white). Perhaps his juvenile institutionalizations exposed him to sexual abuse and further alienated him from society. Perhaps his early career as a burglar gave him the experience of power as he went through the personal belongings of sleeping victims. Perhaps the underwear of sleeping women especially excited him with a sense of power and control. Perhaps this in turn led to rape fantasies—fantasies that were shattered by the resistance of his first victim, Jane, until her brutal destruction restored his sense of potency and established a new behavioral theme for him.[12] As with

---

[12]Schlesinger and Revitch (1999) might suggest that Robert's early burglaries were sexually motivated, perhaps to find a victim, or were sexually stimulating in and of themselves. Robert's sexual murders might also be classified as "acute catathymic" homicides (Schlesinger, 2004).

most serial killers, we do not lack for possible causes; there are more than enough possibilities. The task is to identify those that are operative in a given case and then to integrate them into a coherent model.

THEORIES OF SERIAL SEXUAL SADISTIC KILLING

There has been no shortage of attempts to explain the behavior of serial sexual killers, most of whom are seen as sadists and psychopaths. Many authors get caught up in the issue of whether such killers should be seen as evil versus sick (Knight, 2007; Wilson, 2003), slated for execution and a one-way ticket to Hell or sympathetically confined, perhaps in the hope of rehabilitation, perhaps only awaiting one more development in the knowledge of brain chemistry. Are they themselves not also victims—of society, of bad parenting, or of a capricious gene? Although such philosophical musings can lead to lively debate, they probably do not help understand (let alone apprehend) even one such person. How, then, do we account for individuals who are so perverse as to find their sexual pleasure at the often unspeakable demise of others? Most theorists, in their effort to account for such extreme behavior, have found it necessary to implicate a wide variety of variables. It has become common to organize these variables at the biological, the psychological, and the sociological levels. The theorist's task, then, becomes to show systematically how these three levels interact to produce the serial sexual killer.

BASIC STUDIES

Most studies of serial killers, by necessity, have relied on small samples, with perhaps a dozen or so people interviewed by the researcher. Those researchers with government connections have often been able to achieve sample sizes in the 30s or 40s.[13] Researchers who have gone beyond this have generally had to rely on case files or even media accounts that are very uneven in terms of the quality and quantity of information from case to case. A good example of such case files is the Missen Corpus of Serial Killer data at the University of Liverpool (Canter, Coffee, Huntley, & Missen, 2000). Generalizations across "all" serial sexual killers (even limited to a narrow definition of sadistic killers) are extremely difficult because of the limited nature of the data. Recent studies tend to rely on enlarged databases, but comparisons across studies are difficult because of the high overlap in cases used for obtaining data (see, for example, Kraemer, Lord, & Heilbrun, 2004; Morgenbesser, 2008).

---

[13]According to Beasley (2004), the FBI, through its National Center for the Analysis of Violent Crime, is expanding its database by reviewing case files and conducting additional in-depth interviews of serial killers.

One of the best of the early studies for extensiveness of detail on sexual sadists was conducted by Dietz, Hazelwood, and Warren (1990). Every case studied by the National Center for the Analysis of Violent Crime between 1984 and 1989 that showed a clear element of sexual sadism was included (there is some unclear overlap here with the subjects studied by Ressler et al., 1986). This resulted in a sample of 30 cases on which there was extensive, although varied, documentation. All were male; all but 1 were white. Although all had engaged in intentional torture of their victim(s), only 73% were known to be murderers, and 57% qualified as serial murderers (three or more killings). An additional 9% were suspected of being serial killers. A few findings are used here to illustrate the strengths and weaknesses of this study.

Dietz et al. (1990) report that 30% of their sample had an incestuous involvement with their own child. This seems like a very high figure, and its importance might lie in pointing to a psychodynamic (perhaps Oedipal) origin to the subjects' sadistic rage. But what of the other 70%? It may be that they also had incest-related problems that simply did not surface. Twenty percent of the sample reported that they had been victims of child sexual abuse. Are these the same as the incest abusers, or are they part of the 70% who did not report committing incest? Are these rates of incest and sexual abuse high in comparison to those for other types of violent offenders? This too cannot be answered because no comparison group data is given. Mitchell and Aamodt (2005) explored the child abuse history of 50 serial sexual ("lust") killers. There was a record of at least some abuse in 68% of the cases. Compared to general population norms, the serial sexual killers were much more likely to have been abused psychologically (50% versus 2%), physically (36% versus 6%), and sexually (26% versus 3%).

In addition to their abuse history, the following findings from Dietz et al. (1990) also seem worth noting. A significant number were married (43%) and/or had established reputations as solid citizens (30%); most (57%) had no arrest history prior to the instant case. Drug abuse was fairly high (50%), suggesting either a loss of inhibition or an attempt to self-medicate. A variety of sexual deviance was noted, including cross-dressing, indecent exposure, and wife sharing, in addition to the incest and child sexual abuse noted previously. An intriguing finding was "excessive driving," which was noted for 40% of the sample despite being a variable that would not normally be thought of in the context of sexual homicide. One subject explained his excessive driving as expressing a need for freedom—to go wherever he wanted with no one telling him what to do.

In terms of their criminal behavior, the majority were clearly organized, with 93% showing careful planning. The victim was usually approached using a con or pretext, such as an offer of help or asking directions (90%); only three subjects (10%) preferred a blitz or surprise approach. Thirty-seven percent had the assistance of a partner. Sixty percent of the offenders kept a victim captive for more than 24 hours (and up to 6 weeks). Most offenders (87%) were described as unemotional and detached during the offense. A wide variety of sadistic behaviors were engaged in, both physical and psychological. Sexually, oral (73%) and anal (70%) penetration were more common than vaginal (57%). Dietz et al. (1990) attribute this to the high percentage of offenders with a history of homosexual activity (43%). However, "sexual dysfunction" during the offense was also noted for 43% of the offenders, and this may have played a role in their preferred sexual activity. Or, it may simply be that oral and anal penetration both provide the offender with a greater sense of power over the victim. Ligature (32%) and manual (26%) strangulation were the most common causes of victims' deaths ($N = 130$), but gunshot (25%) and stabbing (10%) were also common. In short, Dietz et al. provide a great deal of heuristic data that are difficult to interpret. The study does not distinguish serial sexual killers from single murderers (Kraemer et al., 2004) and other violent offenders, but it does bring out the variety within sexual killers.

Research by Quinsey, Harris, Rice, and Cormier (1998), although not directly involving serial killers, provides some important data for understanding the psychology of the serial sexual killer. They studied hundreds of violent offenders over a 25-year period. Besides treatment considerations, one of their main goals was predicting risk of recidivism (repeat violence). A subset of their violent offenders was made up of violent sexual offenders, a group whom they studied to develop the Sex Offender Risk Appraisal Guide (SORAG). Myers, Husted, Safarik, and O'Toole (2006) argue that serial sexual killers are primarily a type of sex offender, and they recommend a new *DSM* classification, specifically "sexual sadist, homicide type," thus implying the direct relevance of research on all sadistic rapists. Whereas power and control concerns may be pleasurable and useful in the commission of the rape–murder, sadistic sexual gratification is paramount.

Quinsey et al. (1998) report on a series of studies that used "phallometry" to measure the sexual arousal of convicted rapists to tape recordings of various sexual encounters. This research built on earlier work by Malamuth (1981) that classified subjects as either rape prone or unlikely to rape based on self-reports about their likelihood of committing a rape if they knew they could never be caught. A fairly large subset (35%) of a college male sample was identified as rape prone. Malamuth found that rape-prone subjects did show a different pattern of sexual arousal than the unlikely-to-rape subjects; namely, the rape-prone subjects were more likely to show sexual arousal to a rape scenario than to a consensual sexual encounter. However, rape-prone subjects were more aroused by a rape scenario in which the victim herself became sexually aroused and stopped resisting. With a "victim abhorrent" scenario, in which the victim was clearly distressed throughout the rape, the rape-prone subjects showed a somewhat lower level of arousal, though still much higher than the unlikely-to-rape subjects. A reasonable interpretation of the Malamuth research is that rape proneness is a relatively common characteristic among males, but sadistic rape makes up a small subset of rape proneness.

The Quinsey et al. (1998) studies differ from Malamuth's (1981) earlier research in that convicted rapists were used, most of whom had been involved in violent rapes. Over a number of variations in research methodology, one result stands out. Convicted rapists were found to have a different pattern of sexual arousal than did offenders convicted of nonsexual offenses. Rapists were more aroused by listening to rape scenarios than by a consenting sex scenario, with non-sex offenders showing the opposite pattern. More important, this difference was most clearly found when the rape scenarios portrayed "graphic and brutal rape stimuli" (Quinsey et al., 1998, p. 124). Finally, rapists as a group showed sexual arousal to an audiotape depicting nonsexual violence toward a woman but not to a tape depicting similar violence toward a male (all rapists were heterosexual). These findings do not mean that all rapists pre-fer brutal rape to rape with minimal force, but they do suggest that many, if not most, rapists are not deterred by victim distress and that some rapists, at least, might find that distress arousing. Interestingly, Quinsey et al. found no social skill differences between rapists and non-sex offenders; the rapists, how-ever, did score lower than other offenders on a self-report measure of empathy. The empathy measure, in turn, was correlated with individual differences in arousal to the rape scenarios.

Quinsey et al. (1998) also found that the single best predictor, by far, of violent sexual recidivism was psychopathy, as measured by Hare's (1991) Psychopathy Checklist–Revised (*PCL-R*). Based on Hare's (1993) theory of the *psychopath*, the PCL-R measures a number of personality and background factors of the indi-vidual (extensive background information or interviewing is necessary). The 20 subscales of the PCL-R measure two correlated factors thought to characterize pri-mary and secondary psychopaths. The first factor focuses on such characteristics as cruelty; the absence of feelings such as love, empathy, or guilt; egocentricity; and exploitiveness. In combination, these characteristics lead to the selfish and remorseless use of others. The second factor includes such traits as impulsive-ness, sensation seeking, and lack of socialization (delinquent and criminal behav-ior) and accounts for the unstable and antisocial lifestyle of the psychopath. It is debated as to whether the psychopath represents a distinct personality disorder as opposed to an extreme version of the antisocial personality or perhaps an extreme impulse control disorder (Quinsey et al., 1998; Wiebe, 2003; Zuckerman, 1999).

However it is defined, psychopathy as measured by the PCL-R has proven to be highly predictive of repetitive violent sexual offenders, and psychopaths have been described as "polymorphously perverse" (Meloy, 2002). Hundreds of convicted sex offenders were scored on the SORAG, for which the PCL-R was the main component. Those offenders whose scores placed them in the highest risk category had 100% recidivism for a new violent offense during a 7-year follow-up. In contrast, sex offenders with the lowest SORAG scores had only a 7% recidivism rate (Quinsey et al., 1998, p. 244). The entire SORAG measured 13 variables besides psychopathy (PCL-R). Most of these variables, however, merely reemphasized factors already included in the concept of *psychopath*, such as a disrupted home life, poor school adjustment, a criminal history, early age at first offense, and high alcohol use. The one new variable was phallometrically measured deviant sexual arousal (penile arousal to depictions of violent rape). When combined with this measure of deviant sexual arousal, the PCL-R was highly predictive of repeat violent sexual offenses. The Quinsey et al. research did not include serial sexual killers; however, it does not seem to be much of a conceptual leap to argue that findings on repeat violent sexual offenders would be even more true of the serial sexual killer.

Identifying the serial sexual killer as a psychopath with an additional problem related to deviant sexual arousal opens up a plethora of research on the psychopathic personality in general. Most conclusions, however, can be summed up as viewing psychopathy as an extreme form of egoism lacking in impulse control and having a biological predisposition (or "diathesis") that combines with various childhood trauma or other stressors. Zuckerman (1999) summarizes the research on the biological predisposition to antisocial personality and psychopathy. It is thought that this predisposition may be either genetic or nongenetic (e.g., brain injury or developmental biochemical disorders). Insofar as genes are implicated, it must be stressed that no researchers have identified a "psychopath gene." All geneticists agree that no gene has a one-to-one link to behavior; rather, genes create potentials or tendencies that require specific environmental circumstances for a specific behavior to occur.

Zuckerman (1999) cites a number of twin and adoption studies that support both a biological and an environmental contribution to antisocial personality disorder and, by extension, to psychopathy. A reasonable generalization from these studies is that when the subjects come from a fairly homogeneous socioeconomic background, biology accounts for more of the variance than environment; conversely, when child-rearing practices are very heterogeneous, environment accounts for more of the between-person variance in criminal behavior. A prenatal variable, alcohol exposure via the mother's drinking, was also identified as contributing to childhood aggressiveness and conduct disorder. The implication is that exposure to alcohol in the fetal period may affect frontal lobe development, which in turn suggests loss of impulse control. Likewise, there is evidence that maternal rejection, perhaps linked to a difficult birth, may result in early neglect, which in turn may play a role in poor neuro-logical development.

Numerous studies have identified various hormones (e.g., testosterone) and neurotransmitters (e.g., serotonin) as playing a role in emotional arousal and impulsiveness. Although no specific hormone differences have been linked consistently to specific arousal and behavioral characteristics of psychopaths, a number of studies have shown that criminals identified as psychopaths show lower fear-arousal responses and probably a lower overall emotional arousal. This low arousal, in turn, is thought to be a key factor in the trait of sensation seeking. Where psychopaths differ from normal sensation seekers is in their lack of inhibition toward distress, in turn thought to be connected to their lack of empathy/sympathy (Zuckerman, 1999). The combination of low fear arousal, low empathy, and high need for stimulation would certainly fit the serial sexual killer's linkage of victim pain with his own sexual arousal.

Zuckerman's (1999) theory of psychopathy is that the genetic or at least physi-ological predisposition interacts with the early family environment to produce the adult criminal psychopath. While conceding that there seem to be cases of a full-blown psychopath emerging from a healthy environment, Zuckerman argues that a truly healthy environment is more likely to produce someone with adjustment difficulties that fall short of serious criminal behavior. The emerging psychopath can be fairly well predicted at an early age, with children at risk for antisocial personality and psychopathy being identified as early as age 3 years. The key factors in the family environment are antisocial behavior in the father and (low) nurturance in the mother. Early school failure is both a result of the developing psychopathic personality and a cause of further delin-quent and criminal behavior.

In summary, the bulk of the research that we have reviewed has been done on convicted sex offenders and on general criminals, often using the diagnosis of psychopath to establish a subgroup of more dangerous, high-frequency offend-ers. We believe that serial sexual killers constitute a more extreme group of sex-ual psychopaths, one that is not profoundly different from the violent sexual offenders studied by Quinsey et al. (1998) nor from many of the psychopaths in the studies reviewed by Zuckerman (1999). Furthermore, the general find-ings on psychopaths and psychopathic sex offenders have been supported by more clinically based observations of serial sexual killers (Egger, 2002, 2003; Norris, 1988).

Based on case reviews, clinical observations, and evidence similar to that reviewed previously, a number of different theories of sexual serial killers have been proposed. We briefly review three of them for their similarities and differences.

HICKEY'S TRAUMA CONTROL MODEL OF THE SERIAL KILLER

According to Hickey (2002), there are multiple paths to becoming a serial killer. The predispositions to serial killing can be biological, psychological, sociological, or any combination thereof. No combination of predispositions, however, is likely to produce a serial killer unless some event or series of events, called traumatizations, occur during the person's development. For Hickey, relevant traumas include such things as child abuse (sexual or physical), home life disrupted by death or divorce, ostracism in school, and profuse images of violence (actual or media based). These traumatizations are experienced by many who do not become serial killers, but for those who have a significant vulnerability or predisposition, the effect of the traumas is to create feelings such as rejection, mistrust, confusion, and anxiety, leaving the person unable to adapt to additional stresses. Stresses now have a multiplicative rather than an additive effect. A combination of stresses and negative emotional reactions can lead to a number of responses, both adaptive (help seeking) and maladaptive (from anorexia to suicide). For some reason, however, the evolving serial killer externalizes the blame for his feelings of distress and uses attacks on others as a way of restoring or maintaining self-esteem. Hickey (p. 109) notes the following:

> In an effort to regain the psychological equilibrium taken from them by people in authority, serial offenders appear to construct masks, facades, or a veneer of self-confidence and self-control. The label of psychopath, given to most serial killers, may actually describe a process of maintaining control of oneself, of others, and of one's surroundings.

Various facilitators, such as alcohol or drugs, pornography, and fantasy, then operate to reduce inhibitions and lead to killing, which Hickey believes would usually happen eventually even without the facilitators. Although a killing may fulfill a fantasy and restore a sense of control, this satisfaction eventually wears off, leading to a new killing to reestablish the positive feelings that followed the first one. Differences in the nature of the early traumatizations presumably influence the manner of serial killing (e.g., victim preference, ritualistic behaviors during the killing, or degree of sexualization).

The strength of Hickey's (2002) model is that it provides a framework broad enough to encompass many different types of serial killing, not simply sexual sadistic killing. Also, it does not try to put the serial killer into some narrow classification. Even two sexual sadistic killers might have no particular background variable in common. The nature of their predispositions, their traumas, their adult stressors, and their facilitators may vary greatly from each other, yet their behaviors could be quite similar. Of course, some might find this lack of specificity frustrating, but we see nothing wrong with the idea that there might be multiple routes to the same behavior. If we were to point to a weakness in Hickey's model, it would be the lack of distinction between predispositions and traumas. Because the predispositions can be psychological and sociological as well as biological, it is not clear why child abuse is an example of a trauma and (postnatal) brain damage a predisposition since child abuse may be the cause of the brain damage. Also, it is not clear where traumatizations end and various stresses and facilitators begin. One could just as easily have provided a long menu of contributing factors and argued that a wide variety of combinations could produce a serial killer. Thus, given sufficient social psychological factors, there may be cases in which no physiological diatheses are needed.

THE MOTIVATIONAL MODEL

Ressler et al. (1988) offer what they term a *"motivational model"* that is specific to sexual homicide (see also Burgess, Hartman, Ressler, Douglas, & McCormack, 1986). Data supporting the theory was based on the same 36 convicted sexual killers used in the Ressler et al. (1986) study of organized versus disorganized killers that was reviewed previously. The authors describe their approach as "law enforcement" rather than psychological, meaning that they are attempting to develop a model of the serial sexual killer that would be especially useful for the crime scene profiler. Although the model is not closely tied to established psychological theories, the influence of Erik Erikson's developmental conflicts and Albert Bandura's social learning theory seems evident.

Ressler et al. (1988) describe five components that shape the personality of the serial sexual killer. First, the child is born into an ineffective social environment. This refers primarily to parents who ignore or even accept the typical cognitive distortions of the young child or actively encourage distortions through their own antisocial behavior. The child is met with a combination of unrealistic expectations, lack of emotional support, and discipline that is either absent, harsh, or inconsistent. Within this ineffective environment, the child then faces both the normal and perhaps the non-normative crises of childhood: difficulties at various tasks, witnessing or experiencing violence, and so on. During these formative events, there is a lack of support from his environment, which results in the child retreating into fantasy in the face of these stresses: "Aggressive fantasies, aimed at achieving dominance and control, emerge" (p. 71). This retreat into fantasy leads to a failure to bond to the child's adult caretaker and then to interpersonal failure. The unsupportive environment and the failure to adjust to the formative events combine to form patterned responses: a set of negative personality traits supported by a cognitive structure or belief system. These traits are likely to include autoeroticism and lying (because of the social isolation and reliance on fantasy) and belief in dominance and revenge. These patterned responses then reveal themselves in various negative actions toward others/self, such as cruelty to animals, fire setting, and stealing, which evolve into burglary, arson, abduction, and eventually rape and murder. The actions escalate because of the operation of a feedback filter: This essentially refers to cognitive reinforcements and adjustments (rationalizations) made to fit the behavior into the individual's fantasy system.

The motivational model, which is developed by Ressler et al. (1988) over 6 pages and illustrated in subsequent chapters, reads well, and the foregoing summary does not do it full justice. We believe that the strength of the model lies in its depiction of how a seemingly normal, lovable child can develop into a sadistic "monster" as a result of not-uncommon socialization processes. It is suggestive of a sort of "butterfly effect." That is, a relatively small distortion in development, causing a retreat into fantasy, is not corrected because of inadequate parenting, and this gradually leads to a deep-rooted psychopathic personality. In some ways, this is also a weakness of the model. It would seem to be unable to account for serial sexual killers who emerge from apparently normal family backgrounds, or for those who are highly socially adept and seen as assets to their community until their mask is removed. To be sure, Ressler et al. (1988) make allowances for the socially skilled serial killer, but this part of the model seems a bit ad hoc: They know that there are such cases, so they simply assert that the individual can be superficially sociable (without explaining how these social skills can be developed in the context of the person they describe). This ad hoc nature of the model surfaces in other ways as well. It is asserted that sexual killers "are aroused primarily by high levels of aggressive experience and require high levels of stimulation" (p. 74), but there is no real explanation for this. Elsewhere in the model, it seems to be that tension reduction through fantasy is what motivates the sexual killer. The fact that the model has been developed de novo, as it were, makes it difficult to determine what established psychological constructs are being relied on and thus how the pieces fit together.

ARRIGO AND PURCELL: LUST MURDER AS A PARAPHILIA

Both Ressler et al. (1988) and Hickey (2002) explain the behavior of the serial killer as a result of the interaction between stressful events and a vulnerable personality. The Hickey model is somewhat broader in that it attempts to account for all serial murderers and pays much more attention to biological predispositions. Ressler et al. do not deny possible biological predispositions but focus much more narrowly on personality development specific to the sexual killer. Arrigo and Purcell (2001) narrow the focus still further, specifically to those sexual killers for whom the anticipated killing is clearly a key factor in the sexual arousal, as opposed to either the acting out of simple anger or the instrumental elimination of a witness. Arrigo and Purcell's goal is to add to the motivational model of Ressler et al. and Hickey's *trauma control model* by integrating the concept of a paraphilia to account specifically for the lust murderer. As indicated previously, a paraphilia is sexual arousal to a nonsexual object or behavior. Paraphilias are sustained by fantasies typically reinforced by masturbation. In the case of extremely deviant paraphilias, facilitators or disinhibitors, such as pornography or alcohol, are typically present. Arrigo and Purcell's basic task is to explain how the paraphilia of extreme sadism (or erotophonophilia) becomes established in the serial killer.

Arrigo and Purcell (2001) cite Money's (1990) claim that all paraphilias, especially sexual sadism, are due to a brain disease. The concept of disease here is not meant metaphorically, as in "mental" illness, but means that actual centers and pathways in the limbic system malfunction in the transmission of sexual and aggressive impulses: Messages of attack are linked with messages of arousal and mating. Both the trauma control and the motivational models suggest that paraphilias would result from unresolved traumatic life events early in adolescence. Low self-esteem and lack of attachments have caused the youth to become dependent on fantasizing. Anger over repeated rejection and failure is a common element of the youth's fantasy life. As the youth's sexual feelings arise with puberty, he experiences the same social rejection and failure. Because he has already learned that fulfillment in fantasy is safe, it is only natural that he would turn to fantasy to fulfill sexual desires. The difference now, however, is that with masturbation and release, primary positive reinforcement is present for the fantasies (pp. 23–24):

> Compulsive genital stimulation enables the individual to experience a sexually satisfying result. The person fantasizes and rehearses the paraphilia...to the point of orgasm. This is a conditioning process in which the deviant eventually loses all sense of normalcy....As the nature and content of the fantasy become increasingly violent and sexual, the paraphilias progress in intensity and frequency.

The remainder of Arrigo and Purcell's integrated model relies on the trauma control and motivational models to show how escalation proceeds to more intense fantasies and then spills over into compulsive action.

Arrigo and Purcell (2001) should be credited with two significant contributions. They have shown how two prominent models of serial killing are compatible, and they have greatly elaborated on the nature and dynamics of the sadistic fantasies that drive the serial sexual sadistic killer. We also point to two limitations, however. First, the nature of the "brain disease" underlying the paraphilia is not at all clear. Their citing of Money (1990) makes it seem as if a real, ultimately observable structural problem underlies the erotophonophilia. Their examples, however, seem to follow the motivational model's idea that a physiologically normal person could develop into a sadistic serial killer given the right developmental conditions. Perhaps those developmental conditions may be said to produce deviant neural pathways, but the issue, if not the answer, needs more clarification. Second, it does not seem that this model would account for the case of "Robert" reviewed previously. Although it is certainly possible that Robert was acting out a fantasy, it seems more likely that he was acting on unconscious impulses, at least during his first sexual murder. It is more so the organized sexual murderers who report conscious sadistic fantasies (Ressler et al., 1986). One possibility is the idea of "unconscious fantasies," but this would hardly fit the model put forth by Arrigo and Purcell. Another solution is to relegate Robert to the category of "displaced anger murderer" (Groth et al., 1977), but it seems likely to us that Robert's brutal behavior was connected directly to his sexual arousal. In summary, Arrigo and Purcell have supplied a compelling description of how rape–murder fantasies function as paraphilias, but this may apply to only some sexual killers.

A rival viewpoint to that of Arrigo and Purcell (2001) should also be mentioned. Marshall and Barbaree (1990) present a general model of sex offenders that is based on the biological normalcy of the link between sex and aggression in males. For Marshal and Barbaree, a major developmental task is to learn to inhibit aggression in a sexual context. To some extent, this is a distinction that does not make a difference. The same factors that the previous models point to as leading to the fusion of anger and sex (child abuse, poor attachment, and low self-esteem) are seen by Marshal and Barbaree as interfering with the learning of inhibitions. This does make their model somewhat simpler, however. Rather than having to account for the origin of sexual sadism, it may be the natural consequence of failure to achieve a satisfactory relationship with the opposite sex.

SOCIOLOGICAL FACTORS

The theories of sexual sadistic killing reviewed previously have been primarily biopsychological. Although they have not ignored social factors, such factors have been primarily seen as a source for trauma and conflict that shape the developing personality. Thus, in the case of Robert presented previously, racism is suggested as one source of self-esteem or identity problems that Robert may have had. Interaction with the school system and the juvenile justice system further shaped his personality. His involvement in burglary likely facilitated his fantasizing about sexual encounters with occupants and then gave him his first opportunity to act out his anger. Likewise, Zuckerman's (1999) theory of psychopathy and Hickey's (2002) trauma control model emphasize school experiences and other sources of problems that shape the sexual serial killer. Although important, these variables are "social" mainly in the sense that they are part of the human environment that shapes personality. DeFronzo et al. (2007), however, stress that we need to look at macrolevel social variables to have a more complete picture of serial killing.

DeFronzo et al. (2007) examined a sample of 151 male serial killers, the vast majority of whom were sexual predators. Derived from the work of Rossmo

(2000), the sample represented all known male serial killers active in the United States from 1970 to 1992. DeFronzo et al. found significant variations in the per capita incidence of serial killers from state to state. The purpose of their research was to account for this variation using two macrolevel variables. They first distinguished between a "cultural" and a "structural" variable. The cultural variable that they used was Wolfgang and Ferracutti's (1967) subculture of violence. The structural variable was the opportunity for potential serial killers to obtain victims and escape apprehension, a key aspect of Cohen and Felson's (1979) routine activity theory. DeFronzo et al. argue that although biological and psychological forces may shape the personality of potential serial killers, the environment must still facilitate the expression of that personality. A prehomicidal personality raised in a subculture supportive of aggressive acting out would be more likely to adopt behavioral patterns involving killing. Likewise, a sexual sadist living in an area characterized by anonymity and by many vulnerable people living alone would have more opportunity to act out his fantasies. Using a variety of proxy measures for each of these variables at the state level, DeFronzo et al. found that variations in the strength of the subculture of violence among the 50 states were highly predictive of the number of serial killers who had been born or socialized in each state. Likewise, the availability of vulnerable victims coupled with an environment of anonymity was highly predictive of the number of serial killers active in any given state. Of course, it is possible that sexual serial killers migrate to areas where it is easier to act out their fantasies, but for most of the cases reviewed in the DeFronzo et al. study, the killer was active in the state where he was socialized.

FUTURE DIRECTIONS

Based on our review of the literature and our own casework, we posit a number of directions that future research may be expected to take. It is well accepted that there are significant differences between sexual and nonsexual serial killers. It may also be useful, however, to distinguish serial killers on other dimensions, as a comparison case study by Wolf and Lavezzi (2007) illustrates. For example, there may be significant differences between adolescent and adult serialists, males and females, same-sex and mixed-sex team killers, heterosexual and homosexual killers, and such categories as chronic family killers and medical murderers. Furthermore, serialists may differ based not only on who they are but also on whom they murder. For example, killers of elderly females (Groth, 1978; Muram, Miller, & Cutler, 1992; Safarik, Jarvis, & Nussbaum, 2000) may differ from killers of children, same sex or otherwise. Murderers of prostitutes may differ from killers of gay youth, and interracial murderers may differ from intraracial murderers (Walsh, 2005). Serial murder by health care professionals, in itself highly diverse in methods and motives, presents a markedly different picture from sexual serial killing (Yorker et al., 2006). We can foresee theorists one day establishing a killer–victim matrix that will address these distinctions and determine their significance.[14]

As we learn more about such notorious serial killers as Gary Ridgway (Guillen, 2007; Prothero & Smith, 2006), Dennis Rader (Beattie, 2005; Douglas & Dodd, 2007), and Jeffrey Dahmer (Strubel, 2007), the more apparent it becomes to us that childhood trauma theories are, in themselves, insufficient to explain their depredations. Even "normal" families will have their child-rearing quirks; the early socialization experiences of Ridgway, Rader, and Dahmer, however, were simply not so traumatic as to explain the profundity of their evolving perversions.[15] The neuropsychiatric basis of paraphilia and paraphilia-related disorders, as well as the contribution of autism spectrum disorders to the etiology of serial murder, will receive increasing scientific attention in the future (Briken, Habermann, Kafka, Berner, & Hill, 2006; Haskins & Silva, 2006; Schwartz-Watts, 2005; Silva, Leong, & Ferrari, 2004).

Thus, we believe that the paraphilic nature of serial sexual murder has been reasonably established (Arrigo & Purcell, 2001; Lee, Pattison, Jackson, & Ward, 2001, White, 2007). In keeping with this, we speculate that this brutal act may one day be understood as a perversion of courtship. Freund and colleagues (Freund, Scher, & Hucker, 1983; Freund & Seto, 1998) have analyzed courtship as comprising four phases, each with its unique paraphilia. Thus, the initial phase of courtship, finding a partner, has the corresponding paraphilia of voyeurism. Likewise, the second phase, affiliation, is perverted by exhibitionism; the third phase, touching, by frotteurism; and the fourth phase, copulation, by preferential or compulsive rape. We believe that erotophonophilia can therefore be seen as a particularly virulent subset of this fourth phase of courtship.[16]

Whereas some theorists approach serial murder from a broader, social structural perspective involving alienation and cultural legitimation of violence

---

[14]More complex typologies give rise to the possibility of finding a better fit between offender and crime scene characteristics. We agree with Canter and Wentink (2004), however, that it is critical that typologies of crime scenes be developed more empirically—that is, without trying to make them "fit" some a priori offender typology.

[15]Although some scholars continue to emphasize the role played by poor parenting in the creation of the serial killer (Levi-Minzi & Shields, 2007), we are mindful of the confirmation bias wherein investigators find what they are looking for (Prothero & Smith, 2006; Rossmo, 2006) and the self-serving nature of the recollections of serial killers of their abuse as a child. After all, it benefits the murderer to emphasize his exculpatory victimization as a child in the hope of avoiding execution.

[16]We further speculate that a fifth phase of courtship, separation, can be identified. If so, then stalking may come to be seen as a perversion of the normal phase of mate separation. Stalking, of course, is not unrelated to serial sexual homicide, just as many paraphilias are known to be interrelated (Abel, Becker, Cunningham-Rathner, Mittelman, & Rouleau, 1988; Krueger & Kaplan, 2001; Lehne & Money, 2003).

(DeFronzo et al., 2007; Leyton, 1986), many researchers are turning to more biological and genetic origins. We expect, for example, that future integrated models will blend genetic predispositions (Brennan & Raine, 1997; Money, 1990; Morrison & Goldberg, 2004; Raine, 1993) and hypersexuality (Ellis, 1991; Krueger & Kaplan, 2001) with the neurological insult and anger stemming from child abuse (Pincus, 2001) to one day explain the violent fantasies (Meloy, 2000) so often associated with sadistic serial killers. As the complexities of deviant sexual behavior become more widely known to theorists, the contributions of fixated, regressed, primary, secondary, replacement, cumulative, and collateral paraphilias to serial sexual murder will be magnified (Myers, et al., 2007; White, 2007). Theories centering too narrowly on self-esteem and the adverse impact of early social experiences will be modified accordingly.

We also expect theorizing to continue to be based on increasingly popular evolutionary paradigms. Evolutionary psychologists and criminologists have already explained crime generally (Ellis, 1998; Ellis & Walsh, 1997; Quinsey, 2002) and psychopathy (Pitchford, 2001), sociopathy (Mealey, 1995), homicide (Daly & Wilson, 1988), stalking (Brune, 2002), and rape (Thornhill & Palmer, 2000) particularly. In applying the insights of evolutionary criminology specifically to serial sexual killers, there are two distinct paradigms that may emerge. It might seem evident, for example, that serial sexual killing should be seen as a vestigial pathology—that is, a maladaptive deviation that is simply difficult to eradicate. Given its seeming persistence, however, it is tempting to speculate that there might be some adaptive advantage that leads to the selection of those genetically based traits that underlie serial sexual killing. It will be interesting to note whether the selectionist paradigm can help explain the serial killer or whether the existence of this phenotype is better defined by evolutionary psychiatry (Nesse, 1984; Stevens & Price, 1996), as primarily a vestigial pathology or a by-product of other sexual adaptations.

CONCLUSION: UNDERSTANDING THE SERIAL SEXUAL KILLER

How far have we come in our ability to understand the serial sexual sadistic killer? Do we know why some individuals get so much pleasure and satisfaction from inflicting pain on others that it becomes their preferred method for sexual arousal and release, driving them to overcome taboos against killing, and in most cases eventually subjecting themselves to life in prison or execution?

Although the unmasking of a serial killer is often met with astonishment and disbelief by those who know him, it seems that any time there is the opportunity for detailed inquiry into the person's background, one or more explanations for his deviance arise. On the physiological level, there may be genetic abnormalities, a genetic predisposition to becoming a psychopath, brain injury such as frontal lobe damage (perhaps as a result of physical child abuse), or compulsive masturbation or other evidence of hypersexuality. On the psychological level, that same child abuse may have scarred the personality. There may be severe attachment disorder, child sexual abuse, highly conflicted family relations, antisocial or borderline personality disorder, psychosis, substance abuse, and any of a number of developmental disorders. On the sociocultural level, there may be high exposure to violence and misogyny, poverty, alienation, overemphasis on masculine role taking, gangs and criminal groups that give status for both homicide and dominating women, or simply an environment that presents a number of suitable and unguarded victims. If any theorist's favorite construct is not found in a given case, it may simply be that no one looked for it. Perhaps in most cases one will find the interaction of factors from all three levels of personality formation, whereas in a few cases one particular factor, pushed to an extreme, may be sufficient. Perhaps the use of fantasy combined with rationalization and gradual drift into deviance is enough for a moderately unhealthy personality to become a full-fledged serial sexual killer. If anything, we have too many explanations rather than too few.

Several questions, however, remain unanswered. Are there sufficient differences in the etiology of various serial sexual killers so that meaningful deductions about their individual personalities and lifestyles can be made from their crime scene behavior? Can such a person control his fate? Does he remain morally responsible for his choices, in the sense that society is correct in expecting him to control his deviant impulses, even if he may not be responsible for the deviant desires in the first place? More important, how early in the developmental process does the potential sexual killer need to be identified in order for there to be a reasonable hope of prevention?

Questions

1. Kraft-Ebing originally described how many types of homicide that occurred in connection with rape?

   a. 2

   b. 3

   c. 4

   d. 5

   e. 7

2. Which three of the Holmes and Holmes typology seek to address nonsexual goals?

   a. Vision, mission, sadist

   b. Vision, sadist, comfort

   c. Vision, mission, comfort

d. Mission, sadism, comfort

e. Lust, thrill, power/control

3. Missen found a general decrease in the number of serial killers over time. *True or false?*

4. The classification that has received the most attention is the organized/disorganized serial killer. *True or false?*

5. Select one of the theories of serial sadistic sexual killing and outline its major components and problems.

REFERENCES

Abel, G. G., Becker, J. V., Cunningham-Rathner, J., Mittelman, M., & Rouleau, J. L. (1988). Multiple paraphilic diagnoses among sex offenders. Bulletin of the American Academy of Psychiatry and Law, 16, 153–168.

Abel, G. G., & Osborn, C. (1992). The paraphilias: The extent and nature of sexually deviant and criminal behavior. Clinical Forensic Psychiatry, 15, 675–687.

Alison, L., Bennell, C., Ormerod, D., & Mokros, A. (2002). The personality paradox in offender profiling. Psychology, Public Policy, and Law, 8, 115–135.

American Psychiatric Association. (2000). Diagnostic and Statistical Manual of Mental Disorders (4th ed., text revision). Washington, DC: American Psychiatric Association.

Arrigo, B. A., & Purcell, C. E. (2001). Explaining paraphilias and lust murder: Toward an integrated model. International Journal of Offender Therapy and Comparative Criminology, 45, 6–31.

Bateman, A. L., & Salfati, C. G. (2007). An examination of behavioral consistency using individual behaviors or groups of behaviors in serial homicide. Behavioral Sciences and the Law, 25, 527–544.

Beasley, J. (2004). Serial murder in America: Case studies of seven offenders. Behavioral Sciences and the Law, 22, 395–414.

Beattie, R. (2005). Nightmare in Wichita: The Hunt for the BTK Strangler. New York: New American Library.

Beauregard, E., Proulx, J., Rossmo, K., LeClerc, B., & Allaire, J. (2007). Script analysis of the hunting process of serial sex offenders. Criminal Justice and Behavior, 34, 1069–1084.

Brennan, P., & Raine, A. (1997). Biosocial bases of antisocial behavior: Psychophysiological, neurological, and cognitive factors. Clinical Psychology Review, 17, 589–604.

Briken, P., Habermann, M. A., Kafka, M. P., Berner, W., & Hill, A. (2006). The paraphilia-related disorders: An investigation of the relevance of the concept in sexual murderers. Journal of Forensic Science, 51, 683–688.

Brune, M. (2002). Erotomanic stalking in evolutionary perspective. Behavioral Sciences and the Law, 21, 83–88.

Burgess, A. W., Hartman, C. R., Ressler, R. K., Douglas, J. E., & McCormack, A. (1986). Sexual homicide: A motivational model. Journal of Interpersonal Violence, 13, 251–272.

Canter, D., Alison, L. J., Alison, E., & Wentink, N. (2004). The organized/disorganized typology of serial murder: Myth or model? Psychology, Public Policy, and Law, 10, 293–320.

Canter, D., Coffey, T., Huntley, M., & Missen, C. (2000). Predicting serial killers' home base using a decision support system. Journal of Quantitative Criminology, 16, 457–478.

Canter, D., & Larkin, P. (1993). The environmental range of serial rapists. Journal of Environmental Psychology, 13, 63–69.

Canter, D., & Wentink, N. (2004). An empirical test of Holmes and Holmes's serial murder typology. Criminal Justice and Behavior, 31, 489–515.

Capp, B. (1996). Serial killers in 17th-century England. History Today, 46(3), 21–27.

Cohen, L. E., & Felson, M. (1979). Social change and crime rate trends: A routine activity approach. American Sociological Review, 44, 588–608.

Cooper, A. J. (2000). Female serial offenders. In L. B. Schlesinger (Ed.), Serial Offenders: Current Thoughts, Recent Findings (pp. 263–288). Boca Raton, FL: CRC Press.

Daly, M., & Wilson, M. (1988). Homicide. New York: Aldine.

DeFronzo, J., Ditta, A., Hannon, L., & Prochnow, J. (2007). Male serial homicide: The influence of cultural and structural variables. Homicide Studies, 11, 3–14.

Dietz, P. E. (1986). Mass, serial, and sensational homicides. Bulletin of the New York Academy of Medicine, 62, 477–491.

Dietz, P. E., Hazelwood, R. R., & Warren, J. (1990). The sexually sadistic criminal and his offenses. Bulletin of the American Academy of Psychiatry and Law, 18, 163–178.

Douglas, J., & Dodd, J. (2007). Inside the Mind of BTK: The True Story behind the Thirty-Year Hunt for the Notorious Wichita Serial Killer. San Francisco: Jossey-Bass.

Egger, S. A. (1984). A working definition of serial murder and the reduction of linkage blindness. Journal of Police Science and Administration, 12, 348–357.

Egger, S. A. (2002). The Killers among Us (2nd ed.) Upper Saddle River, NJ: Prentice Hall.

Egger, S. A. (2003). The Need to Kill. Upper Saddle River, NJ: Prentice Hall.

Ellis, L. (1991). A synthesized (biosocial) theory of rape. Journal of Consulting and Clinical Psychology, 59, 631–642.

Ellis, L. (1998). Neo-Darwinian theories of violent criminality and antisocial behavior: Photographic evidence from nonhuman animals and a review of the literature. Aggression and Violent Behavior, 3, 61–110.

Ellis, L., & Walsh, A. (1997). Gene-based evolutionary theories in criminology. Criminology, 35, 229–276.

Ferguson, C. J., White, D. E., Cherry, S., Lorenz, M., & Bhimani, Z. (2003). Defining and classifying serial murder in the context of perpetrator motivation. Journal of Criminal Justice, 31, 287–292.

Fox, J. A., & Levin, J. (1998). Multiple homicide: Patterns of serial and mass murder. In M. Tonry (Ed.), Crime and Justice: A Review of Research (pp. 407–455). Chicago: University of Chicago Press.

Fox, J. A., & Levin, J. (1999). Serial murder: Popular myths and empirical realities. In M. D. Smith & M. A. Zahn (Eds.), Homicide: A Sourcebook of Social Research (pp. 165–175). Thousand Oaks, CA: Sage.

Fox, J. A., & Levin, J. (2005). Extreme Killings: Understanding Serial and Mass Murder. Thousand Oaks, CA: Sage.

Fox, J. A., Levin, J., & Quinet, K. (2008). The Will to Kill: Making Sense of Senseless Murder (3rd ed.). Boston: Pearson.

Freund, K., Scher, H., & Hucker, S. (1983). The courtship disorders. Archives of Sexual Behavior, 12, 369–379.

Freund, K., & Seto, M. C. (1998). Preferential rape in theory of courtship disorder. Archives of Sexual Behavior, 27, 433–443.

Godwin, M., & Canter, D. (1997). Encounter and death: The spatial behavior of U.S. serial killers. Policing, 20, 24–38.

Groth, A. N. (1978). The older rape victim and their assailant. Journal of Geriatric Psychiatry, 2, 203–215.

Groth, A. N., Burgess, A. W., & Holmstrom, L. L. (1977). Rape: Power, anger, and sexuality. American Journal of Psychiatry, 134, 1239–1243.

Guillen, T. (2007). Serial Killers: Issues Explored through the Green River Murders. Upper Saddle River, NJ: Pearson.

Hare, R. D. (1991). The Revised Psychopathy Checklist. Toronto: Multi-Health Systems.

Hare, R. D. (1993). Without Conscience: The Disturbing World of the Psychopath among Us. New York: Guilford.

Haskins, B. G., & Silva, J. A. (2006). Asperger's disorder and criminal behavior: Forensic–psychiatric considerations. Journal of the American Academy of Psychiatry and Law, 34, 374–384.

Hazelwood, R. (1999). Analyzing the rape and profiling the offender. In R. Hazelwood & A. W. Burgess (Eds.), Practical Aspects of Rape Investigation: A Multidisciplinary Approach (4th ed., pp. 155–181). Boca Raton, FL: CRC Press.

Hazelwood, R., & Burgess, A. (1999). The behavioral-oriented interview of rape victims: The key to profiling. In R. Hazelwood & A. Burgess (Eds.), Practical Aspects of Rape Investigation (pp. 139–154). Boca Raton, FL: CRC Press.

Hickey, E. W. (2002). Serial Murderers and Their Victims (3rd ed.). Belmont, CA: Wadsworth.

Hodge, S. (2000). Serial killing. In J. Siegel, G. Knupfer, & P. Saukko (Eds.), Encyclopedia of Forensic Sciences (pp. 1317–1322). San Diego: Academic Press.

Holmes, R. M., & DeBerger, J. (1988). Serial Murder. Newbury Park, CA: Sage.

Holmes, R. M., & Holmes, S. T. (1998). Serial Murder (2nd ed.). Thousand Oaks, CA: Sage.

Holmes, R. M., & Holmes, S. T. (2002). Profiling Violent Crimes: An Investigative Tool (3rd ed.). Thousand Oaks, CA: Sage.

Homant, R. (1980). A theoretical model of anger and aggression. Corrections Today, 42, 32–36.

Homant, R. J., & Kennedy, D. B. (1998). Psychological aspects of crime scene profiling: Validity research. Criminal Justice and Behavior, 25, 319–343.

Keeney, B. T., & Heide, K. M. (1994). Gender differences in serial murder: A preliminary analysis. Journal of Interpersonal Violence, 19, 383–399.

Kelleher, M. D., & Kelleher, C. L. (1998). Murder Most Rare. New York: Dell.

Keppel, R. D., & Walter, R. W. (1999). Profiling killers: A revised model for understanding sexual murder. International Journal of Offender Therapy and Comparative Criminology, 43, 417–437.

Knight, Z. (2007). Sexually motivated serial killers and the psychology of aggression and "evil" within a contemporary psychoanalytic perspective. Journal of Sexual Aggression, 13, 21–35.

Kocsis, R. N., Irwin, H. J., & Hayes, A. F. (1998). Organized and disorganized criminal behavior syndromes in arsonists: A validation study of a psychological profiling concept. Psychiatry, Psychology and Law, 5, 117–131.

Kraemer, G. W., Lord, W. D., & Heilbrun, K. (2004). Comparing single and serial homicide offenders. Behavioral Sciences and the Law, 22, 325–343.

Krafft-Ebing, R. von (1965). Psychopathia Sexualis (F. S. Klaf, Trans.). New York: Bell. (Original work published 1886)

Krueger, R. B., & Kaplan, M. S. (2001). The paraphilic and hypersexual disorders: An overview. Journal of Psychiatric Practice, 7, 391–403.

Lee, J., Pattison, P., Jackson, H., & Ward, T. (2001). The general, common and specific features of psychopathology for different types of paraphilias. Criminal Justice and Behavior, 28, 227–256.

Lehne, G. K., & Money, J. (2003). Multiplex versus multiple taxonomy of paraphilia: Case example. Sexual Abuse: A Journal of Research and Treatment, 15, 61–72.

Levi-Minzi, M., & Shields, M. (2007). Serial sexual murders and prostitutes as their victims: Difficulty profiling perpetrators and victim vulnerability as illustrated by the Green River case. Brief Treatment and Crisis Intervention, 7, 77–89.

Levin, J., & Fox, J. A. (2008). Normalcy in behavioral characteristics of the sadistic serial killer. In R. N. Kocsis (Ed.), Serial Murder and the Psychology of Violent Crimes (pp. 3–14). Totowa, NJ: Humana Press.

Leyton, E. (1986). Hunting Humans: Inside the Minds of Mass Murderers. New York: Pocket Books.

Lykken, D. (1995). The Antisocial Personalities. Hillsdale, NJ: Erlbaum.

Malamuth, N. M. (1981). Rape proclivity among males. Journal of Social Issues, 37(4), 138–157.

Marshall, W. L., & Barbaree, H. E. (1990). An integrated theory of the etiology of sexual offending. In W. L. Marshall, D. R. Laws, & H. E. Barbaree (Eds.), Handbook of Sexual Assault: Issues, Theories, and Treatment of the Offender (pp. 257–275). New York: Plenum.

McNamara, J. J., & Morton, R. J. (2004). Frequency of serial sexual homicide victimization in Virginia for a 10-year period. Journal of Forensic Science, 49, 529–533.

Mealey, L. (1995). The sociobiology of sociopathy: An integrated evolutionary model. Behavioral and Brain Sciences, 18, 523–599.

Meloy, J. (2000). The nature and dynamics of sexual homicide. Aggression and Violent Behavior, 5, 1–22.

Meloy, J. (2002). The "polymorphously perverse" psychopath: Understanding a strong empirical relationship. Bulletin of the Menninger Clinic, 66, 273–289.

Missen, C. G. (2000). Serial murder in the United States, 1860–1995. In L. S. Turnbull, E. H. Hendrix, & B. D. Dent (Eds.), Atlas of Crime: Mapping the Criminal Landscape (pp. 155–161). Phoenix: Oryx Press.

Mitchell, H., & Aamodt, M. G. (2005). The incidence of child abuse in serial killers. Journal of Police and Criminal Psychology, 20, 40–47.

Moffitt, T. E. (1993). Adolescent-limited and life course persistent antisocial behavior: A developmental taxonomy. Psychological Review, 100, 674–701.

Money, J. (1990). Forensic sexology: Paraphilic serial rape (biastophilia) and lust murder (erotophonophilia). American Journal of Psychotherapy, 44, 26–36.

Morgenbesser, L. I. (2008). Sexual homicide: An overview of contemporary empirical research. In R. N. Kocsis (Ed.), Serial Murder and the Psychology of Violent Crimes (pp. 103–117). Totowa, NJ: Humana Press.

Morris, W. (Ed.). (1969). The American Heritage Dictionary of the English Language. Boston: Houghton Mifflin.

Morrison, H., & Goldberg, H. (2004). My Life among the Serial Killers: Inside the Minds of the World's Most Notorious Murderers. New York: Morrow.

Muram, D., Miller, K., & Cutler, A. (1992). Sexual assault of the elderly victim. Journal of Interpersonal Violence, 7, 70–76.

Myers, W. (2004). Serial murder by children and adolescents. Behavioral Sciences and the Law, 22, 357–374.

Myers, W., Bukhanovskij, A., Justen, E., Morton, R., Tilley, J., Adams, K., Vandagriff, V. L., & Hazelwood, R. R. (2007). The relationship between serial sexual murder and autoerotic asphyxiation. Forensic Science International, 176, 187–208.

Myers, W., Gooch, E., & Meloy, J. R. (2005). The role of psychopathy and sexuality in a female serial killer. Journal of Forensic Sciences, 50, 652–662.

Myers, W., Husted, D. S., Safarik, M. E., & O'Toole, M. E. (2006). The motivation behind serial sexual homicide: Is it sex, power, and control, or anger? Journal of Forensic Sciences, 51, 900–907.

Nesse, R. (1984). An evolutionary perspective on psychiatry. Comprehensive Psychiatry, 25, 575–580.

Newton, M. (2000). The Encyclopedia of Serial Killers. New York: Checkmark Books.

Norris, J. (1988). Serial Killers. New York: Anchor Books.

Pallone, N. (2000). Foreword. In L. Schlesinger (Ed.), Serial Offenders: Current Thought, Recent Findings. Boca Raton, FL: CRC Press.

Pincus, J. (2001). Base Instincts: What Makes Killers Kill. New York: Norton.

Pitchford, I. (2001). The origins of violence: Is psychopathy an adaptation? Human Nature Review, 1, 28–36.

Prothero, M., & Smith, C. (2006). Defending Gary: Unraveling the Mind of the Green River Killer. San Francisco: Jossey-Bass.

Quinet, K. (2007). The missing missing. Homicide Studies, 11, 319–339.

Quinsey, V. L. (2002). Evolutionary theory and criminal behavior. Legal and Criminological Psychology, 7, 1–13.

Quinsey, V. L., Harris, G. T., Rice, M. E., & Cormier, C. A. (1998). Violent Offenders: Appraising and Managing Risk. Washington, DC: American Psychological Association.

Raine, A. (1993). The Psychopathology of Crime: Criminal Behavior as a Clinical Disorder. San Diego: Academic Press.

Ressler, R. K., Burgess, A. W., Depue, R. L., Hazelwood, R. R., Lanning, K. V., & Lent, C. (1985). Violent crime. FBI Law Enforcement Bulletin, 8, 1–32.

Ressler, R. K., Burgess, A. W., & Douglas, J. E. (1988). Sexual Homicides: Patterns and Motives. New York: Lexington.

Ressler, R. K., Burgess, A. W., Douglas, J. E., Hartman, C. R., & D'Agostino, R. B. (1986). Serial killers and their victims: Identifying patterns through crime scene analysis. Journal of Interpersonal Violence, 1, 288–308.

Rossmo, K. (1997). Geographic profiling. In J. Jackson & D. Bekerian (Eds.), Offender Profiling: Theory, Research and Practice (pp. 159–175). Chichester, UK: Wiley.

Rossmo, K. (2000). Geographic Profiling. Boca Raton, FL: CRC Press.

Rossmo, K. (2006, September). Criminal investigative failures: Avoiding the pitfalls. FBI Law Enforcement Bulletin, 1–19.

Safarik, M., Jarvis, J., & Nussbaum, K. (2000). Elderly female serial sexual homicide. Homicide Studies, 4, 294–307.

Schechter, H. (2003). The Serial Killer Files. New York: Ballantine.

Schlesinger, L. (1980). Distinction between psychopaths, sociopaths, and antisocial personality disorders. Psychological Reports, 147, 15–21.

Schlesinger, L. (2004). Sexual Murder: Catathymic and Compulsive Homicides. Boca Raton, FL: CRC Press.

Schlesinger, L., & Revitch, E. (1999). Sexual burglaries and sexual homicide: Clinical, forensic and investigative considerations. Journal of the American Academy of Psychiatry and Law, 27, 227–238.

Schwartz-Watts, D. M. (2005). Asperger's disorder and murder. Journal of the American Academy of Psychiatry and Law, 33, 390–393.

Silva, J. A., Leong, M. D., & Ferrari, M. M. (2004). A neuropsychiatric developmental model of serial homicidal behavior. Behavioral Sciences and the Law, 22, 787–799.

Silvio, H., McCloskey, K., & Ramos-Grenier, J. (2006). Theoretical consideration of female sexual predator serial killers in the United States. Journal of Criminal Justice, 34, 251–259.

Stevens, A., & Price, J. (1996). Evolutionary Psychiatry: A New Beginning. New York: Routledge.

Strubel, A. (2007). Jeffrey Dahmer: His complicated, comorbid psychopathologies and treatment implications. The New School Psychology Bulletin, 5, 41–58.

Thornhill, R., & Palmer, C. (2000). A Natural History of Rape: Biological Bases of Sexual Coercion. Cambridge, MA: MIT Press.

Turvey, B. (2002). Criminal Profiling: An Introduction to Behavioral Evidence Analysis (2nd ed.). San Diego: Academic Press.

Walsh, A. (2005). African Americans and serial killing in the media: The myth and the reality. Homicide Studies, 9, 271–291.

White, J. H. (2007). Evidence of primary, secondary, and collateral paraphilias left at serial murder and sex offender crime scenes. Journal of Forensic Sciences, 52, 1194–1201.

Wiebe, R. P. (2003). Reconciling psychopathy and low self-control. Justice Quarterly, 20, 297–336.

Wilson, P. (2003). The concept of evil and the forensic psychologist. International Journal of Forensic Psychology, 1, 1–9.

Wolf, B. C., & Lavezzi, W. A. (2007). Paths to destruction: The lives and crimes of two serial killers. Journal of Forensic Science, 52, 199–203.

Wolfgang, M., & Ferracutti, F. (1967). The Subculture of Violence. London: Social Science Paperbacks.

Yorker, B. C., Kizer, K. W., Lampe, P., Forrest, A. R. W., Path, F. R. C., Lannon, J. M., & Russell, D. A. (2006). Serial murder by health care professionals. Journal of Forensic Sciences, 51, 1362–1371.

Zuckerman, M. (1999). Vulnerability to Psychopathology: A Biosocial Model. Washington, DC: American Psychological Association.

CHAPTER 14

Serial Arson

Ross Brogan

All truths are easy to understand once they are discovered; the point is, to discover them!

—Galileo Galilei

KEY TERMS

Arson: A generic term used for the setting of a deliberate, malicious fire to damage property, generally that of another person.

Serial arson: Two or more deliberate, malicious fires lit by the same person or group.

Bush: An area containing trees, scrub, high vegetation, shrubs, and large amounts of vegetation.

CONTENTS

Arson is a universal problem, and although the psychological motivation behind the arsonist's behavior is discussed in numerous texts and reference materials, questions about why arsonists set fires, and what they get from doing it, are still common. These are, of course, difficult questions to answer (unless you think like an arsonist).

Arson is a generic term used for the setting of a deliberate, malicious fire to damage property, generally that of another person (Bennett & Hess, 2001; Dempsey, 1996). With arson for fraud, however, the target is usually the property of the arsonist, who is seeking to gain an advantage, usually from an insurance policy. With regard to the evolution of an arson definition, DeHaan (2007, p. 648) states the following:

> English common law, on which most American law is based, defines arson as the willful and malicious burning of the dwelling house of another. This made arson a crime against the security of habitation (because loss of habitation could well cost the lives of its dwellers by exposure to weather or enemies). It required certain elements to be

351

present—the structure had to be a dwelling, it had to belong to another, and it had to be burned as a deliberate or intentional act. As the common law concept of arson became inadequate, statutory law (passed by government bodies) expanded the definition to include other buildings and property. By omitting the dwelling or occupancy requirement, other property such as shops, factories, prisons, public buildings, forests, fields, boats and cars are now included in most arson statutes.

The definition will also depend heavily on the criminal statutes of the country or area in which the fire is lit; in some states of Australia, it is referred to as arson, whereas in others it is termed "malicious damage by fire/explosion." In Scotland, it is officially referred to as "willful fire-raising," and in the United States there are very fine parameters used to define what actually constitutes an arson event. Arsonists are quite often referred to in texts on psychiatry or psychology as "malicious fire-raisers" or "fire-setters," among other common terms.

A prime example of the difficulties faced by arson investigators is contained in a California newspaper article titled "The Life and Death of a Serial Arsonist" (2007). The article tells the story of a typical family man, married with adult children, who was charged with setting fires over a 3-year period. His wife said,

> There was nothing in his past suggesting he could be an arsonist. He had no interest in firefighting, no fascination with the many campfires they enjoyed over the years, no recognizable twist of personality that hinted at arson. The whole thing makes so little sense that I can't help but think that investigators made a terrible mistake.

Unfortunately, the investigators not only had convincing physical evidence but also had obtained a taped admission from the husband as to his guilt. Investigators had tracked his vehicle by sight and by GPS locator, and they had carried out surveillance to gather the evidence that eventually led to his arrest and charges. No people were injured in any of the fires, but it soon became evident that the fire-lighting activity was escalating and it was becoming too dangerous to allow it to continue. He was arrested with the prospect of charges in relation to 46 fires.

In continuing discussions with the accused, there was no explanation offered for his actions, no recognizable motive or reasoning behind why he had acted this way. Given his background, investigators were baffled by why he had set so many fires—and why he had set fires at all. While in jail awaiting trial, the accused took his own life, leaving a message for his family: "I'm sorry I let you down and ruined your lives." No plausible explanation was ever obtained for his actions or motivation in setting so many fires ("The Life and Death," 2007).

One difficulty faced by arson investigators and researchers is that our under-standing of the fire setter's behavior is still developing. Dickens et al. (2007) conducted a study on the gender differences among adult arsonists using data collected from the West Midlands (United Kingdom) Psychiatry Service during a 24-year period. This study sampled 167 adult arsonists, of which 129 were male and 38 female. Data showed that female arsonists had a history of sex-ual abuse, whereas males had a more varied criminal background, with associ-ated substance abuse problems. The study found significant gender differences among the arsonists studied, suggesting that different treatment may be required for males and females. These differing treatment requirements suggest that, for gender at least, fire setting behavior serves different needs. It stands to reason that the arson investigator would be well served in understanding these needs, which demands training and education directed toward this goal.

Arson is also a difficult crime to investigate because of its destructive nature (Saferstein, 2004), and this also calls for a great deal of training and knowl-edge on the part of those who seek to research the act and catch the actor. With regard to training of investigators, the following comment on the reason for effective training is provided in the training manual for fire investigators trained through Charles Sturt University (Jacobson & Brogan, 2004, p. 4):

> To effectively confront the issue of arson it is important that fire investigators have a sound appreciation of the reasons why people commit this offense. It is also useful for investigators to be aware of the latest developments in the psychological research that might provide additional tools to assist in the detection, investigation, and apprehension of arsonists.

The investigation of fires involves not only arson but also accidental and natural fires (e.g., those that occur through lightning and spontaneous self-heating). Fire services rely on an accurate appraisal of how and where a fire started for many reasons, the most important of which is that this assists their objective of protecting the community from the ravages of fire:

- Fire safety legislation relies on accurate fire statistics to determine building safety regulations, placement of fire safety exits, and placement of sprinklers and hoses to protect the occupants (if the determination of the cause is incorrect, the statistics are incorrect; if the statistics are incorrect, the safety rules may be incorrect).

- The placement of fire stations and specialized fire engines relies on efficient response times to reach areas of greatest risk to the community. The quicker the fire engine arrives, the less damage will occur to the property and the fewer injuries to the community. Accurate statistics assist with effective placement of fire stations.

- If fires continually occur in electrical appliances or machinery or involve similar items, an accurate cause determination may find a fault in that item that can be rectified and eventually make for a safer community.

- If the fire is determined to be incendiary, or a deliberate case of arson, the police can be involved early and evidence collected to prove who might have been involved. The earlier a criminal investigation is started, the better the chance of success—either catching the offender or deterring the criminal activity.

The investigation of a fire is conducted by operational fire officers attending the fire in the first instance, making determinations on cause based on their observations and knowledge of fire behavior. If the task of fire cause determination proves beyond their knowledge, experience, and capability, there are generally specialist fire investigators[1] in fire service units with greater knowledge and expertise capable of attending to a more detailed examination of the scene to make an expert determination of the fire's cause.[2] According to the Australian Institute of Criminology (2008), approximately 280,000 vegetation fires were analyzed in a study of fire statistics from 18 Australian fire and land management authorities. The study concluded that for all vegetation fires for which a cause was recorded, 50% were considered deliberately lit. It was also found that different agencies have differing thresholds for classifying the cause of the fire, and although it became clear that a fire starting from a natural event is rare, a vast majority of fires are related to human causes (Australian Institute of Criminology, 2008).

Once the fire is determined to be deliberate or incendiary in nature (and therefore arson), police service resources are generally brought in to assist or take over the investigation. Specialist police forensic officers, trained to collect and preserve evidence, assist with the scene examination, collection, and documentation of physical evidence.

Evidence samples are collected and sent to selected laboratories for forensic examination or analysis. This evidence and the sampling results then become part of an overall brief of evidence, compiled by trained police detectives from arson squads for presentation in criminal or civil hearings. Insurance companies also have a vested interest in the outcome of the investigation because of insurance policies covering the fire damage. They will often have their own

---

[1] It is interesting to note that in most states of the United States, fire investigation is conducted by specialist officers called fire marshals. These marshals are fire officers sworn as police officers. They carry weapons; have powers of arrest, search, and seizure; and carry the fire matter through to the court system, conducting the investigation from start to finish.

[2] Throughout the world, there are many different ways in which fire and police services conduct specialist fire investigations. The methodology of conducting an investigation does not vary—it is a well-recognized and accepted method. It is the makeup of the investigating authority that changes.

trained forensic investigators or contract specialists from private fire investigation companies to conduct independent investigations into the origin and cause of the fire. Occasionally, all three bodies (fire, police, and insurance) work together on a case to pool their resources and data or information.

To provide central control for directing efforts to combat arson, the government in the United Kingdom has established the Arson Control Forum. The Forum provides the strategic direction to the government-led arson control/prevention program and was established to address the many facets of the menace of arson. To this point, the Forum has

- Issued improved guidance on investigating fires
- Published research into what motivates the arsonist
- Commissioned research aimed at achieving more arson prosecutions

A document on arson control written by the Forum and commissioned by the Office of the Deputy Prime Minister details what is required when faced with an arson problem. Under "Establishing the Need," it states the following (Arson Control Forum, 2003):

> All deliberate fire reduction strategies must start with an analysis of local fire problems and an appraisal of the communities' needs. This can then be addressed by the provision of the required methodology and resources in terms of finance, personnel, and the construction of partnerships.

The strategy should revolve around four proven strands, which stem from the collection of statistical data that can be accurately analyzed to provide evidence in terms of need, response, and effect. These data, with the addition of time and cost elements, will provide a valuable tool in supporting the strategy. The four strands are

- Prevention
- Education
- Detection
- Investigation

The primary aim of the strategy should be to reduce deliberate fires. The current aim of the Forum (2006) is to reduce arson attacks by 10% by March 31, 2010.

Clearance rate in this crime is generally low; for example, in the United States approximately 100,000 arsons are reported to the police each year, but only 15% of these are solved (Dempsey, 1996). Deliberately lit fires are on the increase throughout the world, but it is not just the number of fires that is a problem. One data set suggestive of the increase in arson is from the Arson Control Forum (2004). The data for the period 1994–2003 demonstrate the following[3]:

---

[3]Statistics from the 2006 report do not show a great deal of difference from the figures above.

- In the past decade, there have been approximately 2.4 million deliberate fires in the United Kingdom.
- Arson involving vehicles has doubled in those same 10 years.
- These fires caused 32,000 injuries and 1,200 deaths.
- In an average week, there are 2,100 arson fires resulting in two deaths, 55 injuries, and a cost to society of 40 million pounds sterling or 72 million euros.

Further statistics available from the British Government/British Insurers Association Arson Prevention Bureau (2004) show the following:

- Each week, 20 schools are damaged or destroyed by arson.
- Each week, there are 2,213 arson attacks in the United Kingdom.
- Each week there are 53 injuries and two deaths.
- Each week, four churches or places of worship are damaged or destroyed.
- Teenagers (10- to 17-year-olds) comprise 40% of those prosecuted or cautioned for arson offenses.
- Arson fires have doubled since 1991.
- Vehicle arson has tripled since 1991.

These statistics suggest a much worse problem than the data from the Arson Control Forum.

In New South Wales (NSW), Australia (which contains the largest population mass of all states in the country), fire statistics show the following for the years 2006 and 2007 (New South Wales Fire Brigades, 2008):

- 138,021 incidents were attended as fire calls.
- 33,118 of these proved to be actual fires.
- 32.92% were bush and grass fires.
- 23.3% were building fires.
- 14.9% were mobile property fires (cars and other vehicles).
- 28.8% were rubbish and other fires.
- Of all actual fires, 39% were attributed to arson causes.

Incendiary/arson causes were the second highest cause allocated to building fires.

Since 1988, the state government of NSW has established several committees and inquiries examining the problem of arson, with recommendations made and implemented over the ensuing years in an effort to reduce the problem. As recently as 2002 and 2003, there were Federal Committees of Inquiry into the large *bush* fires that ravaged many states and the Australian Capital Territory (ACT) during those years. In the ACT, the McLeod Inquiry resulted in many changes to government bodies and emergency services and the way they handle emergencies. To date, no organization in Australia (similar to the British Arson

Control Forum) has been formed as a result of any of the inquiries, although these did bring about changes to the way in which fire and police authorities conduct their fire investigations and evidence-gathering techniques.

Although the exact number of serial arsonists is not known, from my experience with arson, a certain number of fires occur in a community that are lit by the same person or persons, and these fires can be documented and determined to be serial in nature by the astute fire investigator. Until several fires of the same type occur, one cannot determine that the fires are due to serial involvement; determination of serial fires relies on accurate cause determination, accurate documentation, and efficient evidence collection and interpretation.[4]

METHODOLOGY OF FIRE INVESTIGATION

To successfully conduct a fire investigation, one must follow a recognized methodology to ensure that all facets of the investigation have been covered adequately. The National Fire Protection Association's (NFPA, 2008) document No. 921 provides a basic methodology for fire investigation that is recognized in most countries throughout the world and followed by professional fire investigators. It states the following (p. 16):

> A fire or explosion investigation is a complex endeavor involving skill, technology, knowledge, and science. The compilation of factual data, as well as an analysis of those facts, should be accomplished objectively and truthfully. The basic methodology of the fire investigation should rely on the use of a systematic approach and attention to all relevant details.

The systematic approach recommended in the text employs the scientific method. This approach is not only desirable when carrying out any analytical process but also necessary for a successful conclusion to the investigation.

The scientific method recommended by NFPA 921 (NFPA, 2008) contains the following steps:

- Recognize the need (identify the problem).
- Define the problem.
- Collect data.
- Analyze the data (inductive reasoning).

---

[4]I use the word "interpretation" because the determination of serial fires is reliant on the investigator's intimate knowledge and experience of fire scenes to inspect a fire-damaged object and interpret what it was before the fire caused it to melt, decay, or become blackened. Once the investigator has determined what it was, the interpretation has to be made as to how this object was involved in the fire cause.

- Develop a hypothesis.
- Test the hypothesis (deductive reasoning).
- Select the final hypothesis.[5]

Note that NFPA 921 (NFPA, 2008) is a guide only and not a standard; therefore, it is used to guide people conducting fire investigations. NFPA 1033 (NFPA, 2009) is a standard. As a standard, the document details qualities and knowledge required of a person to fulfill the necessary qualifications to carry out the role of a professional fire investigator. Both documents are well recognized and have been adopted by many fire authorities throughout the world.

Specialist fire investigators must be highly trained and knowledgeable in all aspects of firefighting tactics and fire service operations, fire behavior, fire science, materials behavior, building construction, the effects of fire on buildings and building materials, and physical evidence collection and preservation. They must also be able to apply this vast amount of knowledge to writing expert reports and giving testimony on these findings and theories in a court of law or before any other inquiry. In addition to these qualities that are necessary for a successful investigation to be conducted, the investigator needs to be well read in aspects of human behavior related to fires and fire setting. All these are areas of special significance when determining a motive for the fire starting, along with how it was lit and where.

Jacobson and Brogan (2004) cite Prins (1994) when discussing the motivation of fire setters and arsonists. The following quotation regarding motive relates to the requirement for a fire investigator to have specialist knowledge not only of investigative procedures but also of the behavioral aspects of arson (Jacobson & Brogan, p. 142):

> Prins contends that fire as a phenomenon has always played an important and significant part in human history. It has been put to many uses, the least of which is fire's use as a destructive force. This destructive capacity however is only too evident in today's world with everyday reports of fire, bombings, and incendiarism. Fire, as a phenomenon, has held, and continues to hold, a fascination every bit as powerful as that evoked by life and death. To successfully operate in this environment it is essential that one understands the complex nature and behavior of people who use fire for destruction and the motives behind their behavior.

When *serial arson* is suspected, it is imperative that an investigation be conducted into every case in which the suspect is allegedly involved. The details of

---

[5]It is vital that the final hypothesis be able to withstand rigorous scrutiny in the courtroom.

each of the fires and the findings of the investigator must be thoroughly documented to accurately record the serial nature of these crimes and establish that the fires are in fact linked.

First, the investigator must inspect the fire scene, investigate the circumstances of each fire, and establish that each is a deliberate fire. Once arson has been established, scrupulous attention must be paid to the effective, efficient, and legal gathering of relevant evidence that will prove arson has been committed. Second, there must be a concerted effort to establish evidence that proves involvement by the person suspected as the serial arsonist. Evidence must be available to show that this person has been directly involved in each case. Third, there must be evidence showing a direct link between the person of interest and each of the arson fires that constitutes the serial activity. Without a direct link to a particular person, one may be able to prove serial arson activity but not who the serial arsonist actually is. This is the objective of the exercise.

When serial arson is suspected, it is usually prudent to set up a specialized task force. Guidance on how this is done is provided by the Arson Control Forum (2003); under the heading "Detection," there are several areas of interest that should be taken into consideration:

- A police presence is advised and considered essential.
- Fire and police personnel should be involved in any interviews because it has been found that most young suspects will talk to a firefighter, and not a police officer, in a street location.
- A highly visible vehicle is a valuable tool.
- Training in cognitive interviewing skills is a distinct advantage, as is a background in fire behavior.
- Best practice should be established with the investigation; this should include all available investigative sources being at the scene at the same time—fire investigator, police forensic, police, canine accelerant detector, and so on.

The text contains one piece of advice classified as essential for success: "Training for firefighters in crime scene management and preservation is essential, as it is possible that vital evidence can be missed during the early stages of an incident" (Arson Control Forum, 2003, p. 18).

A similar document published by the U.S. Federal Emergency Management Agency (FEMA, 1989) details ways in which to form an arson strike force. This document also mentions the following benefits of an arson strike force (pp. 4–5):

- Greater productivity with existing resources
- Better interagency coordination and cooperation
- Stronger prosecutions

THE ARSONIST

It is important to note that most classification systems provide a starting point only, and that we should be cautious in the application of rigid typologies. Canter and Almond (2002, p. 11) state the following:

> It is recognized by psychologists that assigning individuals to one of a few "types" is likely to be very crude and that any such classification process can only be approximate. However, in order to develop a strategy for dealing with arson some attempt must be made to identify the different forms it can take in order to facilitate the targeting of appropriate policies and interventions. It is important to develop a framework that will reduce ambiguities and provide a way of distinguishing between the acts of arson and that takes account of both the characteristics of the arsonist and the property that is the target.

Table 14.1 provide the proportion of property and vehicle arson for 2000 (Canter & Almond, 2002, p. 11). It is interesting to note the view of Canter and Almond of the "malicious" type (p. 14):

> It is often assumed that arson is a crime against property. However, it does share some of the characteristics of personal or violent crimes in often being an attack against a person or group of people. Put simply, fire is sometimes used as a weapon.

This proposition is also supported by Turvey (2008).

Some motives can be multifaceted or obscure in their reasoning. A newspaper article relating to arson in Israel discusses a fire set by a suspect who used gasoline and spray paint in an attempt to both destroy and deface a synagogue. It was considered by local police authorities that this might have been the same person who lit other fires in synagogues prior to this event. On the prior occasion, the perpetrator informed police his actions were in protest of religious women wearing wigs because some rabbis had ruled that wigs were immodest and that women must use cloths to cover their hair ("Serial Arsonist," 2008).

Table 14.1 Arson by Type and Quantity, 2000

Type of Arson	Property	Vehicle
Youth disorder	36%	39%
Malicious	25%	3%
Emotional expression	27%	13%
Criminal	13%	45%
Total fires	32,200	70,800

From Canter and Almond (2002).

A useful online resource for fire investigators is interFIRE Online (http://www.interfire.org), which provides training, education, and resources for investigators to improve their skills. An article titled "The Study of Serial Arsonists" (2004) contains information compiled by a team from the Federal Bureau of Investigation's (FBI) National Center for the Analysis of Violent Crime (NCAVC) (Sapp et al., 2004). The study was conducted in an attempt to find solutions to problems confronting police authorities, such as serial arson, which had reached epidemic proportions throughout the United States. The research was conducted and the project planned and implemented with several goals in mind. In relation to this, Sapp et al. state that "these goals are based on the belief that any understanding of the typology of arsonists, particularly typological classification based on motivations, may enhance investigative efforts and provide a focus for intervention efforts" (p. 2).

Some interesting results came from the NCAVC study, some of which are mentioned in the case studies detailed later in this chapter (Sapp et al., 2004). Regarding methods of setting fires, the study found that almost all of the arsonists used "unsophisticated" methods, which included available materials such as trash, paper, gasoline, and, most commonly, matches or cigarette lighters for the ignition source (see the "Hurricane Harry" case study discussed later). It was noted that few used any sort of handmade device to light their fires, and nearly half left some kind of evidence that could have been used to link them with the fire (p. 3). Regarding mobility, the study found that 61% walked to the scene and 70% of the fires were set within a 2-mile radius of their residence. Almost all fires were found to have been lit within an area that the arsonist was familiar with, suggesting that the arsonist was comfortable with these surroundings. The study also showed that few owned motor vehicles and most set fires in their own neighborhood (p. 3).

In 2006, Edwards and Grace conducted an analysis of data, based on New Zealand arson statistics, to test Canter and Larkin's 1993 "circle theory of environmental range for offending by serial arsonists." The offenders were classified as marauders or commuters, depending on whether or not their home base was within the criminal range circle. Their study did not reliably differentiate between characteristics applicable to either marauders or commuters, and they stated, "Overall, these results suggest that the criminal range circle may provide only limited information for predicting the home base of serial arsonists in New Zealand" (p. 1) (see also the case studies in this chapter, with the exception of "Sean Broom").

Another issue arising from the NCAVC study is that approximately one-third of the serial arsonists remained at the scene to watch the fire and the subsequent commotion. This proved useful in setting the parameters for investigation into the "city" arsonist, who was thought to be within the crowd watching the fires that he had lit. Approximately one-fourth leave the scene and go to another location from where they can observe the results of their fire and the firefighters fighting it.

CASE STUDIES

During more than 20 years as a fire investigator, I have been involved with a number of serial arsonists: investigating their fires and ensuring the evidence was gathered to prove their arson and their particular involvement with each fire. This has also involved assisting other investigators with the same goals and assisting investigating police officers in compiling a brief of evidence in these serial offenses. Later involvement with some cases has also included attending court and presenting evidence to show the results of the fires and the direct links between them.

The following case histories are provided to illustrate some of the methods used by arsonists and some of the traits displayed that in some cases were used to apprehend and convict them. I was involved in all of these cases in some way, and the facts are from my personal files maintained over many years.[6]

The "City" Arsonist

The "city" arsonist was so named because of the location of his fires, all set within the central business district of the city of Sydney.

Twenty-six-year-old Gregory Alan Brown—a white Caucasian male—started lighting fires in 1987 within the buildings of the inner-city business district. It has since become known that he started lighting fires when he was only 12 years old, admitting that he set fire to the garage of the house next door to where he lived with his adopted parents. This was apparently the start of his criminal career. It was also revealed that he was a bed wetter when he was young. Brown was described as borderline retarded, having suffered brain damage at an early age. There are also indications that he was a drug and alcohol abuser.

Within the city area, the fire service attends a great number of calls directly related to automatic fire alarms, many proving to be false alarms. Many hours of fire service time are spent attending these calls, day and night, with the firefighters becoming frustrated at not seeing any actual fires. Because of the high risk involved with fires in inner-city buildings, old buildings, densely populated areas, and high-rise buildings, the fire service responds with a large number of fire engines and firefighters. Rarely do fires actually break out (compared to the percentage of false alarm calls), and when numerous fires occur, it becomes a topic of animated discussion, drawing much attention. This was the case with the fires attributed to Brown.

Fires were lit in businesses, offices, and commercial buildings throughout the city. They invariably occurred in morning or afternoon peak hours, when many people were moving about the city. As a result, they drew large crowds, with large num-

---

[6] I recognize several people in the Acknowledgments who were also involved with these cases, in many cases playing much more important roles than I did.

bers of fire engines, police vehicles, and ambulances that attended. The fires were located in exit stairs, exit passages, and public access areas of these buildings and were almost always lit using trash or discarded items found in these areas. The fires were set beneath a fire sprinkler or in an area covered by a fire detector where they would be discovered and reported to the fire service immediately (usually by an automatic alarm system). Because of their location beneath a fire sprinkler, they were easily contained and did not spread to become a hazard. Also because of their location, the fires would produce a great deal of smoke once the sprinkler activated. Immediate and rapid response by the fire engines contributed to early intervention in these fires, stopping their progress and ensuring the safety of the building occupants. The fires achieved one main aim, and it was suspected that the arsonist was seeking attention. The large emergency service attendance, large crowds, and evacuation of buildings caused havoc in the city center at peak periods of the day. Minor injuries occurred, mainly from smoke inhalation, although no serious injuries occurred until one of the fire events in 1989.

On September 17, 1989, a fire occurred in the "Downunder" backpackers hostel in the suburb of Kings Cross, this time taking the lives of six tourists who were trapped inside the building by a fire lit in the entry foyer, preventing safe exit from the building. Most of the victims were trapped in their rooms, unable to escape the smoke and toxic gases rising up through the single stairway from the foyer. In this instance, no fire sprinklers were fitted to the building to hold the fire in check or automatically alert the fire service.

Because of the serial nature of these fires and the research suggesting that this person was probably remaining at the scene, standing in the crowd watching the results of his handiwork, the fire and police services made a concerted effort to apprehend the suspect. Undercover operatives from the police worked throughout the city areas where the fires were occurring, hoping to catch the offender in the act. Fire service investigators transferred to inner-city fire stations and responded with fire crews on the first call to fires, carrying video cameras and videotaping the crowd in case a familiar face was sighted at a number of fire scenes. However, all these attempts were fruitless and frustrating.

Within a short period of time after the 1989 tragedy, Brown was arrested and charged with the arson resulting in the fatalities. As a result of ongoing investigations into all the fires, he was eventually charged with lighting approximately 158 fires and the murder of six victims. Brown confessed to his involvement in the fires and participated in a drive-around with police to show them where the fires had been lit. He was found guilty of manslaughter and convicted of his crimes; he was sentenced to 18 years in jail. After his conviction in NSW, he was charged in Victoria with a multitude of fires in the St. Kilda area (a suburb of Melbourne). These charges resulted in his conviction and a sentence of 12 months.

"Hurricane Harry"

From early 1993 to late 1995, a series of fires occurred in a southern suburb of Sydney. These fires involved motor vehicles, trash bins, houses, fences, grass, stacked tires, and other small items. Each of the fires was determined to have been deliberately lit, and a pattern started to emerge in relation to these fires, all in close proximity to each other. Similar evidence was located at many of the fires, which began to suggest they were all lit in the same manner.

A suspect emerged and further investigation revealed certain facts about him and the fires that were lit. This suspect was a 51-year-old male of slight build, unemployed, unshaven, who had an appearance similar to a "homeless" individual (although he did in fact have his own residence). He had a prior history of criminal activity for unauthorized entry to property with intent, and the police nicknamed the suspect "Hurricane Harry."

Fires kept occurring and the pattern that emerged showed that the arsonist either was very fast on his feet (to get around such a wide area in a short period of time) or had some form of transportation. The fires were all linked, and several were lit in a very short period of time, usually in a geographically circular pattern (the last fire was always very close to where the suspect lived). Plastic soft drink bottles containing paper of different types, determined to have been used to start the fire, were found at many fire sites. Once the pattern was discovered, it became vital for the police to try to get to the suspect's address first, before he returned from starting fires; unfortunately, he was extremely fast and apparently wily, and he was never caught returning to his residence at these times.

On one occasion, this suspect was caught entering a property by police. He was carrying a bag that was found to contain advertising leaflets, papers, plastic soft drink bottles, and plastic carry bags—all that one would need to start a fire. No fire was started in this case, and police had no evidence to arrest him.

After this incident, the fires appeared to cease and no further serial activity came to the attention of fire or police authorities. The suspect was never arrested and charged with any of the fires because of the lack of sufficient evidence.[7]

---

[7]During unusually high bush fire activity throughout the suburbs of Sydney and in the rural areas of the state in December 2001 and January 2002, I worked on Police Strike Force "Tronto," established to investigate the high incidence of arson reported with these fires. One fire being investigated in a national park close to the southern suburbs of Sydney came to my attention when a report from a fire officer came to my desk. This report contained a description of a male person observed acting suspiciously at one of the fires by an eyewitness—male, approximately 50 years of age, thin, unshaven, with the appearance of being homeless and riding a bicycle.

Sean Broom

Sean Broom is a white Caucasian male who was 34 years old at the time of his sentencing in 2003.

Between May 1999 and August 2000, approximately 16 fires occurred in a wide area across the suburbs of Sydney. These fires involved motor vehicles, caravans, tire storage premises, factories, warehouses, and other properties in industrial areas. One thing these fires had in common was that at each fire the attending fire brigades would be met by a male person who then informed them of the whereabouts of the fire and, in some cases, assisted them in finding it. One of the early fires involved a factory where fiberglass swimming pools were manufactured; this was the largest of the fires, causing more than $1 million in damage.

This individual had a prior criminal history of lighting fires (or at least being caught for it) but continued with his activities. One of the main pieces of incriminating evidence was the fact that recordings of the emergency phone calls made to the fire brigade reporting these fires were proven by voice recognition to be the voice of Sean. He had not only lit fires to bring the fire brigade to his area but also was one of the first to phone in the emergency call to ensure that the fire brigade arrived at the correct address. Fire officers gave descriptions of a male observed at the scene of many of the fires, who met them on arrival and was very helpful in assisting them to find the fires, which were usually in remote locations.[8]

On one occasion, Campbelltown Fire Station attended three fires in the same street, during the same night, all involving motor vehicles or caravans in an industrial area, and all were considered to be deliberately lit. In each case, they were met by the same male person who showed them the location of each fire. He also informed them that he had made the emergency call regarding each fire. The firefighters considered his actions suspicious because this was an industrial area late at night and it would be unusual for anyone to be in the area at this time, even more so when this occurred on three separate occasions. The fire brigade investigator was summoned to look into the incidents, and this led to police involvement for further investigation.

The fire brigade investigation unit alerted police to the possibility that a serial arsonist was at work in several areas. It was amazing that these areas were linked to just the one person, and police investigations revealed that, in all, the fires covered a distance of travel across Sydney of approximately 70 km involving five separate suburbs.

---

[8]I was involved in the investigation of many of the fires suspected as being this person's work. The main thrust of the investigations was to obtain eyewitness accounts and descriptions of this male from attending firefighters. Once obtained and compared, the descriptions linked him to the other fires.

During initial investigations by police, the suspect maintained his innocence, but once charged and confronted with court appearances, he pleaded guilty to many of the fires. In 2003, he was sentenced to serve 4 years and 9 months for his crimes. The reason behind this activity has not been revealed, but it could be theorized that this arsonist was looking for personal recognition and kudos, in his own distorted way, for summoning and assisting the fire brigade, thereby helping the community.

Cameron Burgess

Cameron Burgess is the most stereotypical arsonist I have encountered in my career, for many reasons. He was approximately 20 years of age and had been (prior to Christmas 2001) under surveillance by the police for suspicion of lighting fires in bush in the southern part of NSW in a town called Albury. After several months, he left Albury and went to a village north of Sydney named Dooralong. Here, he again came to the attention of the police for lighting fires in the bush. After a short period, he left Dooralong and went to stay with relatives in a village west of Sydney, within the Lapstone area of the Blue Mountains. It was Christmas when he came to Lapstone, and therefore midsummer in Australia. This particular summer had been very dry as a result of a long drought in the southern states, and high-strength hot winds were drying the bush areas across the state. Many bush fires were starting to cause fire authorities concern.[9]

During the short period between Christmas Eve 2001 and mid-January 2002, an unusually large number of bush fires raged across the state of NSW, stretching firefighting resources to the limit. Many fires were found to be deliberately lit, and evidence existed to show that serial arsonists were involved in many cases. New South Wales Fire Brigade (NSWFB) statistics indicated in excess of 1,000 fires attended during this period—just those involving grass, bush, and vegetation and just those fires attended by NSWFB resources. Rural fire services, National Parks staff, and other services attended many more. As a result of this unusual activity and the threat that serial arsonists posed to the community, the NSW government formed a police strike force to investigate the fires and charge and prosecute any offenders caught through the mechanism of these investigations. The strike force was called "Tronto" and consisted of NSW police detectives, forensic specialists, and NSWFB and rural fire service members (Strike Force Tronto still exists today, reforming when the need arises because of serial arson activity).

---

[9]In Australia, the term *bush* is used to refer to areas containing trees, scrub, high vegetation, shrubs, and large amounts of vegetation. In other countries, these would be referred to as forests, woodland, wildland, etc. In fact, all of the areas outside the major cities are referred to as "the bush," meaning unsettled areas, not necessarily areas containing vegetation. It is from this term that Australians refer to fires in vegetation as bush fires.

Burgess had been a member of the rural fire service in Albury, a volunteer association formed to assist with bush fires in areas not covered by established fire services. When he came to Lapstone, he joined the local volunteer brigade. At this time, because of extreme weather and fire conditions, the local fire services were on high alert.

Being associated with Police Strike Force Tronto, I became aware of investigations into fires in the Lapstone area and an adjoining area named Glenbrook. When notified that police were conducting a surveillance operation on a suspect in the area of Lapstone and Glenbrook, I was particularly interested because of my knowledge of members of the local fire brigade. Burgess had become a person of interest because of the number of calls he had made to the fire brigade communications center, and apparently he had been making regular calls to report fires in the Lapstone area. Not only had they been able to recognize the phone number from Burgess' personal phone[10] but also he identified himself when calling. This information had been provided to investigating police.

Burgess' modus operandi (MO) was to light a fire in a remote area of the bush near his home. He would then call the fire brigade to report the fire's location. On arrival of the fire brigade, he would show them where the fire was and, on many occasions, he would depart and return soon after clothed in his volunteer firefighting uniform.

In *The Australian*, journalist Martin Chulov (2004) said the following about Burgess in a piece titled "Firebugs in Fire Engines":

> Peter Cameron Burgess is a textbook example. In early 2002 Burgess was a 20 year-old loner with good parents and a penchant for action games. He told his lawyer his life had become mundane. He wanted to be just like the New York firemen who months before he had seen as the heroes of September 11. Later that year and in early 2002, he became the face of pyromania in regional NSW, an immature, attention-seeking drifter, who was single-handedly responsible for many of the fires that scorched the state—in Albury, the Blue Mountains, and the NSW Central Coast.

John Laycock, Assistant Commissioner of Police in NSW and Commander of Strike Force Tronto, was quoted in Chulov's article as saying that Burgess' repeated offending was typical of many of the people Tronto had put before the courts: "The thing we have found is that they don't stop lighting fires until they are caught.... They become very serial in nature."

---

[10]Modern communications centers for police and fire brigades are fitted with technology that recognizes telephone numbers from calling handsets.

One of the "good" things about Burgess' MO was that, if true to predictions based on research on his type of behavior, he would only light a fire that would stay small and not get out of control (of course, this is in a perfect world, and fire is an unpredictable entity). His MO was to light a fire, call the fire brigade, greet them on arrival, and show them the location of the fire. According to research, he was looking for attention and wished to be viewed as a hero to the community. Thus, if the fire got larger than he wanted, there was likely to be someone other than him who would see it and report it. If this happened, the adulation that followed was not likely to be forthcoming, so he would remain vigilant at the fire scenes.

In 2002, Peter Cameron Burgess was charged and convicted of 26 counts of "maliciously damage property by fire" and three counts of "false representation" (false alarm calls). He pleaded guilty to the charges and was sentenced to a 2-year custodial sentence.[11]

FIREFIGHTERS AND ARSON

Chulov (2004) discusses the multitude of fires throughout NSW that have been described by police as being deliberately lit by Rural Fire Service (RFS) volunteer firefighters, stating, "A NSW police investigation team estimates that close to one in five of the bushfires to have blazed across NSW during the past 3 years was lit by an RFS volunteer." Further discussion on the matter brought RFS Commissioner Phil Koperberg into the debate. Quoted on the matter, he stated, "I am not surprised by it, but I am disappointed. If you look at any large fire service anywhere on the planet you will find the same problem in the same way that large corporations attract embezzlers."

Chulov's (2004) article contains a list of arsonists and their crimes, including the following:

- Joshua Brook: Malicious damage to property by fire (18 counts).
- Petar Belobrajdic: Intentionally cause fire and be reckless as to its spread (16 counts). The result of this was community service and custodial bonds totaling 6½ years.
- Martin Melbourne: Malicious damage to property by fire (5 counts). Melbourne received a 10-month suspended sentence.
- David Mills: Intentionally cause fire and be reckless as to its spread (7 counts) and set fire to property (3 counts).
- Michael Richardson: Malicious damage to property by fire (8 counts). Richardson was sentenced to 400 hours of community service.

---

[11]Burgess was released from prison after serving his custodial sentence, moved away from NSW, and currently resides in another state of Australia.

Throughout the world, this is a particular problem given the sheer number of volunteer firefighters, although fire services are attempting to eliminate this problem when recruiting new staff. A representative of the New South Wales Police Service (Laycock) notes that "police are working closely with the RFS, who are also very keen to eliminate these people from their ranks" but also remains doubtful about "whether the firebug vetting process can ever be foolproof" (Chulov, 2004, p. 12).

After the tragic September 11, 2001, terrorist attacks in the United States, the U.S. government instituted a new department to oversee security throughout the country—the Department of Homeland Security. Because firefighters are usually the first emergency service workers to attend any terrorist event, a need arose for screening of those firefighters to ensure security of scenes. In a thesis on the screening of firefighter candidates, Pope (2006, p. 1) stated,

> While billions of dollars are spent on buying new homeland security equipment to enhance response and training the workforce to use it, little time and attention has been paid to whom we are choosing to perform the mission.

Pope considered that it was essential, and critical, for the success of the Homeland Security mission that the fire services in the United States had "a sound workforce, mentally and physically prepared to manage the new challenges they will confront" (Abstract).

A SPECIAL CASE: JOHN LEONARD ORR

John Orr was a dedicated fire investigator and career fire officer, attached to the Glendale (California) Fire Department. He had wanted to be a police officer but had failed in his efforts to join.[12] Orr has become one of the most recognized serial arsonists of our time, even if only by his peers (and the communities of Southern California where he lit his fires). Orr's fires have also been the subject of much popular media coverage, including a documentary on the Odyssey Channel and a special program on U.S. Court TV titled *The Firestarter—John Orr* (2004).

Throughout the 1980s and 1990s, Los Angeles was plagued by a series of fires that caused millions of dollars of damage and killed four people. The serial arsonist clearly knew what he was doing. Forensic investigators realized he was employing time-delay incendiary devices so he could flee before the fires erupted. From the January 1987 fires, investigator Marvin Casey recovered a single fingerprint and developed a theory that the fires were somehow

---

[12]John Orr's story is subject of a book, *Fire Lover*, by Joseph Wambaugh (2002).

connected to local firefighter conferences. The fingerprint, however, did not match any of the attendees. Two years later, another string of fires was set during another arson investigators' conference. A comparison of the attendance rosters at both conferences produced 10 common names, but no one matched the fingerprint from the previous fire.

In 1991, an arson task force was formed and began working with Casey. With advanced fingerprint technology, the forensic team finally identified the culprit and realized it was one of their own—John Orr, a fire captain and renowned arson investigator. A search of Orr's residence revealed videos of fires that Orr had set before the fire trucks arrived. Also found was a manuscript titled "Points of Origin" that provided details of many fires under investigation, including information only the culprit could know.

The manuscript found in Orr's home related the story (supposedly about a fictitious character) of a fire investigator turned arsonist who was lighting fires across an area of Southern California. Police and prosecutors used the content of the manuscript against Orr in his trial because it matched with uncanny accuracy the fires that were attributed to Orr.

He would set fires using an incendiary timing device (typically a cigarette with a rubber band wrapped around the end wedged in a matchbook) in stores during business hours. He would also set other fires in the same manner in an effort to draw firefighters to small fires. At the same time, another larger fire set in another area would not be attended as quickly, thereby becoming fully involved very quickly. This MO reached epic proportions at a fire set in an Ole's Home Improvement Store, which was set in a display area containing block foam products. The fire spread so quickly that four people were trapped inside, with all losing their lives despite the desperate efforts of attending firefighters. This fire was one of three set on that day. John Orr attended all three.

Ironically, the investigator who initiated the investigation into Orr's fires and assisted in his arrest and conviction was one of his former students. Orr was arrested, charged, and convicted of his crimes. He is currently serving four life terms in a California state penitentiary, with no possibility of parole. Orr was also charged with setting fires in brush (bush/forest) country around the same area and convicted of many of these fires, with one causing millions of dollars worth of damage when it destroyed 67 homes in the College Hills area. There are indications that after he was arrested, bush fires dropped by 90% in the area.

CONCLUSION

It is quite clear that arson is a huge problem, a universal problem that has no state or country boundaries, and serial arson is "a problem within a problem." The solution is a "team-based effort," as stated by the FBI, FEMA, and the UK-based

Arson Control Forum. In addition to this is the necessity for continued research into the psychological aspects of arson and arsonist activity, which will support the physical investigation conducted by fire investigators and forensic examiners, the ongoing investigative efforts of detectives, and the prosecution of those offenders in the courtroom. The overall objective is to stop arson, and particularly serial arson activity, to provide a safer community.

Fire investigators in particular need to be ever vigilant in their fire scene inspections and ongoing investigations into fires occurring in their areas of responsibility. Patience and perseverance are the key factors where there is suspicion of arson, and especially when serial arson is suspected. Without the initial identification of serial activity by the fire investigator in the early stages of the offense, the offender will continue his or her activity until it leads to a serious fire or, worse, a fire fatality.

Taking an open-minded approach to all fire scenes cannot be overemphasized. The approach should be that each fire is a separate, unique incident; there should be no bias regarding the origin and cause of the event. Once the physical inspection has been conducted and evidence gathered, if evidence indicates a link between this and other fire events, then an effort should be made to pursue this avenue of investigation. It should be accepted that this single event could be part of a series of events, linked by physical evidence, methods of ignition, people, motives, and circumstance.

Acknowledgments

I thank the following police officers for their contributions to the case histories contained in this chapter: Detective Sgt. Thomas (NSW Police, Camden), Detective Senior Constable Parish (Sydney South Region Arson Unit, NSW Police), Detective Sgt. Horne (Hurstville Forensic Services, NSW Police), Sgt. Green (NSW Police Strike Force Tronto), Inspector Jacobson (NSW Fire Brigades), and Inspector Powell (NSW Fire Brigades Fire Investigation Unit).

Questions

1. The study by Dickens et al. (2007) showed that there were significant gender differences in the fire-setting crimes of males and females. *True or false?*
2. List and briefly describe some of the reasons why fire services rely on an accurate appraisal of how and where a fire started.
3. NFPA 912 contains a basic methodology for fire investigation recognized in countries throughout the world. *True or false?*
4. The definition of arson depends heavily on the jurisdiction in which the crime occurs. *True or false?*
5. What about the case study on John Orr is of interest and why?

REFERENCES

ACT government inquiry into the operational response to the January 2003 bushfires. (2003). Available at http://www.cmd.act.gov.au/publications/archived_publications/mcleod_inquiry. Accessed on June 12, 2008.

Arson Control Forum. (2003). Working Together: How to Set Up an Arson Task Force. London: Office of the Deputy Prime Minister.

Arson Control Forum. (2004). Annual Report. London: Office of the Deputy Prime Minister.

Arson Control Forum. (2006). Annual Report. London: Office of the Deputy Prime Minister. Available at http://www.crimereduction.homeoffice.gov.uk/arson/arson8.htm. Accessed June 16, 2008.

Arson Prevention Bureau. (2004). Key facts—Key facts about arson. Available at www.arsonpreventionbureau.org.uk. Accessed June 12, 2008.

Australian Institute of Criminology. (2008, March 6). Bushfire arson bulletin (No. 51). Canberra: Australian Institute of Criminology.

Bennett, W. W., & Hess, K. M. (2001). Criminal Investigation (6th ed.). Belmont, CA: Wadsworth.

Canter, D., & Almond, L. (2002). The burning issue: Research and strategies for reducing arson. Arson Control Forum. London: Office of the Deputy Prime Minister.

Chulov, M. (2004, August 23). Firebugs in fire engines. The Australian.

DeHaan, J. D. (2007). Kirk's Fire Investigation (6th ed.). Upper Saddle River, NJ: Prentice Hall.

Dempsey, J. S. (1996). An Introduction to Public and Private Investigations. Minneapolis: West.

Dickens, G., Sugarman, P., Ahmad, F., Edgar, S., Hofberg, K., & Tewari, S. (2007). Gender differences amongst adult arsonists at psychiatric assessment. Medicine, Science and the Law, 47(3), 233–238.

Edwards, M., & Grace, R. (2006). Analysing the offence locations and residential base of serial arsonists in New Zealand. Australian Psychologist, 41(3), 219–226.

Federal Emergency Management Agency, United States Fire Administration. (1989). Establishing an arson strike force (Report No. FA-88). Emmitsburg, MD: Federal Emergency Management Agency, United States Fire Administration.

Jacobson, G., & Brogan, R. (2004). Fire Investigation Training Manual [electronic resource]. Sydney, Australia: Charles Sturt University.

The life and death of a serial arsonist. (2007). CN&R Newsreview. Available at http://www.newsreview.com/chico. Accessed June 12, 2008.

National Fire Protection Association. (2008). NFPA 921: A Guide to Fire and Explosion Investigation. Battery March Park, Quincy, MA: National Fire Protection Association. Available at http://www.nfpa.org.

National Fire Protection Association. (2009). NFPA 1033: Standard for Professional Qualifications for Fire Investigator. Battery March Park, Quincy, MA: National Fire Protection Association.

New South Wales Fire Brigades. (2008). 2006/07 Annual Report. Sydney: New South Wales Government.

Pope, C. M. (2006). A model strategy and policy for screening firefighter candidates. Monterey, CA: Naval Postgraduate School.

Prins, H. A. (1994). Fire-raising: It's Motivations and Management. New York: Routledge.

Saferstein, R. (2004). Criminalistics: An Introduction to Forensic Science (8th ed.). Upper Saddle River, NJ: Prentice Hall.

Sapp, A. D., Huff, T. G., Gary, G. P., & Icove, D. J. (2004). A motive based offender analysis of serial arsonists. Interfire. Available at http://www.interfire.org/features/serialarsonists/Motive_based/cover.asp. Accessed November 23, 2004.

Serial arsonist who hit 3 synagogues may have struck again. (2008). Haaretz Newspaper. Available at http://www.haaretz.com. Accessed June 12, 2008.

The study of serial arsonists. (2008). Interfire Online. Available at http://www.interfire.org. Accessed June 12, 2008.

Turvey, B. E. (2008). Criminal Profiling: An Introduction to Behavioral Evidence Analysis (3rd ed.). Burlington, MA: Academic Press.

Wambaugh, J. (2002). Fire Lover. New York: HarperCollins.

Index

Note: Page numbers followed by *t* indicates table.

C